FIRE FORCE

25

ATSUSHI
OHKUBO

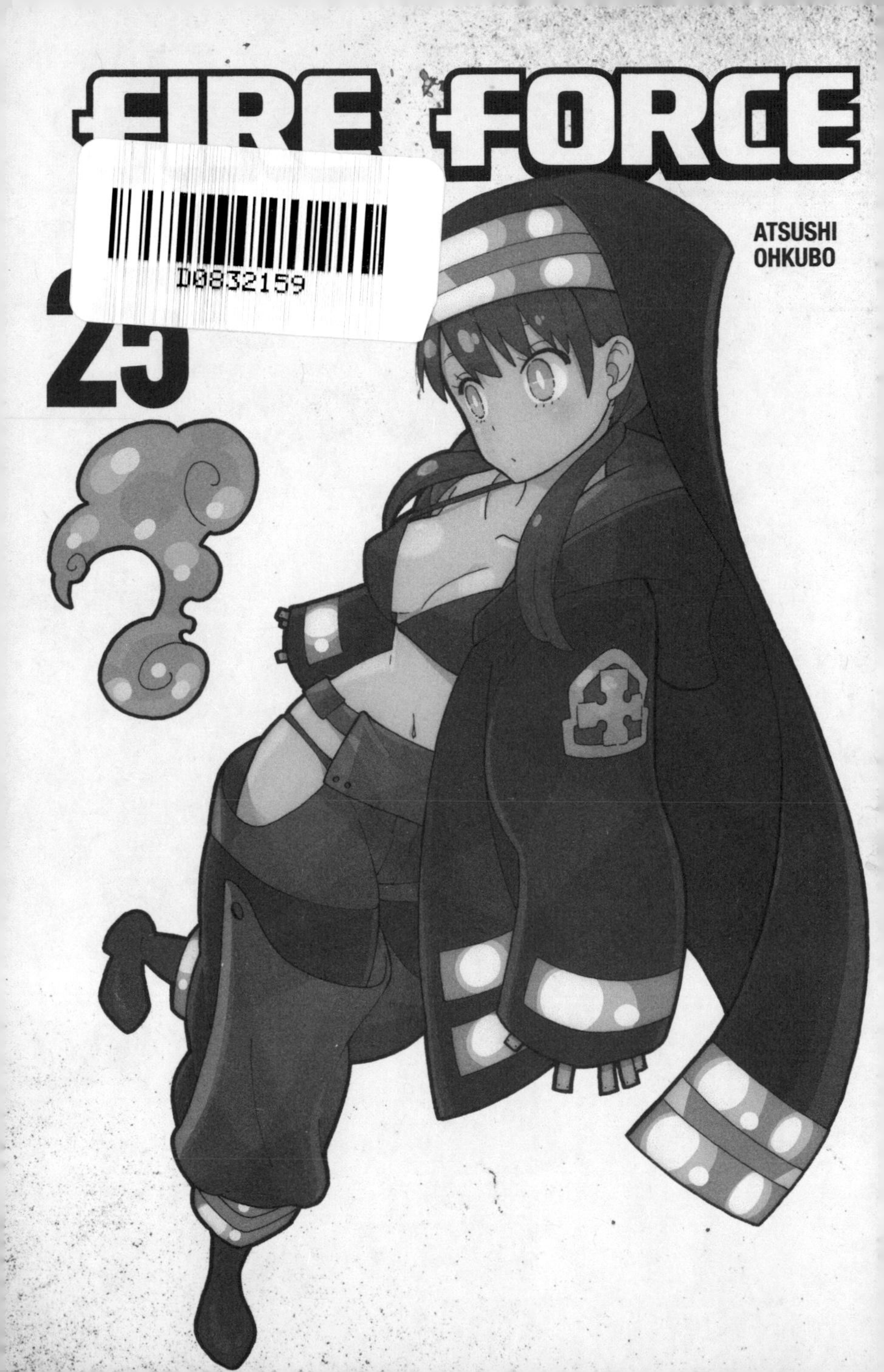

you?
me?

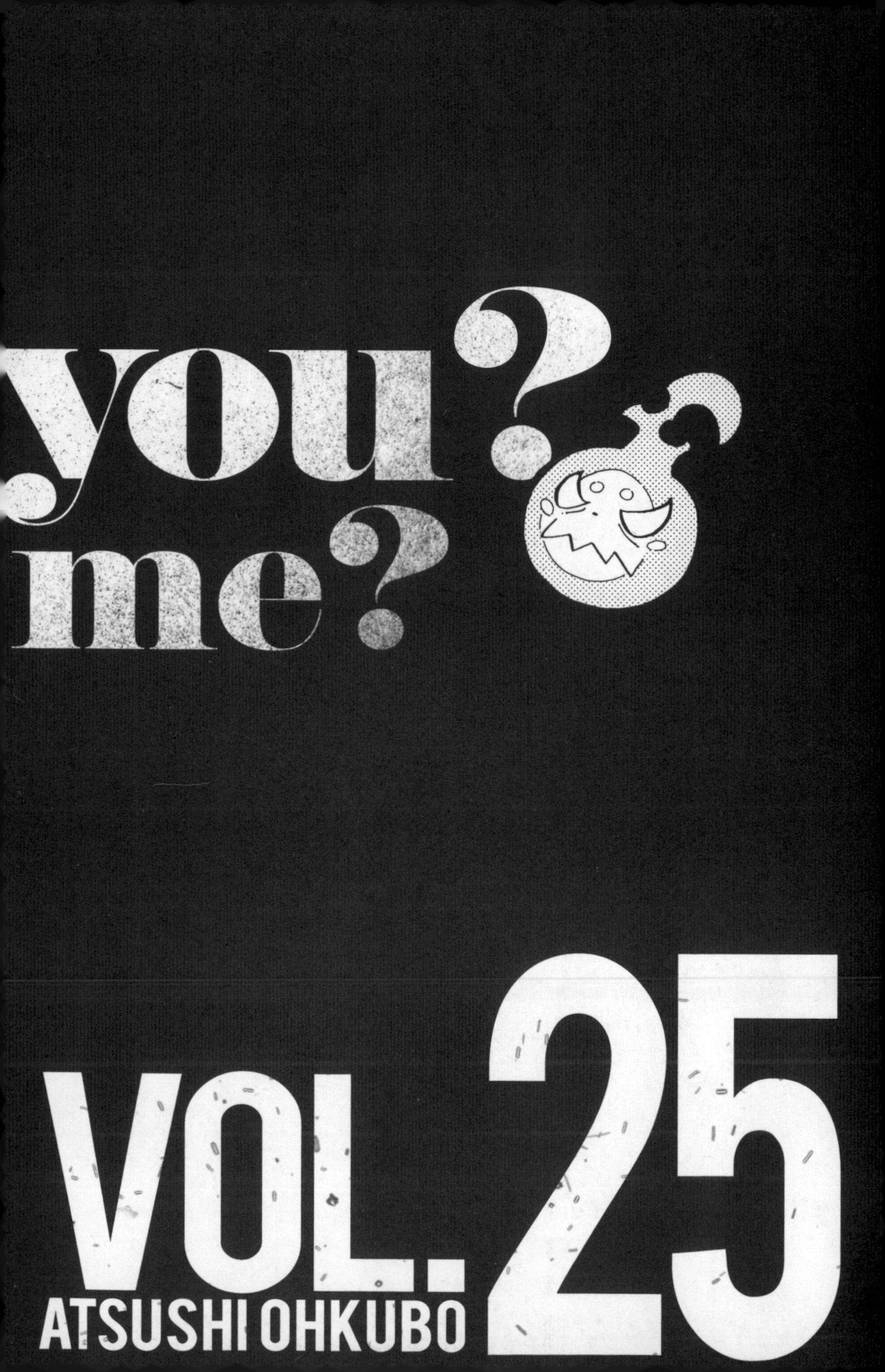

VOL. 25

ATSUSHI OHKUBO

Who are Are you

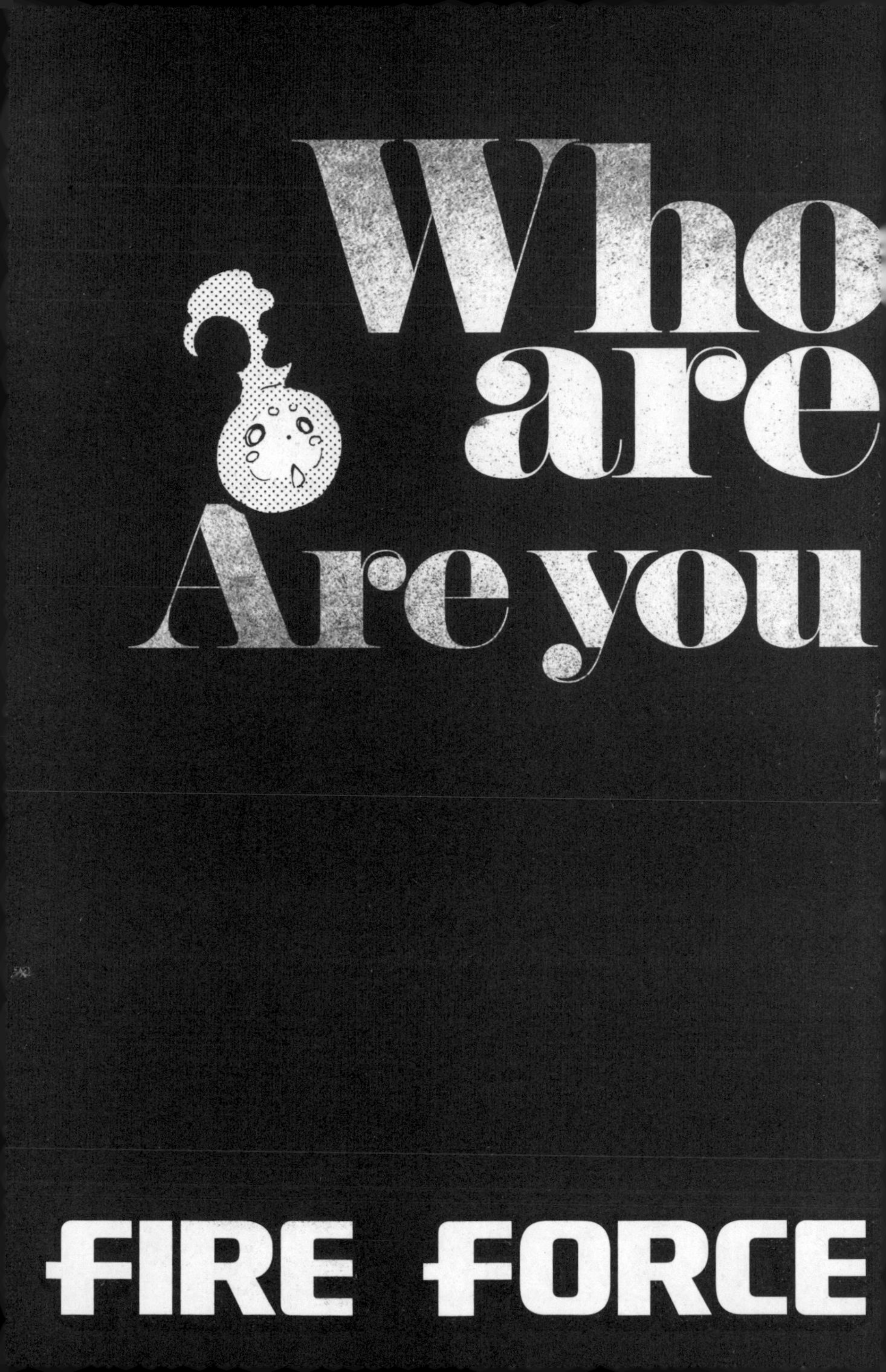

FIRE FORCE

SPECIAL FIRE FORCE COMPANY 8

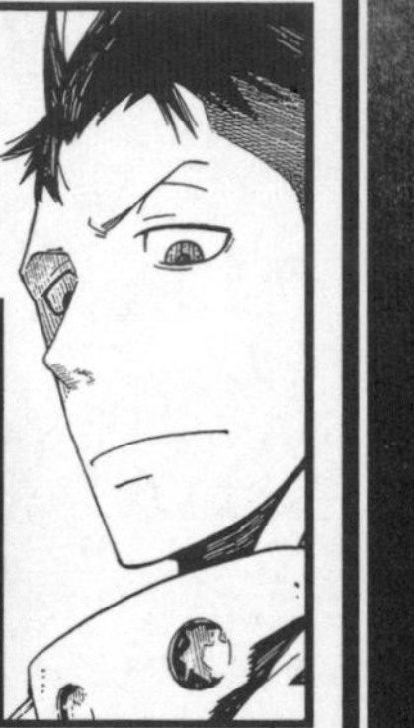

CAPTAIN
(NON-POWERED)
AKITARU ŌBI

The caring leader of the newly established Company 8. He has no powers, but uses his finely honed muscles as a weapon in a battle style that makes him worthy of the Captain title. He is taking action to prepare for the Great Cataclysm that is to come.

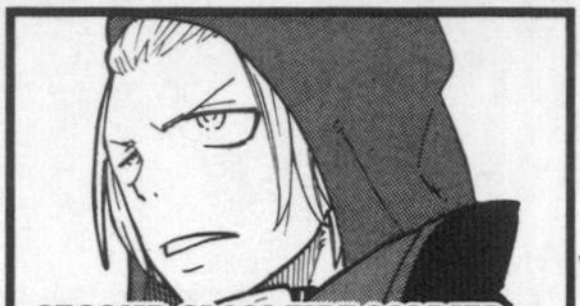

SECOND CLASS FIRE SOLDIER
(THIRD GENERATION PYROKINETIC)
ARTHUR BOYLE

Trained at the academy with Shinra. He follows his own personal code of chivalry as the self-proclaimed Knight King. He's a blockhead who is bad at mental exercise. He's a weirdo who grows stronger the more delusional he gets. While on a quest to find orichalcum for the rebirth of Excalibur, he went to the Nether, where he was reunited with his long-lost parents!!

WATCHES OUT FOR

TRUSTS

IDIOT!!

WATCHES OUT FOR

TRUSTS

STRONG BOND

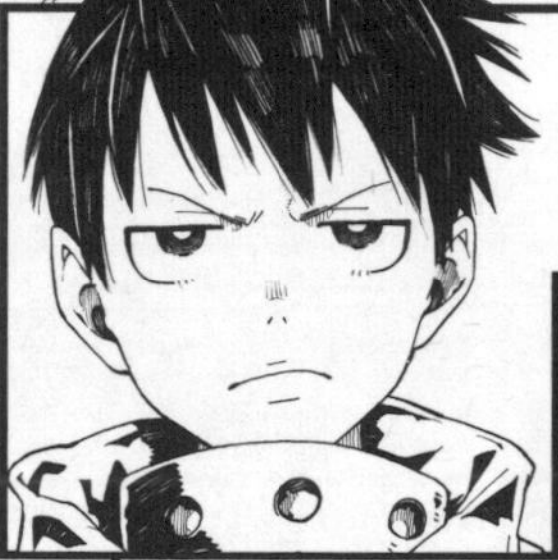

SECOND CLASS FIRE SOLDIER
(THIRD GENERATION PYROKINETIC)
SHINRA KUSAKABE

Dreams of becoming a hero who saves people from spontaneous combustion! His weapon is a fiery kick. He wields a special flame called the Adolla Burst. Has undergone training from Company 7 Captain Shinmon to hone his senses in an effort to take the fight to Adolla.

A NICE GIRL

LOOKS AWESOME ON THE JOB

A TOUGH BUT WEIRD LADY

HANG IN THERE, ROOKIE!

TERRIFIED

STRICT DISCIPLINARIAN

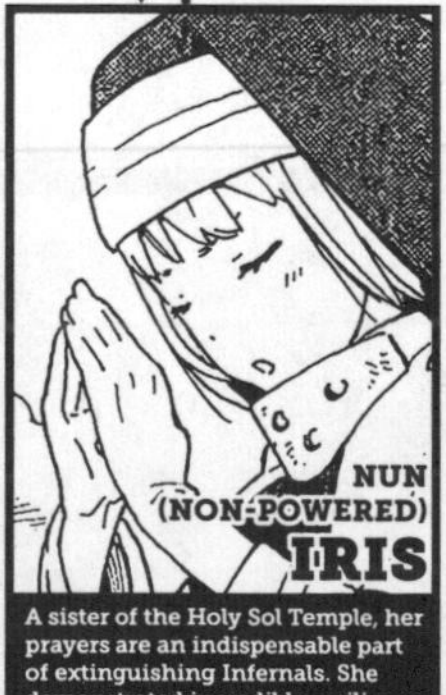

NUN
(NON-POWERED)
IRIS

A sister of the Holy Sol Temple, her prayers are an indispensable part of extinguishing Infernals. She demonstrated incredible resilience in facing the Infernal hordes.

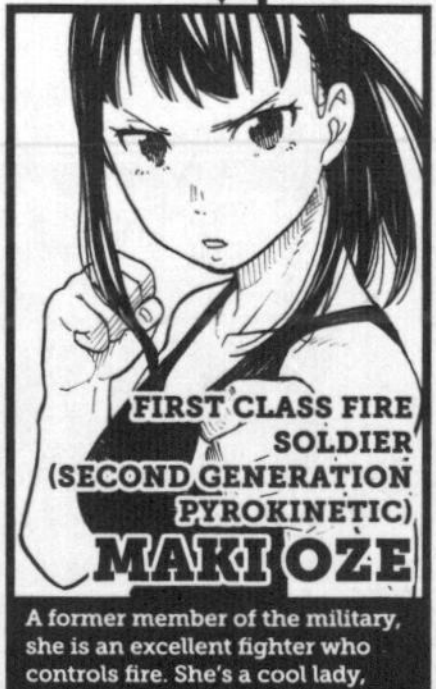

FIRST CLASS FIRE SOLDIER
(SECOND GENERATION PYROKINETIC)
MAKI OZE

A former member of the military, she is an excellent fighter who controls fire. She's a cool lady, but is mad about love stories, and her beauty is overshadowed by her "head full of flowers and wedding bells."

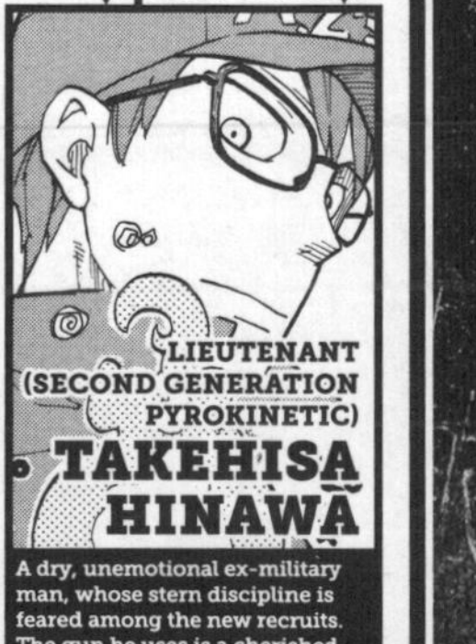

LIEUTENANT
(SECOND GENERATION PYROKINETIC)
TAKEHISA HINAWA

A dry, unemotional ex-military man, whose stern discipline is feared among the new recruits. The gun he uses is a cherished memento from his friend who became an Infernal.

THE GIRLS' CLUB

RESPECTS

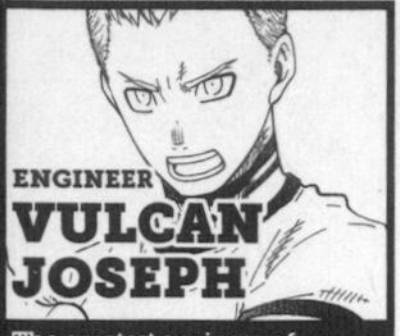

ENGINEER
VULCAN JOSEPH

The greatest engineer of the day, renowned as the God of Fire and the Forge. As promised, he has forged a brilliant new Excalibur for Arthur.

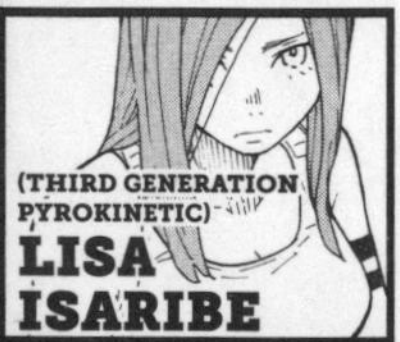

(THIRD GENERATION PYROKINETIC)
LISA ISARIBE

Formerly a spy sent by Dr. Giovanni, she is now a member of Company 8. She controls tentacles of flame.

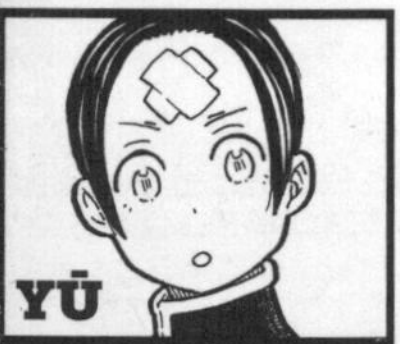

YŪ

A self-proclaimed apprentice of Vulcan's. Has now recovered from the injuries inflicted by Dr. Giovanni.

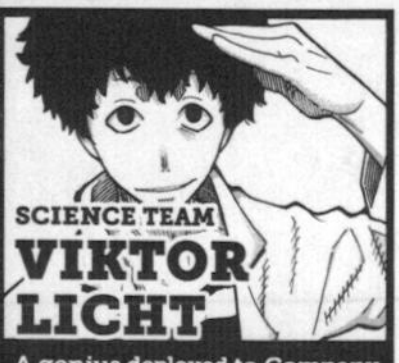

SCIENCE TEAM
VIKTOR LICHT

A genius deployed to Company 8 from Haijima Industries. Has confessed to being a Haijima spy.

HAS HIM ON HER MIND

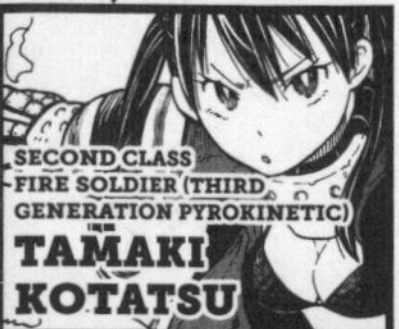

SECOND CLASS FIRE SOLDIER (THIRD GENERATION PYROKINETIC)
TAMAKI KOTATSU

A rookie from Company 1 currently in Company 8's care. She controls nekomata-like flames.

HOLY SOL TEMPLE + "EVANGELIST"

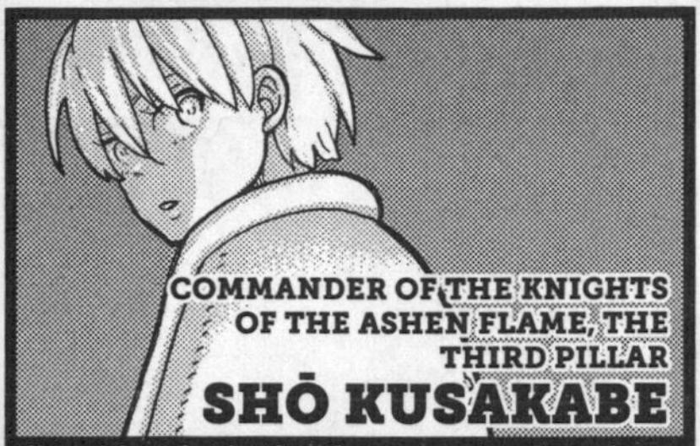

COMMANDER OF THE KNIGHTS OF THE ASHEN FLAME, THE THIRD PILLAR

SHŌ KUSAKABE

Shinra's long-lost brother, the commander of an order of knights that works for the Evangelist. He can use his powers to stop time for all but himself. He was made into a doll for Haumea, but is impelled to leave the Church when he feels his brother's warmth through an Adolla Link.

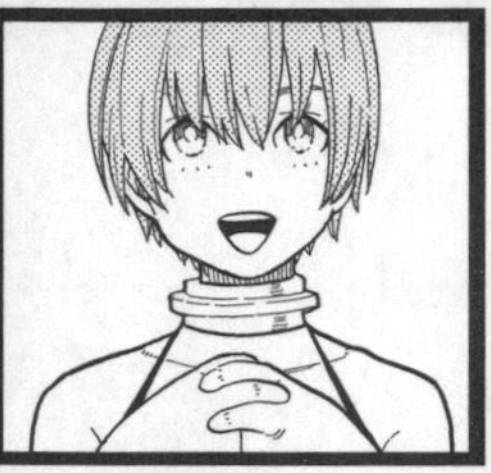

THE FIFTH PILLAR

INCA

Can predict the course of the flames. She joined the Evangelist out of her hatred of boredom.

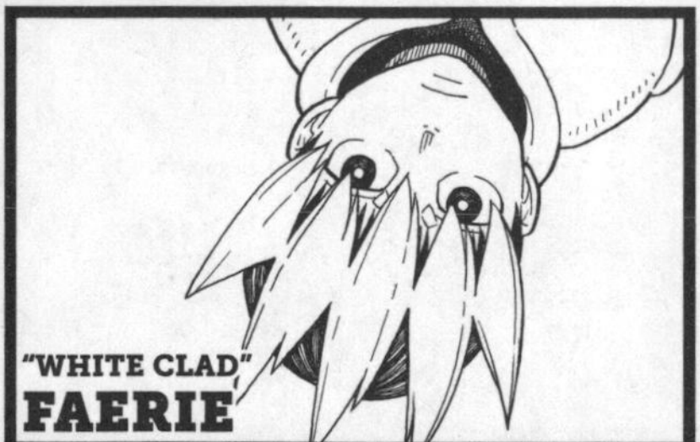

"WHITE CLAD"

FAERIE

A boy who suddenly appeared in midair. A member of the Cataclysm Squad. He is constantly egging humans on, insisting they stop the giant Infernal. Shō has sliced him in two, but...

SPECIAL FIRE FORCE COMPANY 7

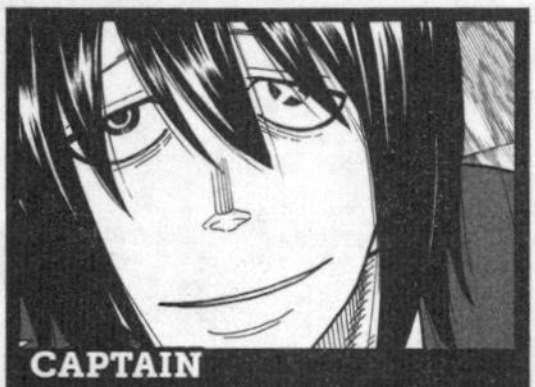

CAPTAIN

SHINMON BENIMARU

A composite fire soldier, with the powers of a second gen and a third gen pyrokinetic. Rescued Company 8 under the guise of Moonlite Mask, and has been sheltering the company ever since.

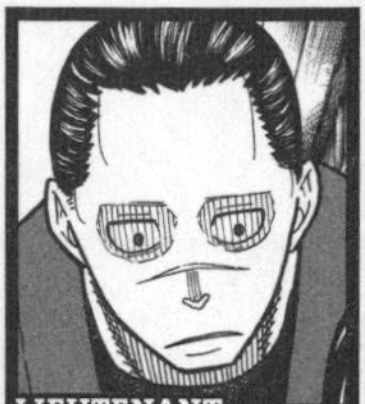

LIEUTENANT

SAGAMIYA KONRO

Has the "holy scar" of one who has experienced an Adolla Link. Refers to Benimaru as Waka.

HAIJIMA INDUSTRIES

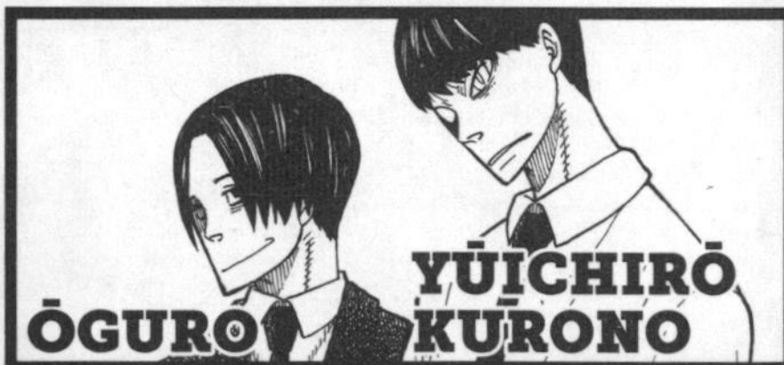

ŌGURO

An elite Haijima executive who climbed the corporate ladder faster than anyone in history. A horrible human being who nevertheless silences all complaints by continually achieving better-than-perfect results. Non-powered.

YŪICHIRŌ KURONO

The man known as Death, he adores weaklings. Will only take orders from Ōguro and Haijima's CEO, thus forcing Ōguro to accompany him to the field. Third-generation pyrokinetic.

SPECIAL FIRE FORCE COMPANY 2

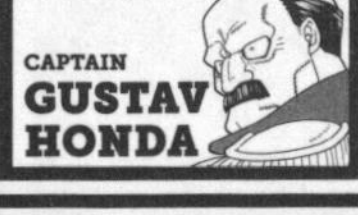

CAPTAIN

GUSTAV HONDA

SPECIAL FIRE FORCE COMPANY 4

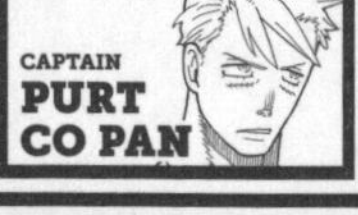

CAPTAIN

PURT CO PAN

SUMMARY

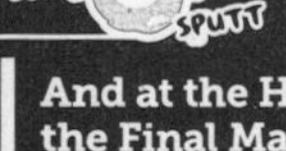
SPUTT
SPUTT

Using a fairing that he found in the Nether, Vulcan masterfully reconstructs Arthur's sword Excalibur after it was lost in the battle at Fuchū. In the meantime, Shinra feels the need to take the fight to Adolla, and trains with Benimaru to hone his senses. Meanwhile, there are stirrings in the heart of Shinra's brother Shō that lead him to desert the Church.

And at the Holy Sol Temple, they hold the Final Mass and raise the curtain on the Great Cataclysm. During a massive earthquake, an enormous Infernal appears in the waters of the Pacific Ocean. The Fire Force puts their lives on the line to fight it, while on the sidelines, a White Clad boy named Faerie appears and goes head-to-head with Shō!

FIRE FORCE 25

CONTENTS

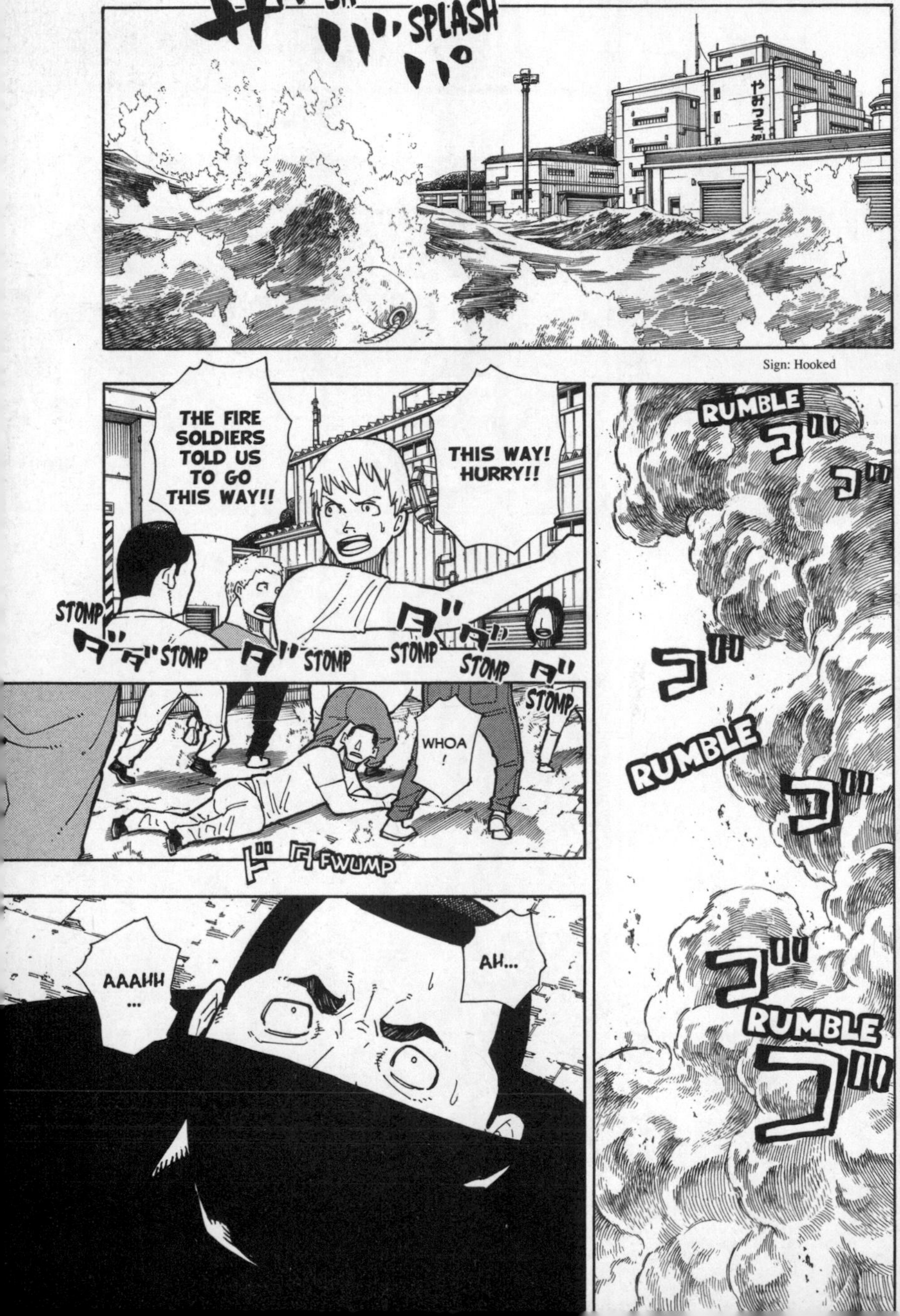
SA-SPLASH
RUMBLE
RUMBLE
RUMBLE
THIS WAY! HURRY!!
THE FIRE SOLDIERS TOLD US TO GO THIS WAY!!
STOMP
STOMP
STOMP
STOMP
STOMP
STOMP
STOMP
WHOA!
FWUMP
AH...
AAAHH...

Sign: Hooked

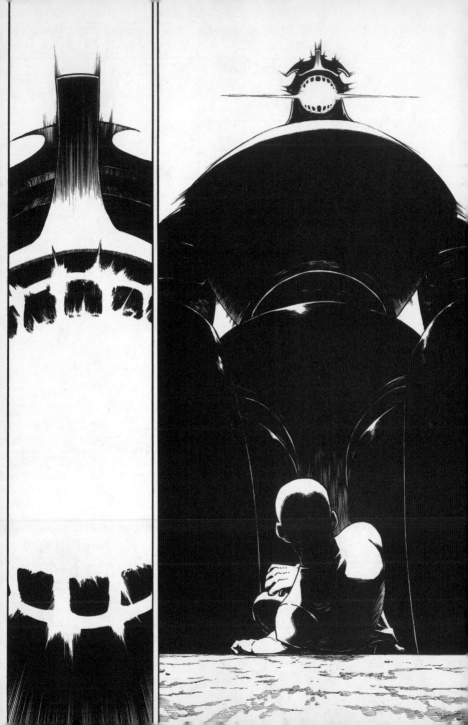

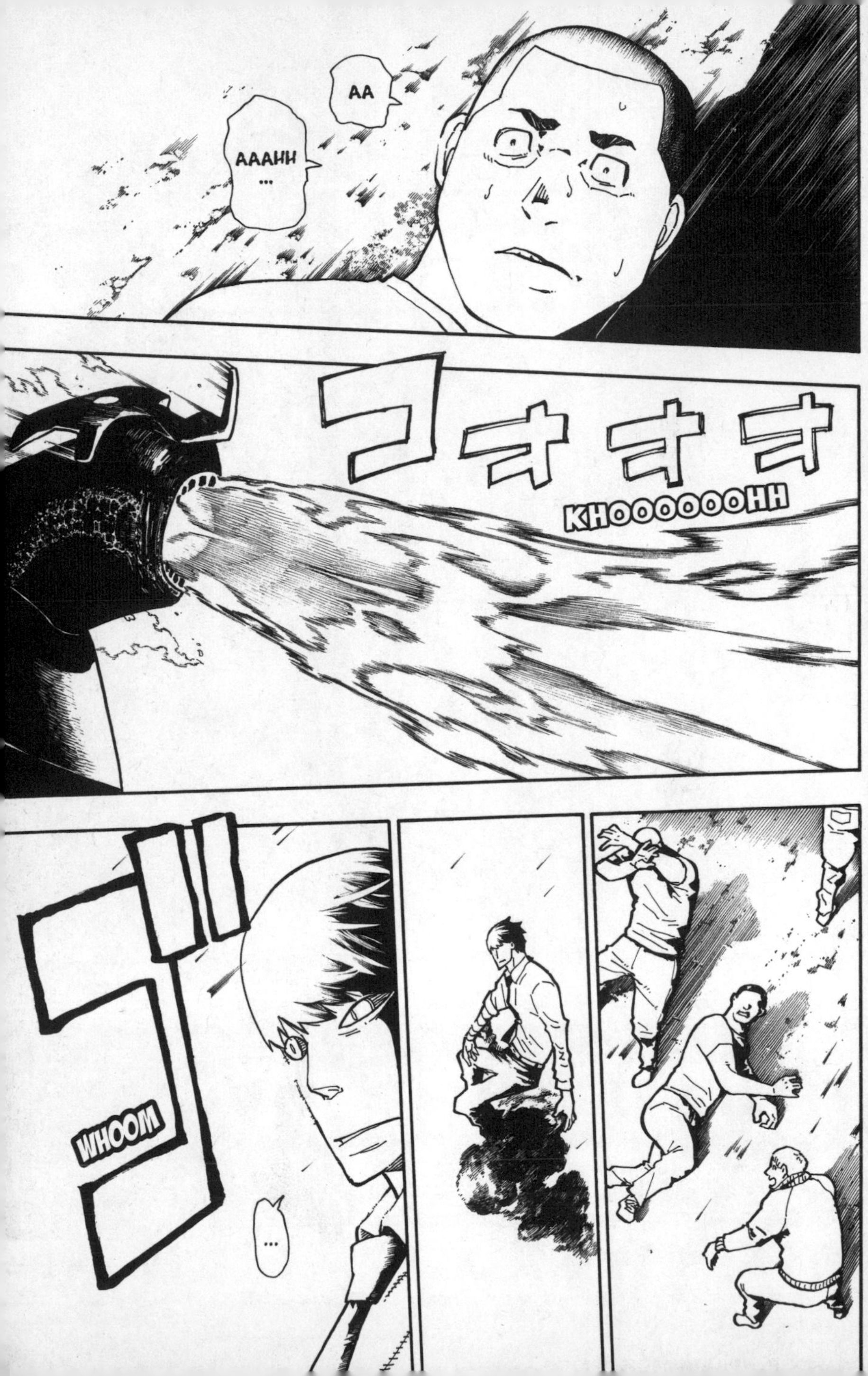
AA
AAAHH ...
コォォォ
KHOOOOOOHH
ゴ
WHOOM
...

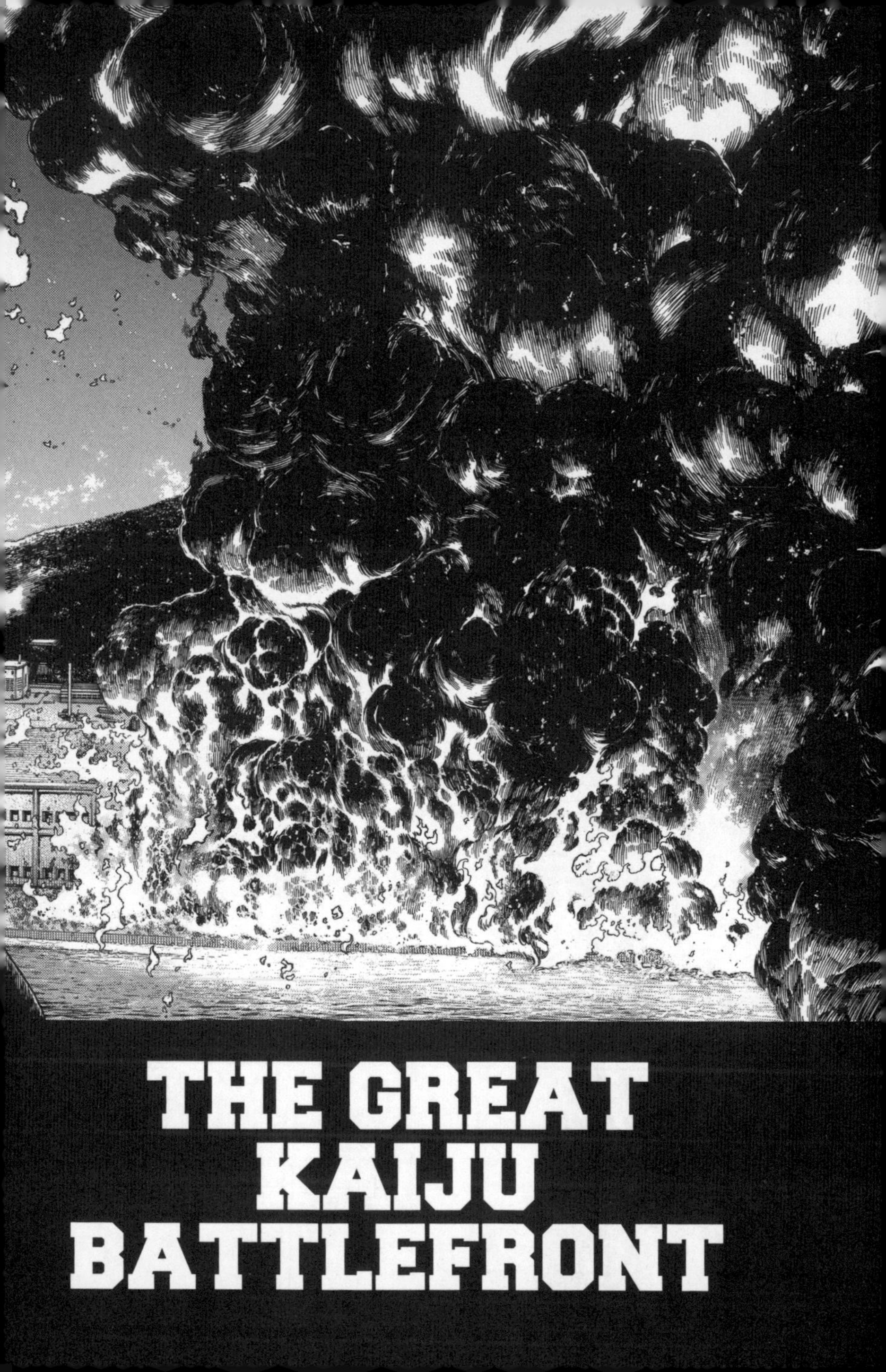

THE GREAT KAIJU BATTLEFRONT

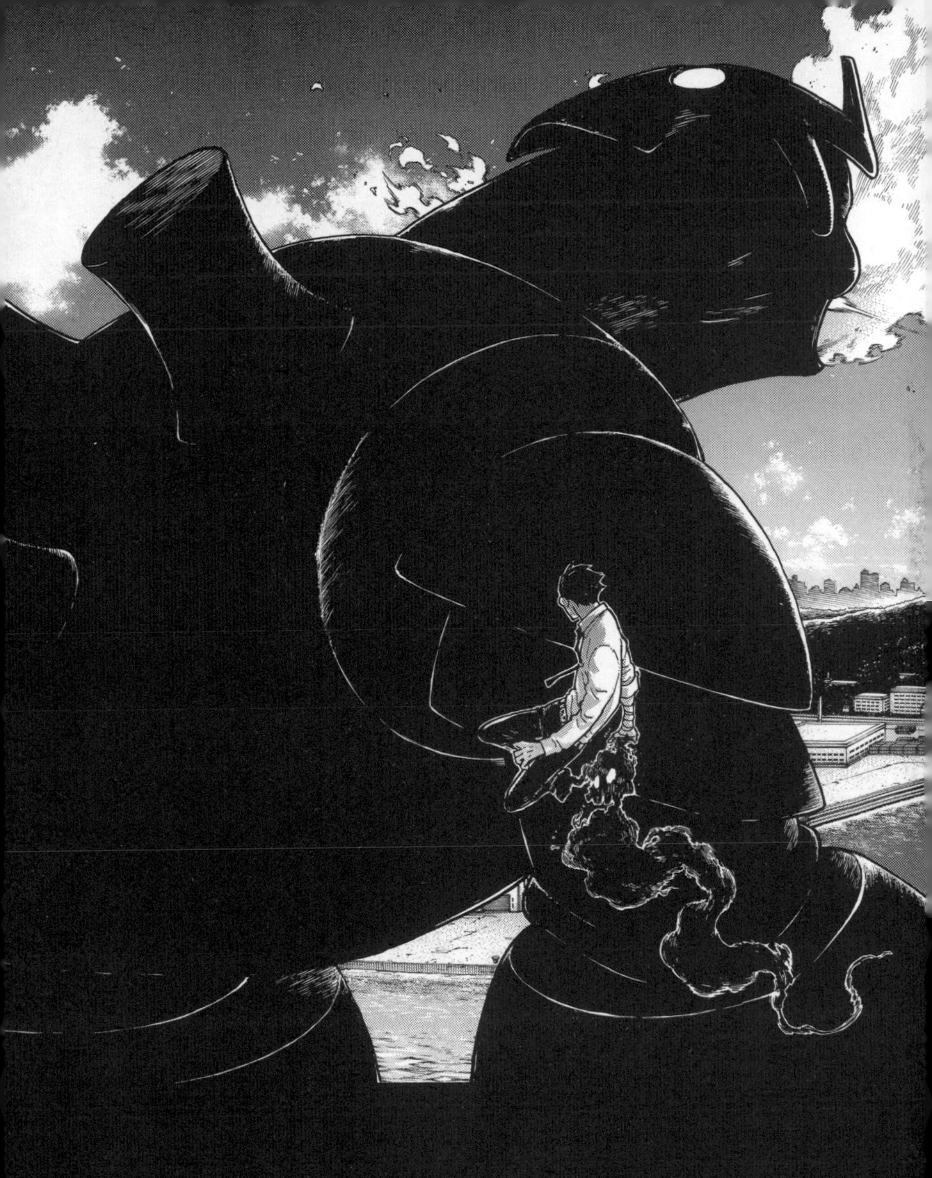

CHAPTER CCXIV:

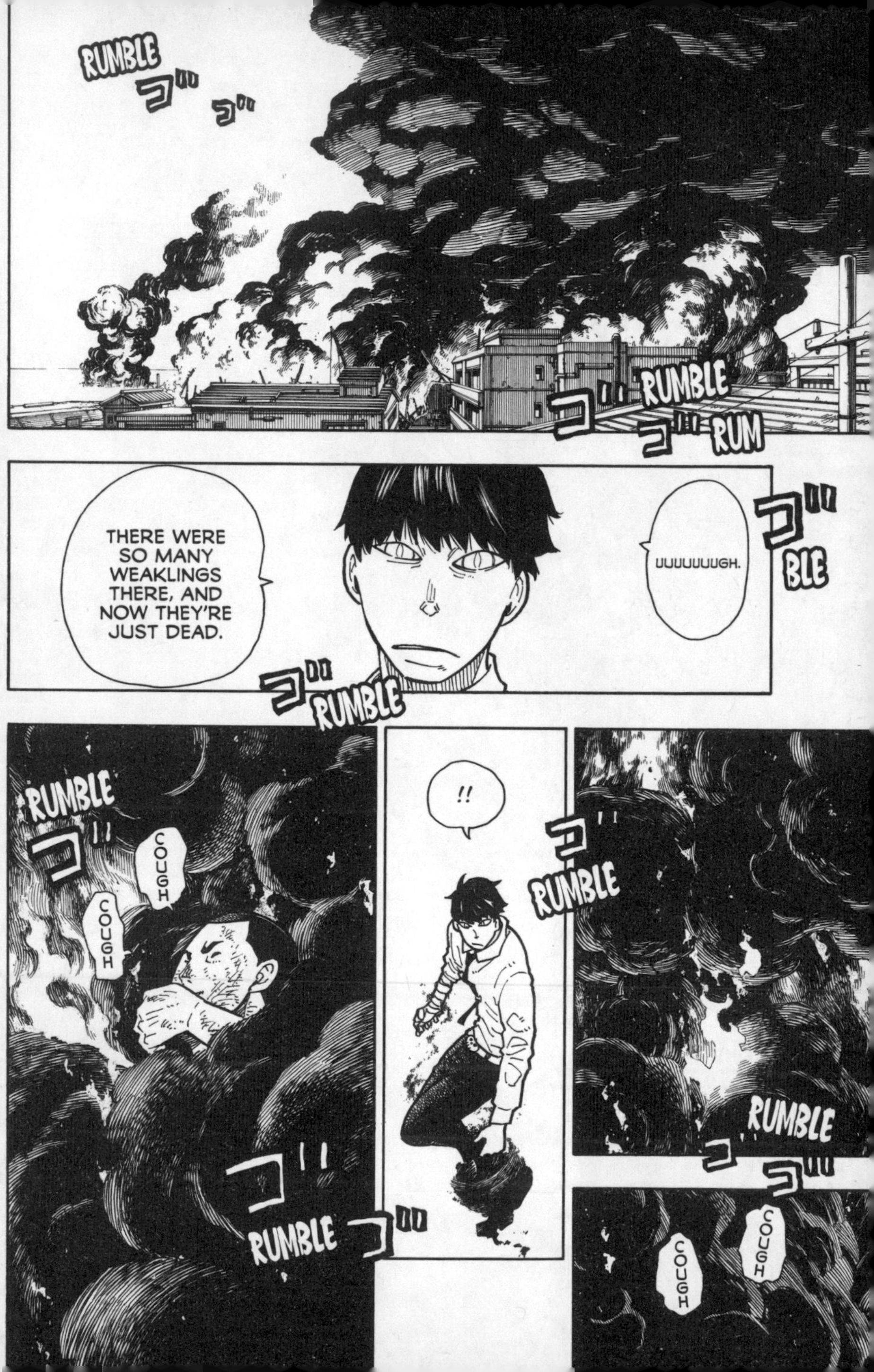
RUMBLE
ゴ ゴ
ゴ RUMBLE
ゴ RUM
ゴ BLE
UUUUUUUGH.
THERE WERE SO MANY WEAKLINGS THERE, AND NOW THEY'RE JUST DEAD.
ゴ RUMBLE
RUMBLE
ゴ ゴ
COUGH
COUGH
!!
ゴ RUMBLE
RUMBLE
ゴ
COUGH
COUGH
ゴ
RUMBLE ゴ

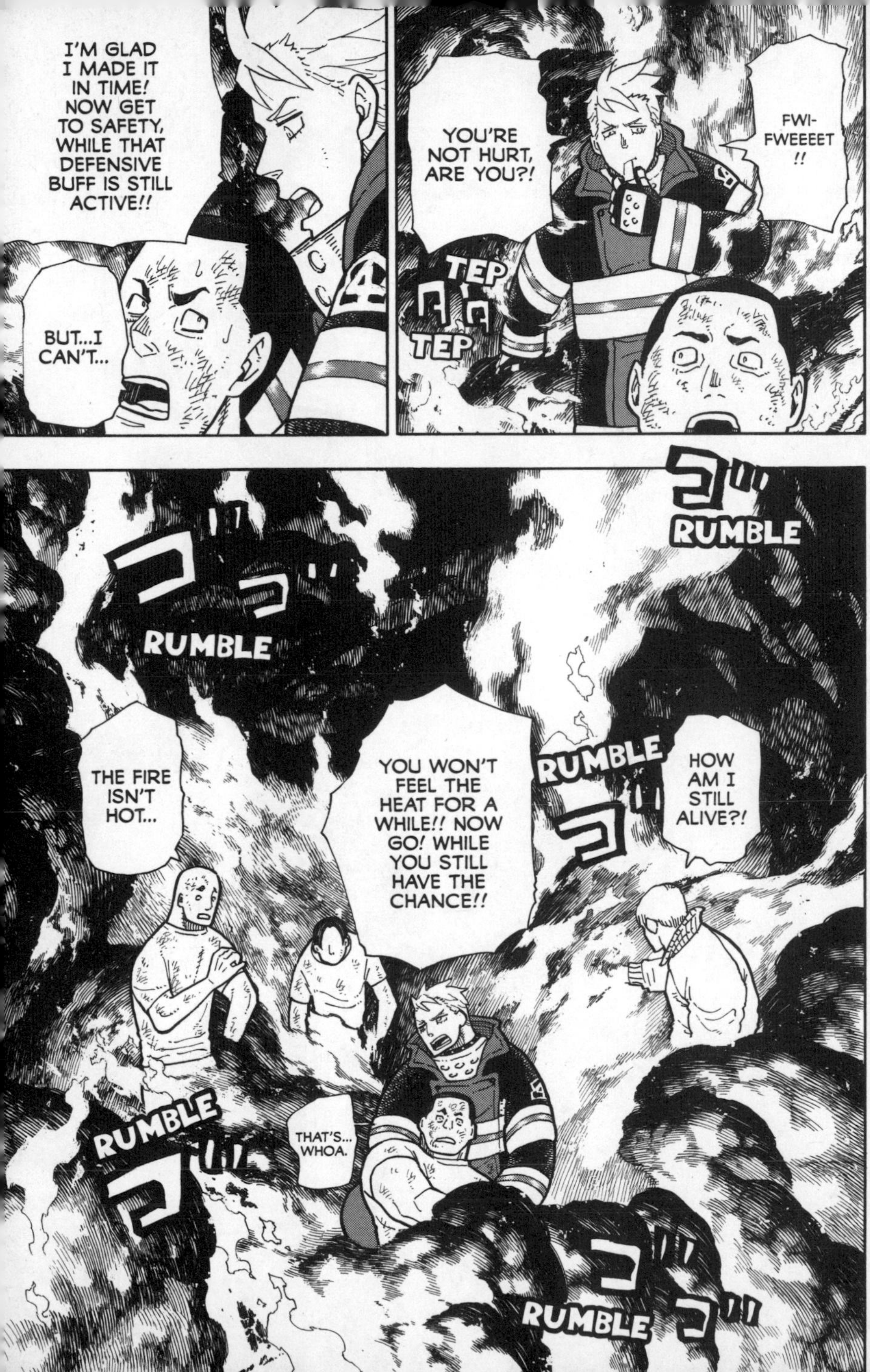
FWI-FWEEEET!!
YOU'RE NOT HURT, ARE YOU?!
TEP TEP
I'M GLAD I MADE IT IN TIME! NOW GET TO SAFETY, WHILE THAT DEFENSIVE BUFF IS STILL ACTIVE!!
BUT...I CAN'T...
RUMBLE
HOW AM I STILL ALIVE?!
RUMBLE
YOU WON'T FEEL THE HEAT FOR A WHILE!! NOW GO! WHILE YOU STILL HAVE THE CHANCE!!
RUMBLE
THE FIRE ISN'T HOT...
THAT'S... WHOA.
RUMBLE
RUMBLE

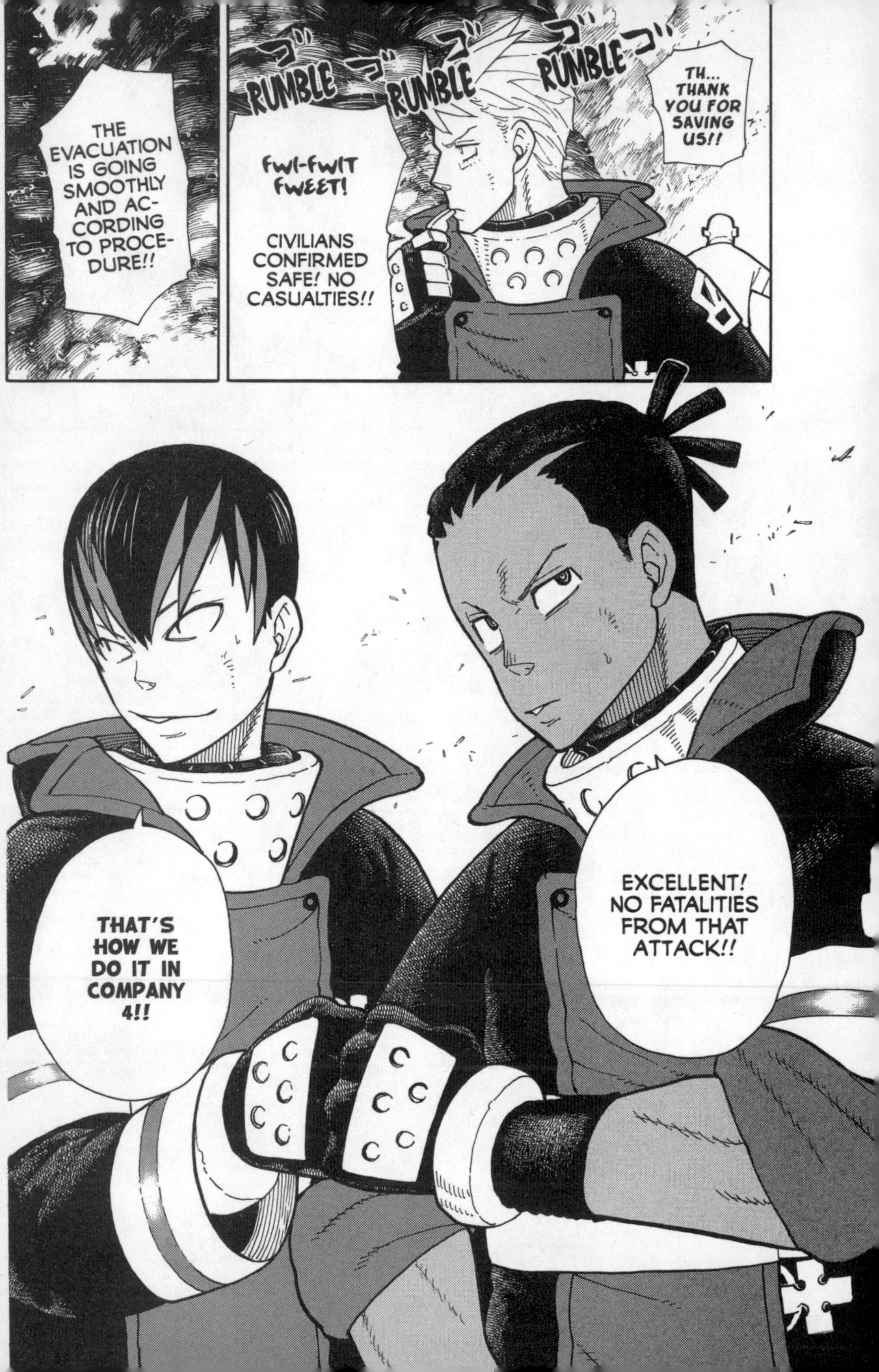
RUMBLE RUMBLE RUMBLE
TH... THANK YOU FOR SAVING US!!
FWI-FWIT FWEET!
CIVILIANS CONFIRMED SAFE! NO CASUALTIES!!
THE EVACUATION IS GOING SMOOTHLY AND ACCORDING TO PROCEDURE!!
EXCELLENT! NO FATALITIES FROM THAT ATTACK!!
THAT'S HOW WE DO IT IN COMPANY 4!!

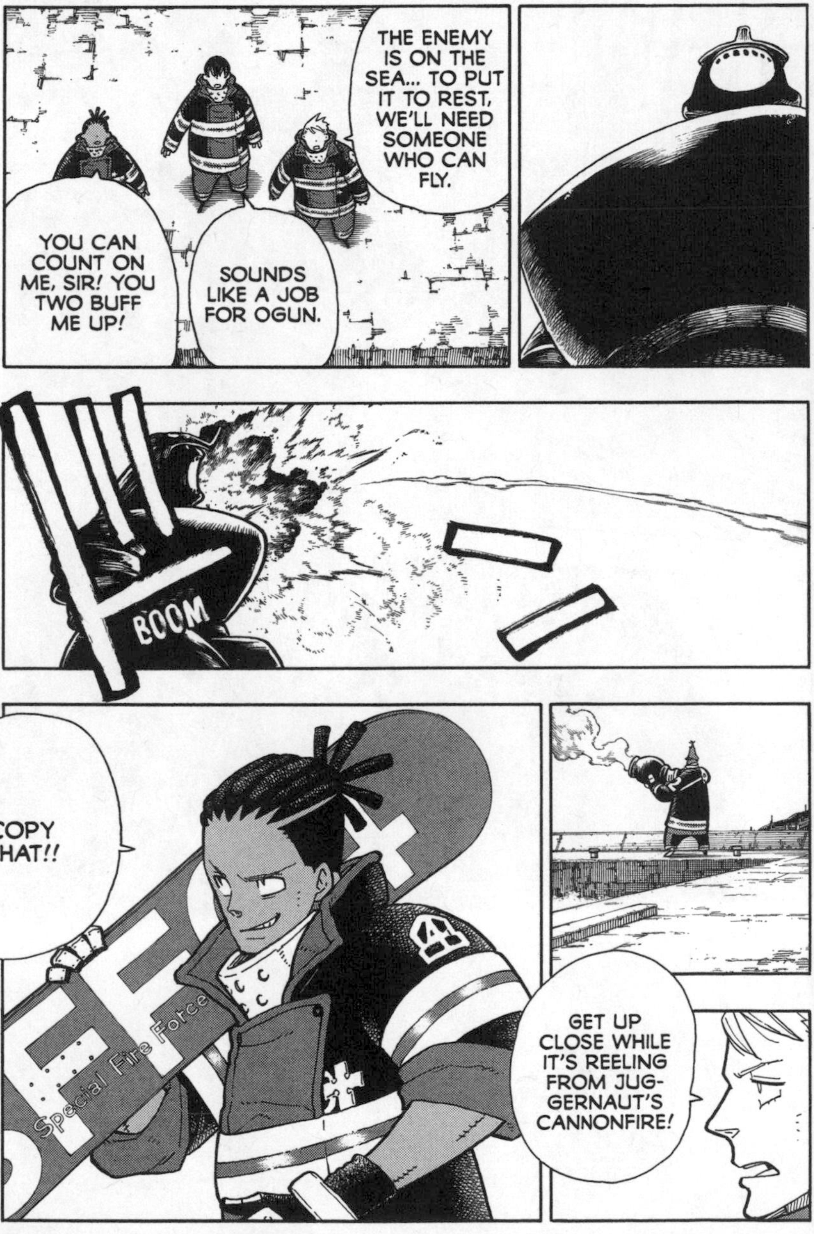
THE ENEMY IS ON THE SEA... TO PUT IT TO REST, WE'LL NEED SOMEONE WHO CAN FLY.
SOUNDS LIKE A JOB FOR OGUN.
YOU CAN COUNT ON ME, SIR! YOU TWO BUFF ME UP!
BOOM
GET UP CLOSE WHILE IT'S REELING FROM JUG-GERNAUT'S CANNONFIRE!
COPY THAT!!
Special Fire Force

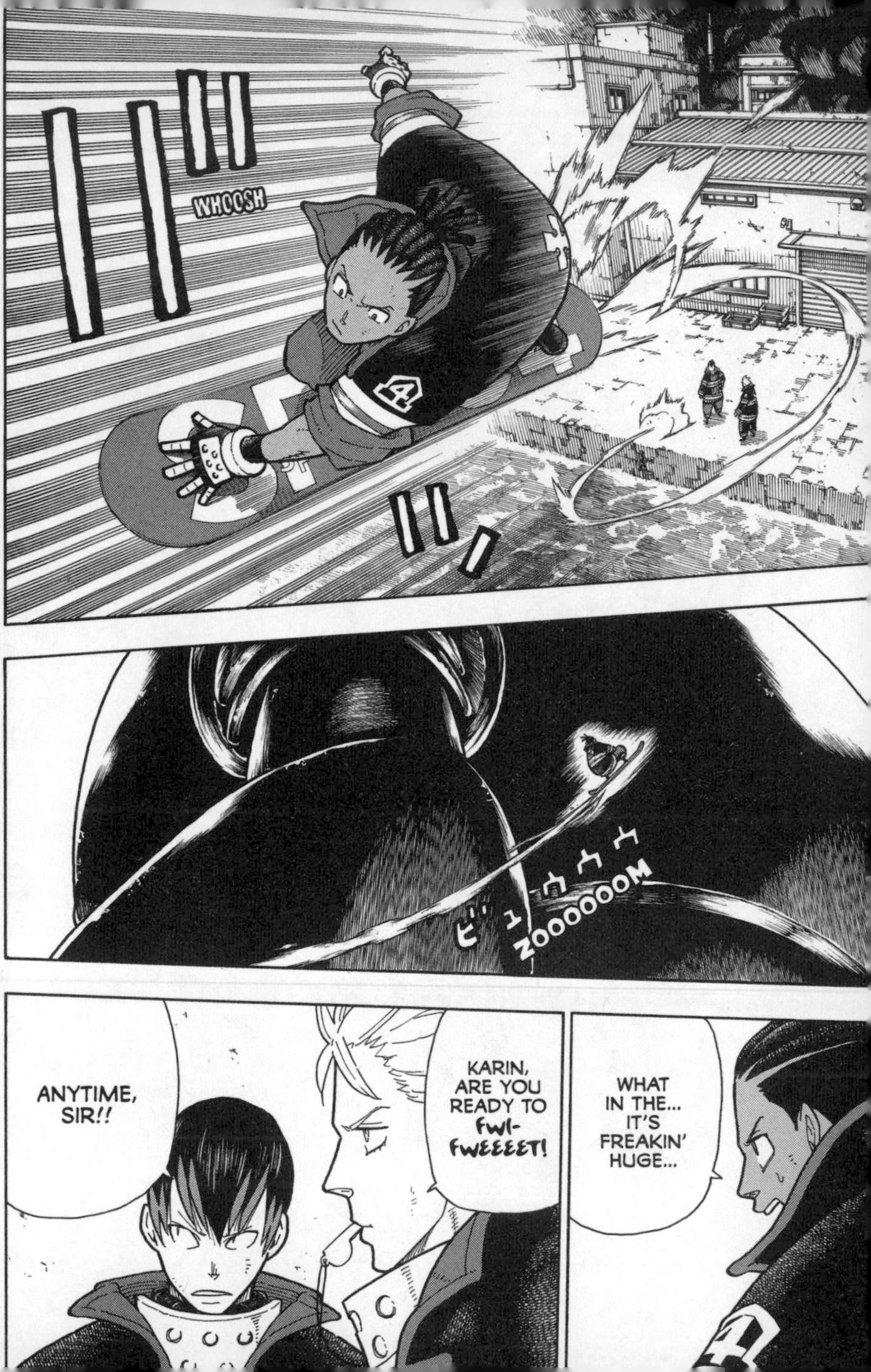

WHOOSH
ZOOOOOOM
WHAT IN THE... IT'S FREAKIN' HUGE...
KARIN, ARE YOU READY TO FWI- FWEEEET!
ANYTIME, SIR!!

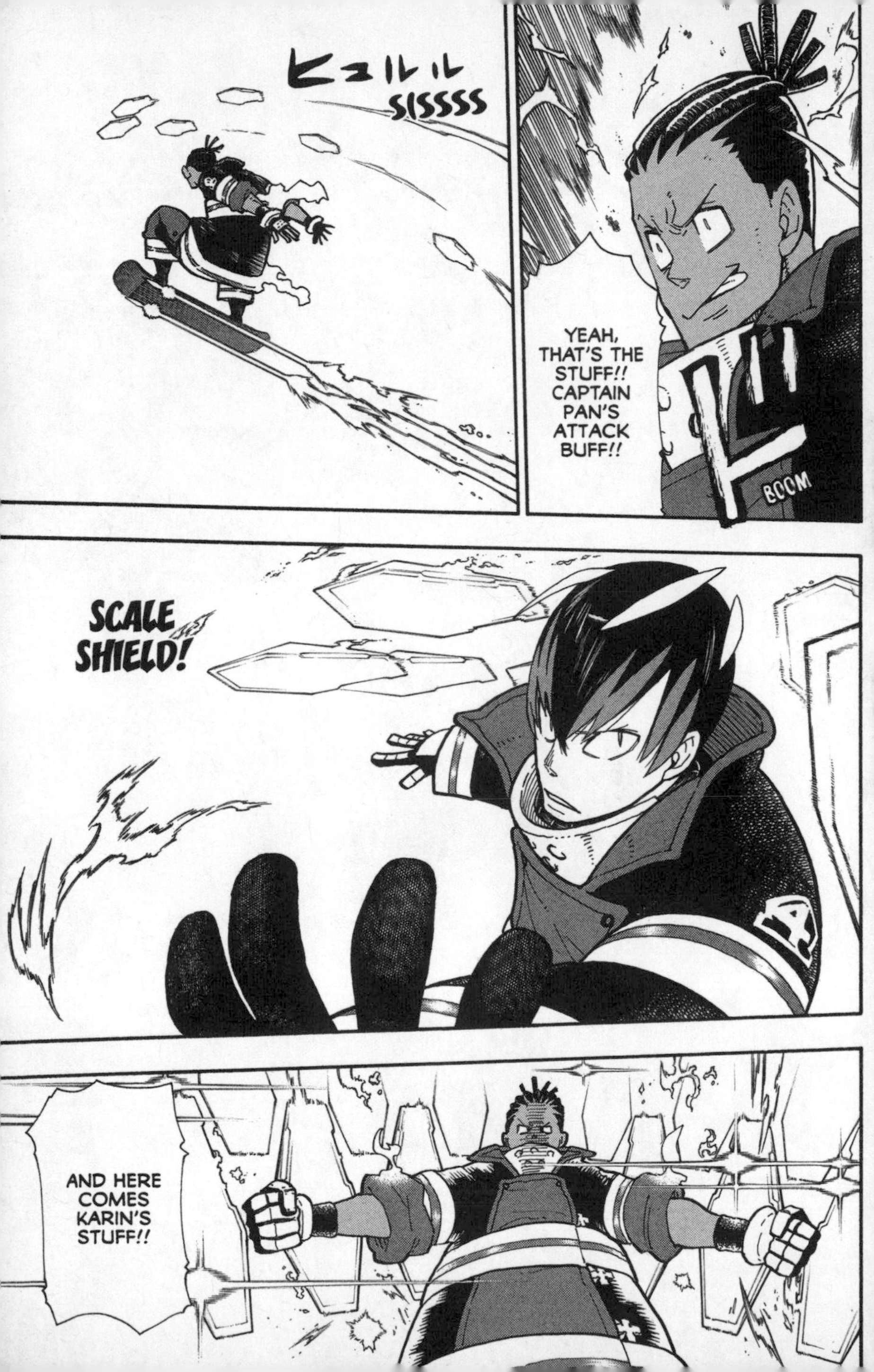
YEAH, THAT'S THE STUFF!! CAPTAIN PAN'S ATTACK BUFF!!
BOOM
ヒュルル
SISSSS
SCALE SHIELD!
AND HERE COMES KARIN'S STUFF!!

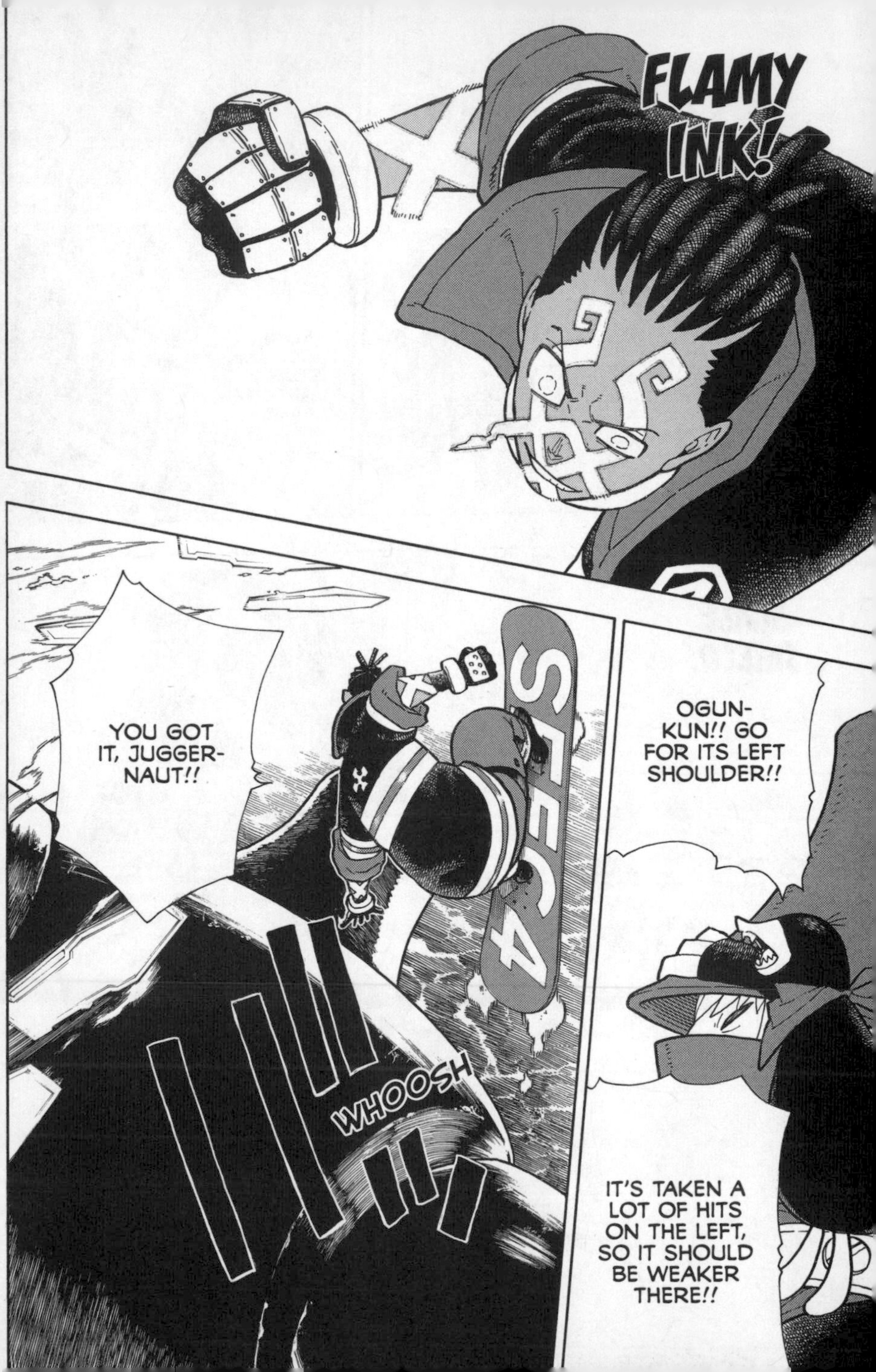
FLAMY INK!
OGUN-KUN!! GO FOR ITS LEFT SHOULDER!!
IT'S TAKEN A LOT OF HITS ON THE LEFT, SO IT SHOULD BE WEAKER THERE!!
YOU GOT IT, JUGGERNAUT!!
WHOOSH

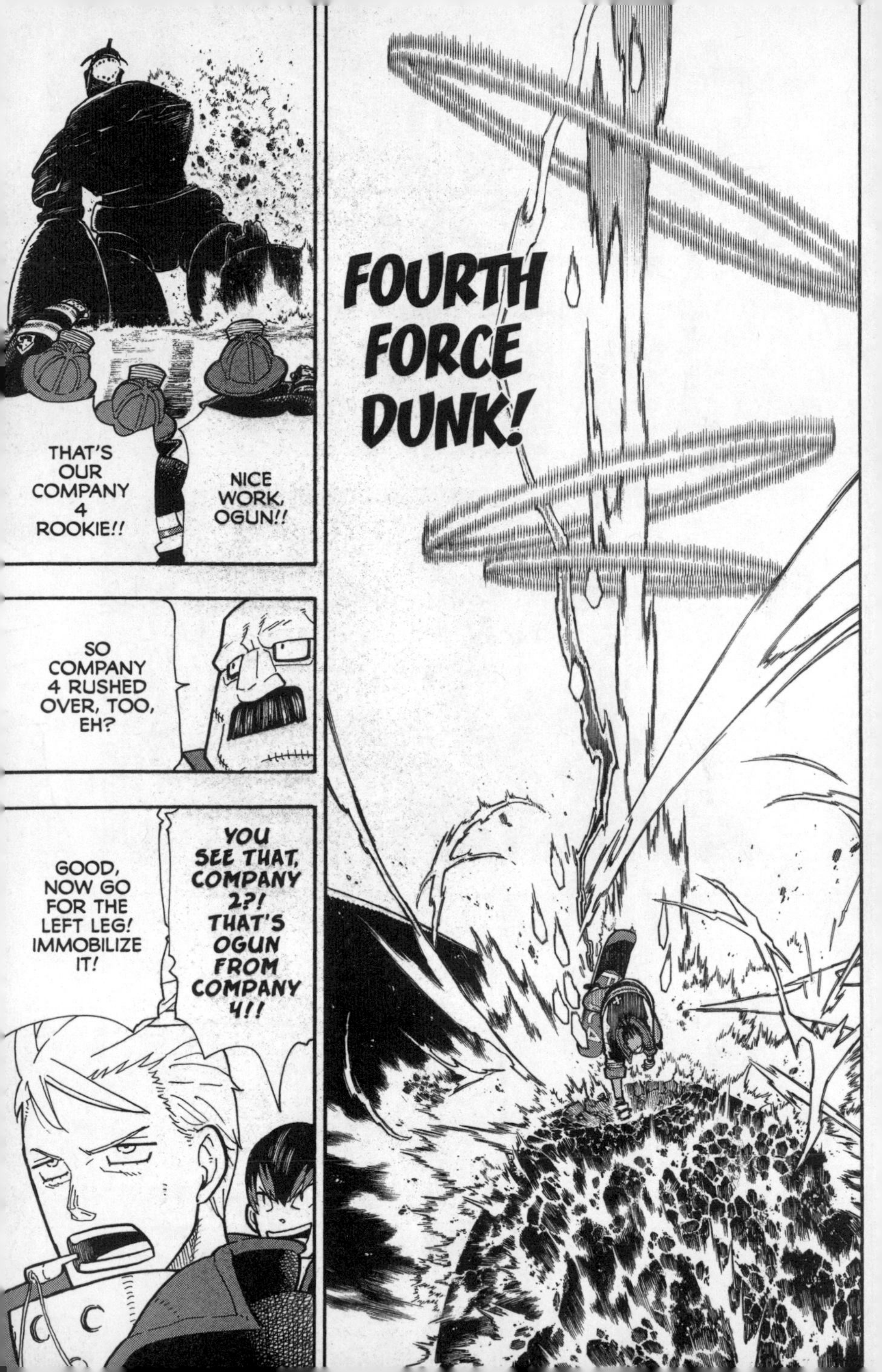
FOURTH FORCE DUNK!
NICE WORK, OGUN!!
THAT'S OUR COMPANY 4 ROOKIE!!
SO COMPANY 4 RUSHED OVER, TOO, EH?
YOU SEE THAT, COMPANY 2?! THAT'S OGUN FROM COMPANY 4!!
GOOD, NOW GO FOR THE LEFT LEG! IMMOBILIZE IT!

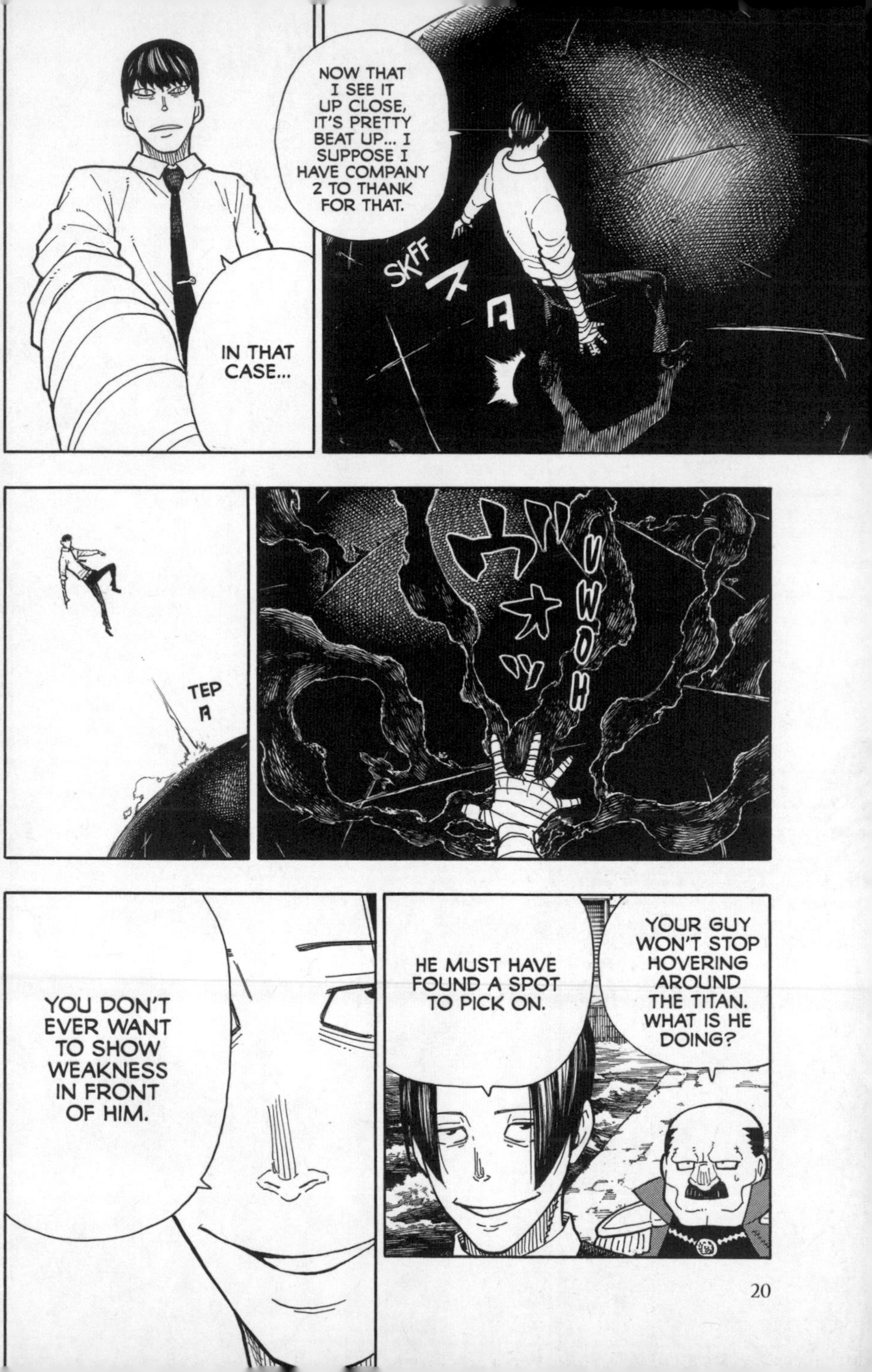
NOW THAT I SEE IT UP CLOSE, IT'S PRETTY BEAT UP... I SUPPOSE I HAVE COMPANY 2 TO THANK FOR THAT.
SKFF
IN THAT CASE...
UWOOH
TEP
YOUR GUY WON'T STOP HOVERING AROUND THE TITAN. WHAT IS HE DOING?
HE MUST HAVE FOUND A SPOT TO PICK ON.
YOU DON'T EVER WANT TO SHOW WEAKNESS IN FRONT OF HIM.

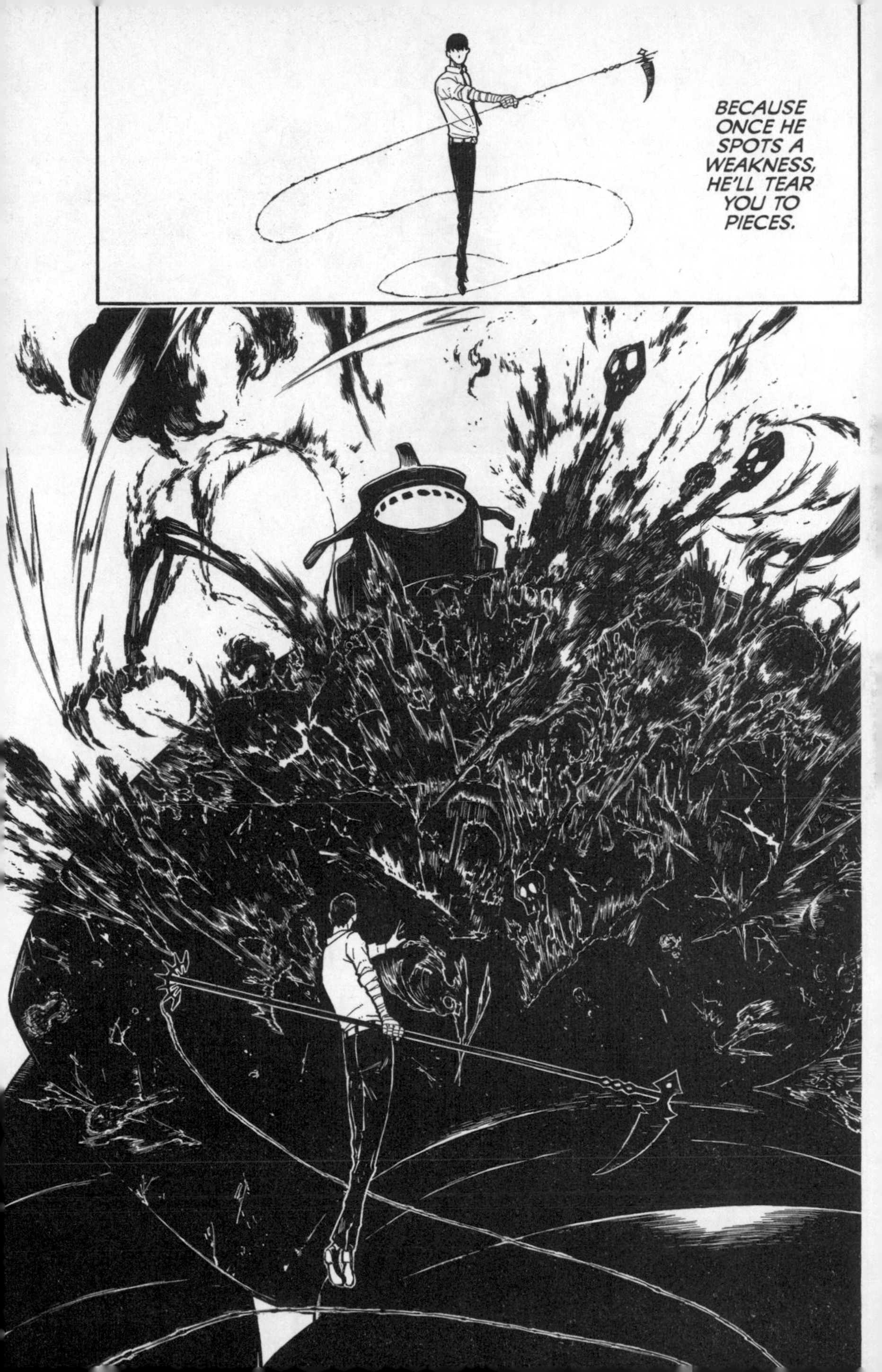
BECAUSE ONCE HE SPOTS A WEAKNESS, HE'LL TEAR YOU TO PIECES.

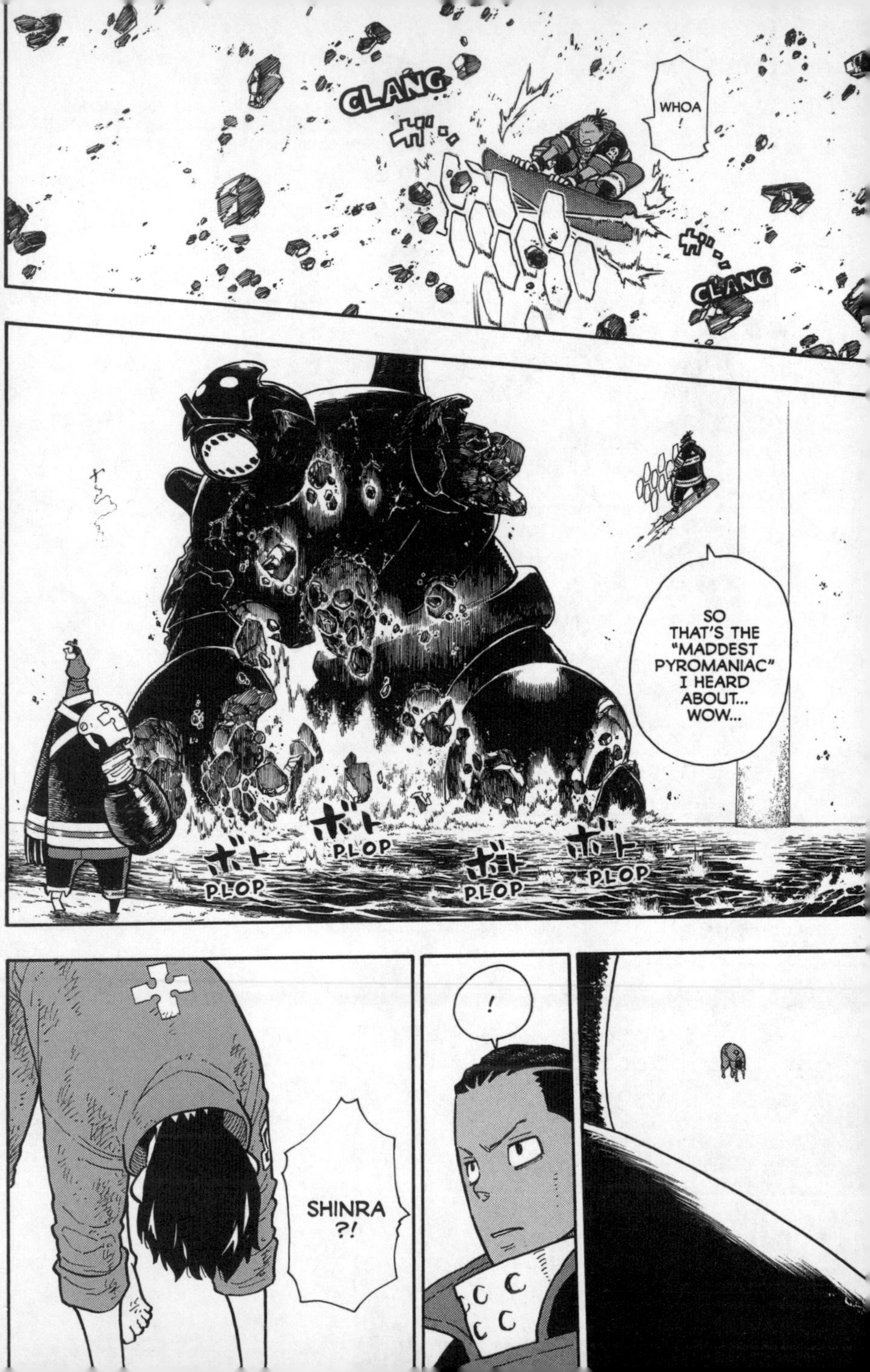
WHOA
!
CLANG
CLANG
SO THAT'S THE "MADDEST PYROMANIAC" I HEARD ABOUT... WOW...
PLOP
PLOP
PLOP
PLOP
!
SHINRA
?!

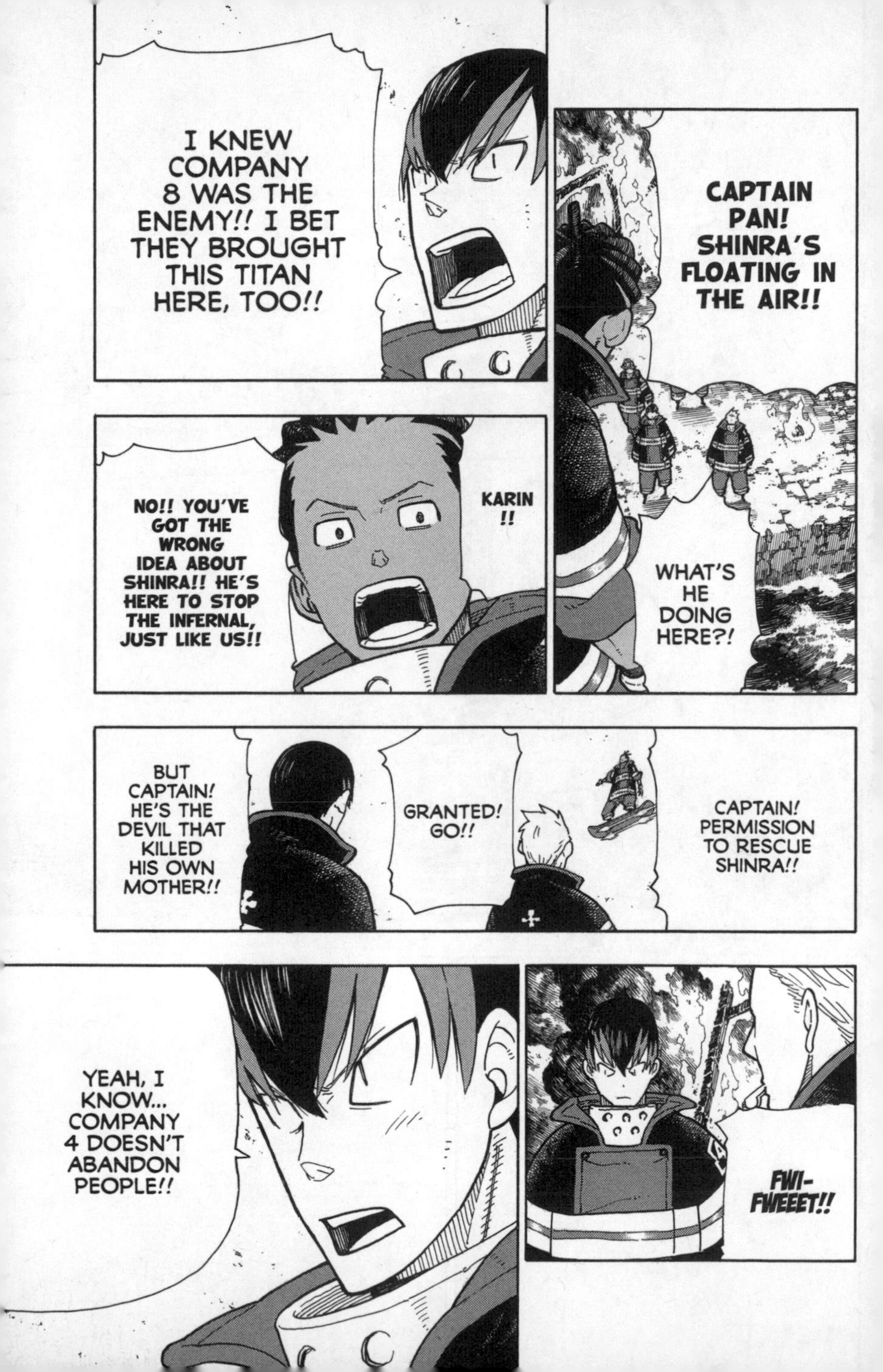
CAPTAIN PAN! SHINRA'S FLOATING IN THE AIR!!
WHAT'S HE DOING HERE?!
I KNEW COMPANY 8 WAS THE ENEMY!! I BET THEY BROUGHT THIS TITAN HERE, TOO!!
KARIN !!
NO!! YOU'VE GOT THE WRONG IDEA ABOUT SHINRA!! HE'S HERE TO STOP THE INFERNAL, JUST LIKE US!!
CAPTAIN! PERMISSION TO RESCUE SHINRA!!
GRANTED! GO!!
BUT CAPTAIN! HE'S THE DEVIL THAT KILLED HIS OWN MOTHER!!
FWI-FWEEET!!
YEAH, I KNOW... COMPANY 4 DOESN'T ABANDON PEOPLE!!

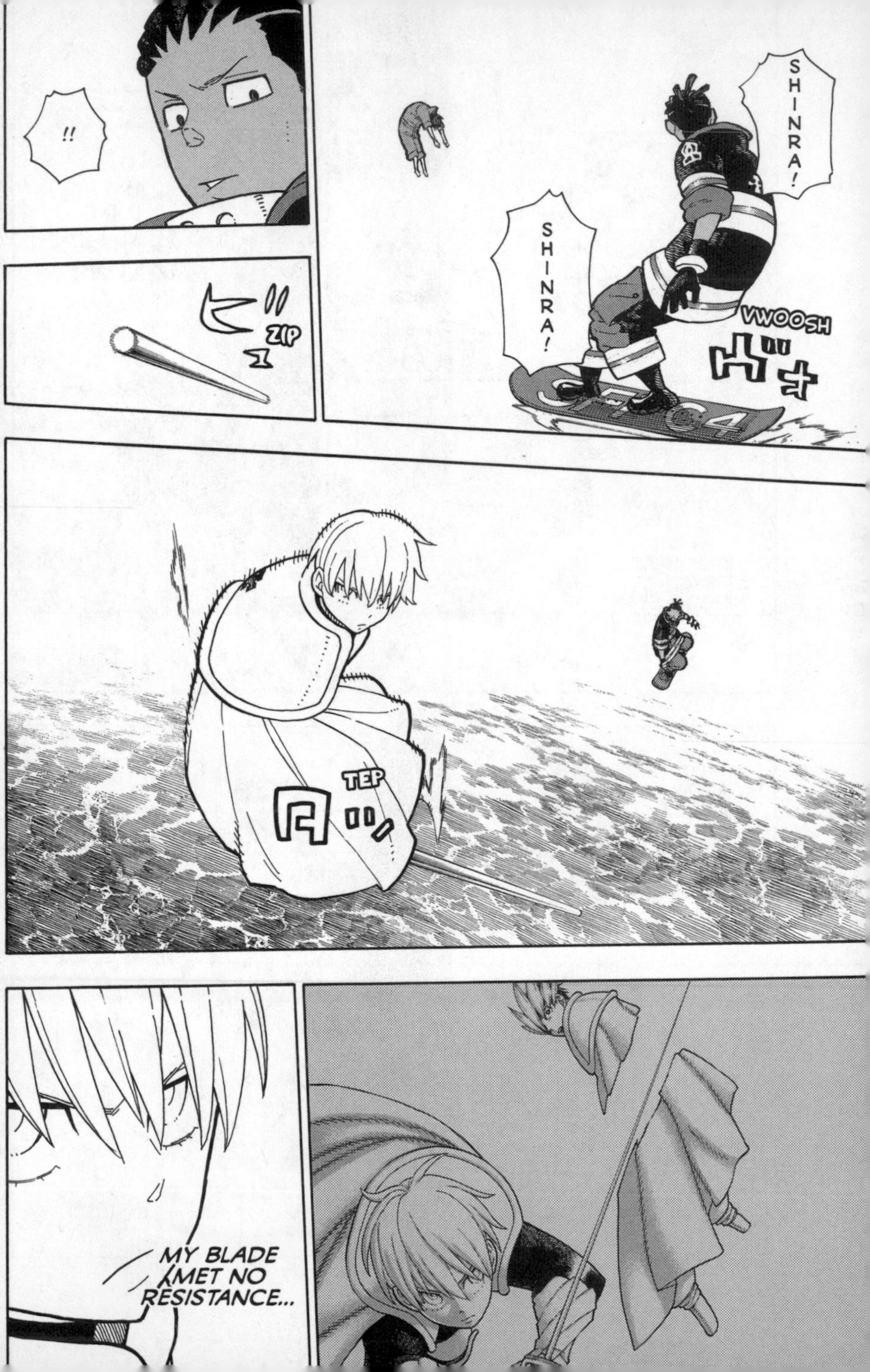
SHINRA!
SHINRA!
VWOOSH
!!
ZIP
TEP
MY BLADE MET NO RESISTANCE...

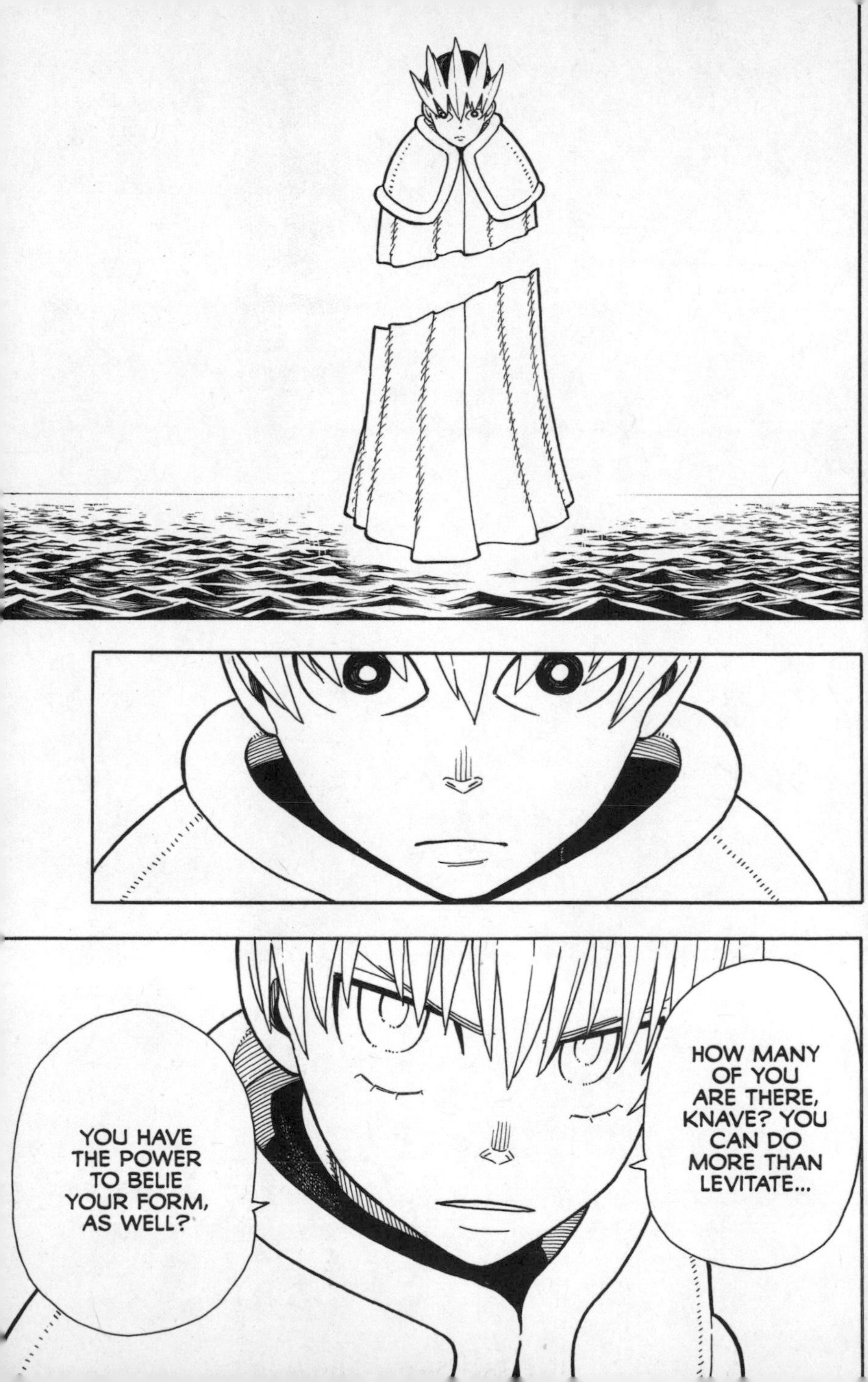
HOW MANY OF YOU ARE THERE, KNAVE? YOU CAN DO MORE THAN LEVITATE...
YOU HAVE THE POWER TO BELIE YOUR FORM, AS WELL?

FIRE FORCE

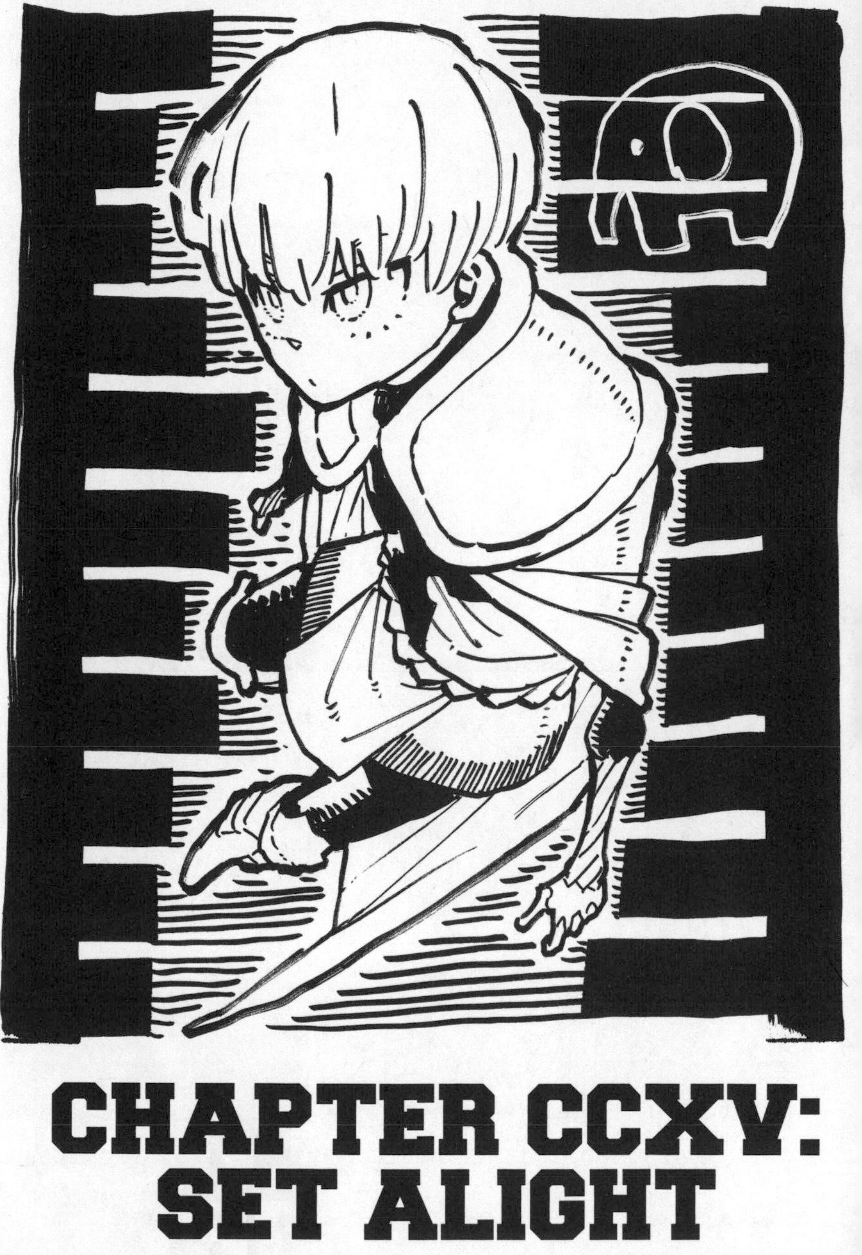

CHAPTER CCXV: SET ALIGHT

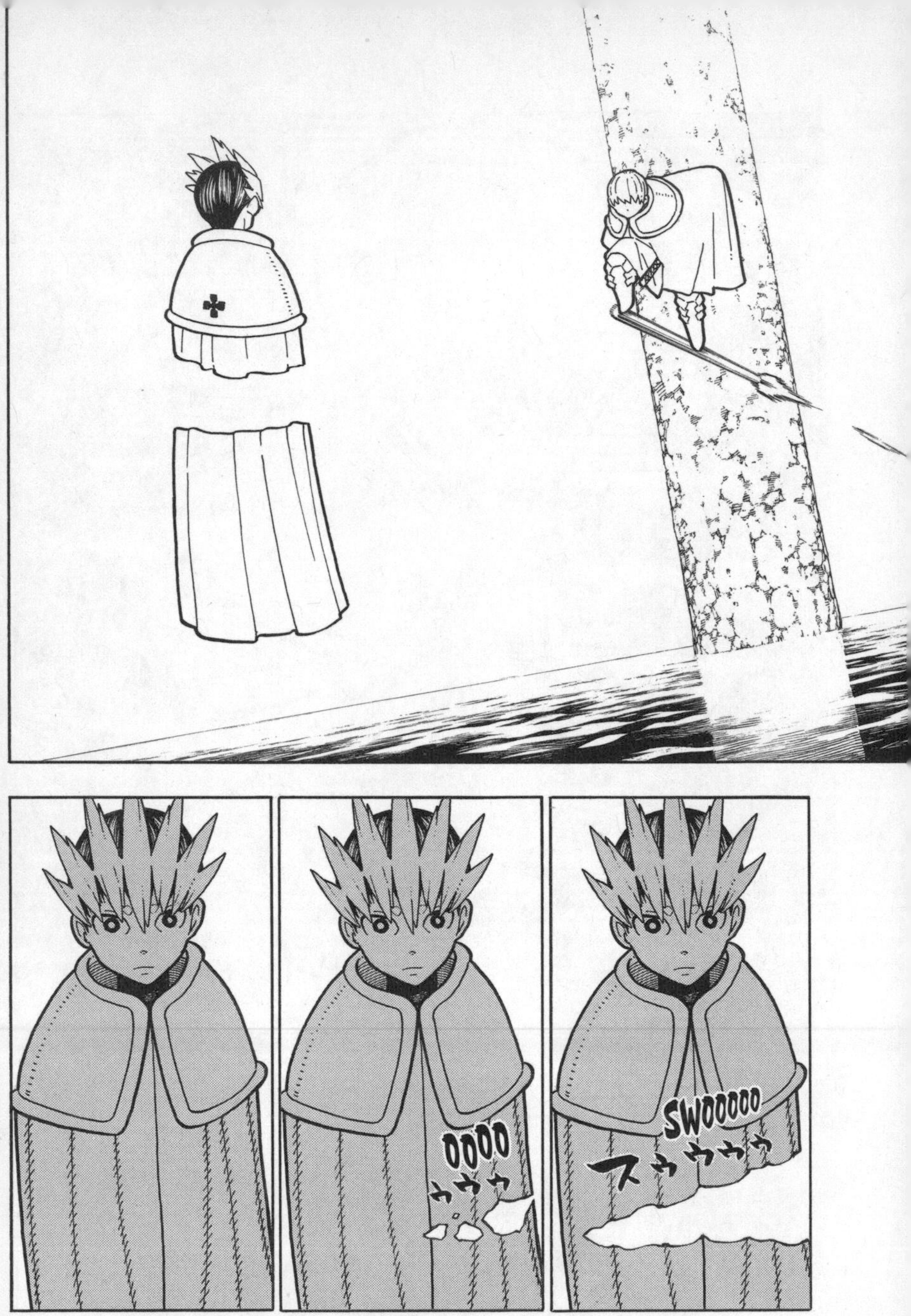
SWOOOOO
スゥゥゥゥ
OOOO
ゥゥゥ

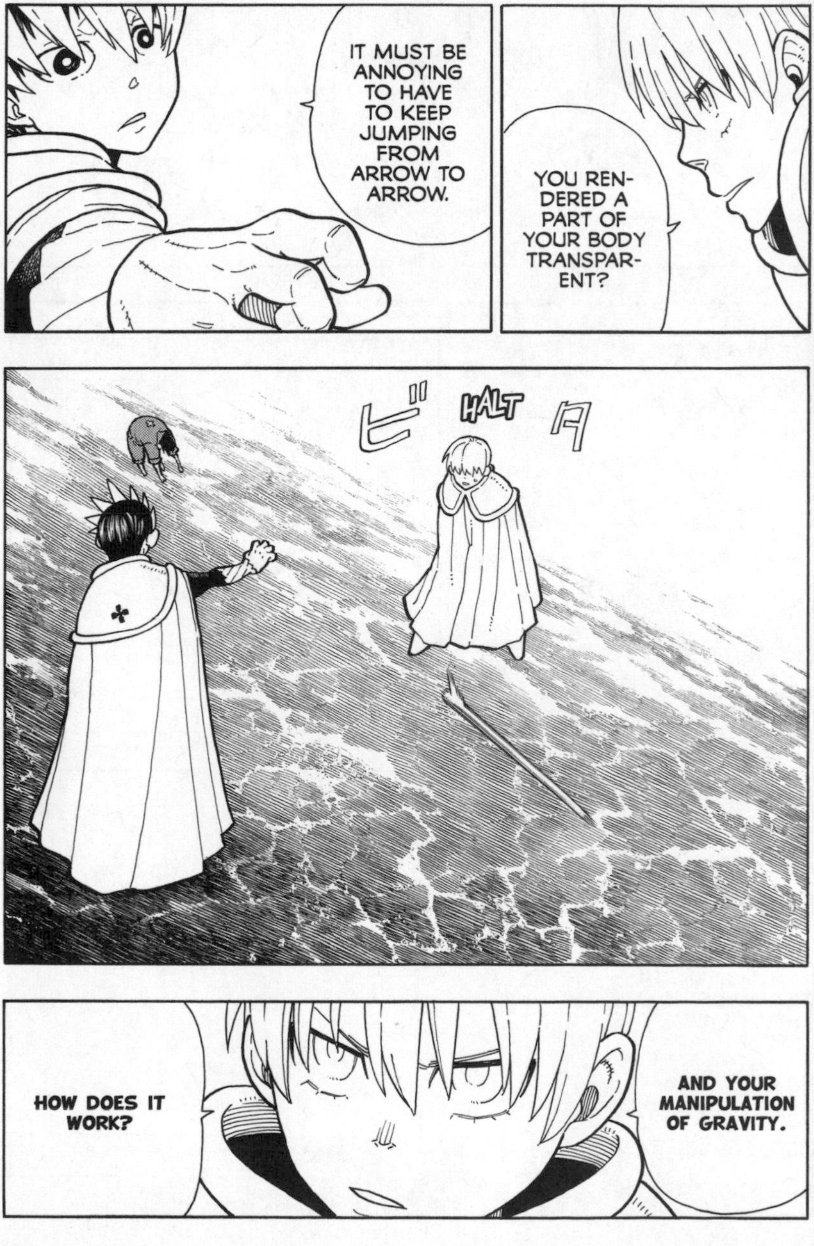
YOU RENDERED A PART OF YOUR BODY TRANSPARENT?
IT MUST BE ANNOYING TO HAVE TO KEEP JUMPING FROM ARROW TO ARROW.
HALT
AND YOUR MANIPULATION OF GRAVITY.
HOW DOES IT WORK?

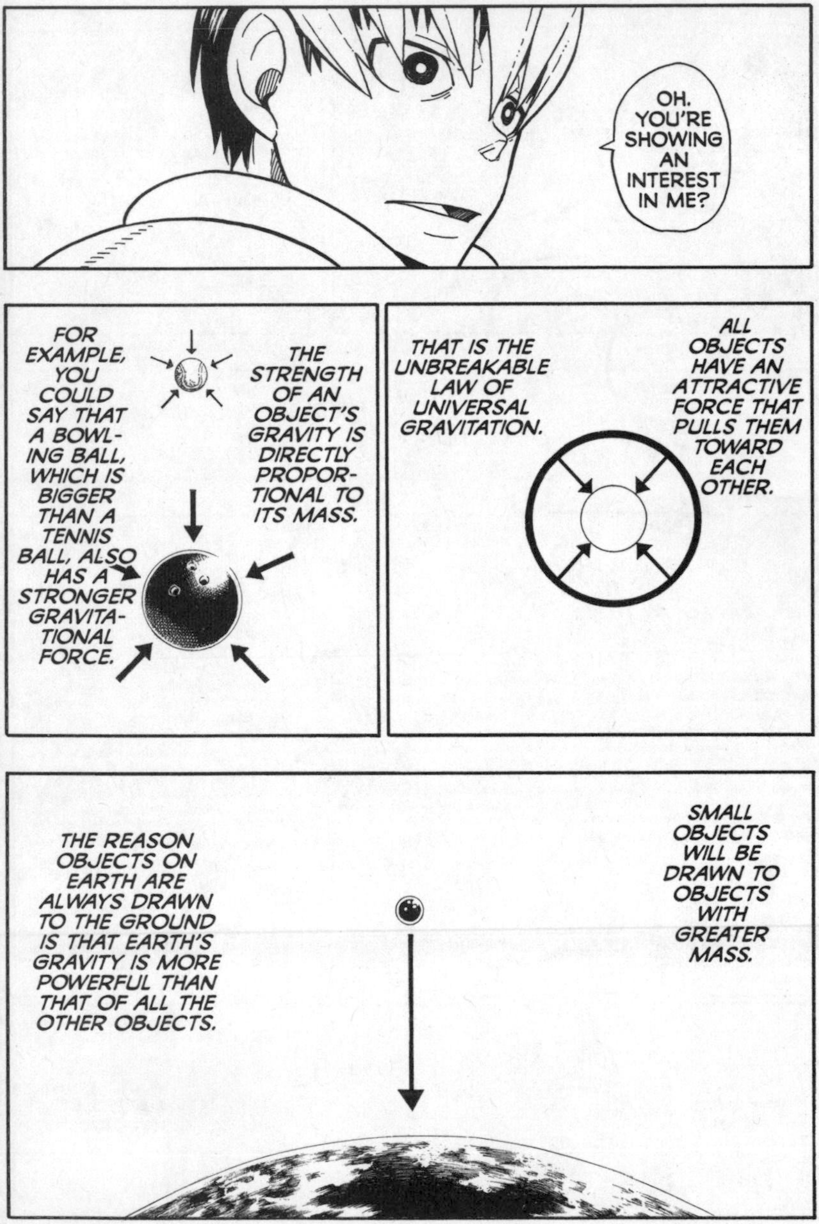
OH. YOU'RE SHOWING AN INTEREST IN ME?
ALL OBJECTS HAVE AN ATTRACTIVE FORCE THAT PULLS THEM TOWARD EACH OTHER.
THAT IS THE UNBREAKABLE LAW OF UNIVERSAL GRAVITATION.
THE STRENGTH OF AN OBJECT'S GRAVITY IS DIRECTLY PROPOR-TIONAL TO ITS MASS.
FOR EXAMPLE, YOU COULD SAY THAT A BOWL-ING BALL, WHICH IS BIGGER THAN A TENNIS BALL, ALSO HAS A STRONGER GRAVITA-TIONAL FORCE.
SMALL OBJECTS WILL BE DRAWN TO OBJECTS WITH GREATER MASS.
THE REASON OBJECTS ON EARTH ARE ALWAYS DRAWN TO THE GROUND IS THAT EARTH'S GRAVITY IS MORE POWERFUL THAN THAT OF ALL THE OTHER OBJECTS.

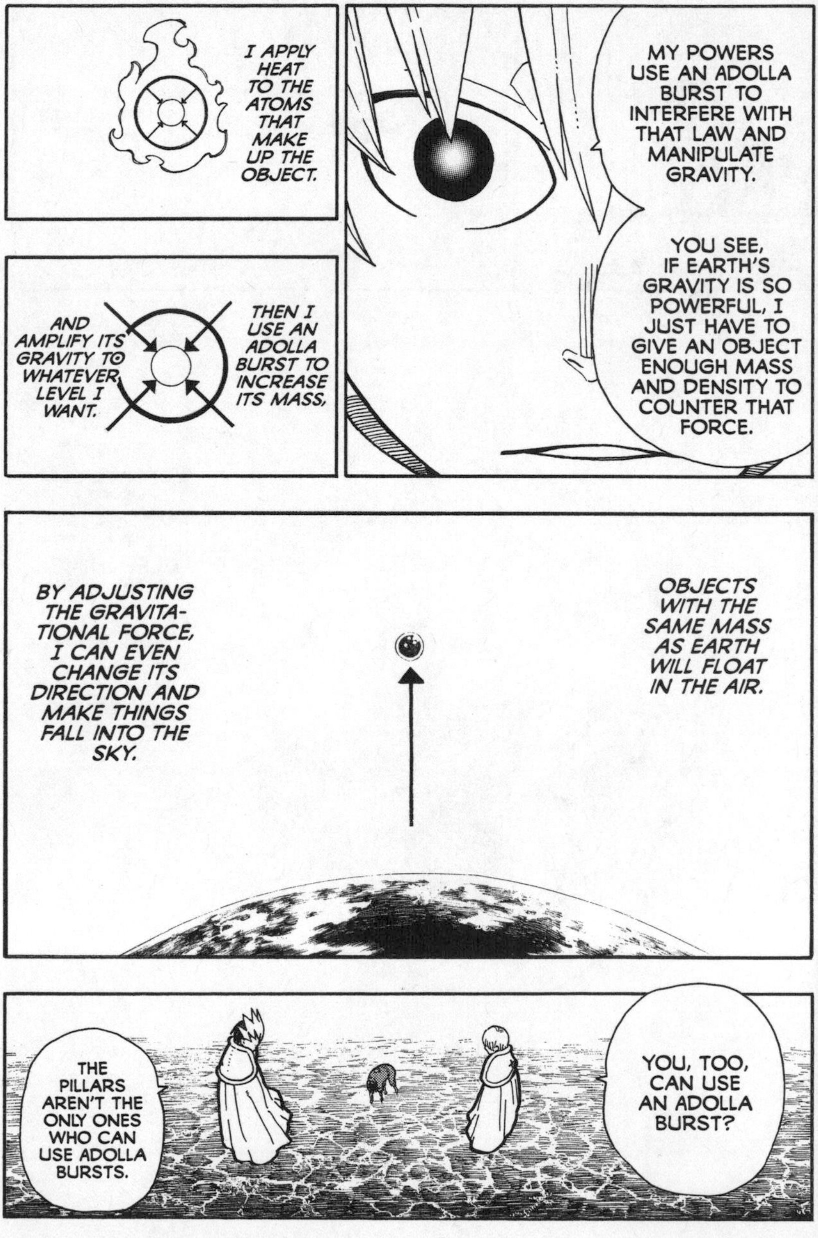
MY POWERS USE AN ADOLLA BURST TO INTERFERE WITH THAT LAW AND MANIPULATE GRAVITY.
YOU SEE, IF EARTH'S GRAVITY IS SO POWERFUL, I JUST HAVE TO GIVE AN OBJECT ENOUGH MASS AND DENSITY TO COUNTER THAT FORCE.
I APPLY HEAT TO THE ATOMS THAT MAKE UP THE OBJECT.
THEN I USE AN ADOLLA BURST TO INCREASE ITS MASS,
AND AMPLIFY ITS GRAVITY TO WHATEVER LEVEL I WANT.
OBJECTS WITH THE SAME MASS AS EARTH WILL FLOAT IN THE AIR.
BY ADJUSTING THE GRAVITA-TIONAL FORCE, I CAN EVEN CHANGE ITS DIRECTION AND MAKE THINGS FALL INTO THE SKY.
YOU, TOO, CAN USE AN ADOLLA BURST?
THE PILLARS AREN'T THE ONLY ONES WHO CAN USE ADOLLA BURSTS.

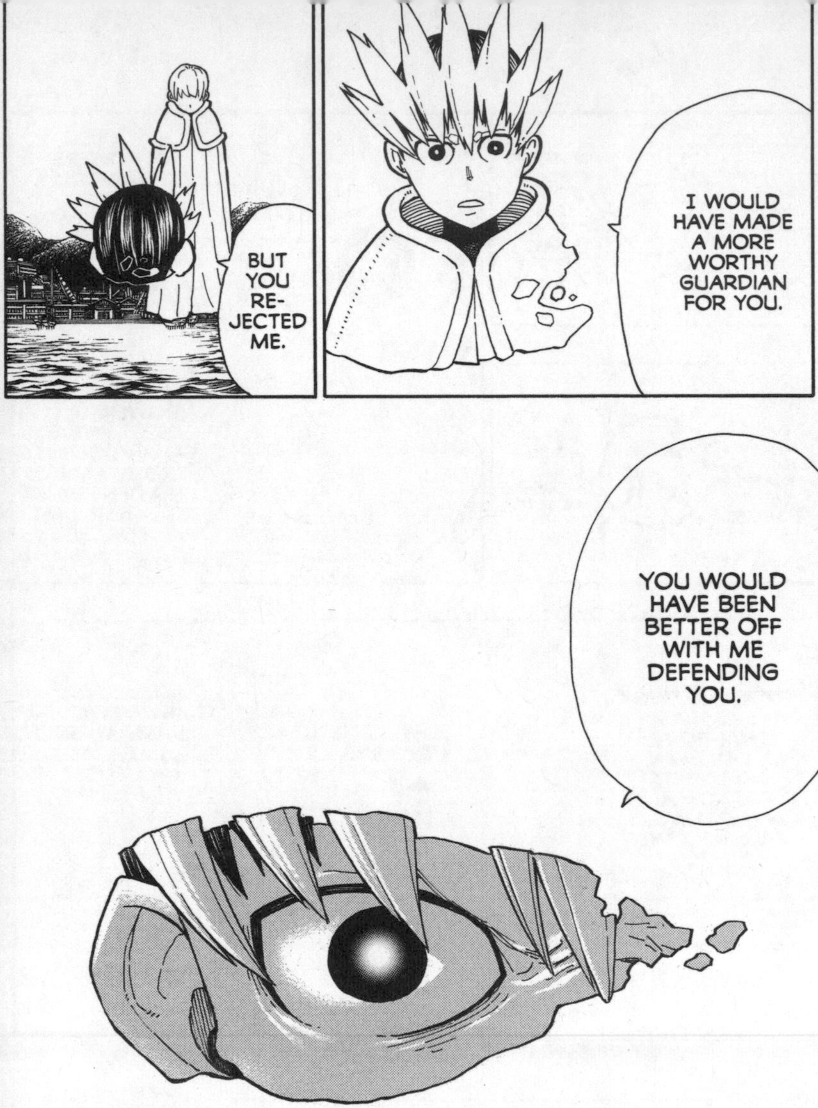
I WOULD HAVE MADE A MORE WORTHY GUARDIAN FOR YOU.
BUT YOU RE-JECTED ME.
YOU WOULD HAVE BEEN BETTER OFF WITH ME DEFENDING YOU.

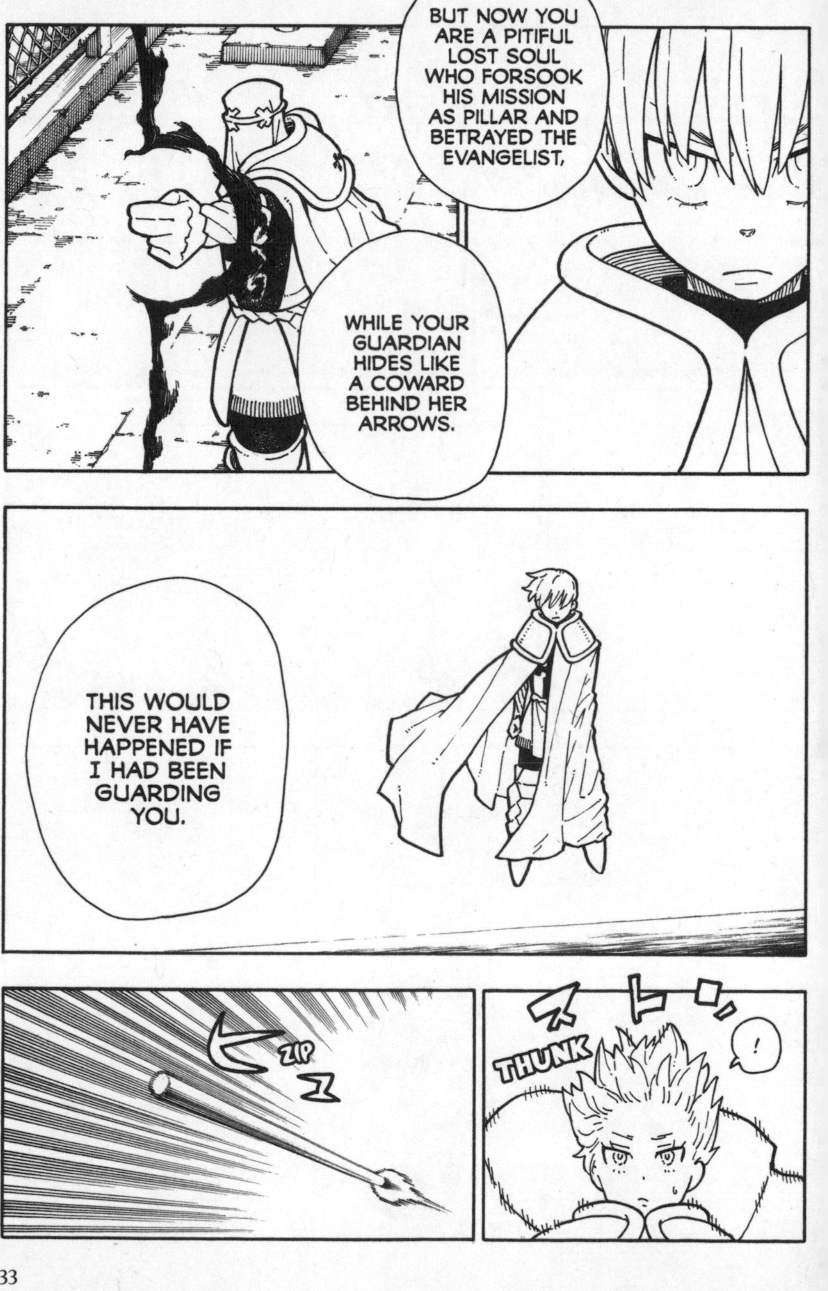
BUT NOW YOU ARE A PITIFUL LOST SOUL WHO FORSOOK HIS MISSION AS PILLAR AND BETRAYED THE EVANGELIST,
WHILE YOUR GUARDIAN HIDES LIKE A COWARD BEHIND HER ARROWS.
THIS WOULD NEVER HAVE HAPPENED IF I HAD BEEN GUARDING YOU.
THUNK
!
ZIP

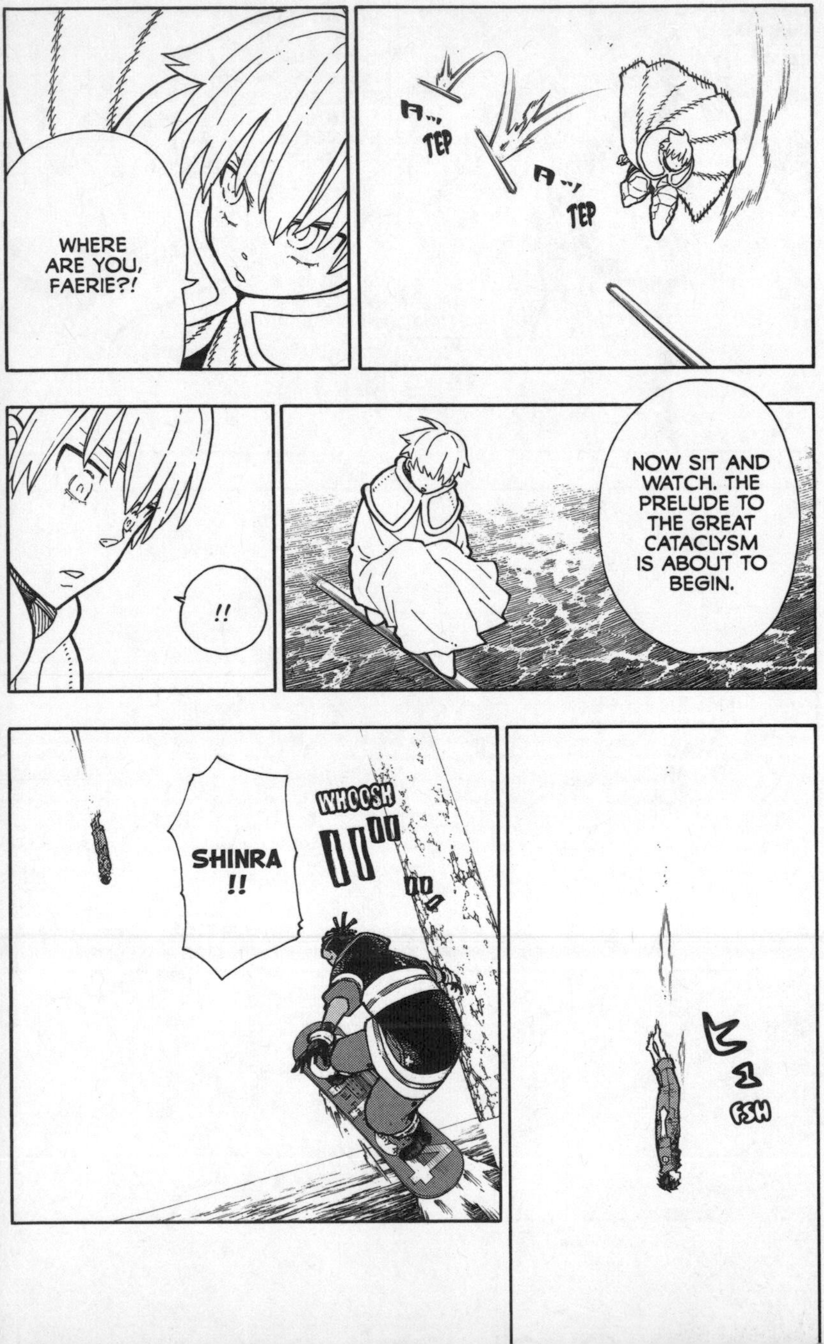
TEP
TEP
WHERE ARE YOU, FAERIE?!
NOW SIT AND WATCH. THE PRELUDE TO THE GREAT CATACLYSM IS ABOUT TO BEGIN.
!!
FSH
WHOOSH
SHINRA!!

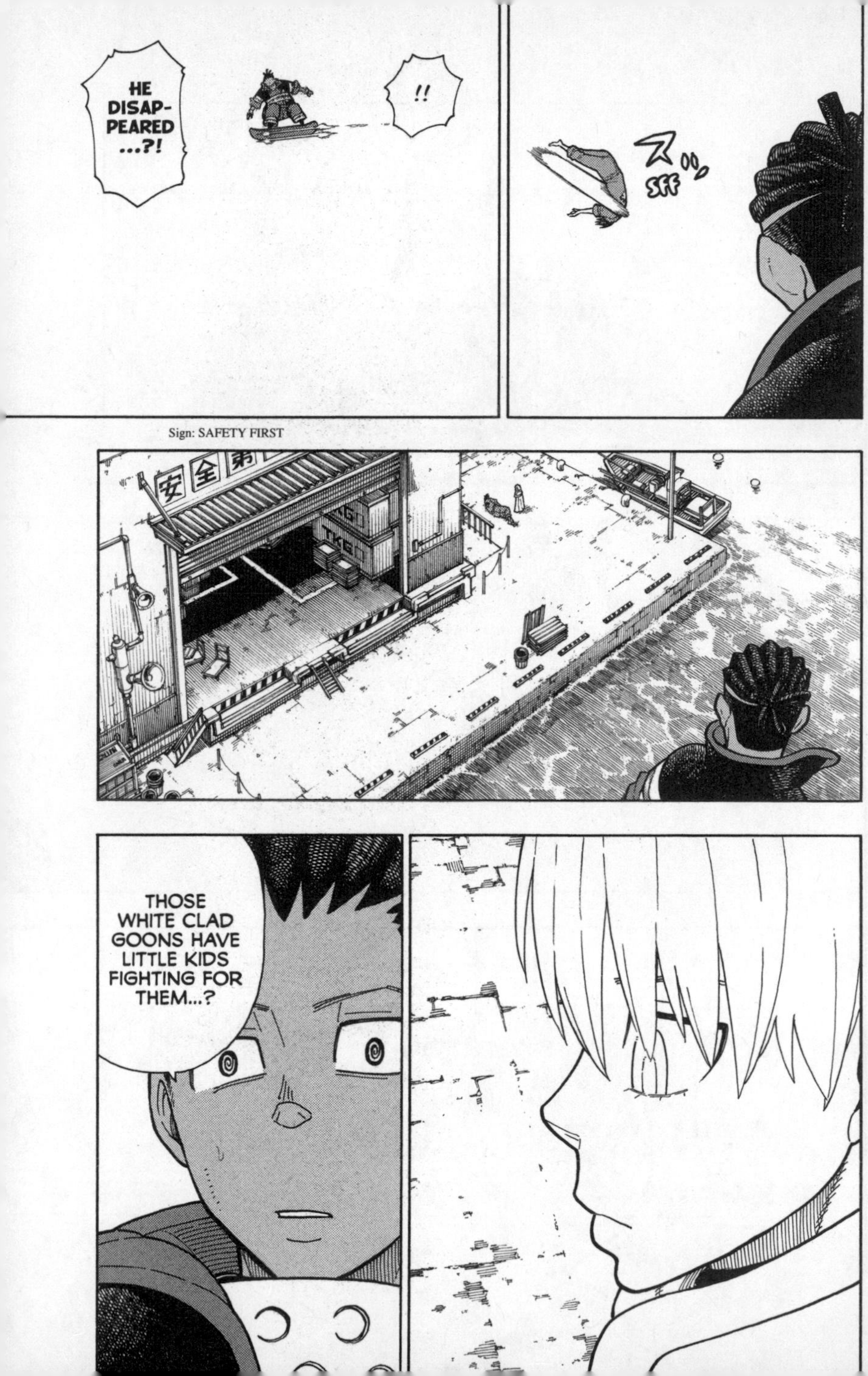
SFF
!!
HE DISAP-PEARED ...?!
Sign: SAFETY FIRST
安全第
THOSE WHITE CLAD GOONS HAVE LITTLE KIDS FIGHTING FOR THEM...?

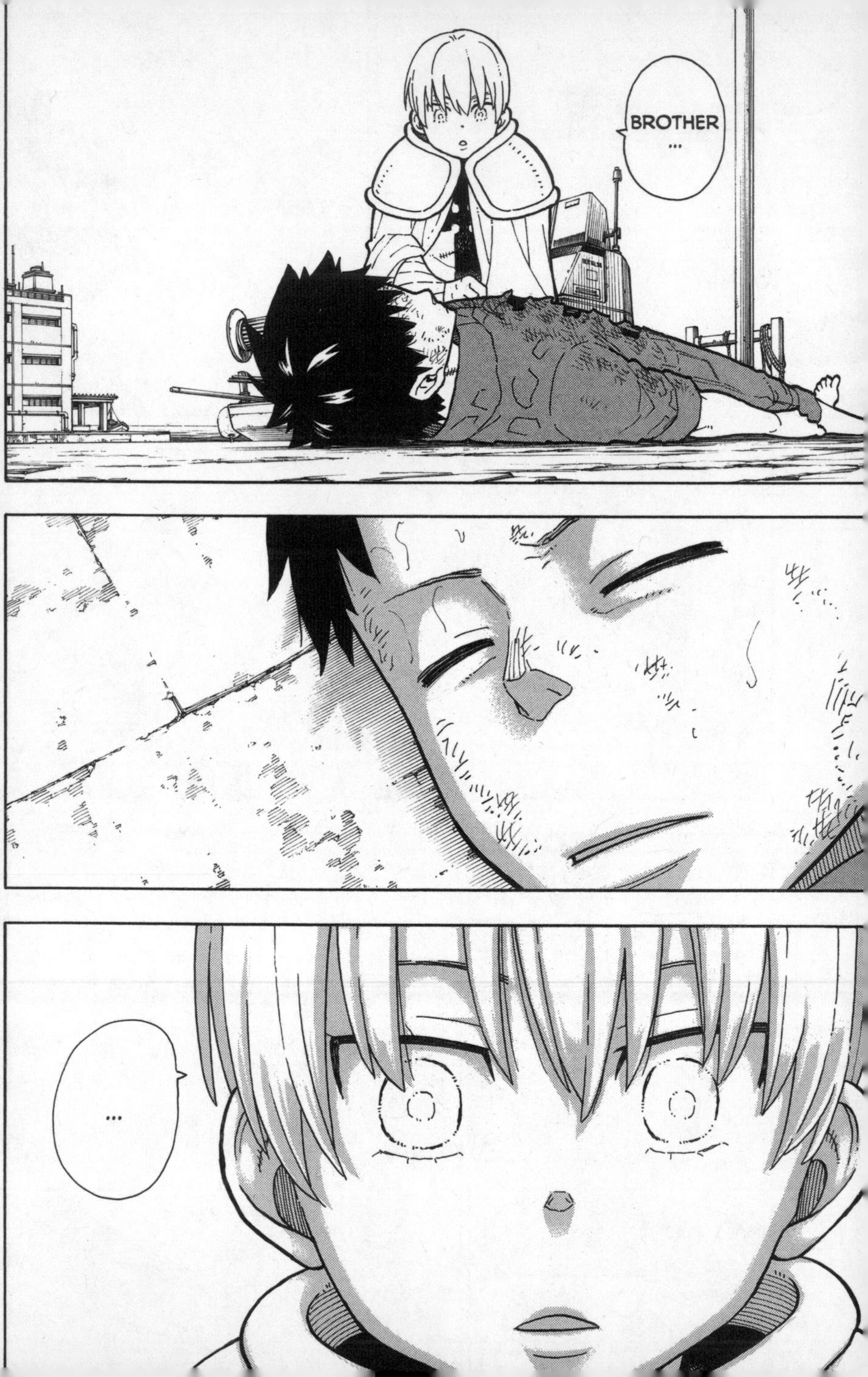
BROTHER
...
...

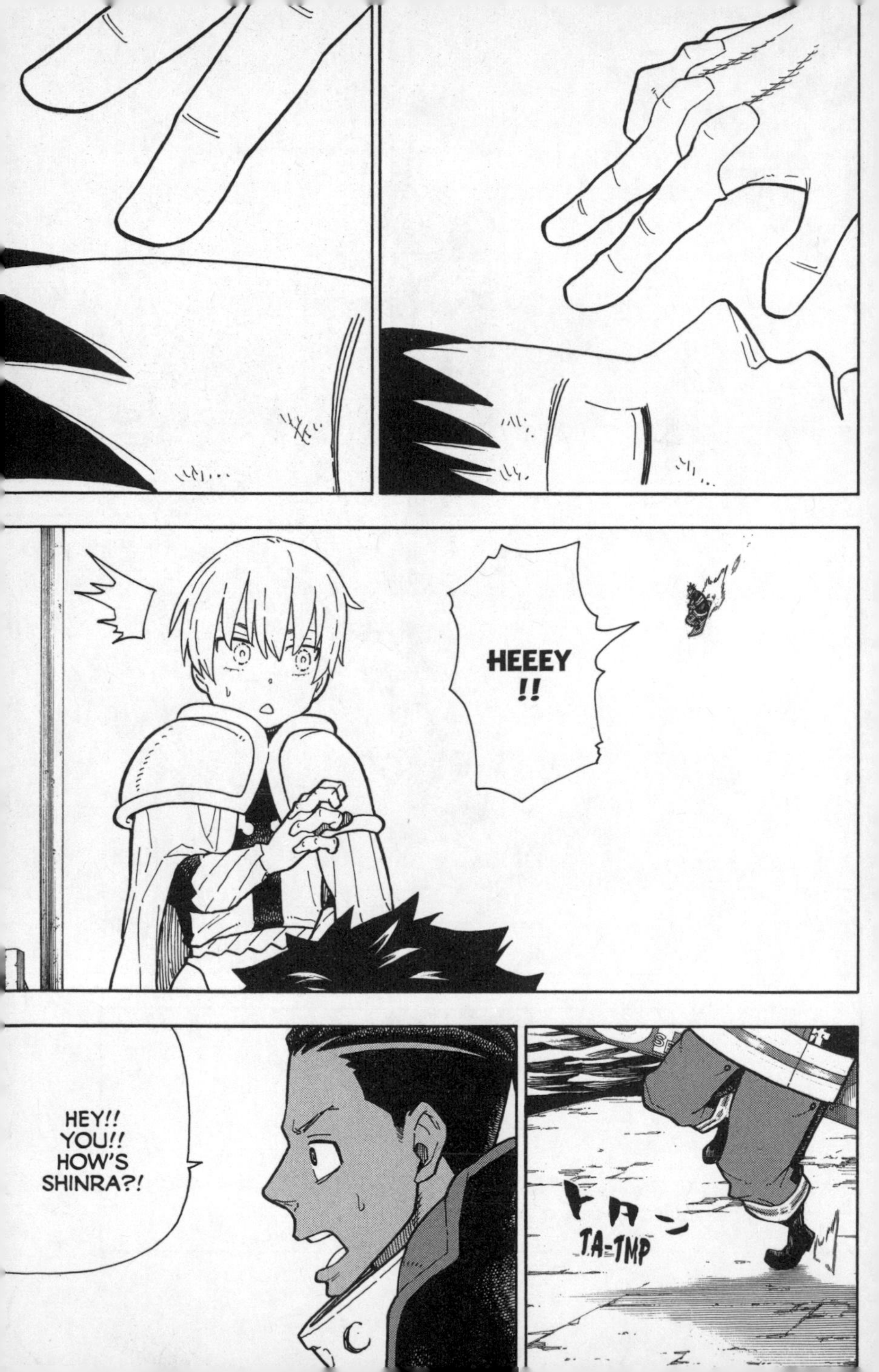
HEEEY!!
T.A-TMP
HEY!! YOU!! HOW'S SHINRA?!

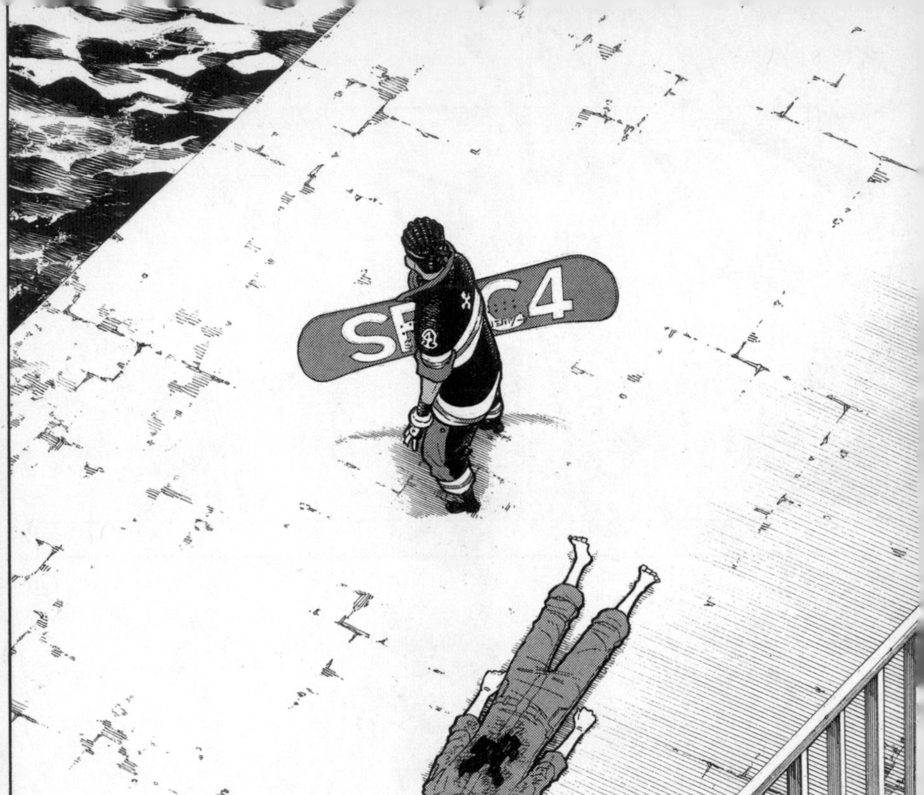

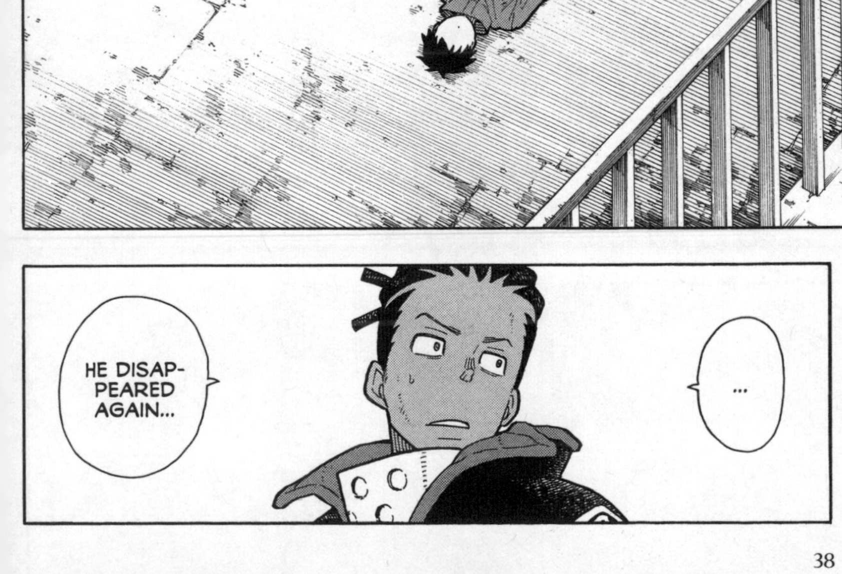
...
HE DISAPPEARED AGAIN...

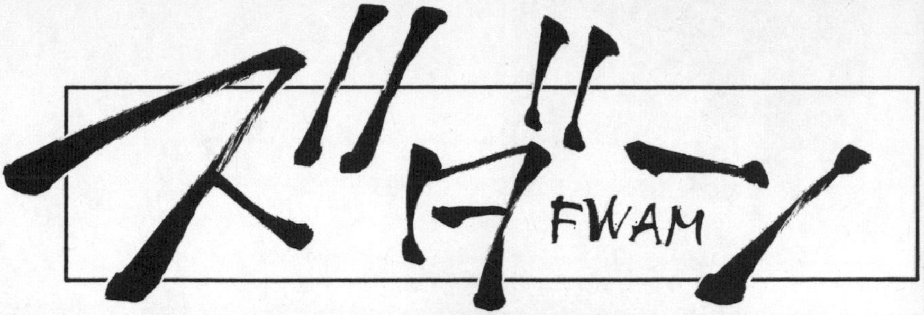
FWAM
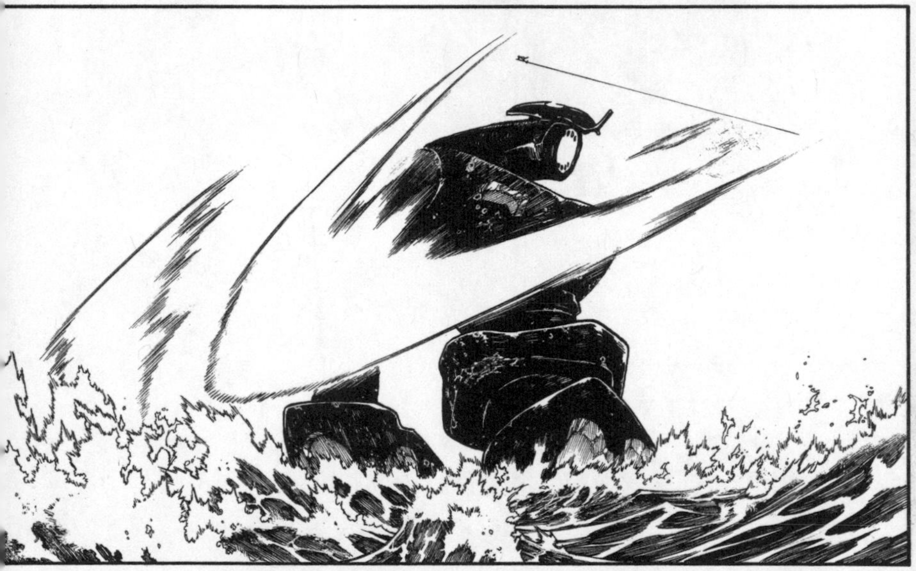
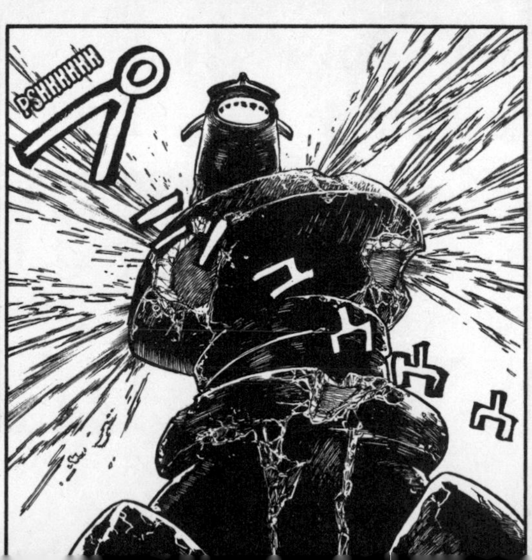
PSHHHHHH
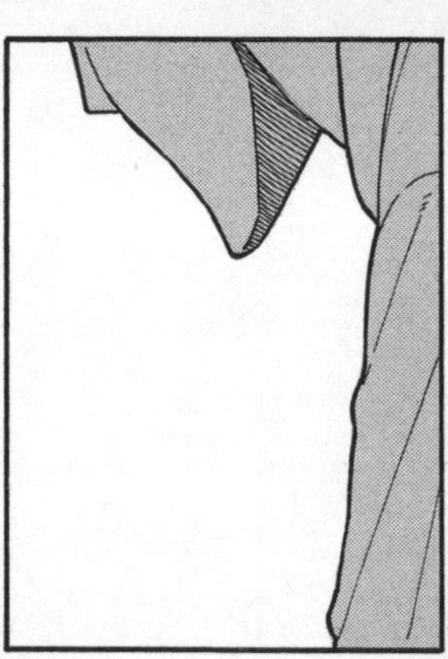

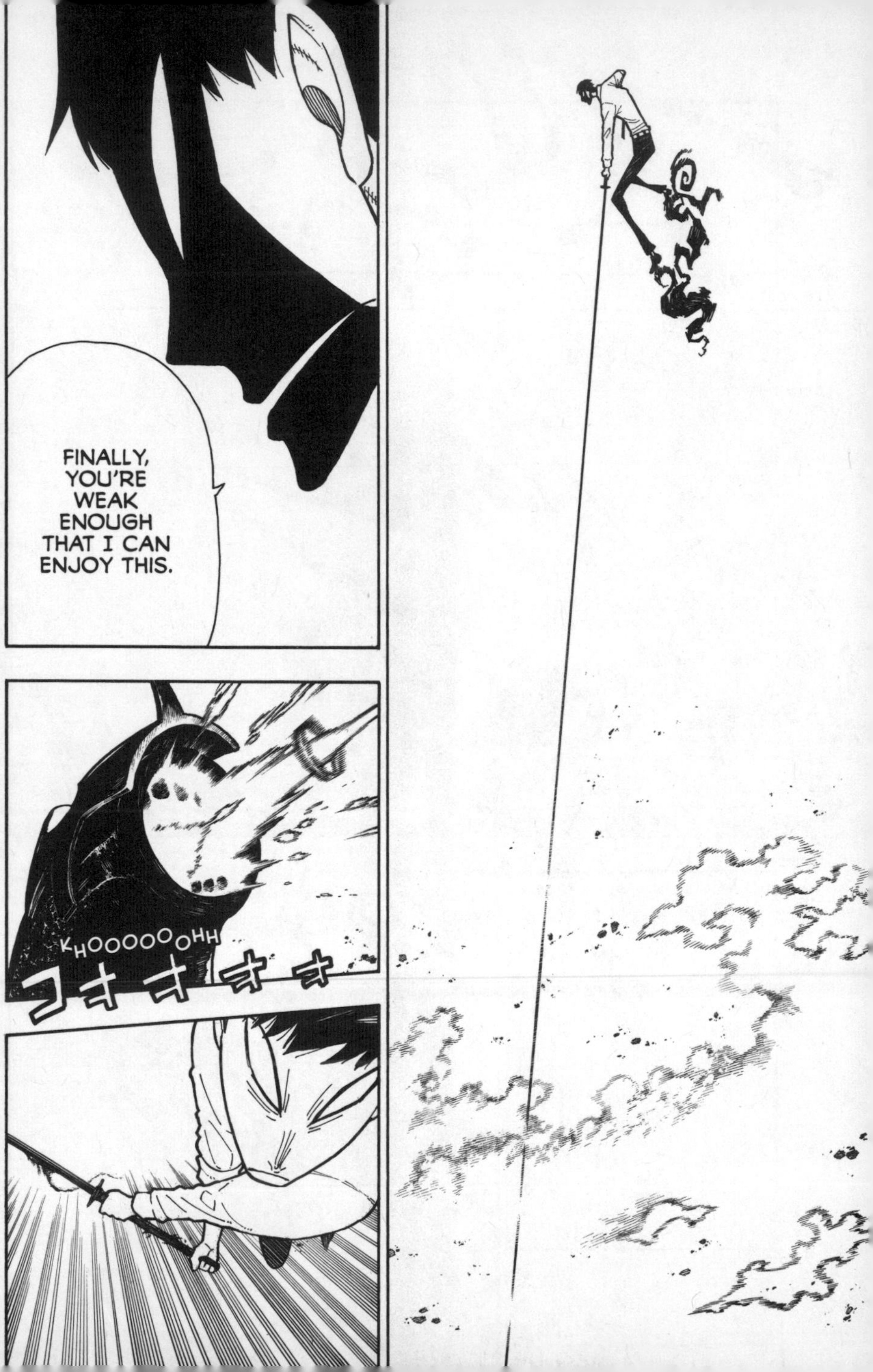
FINALLY, YOU'RE WEAK ENOUGH THAT I CAN ENJOY THIS.
KHOOOOOOHH
コオオオオ

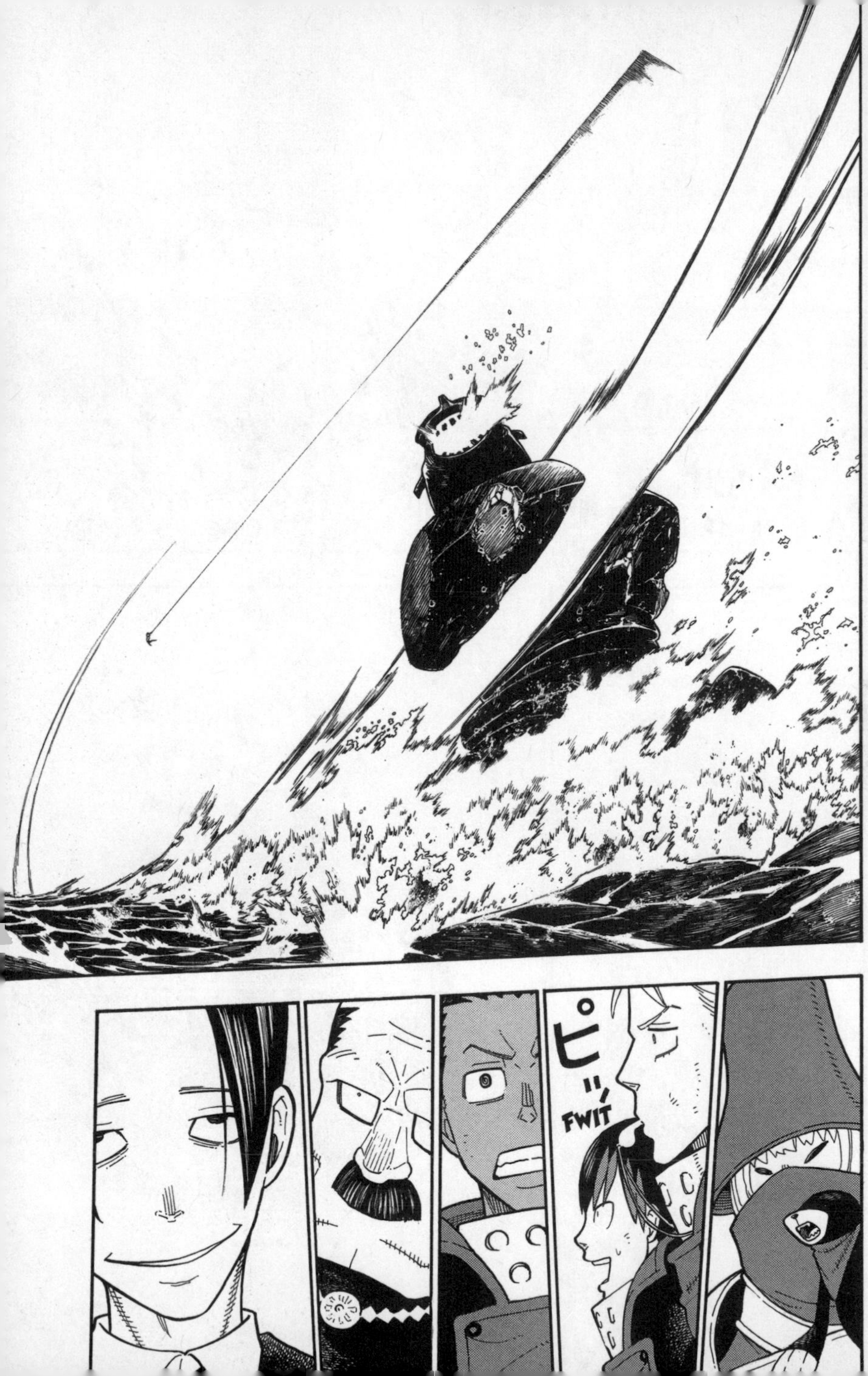
ピッ
FWIT

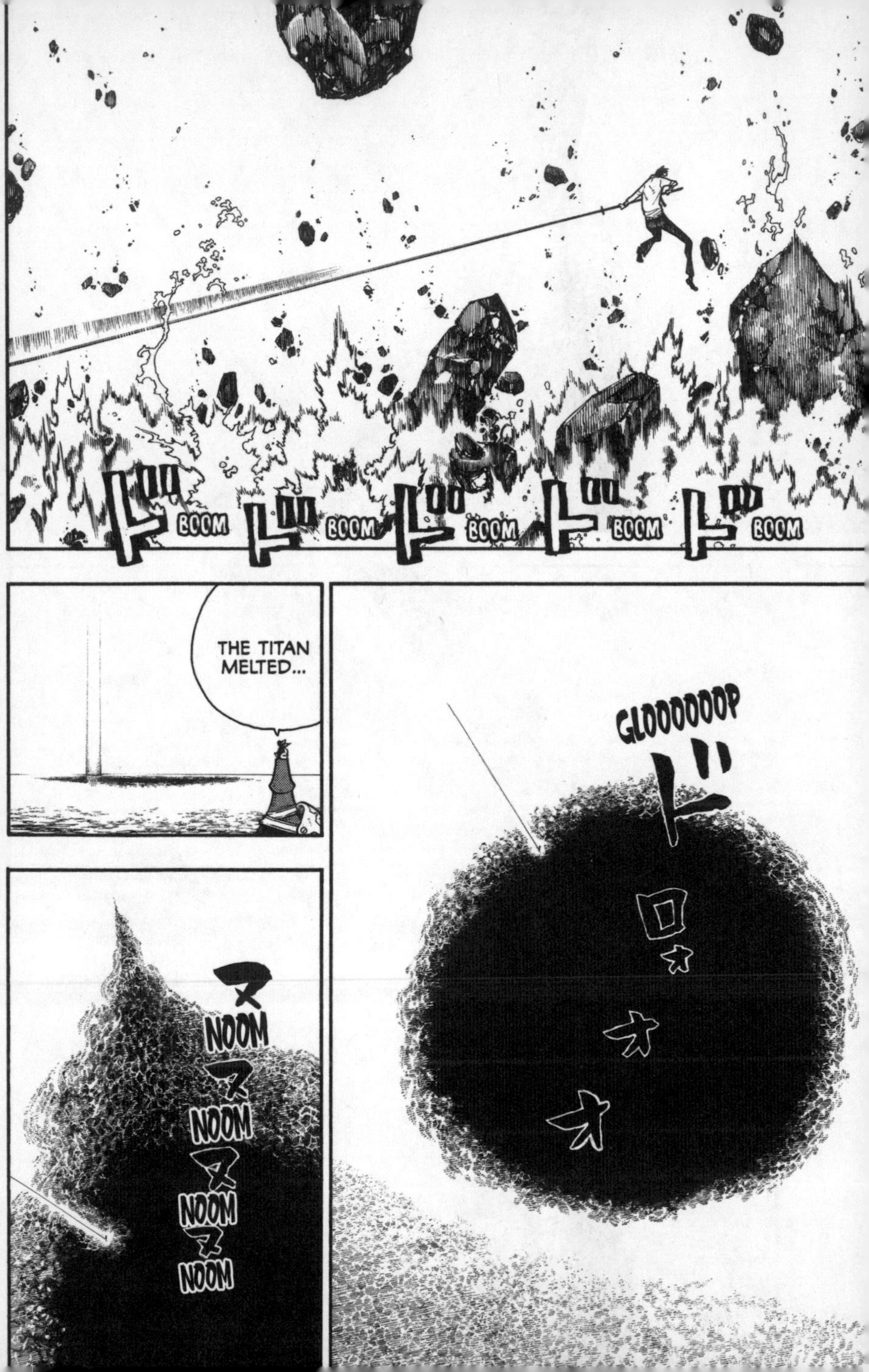

ド BOOM
ド BOOM
ド BOOM
ド BOOM
ド BOOM
GLOOOOOOP
ドロォオオ
THE TITAN MELTED...
ヌ NOOM
ヌ NOOM
ヌ NOOM
ヌ NOOM

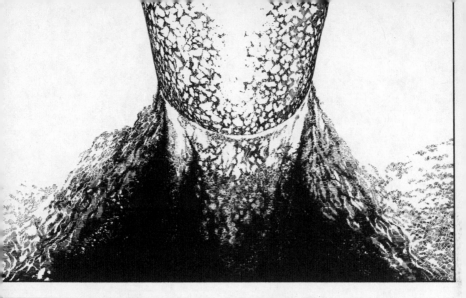

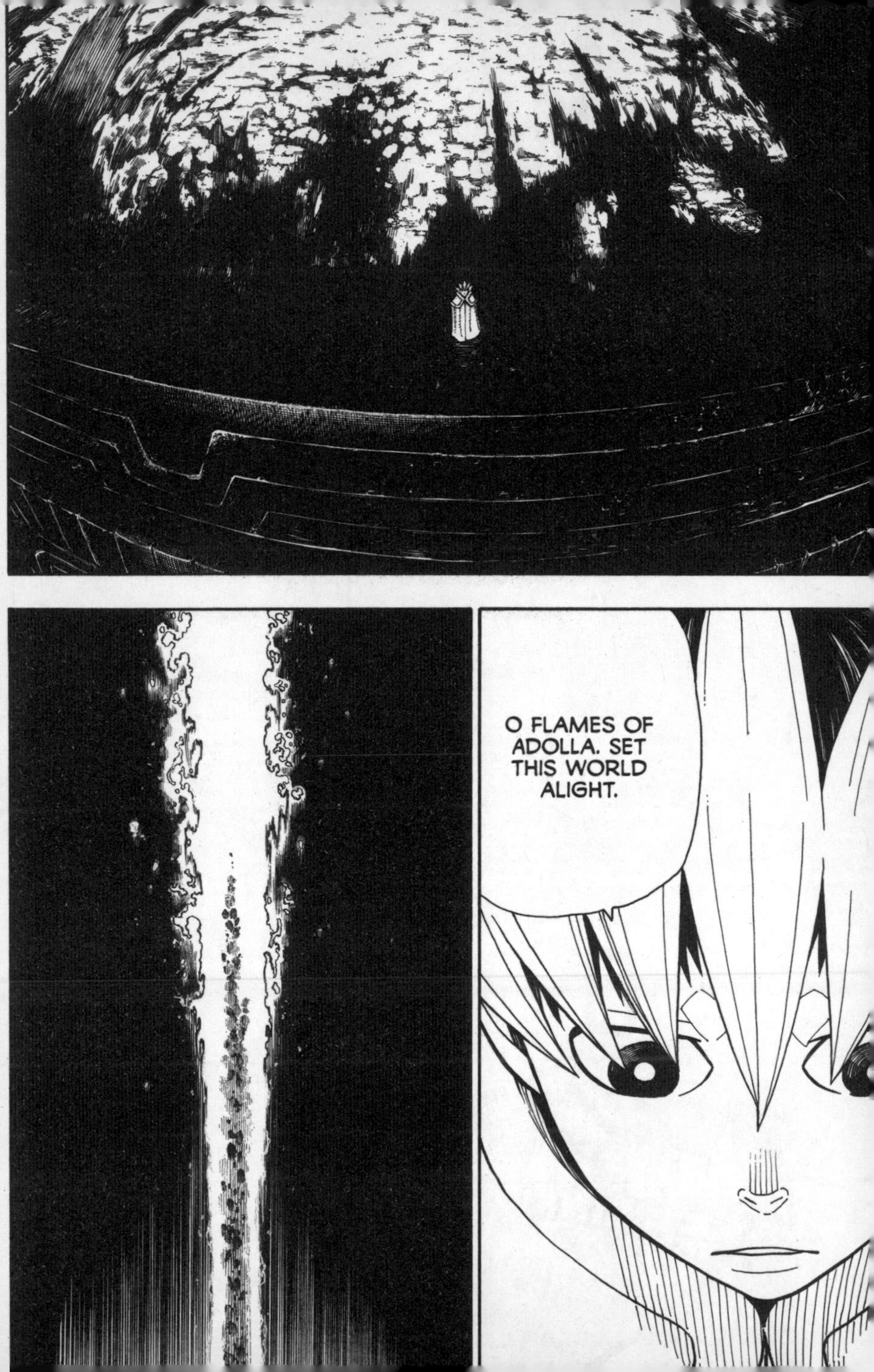
O FLAMES OF ADOLLA. SET THIS WORLD ALIGHT.

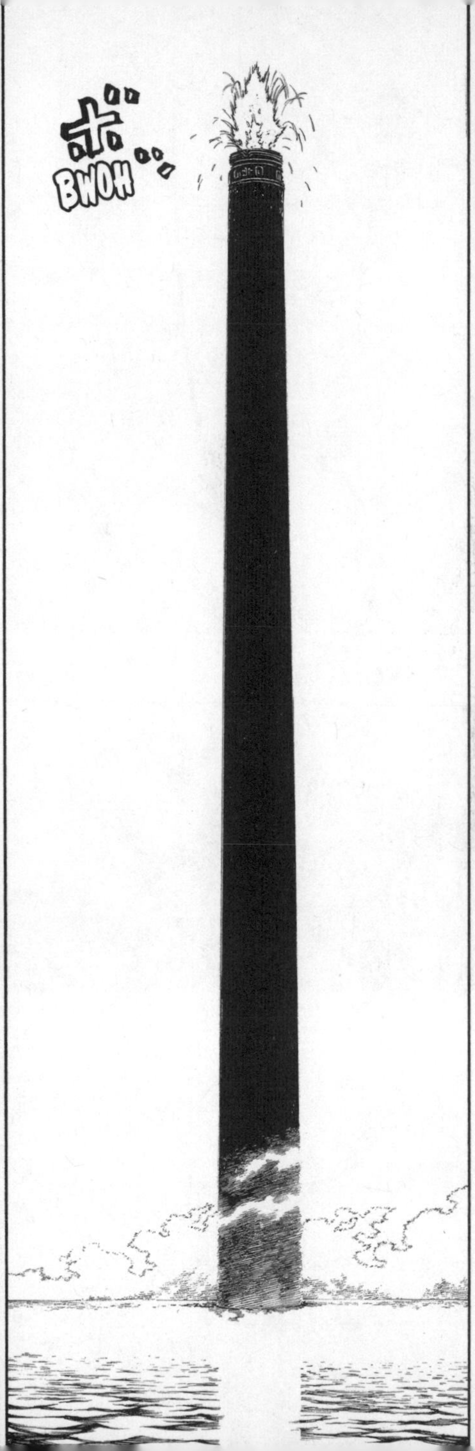
ボ
BWOH

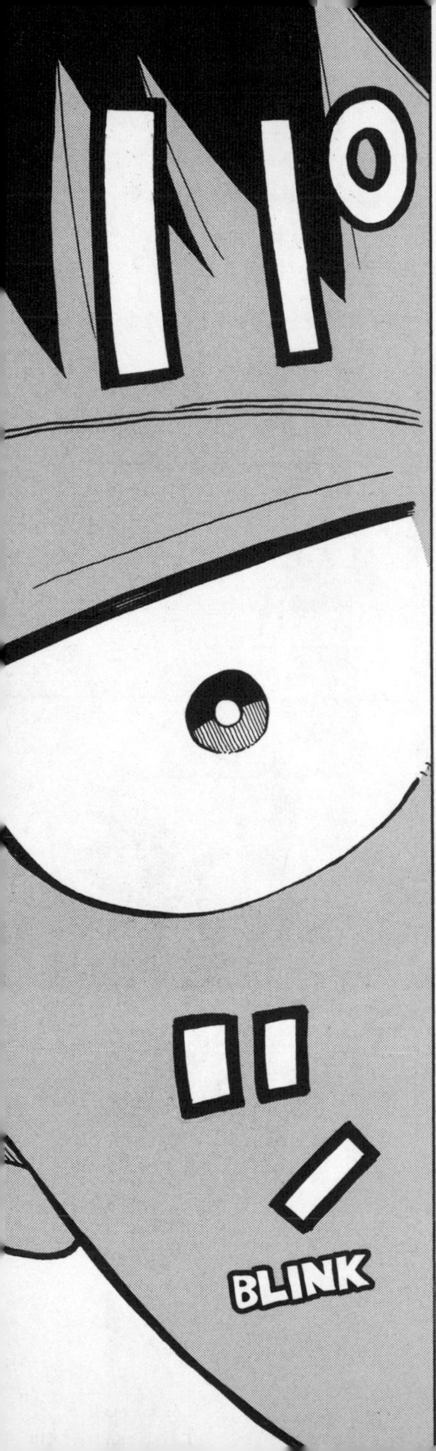
BLINK

THIS PLACE...

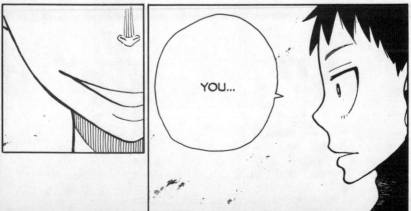

YOU...

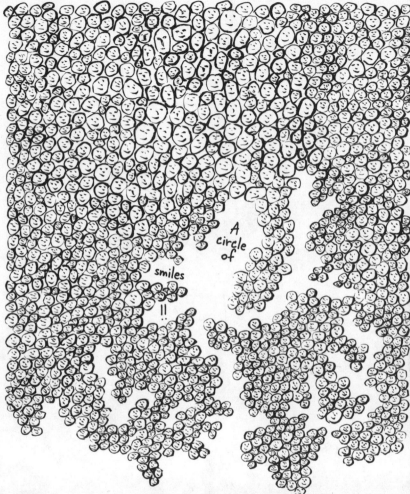

CHAPTER CCXVI: ANCIENT MADNESS

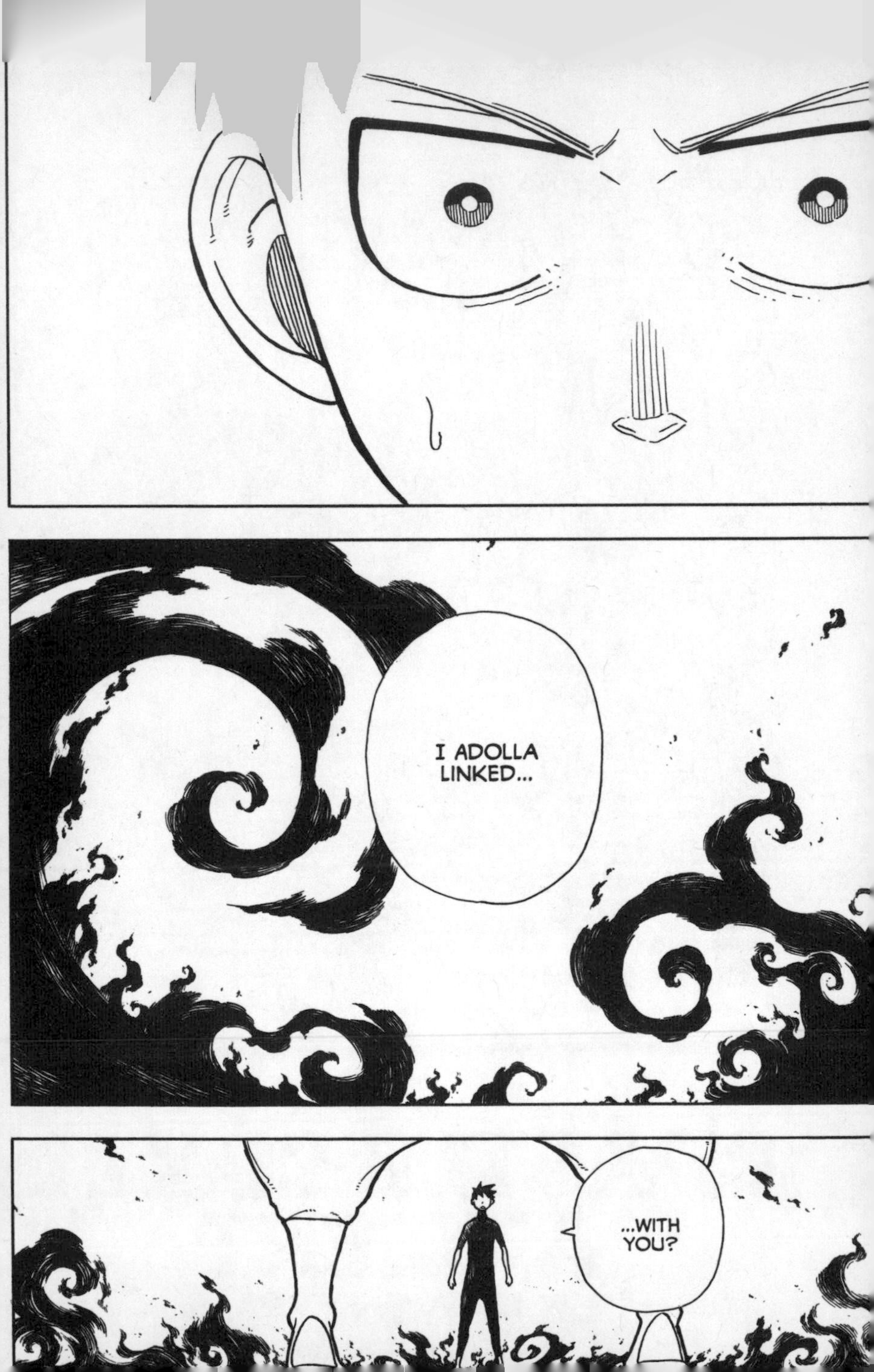
I ADOLLA LINKED...
...WITH YOU?

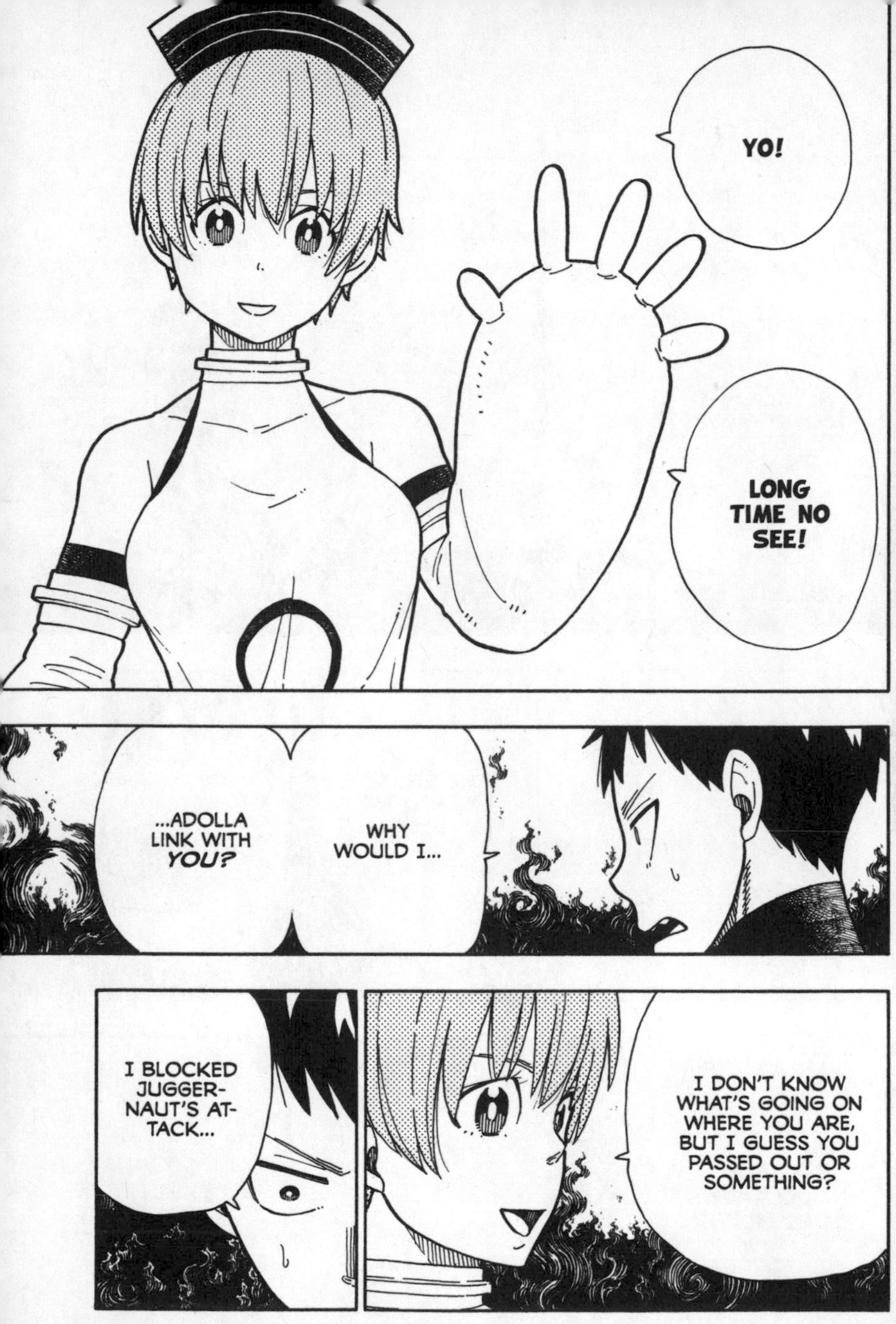
YO!
LONG TIME NO SEE!
WHY WOULD I...
...ADOLLA LINK WITH *YOU?*
I DON'T KNOW WHAT'S GOING ON WHERE YOU ARE, BUT I GUESS YOU PASSED OUT OR SOMETHING?
I BLOCKED JUGGER-NAUT'S AT-TACK...

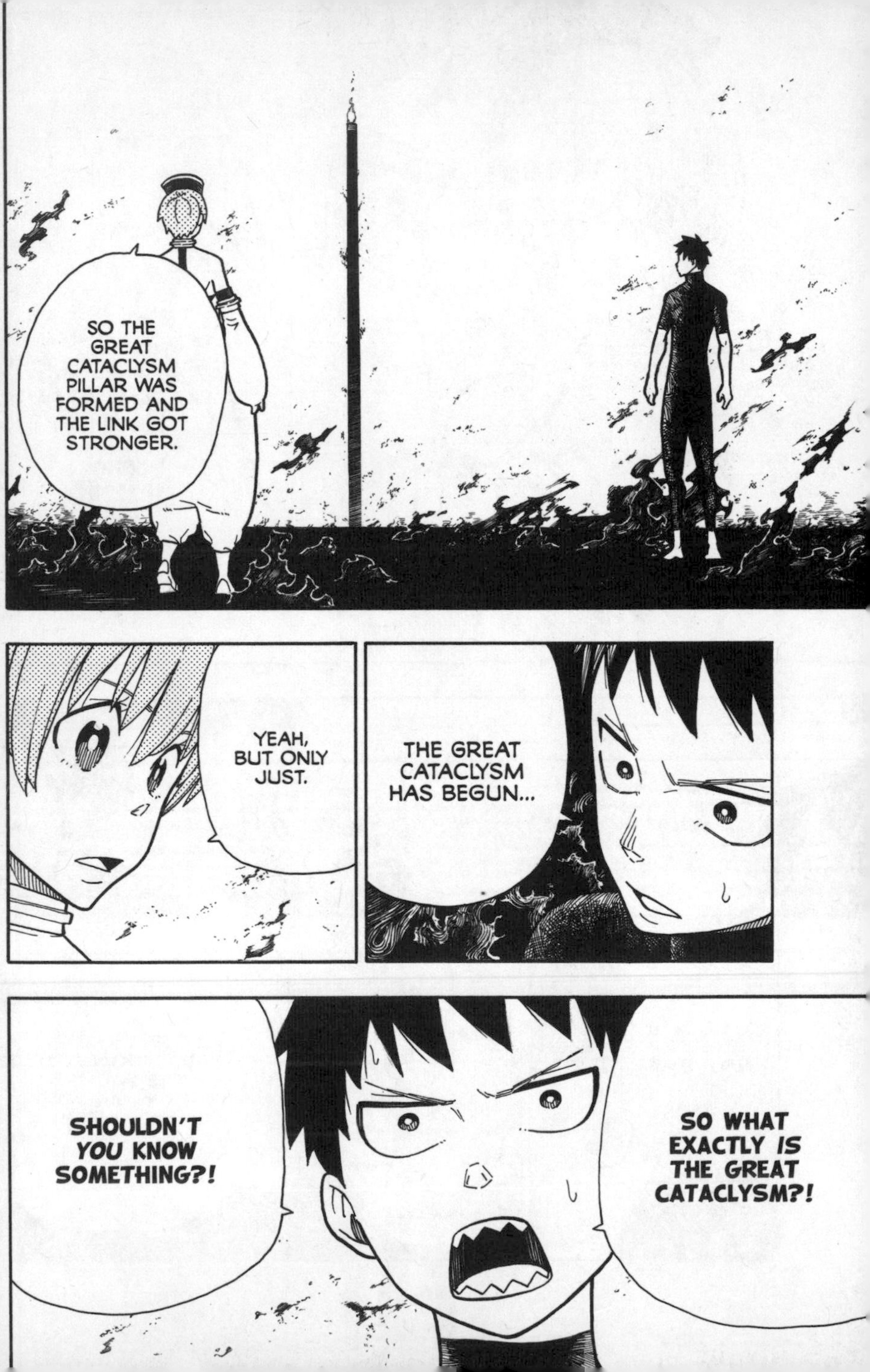
SO THE GREAT CATACLYSM PILLAR WAS FORMED AND THE LINK GOT STRONGER.
THE GREAT CATACLYSM HAS BEGUN...
YEAH, BUT ONLY JUST.
SO WHAT EXACTLY *IS* THE GREAT CATACLYSM?!
SHOULDN'T *YOU* KNOW SOMETHING?!

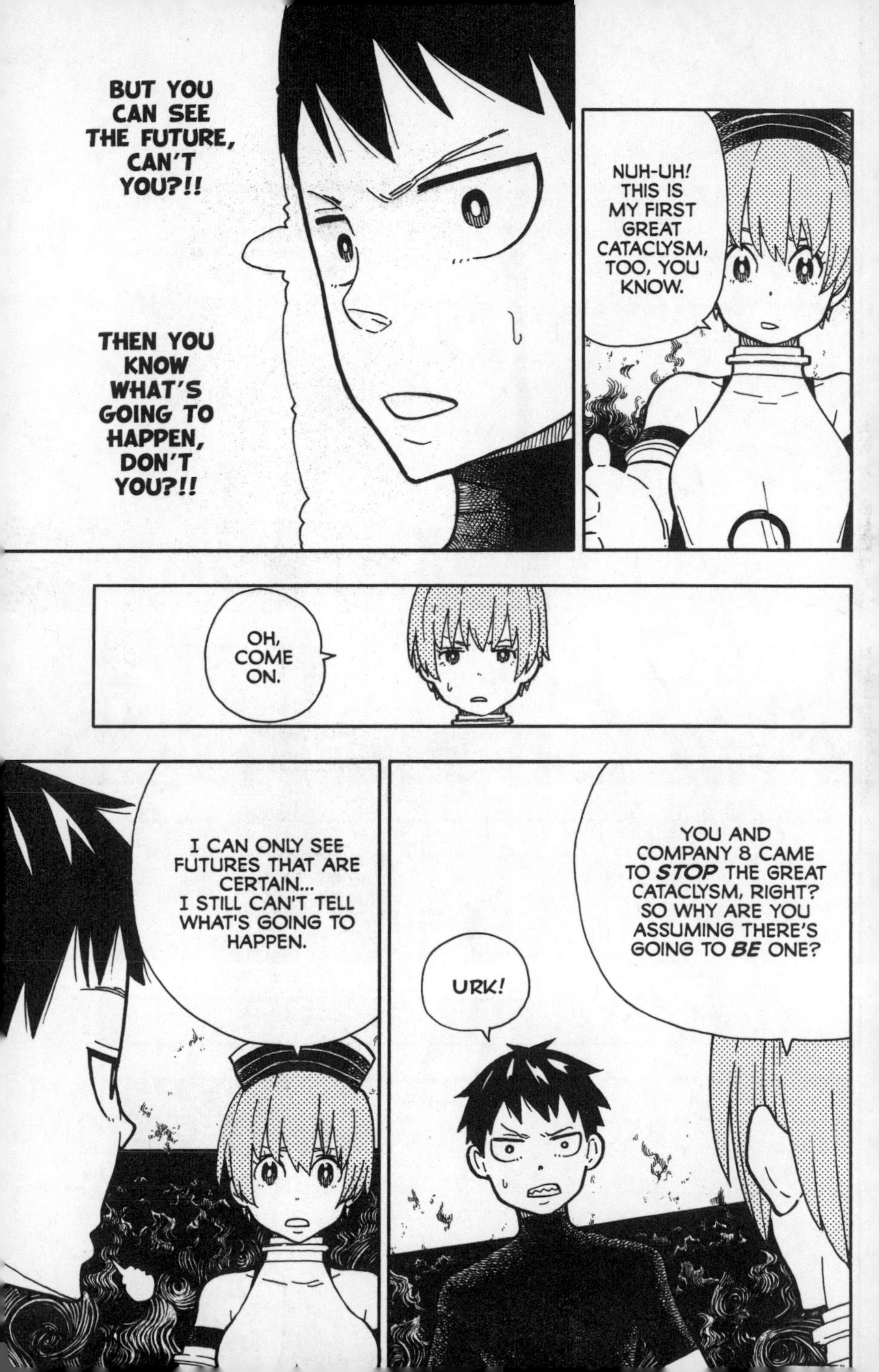
BUT YOU CAN SEE THE FUTURE, CAN'T YOU?!!
THEN YOU KNOW WHAT'S GOING TO HAPPEN, DON'T YOU?!!
NUH-UH! THIS IS MY FIRST GREAT CATACLYSM, TOO, YOU KNOW.
OH, COME ON.
I CAN ONLY SEE FUTURES THAT ARE CERTAIN... I STILL CAN'T TELL WHAT'S GOING TO HAPPEN.
YOU AND COMPANY 8 CAME TO *STOP* THE GREAT CATACLYSM, RIGHT? SO WHY ARE YOU ASSUMING THERE'S GOING TO *BE* ONE?
URK!

YOUR SUPER LIGHTSPEED THING LETS YOU SEE THE PAST, RIGHT?

IF YOU TAKE A LOOK AT THE PAST AND THE WORLD BEFORE THE LAST CATACLYSM, MAYBE YOU CAN FIGURE OUT WHAT'S GOING TO HAPPEN WITH THIS ONE.

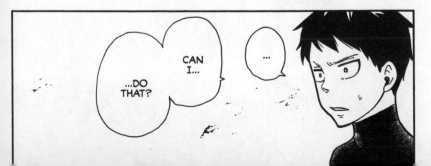

CAN I...

...

...DO THAT?

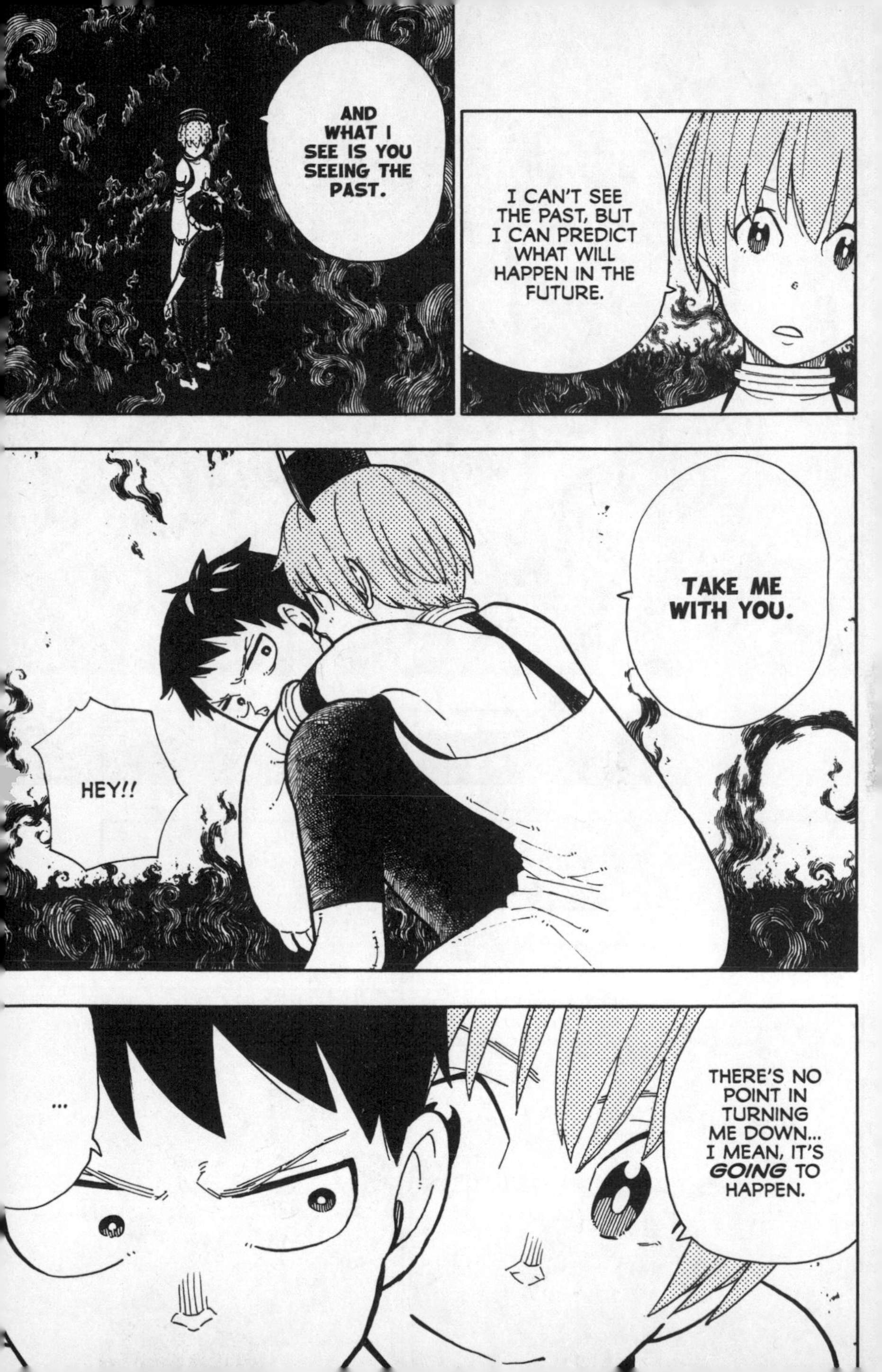
I CAN'T SEE THE PAST, BUT I CAN PREDICT WHAT WILL HAPPEN IN THE FUTURE.
AND WHAT I SEE IS YOU SEEING THE PAST.
TAKE ME WITH YOU.
HEY!!
THERE'S NO POINT IN TURNING ME DOWN... I MEAN, IT'S *GOING* TO HAPPEN.
...

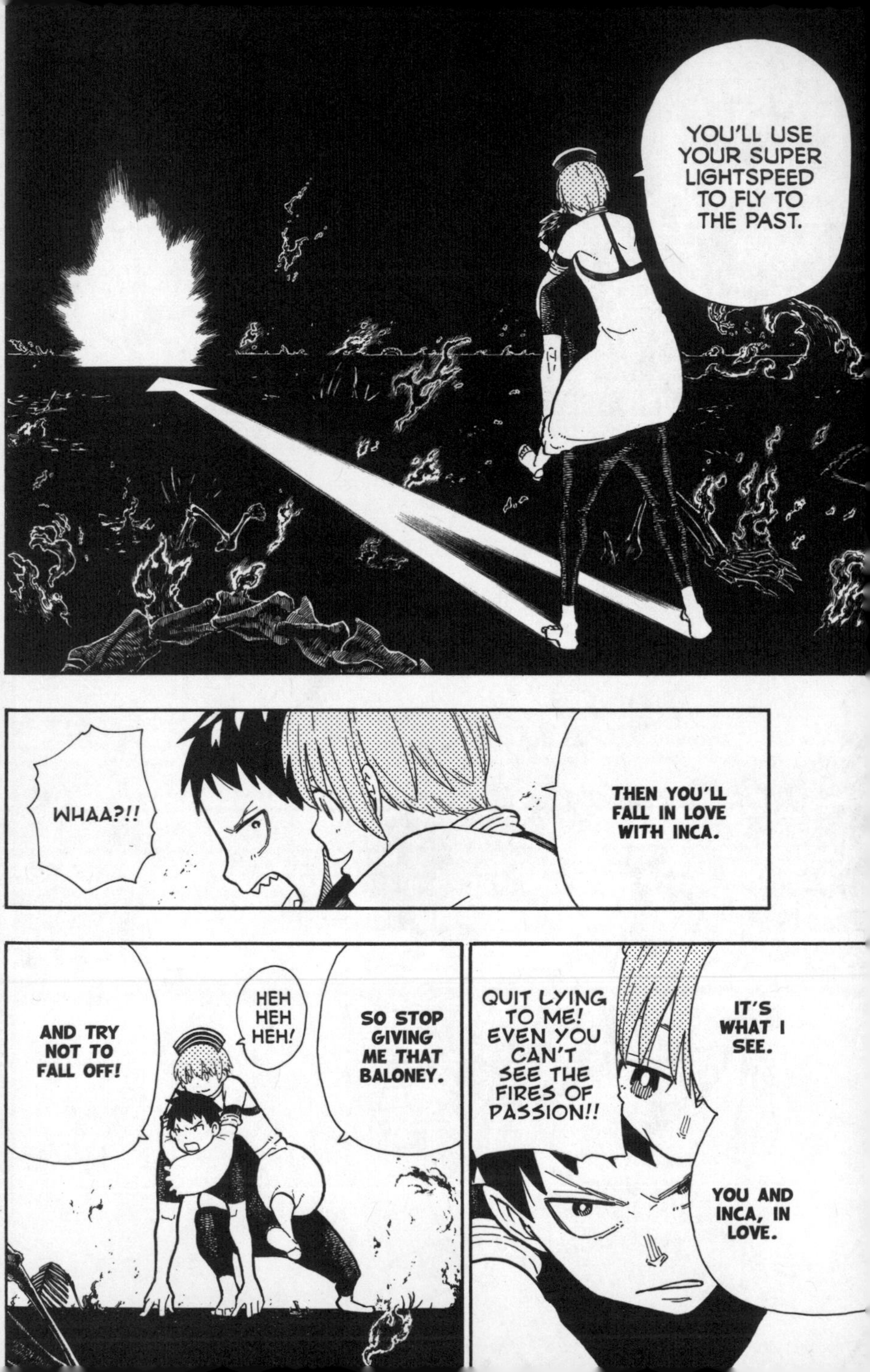
YOU'LL USE YOUR SUPER LIGHTSPEED TO FLY TO THE PAST.
THEN YOU'LL FALL IN LOVE WITH INCA.
WHAA?!!
IT'S WHAT I SEE.
QUIT LYING TO ME! EVEN YOU CAN'T SEE THE FIRES OF PASSION!!
YOU AND INCA, IN LOVE.
SO STOP GIVING ME THAT BALONEY.
HEH HEH HEH!
AND TRY NOT TO FALL OFF!

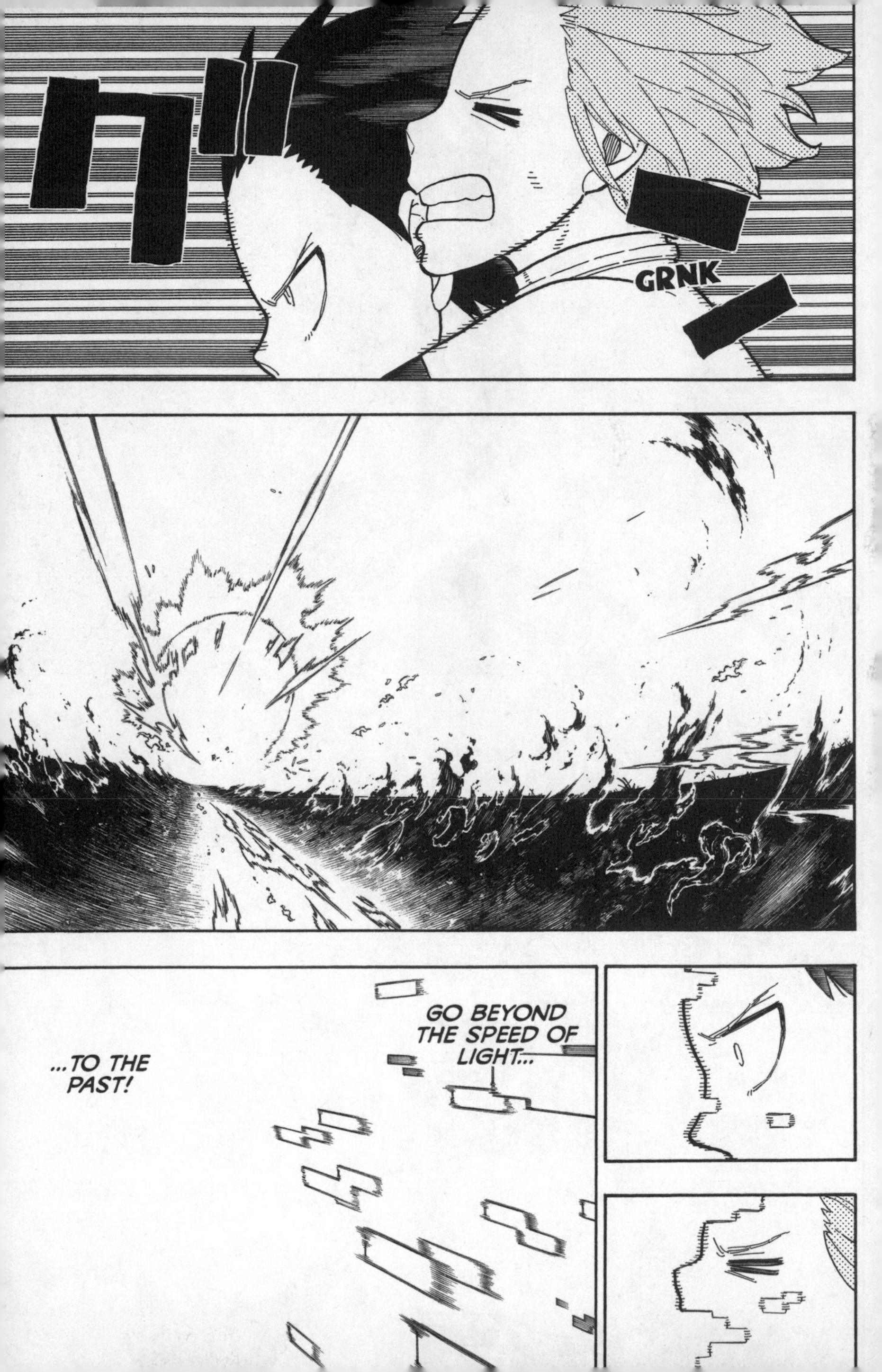
GRNK
GO BEYOND THE SPEED OF LIGHT...
...TO THE PAST!

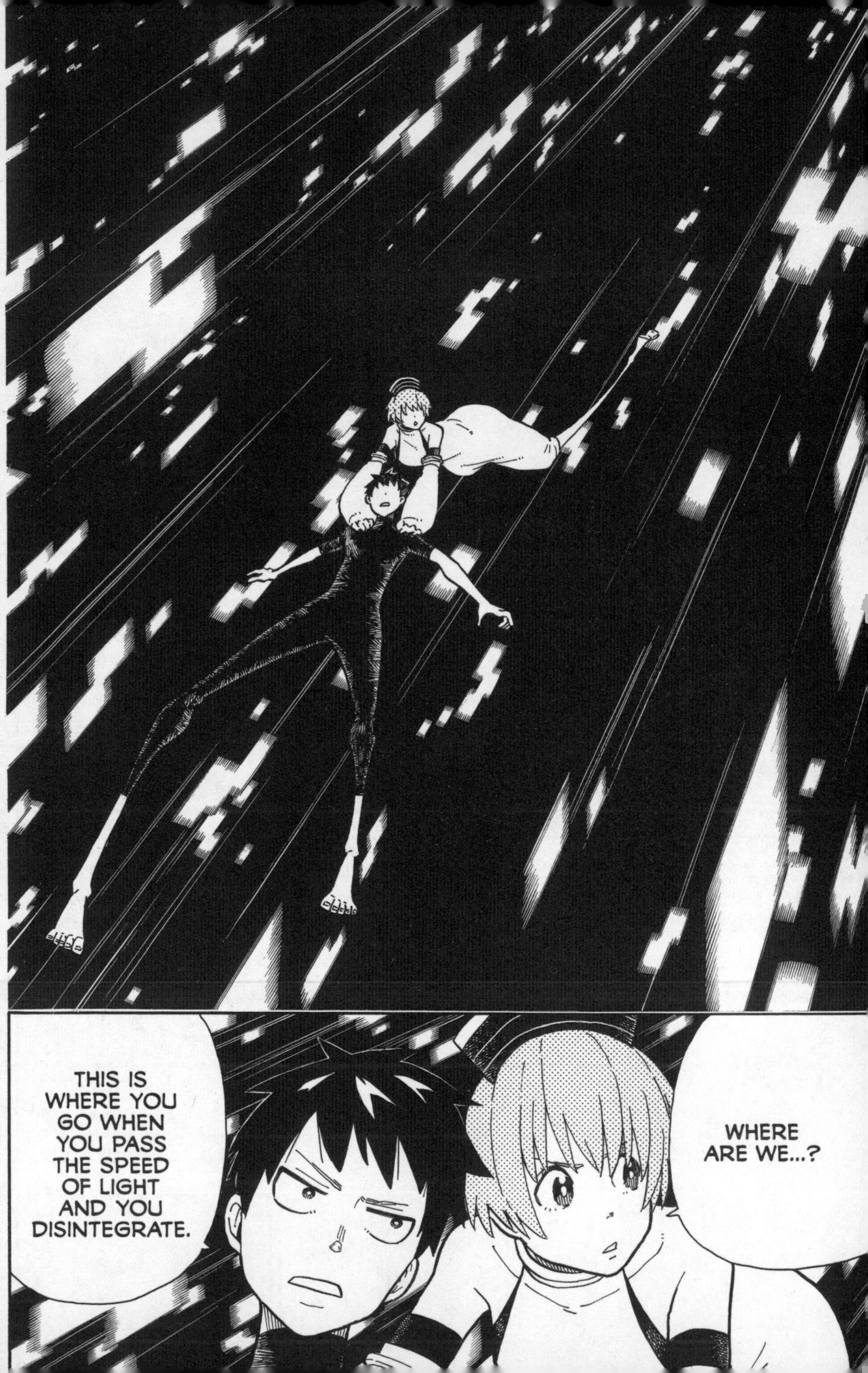
WHERE ARE WE...?
THIS IS WHERE YOU GO WHEN YOU PASS THE SPEED OF LIGHT AND YOU DISINTEGRATE.

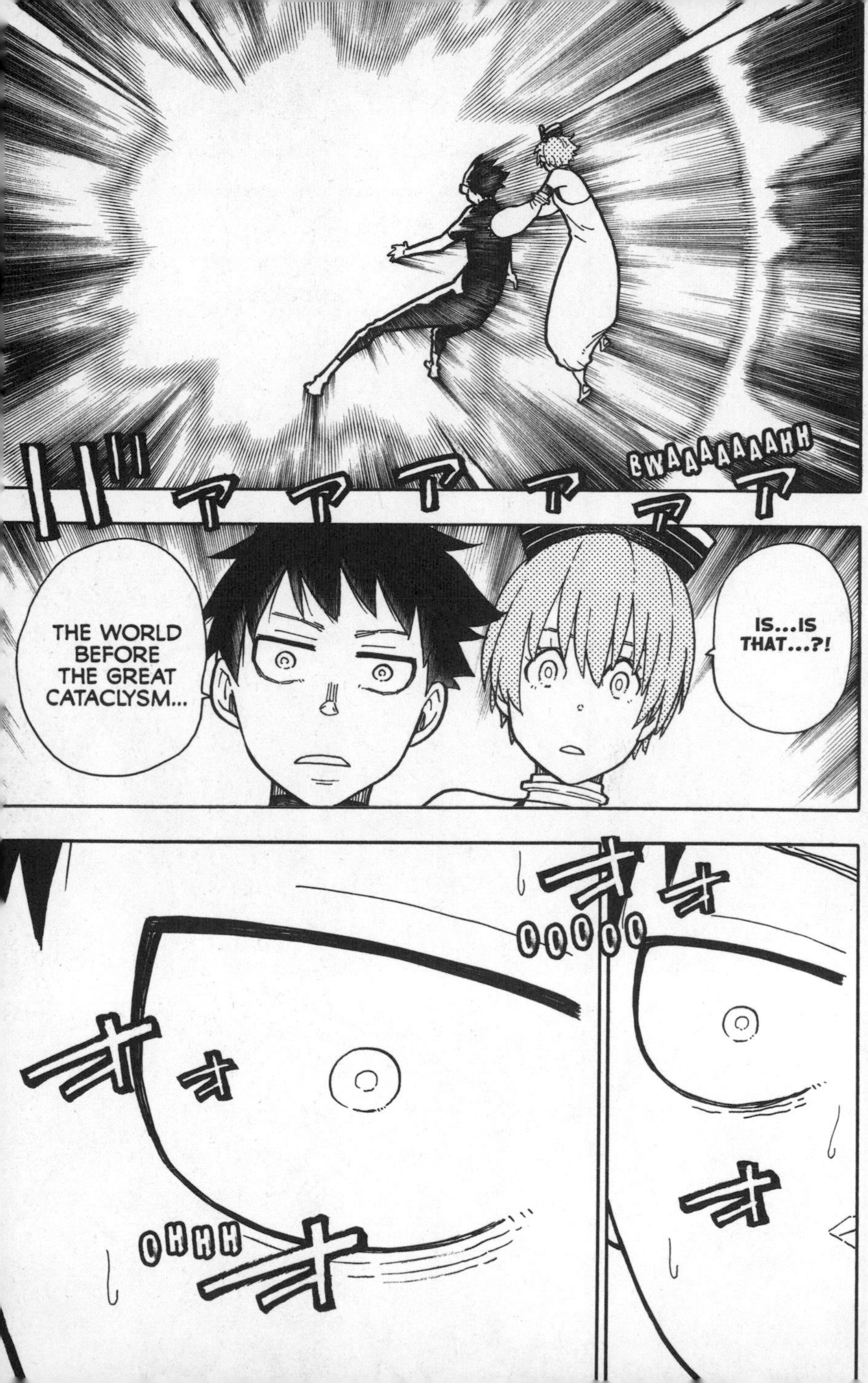
BWAAAAAAAHH
IS...IS THAT...?!
THE WORLD BEFORE THE GREAT CATACLYSM...
OOOOO
OHHH

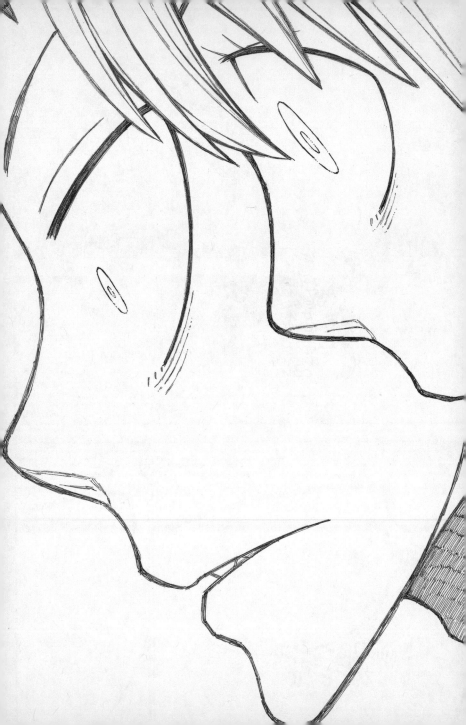

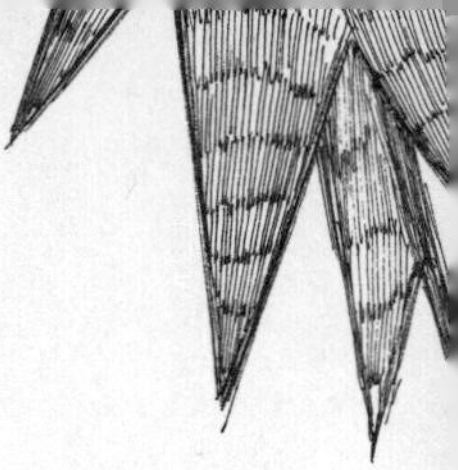

I HAD IMAGINED IT BEFORE–THE PAST...WHAT TOKYO WAS LIKE BEFORE THE GREAT CATACLYSM... I FIGURED IT WAS PEOPLE NO DIFFERENT FROM US, LIVING THEIR LIVES JUST LIKE WE DO... I THOUGHT THE ONLY DIFFERENCE WAS THAT THERE WAS NO SPONTANEOUS HUMAN COMBUSTION...THAT WAS ALL.

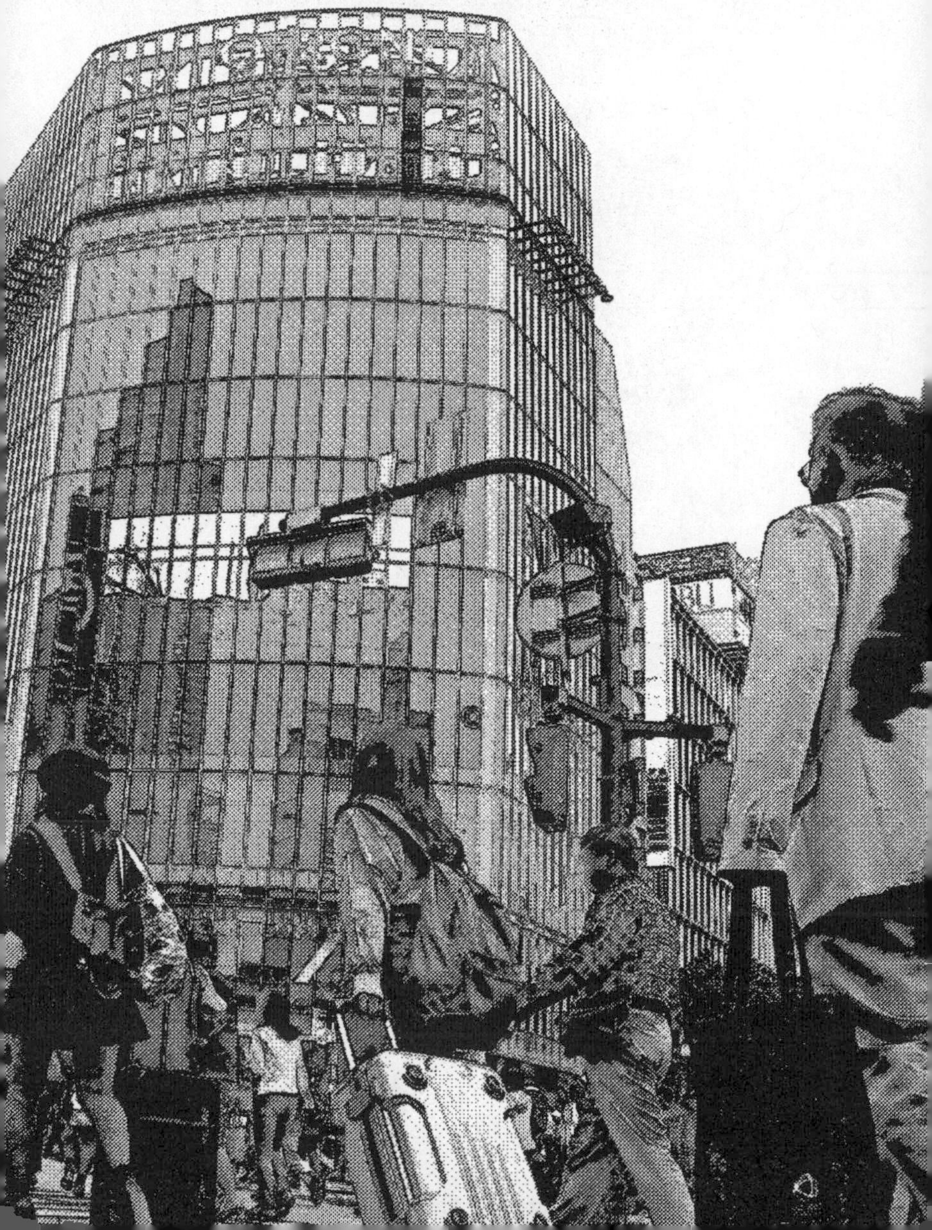

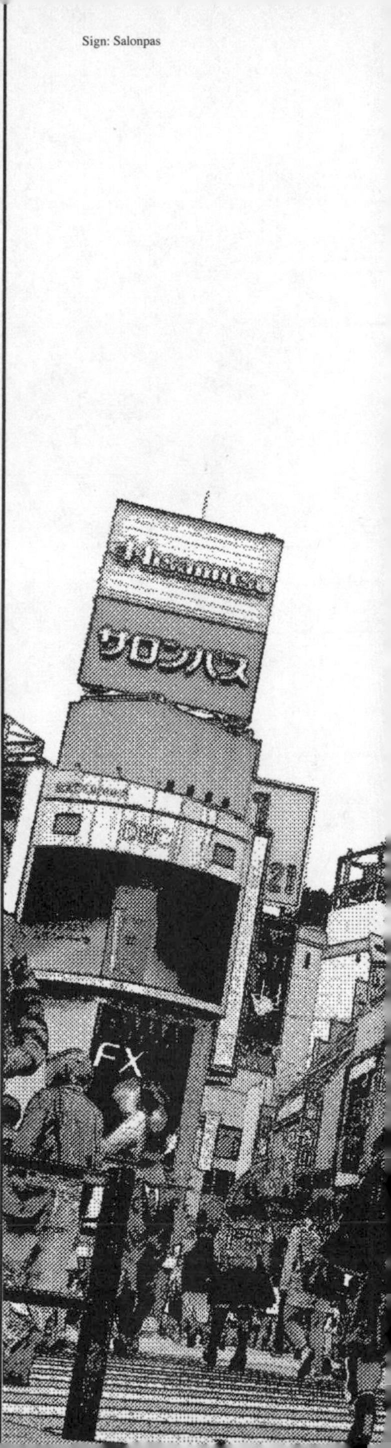
Sign: Salonpas
サロンパス
FX
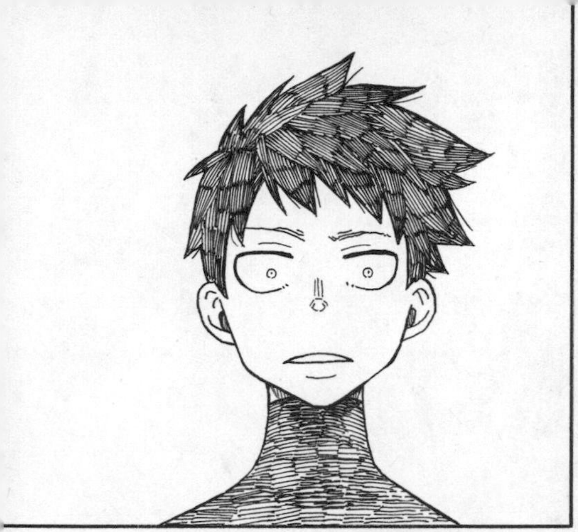
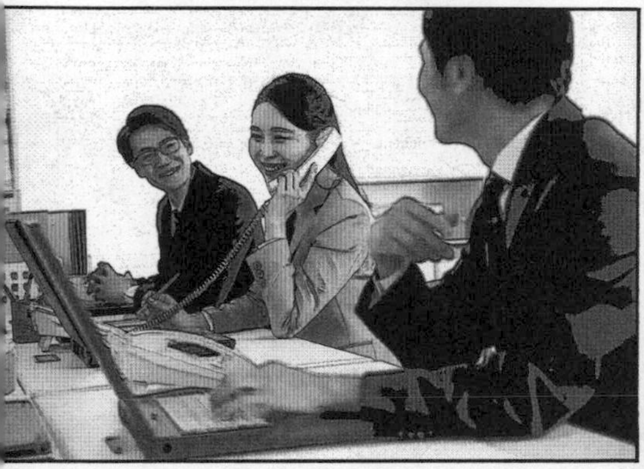
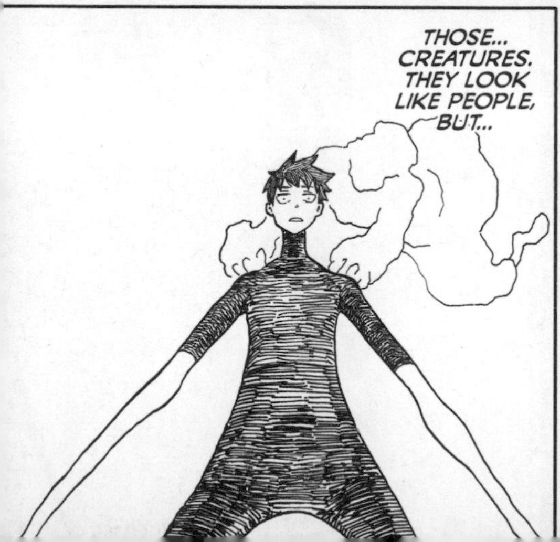
THOSE... CREATURES. THEY LOOK LIKE PEOPLE, BUT...

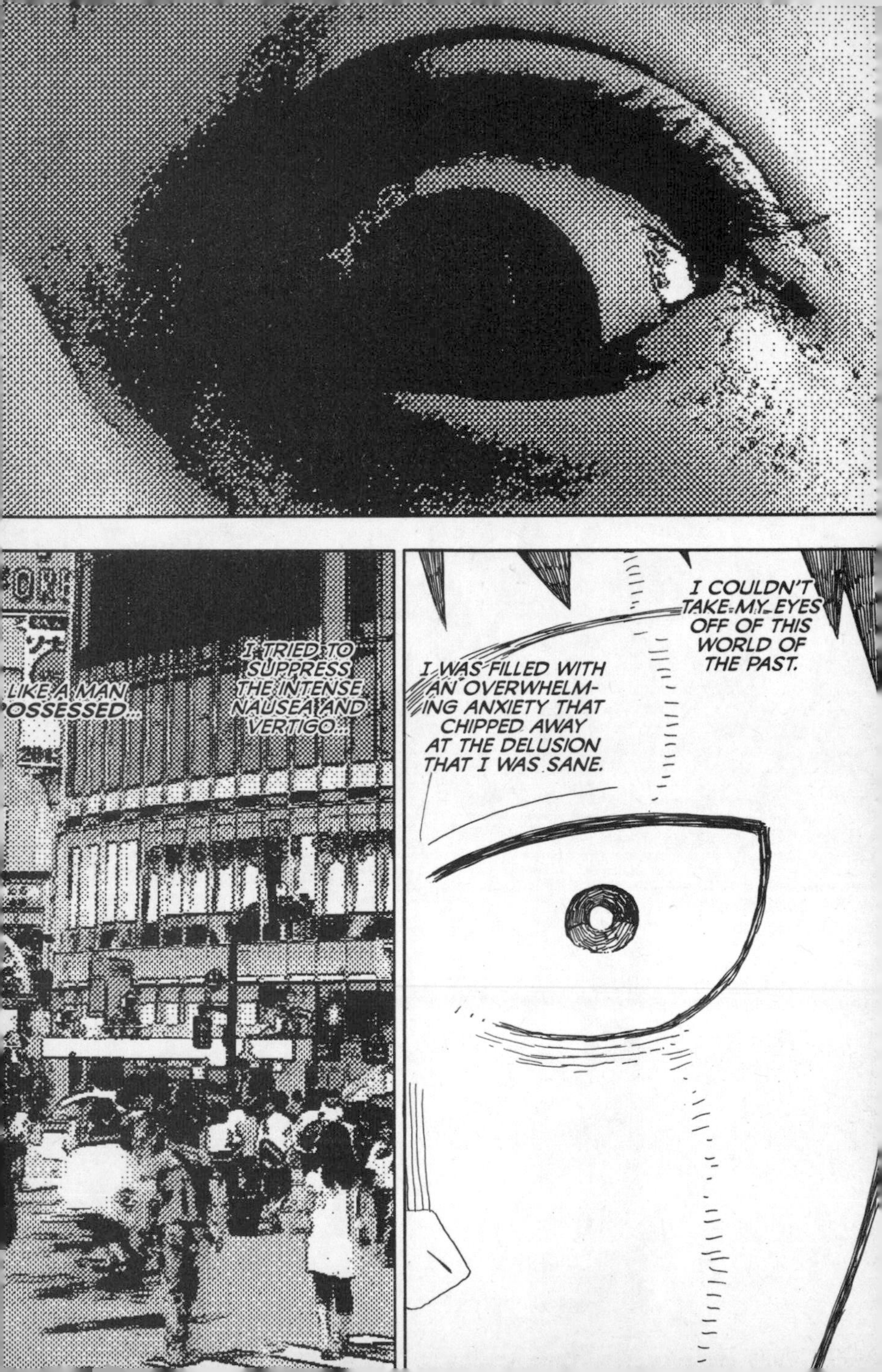
I COULDN'T TAKE MY EYES OFF OF THIS WORLD OF THE PAST.
I WAS FILLED WITH AN OVERWHELM-ING ANXIETY THAT CHIPPED AWAY AT THE DELUSION THAT I WAS SANE.
I TRIED TO SUPPRESS THE INTENSE NAUSEA AND VERTIGO...
LIKE A MAN OSSESSED...

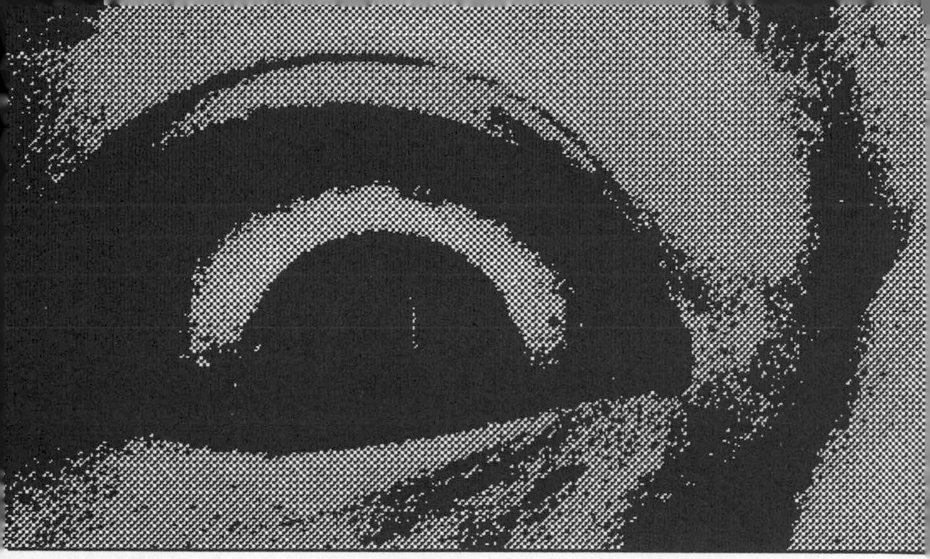

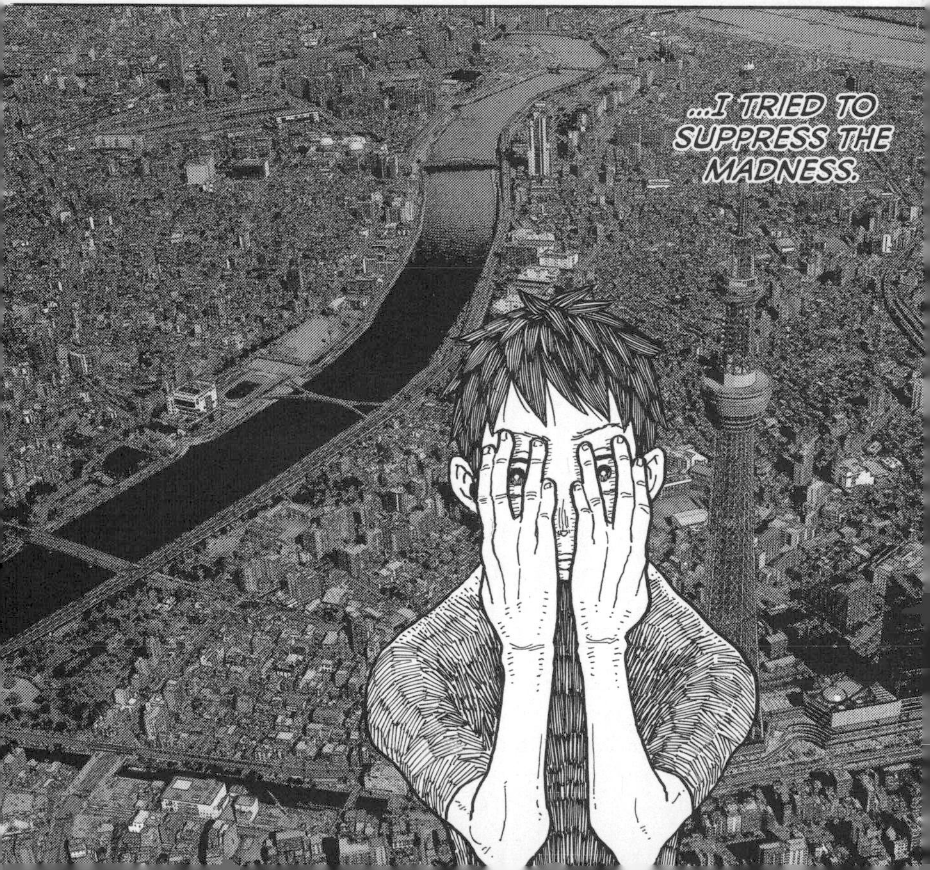
...I TRIED TO SUPPRESS THE MADNESS.

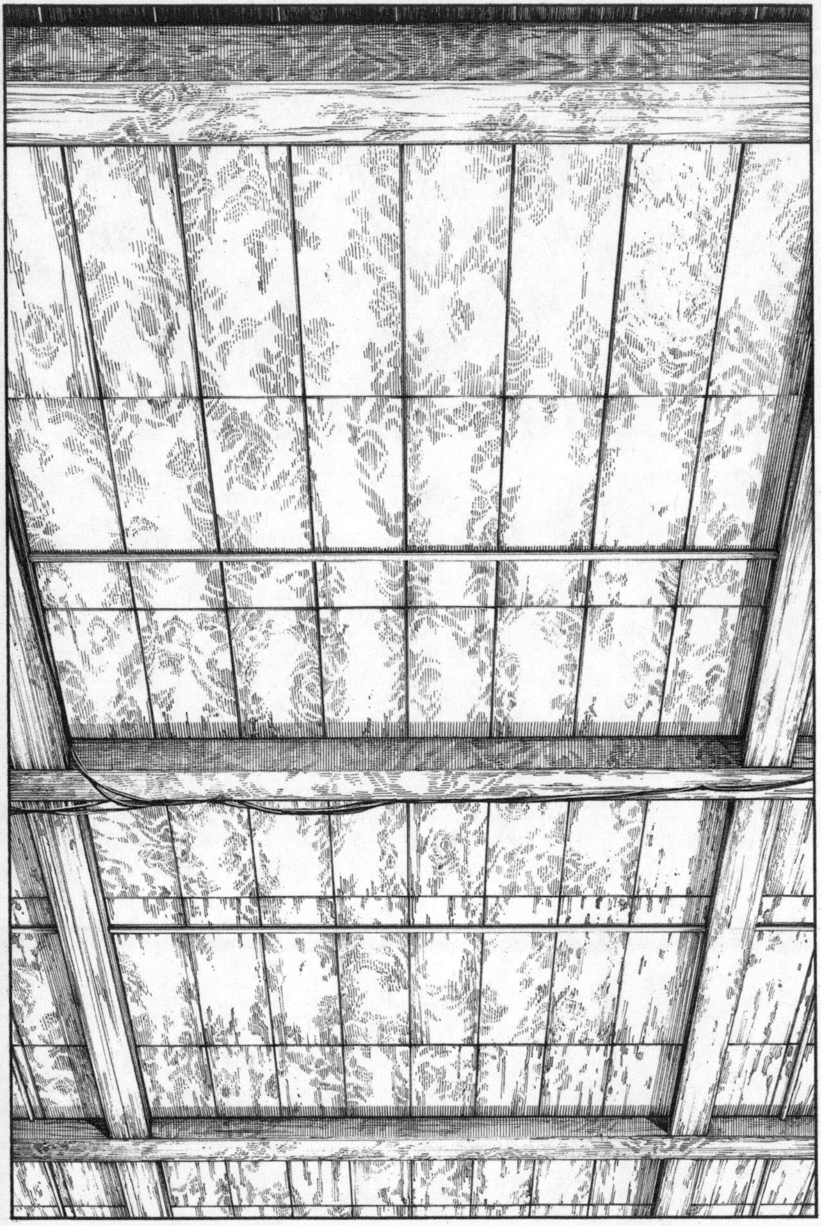

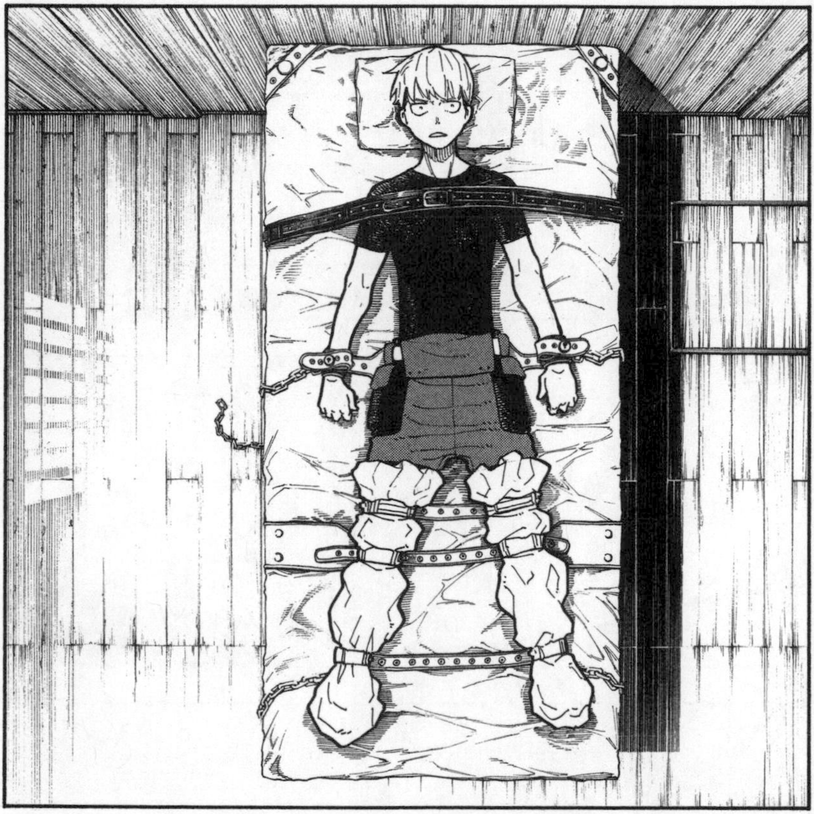
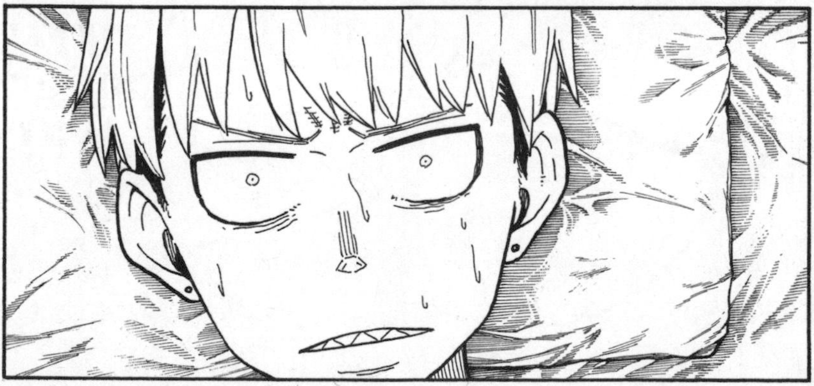

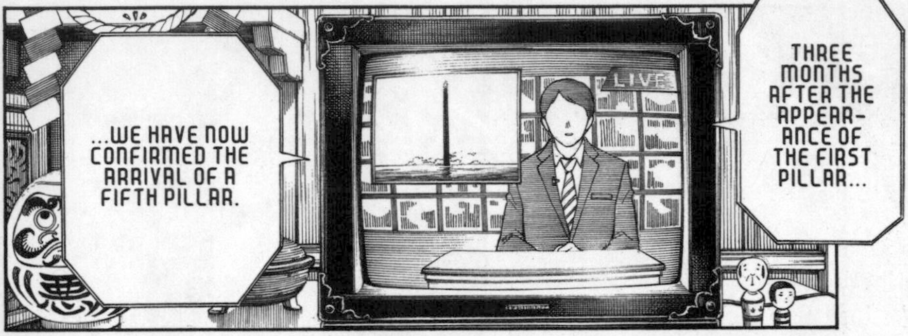
THREE MONTHS AFTER THE APPEARANCE OF THE FIRST PILLAR...
...WE HAVE NOW CONFIRMED THE ARRIVAL OF A FIFTH PILLAR.
LIVE

Daruma: Evil

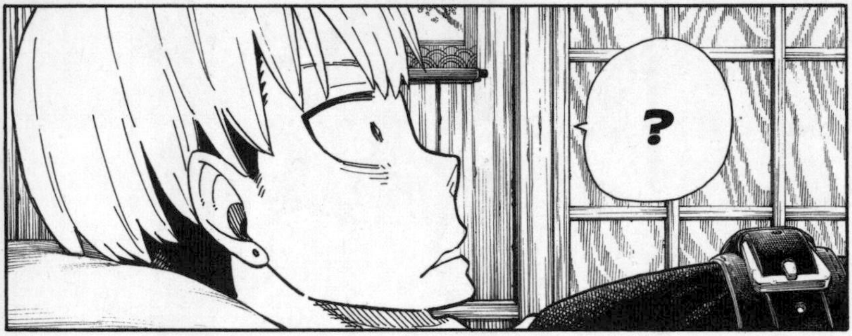
?

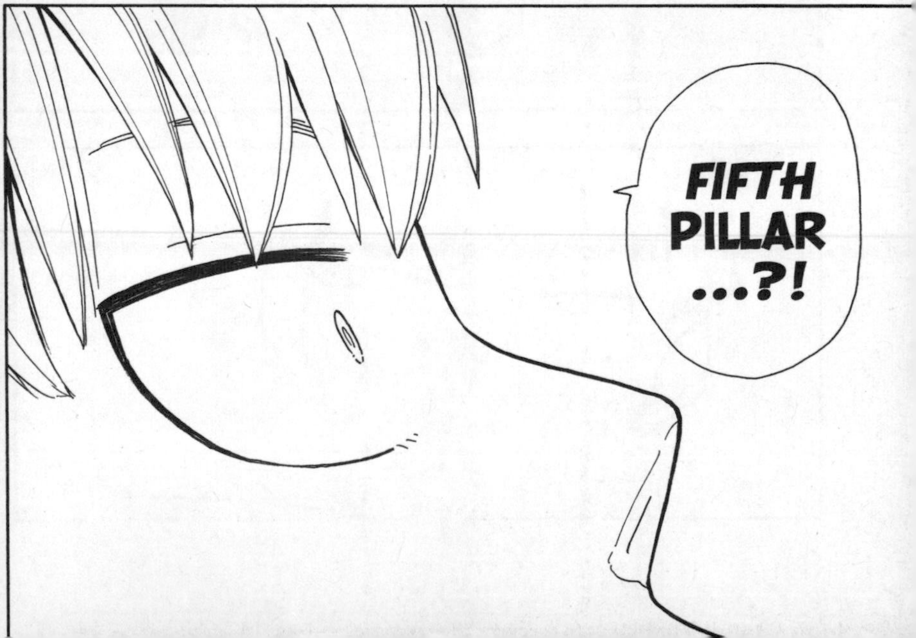
FIFTH PILLAR ...?!

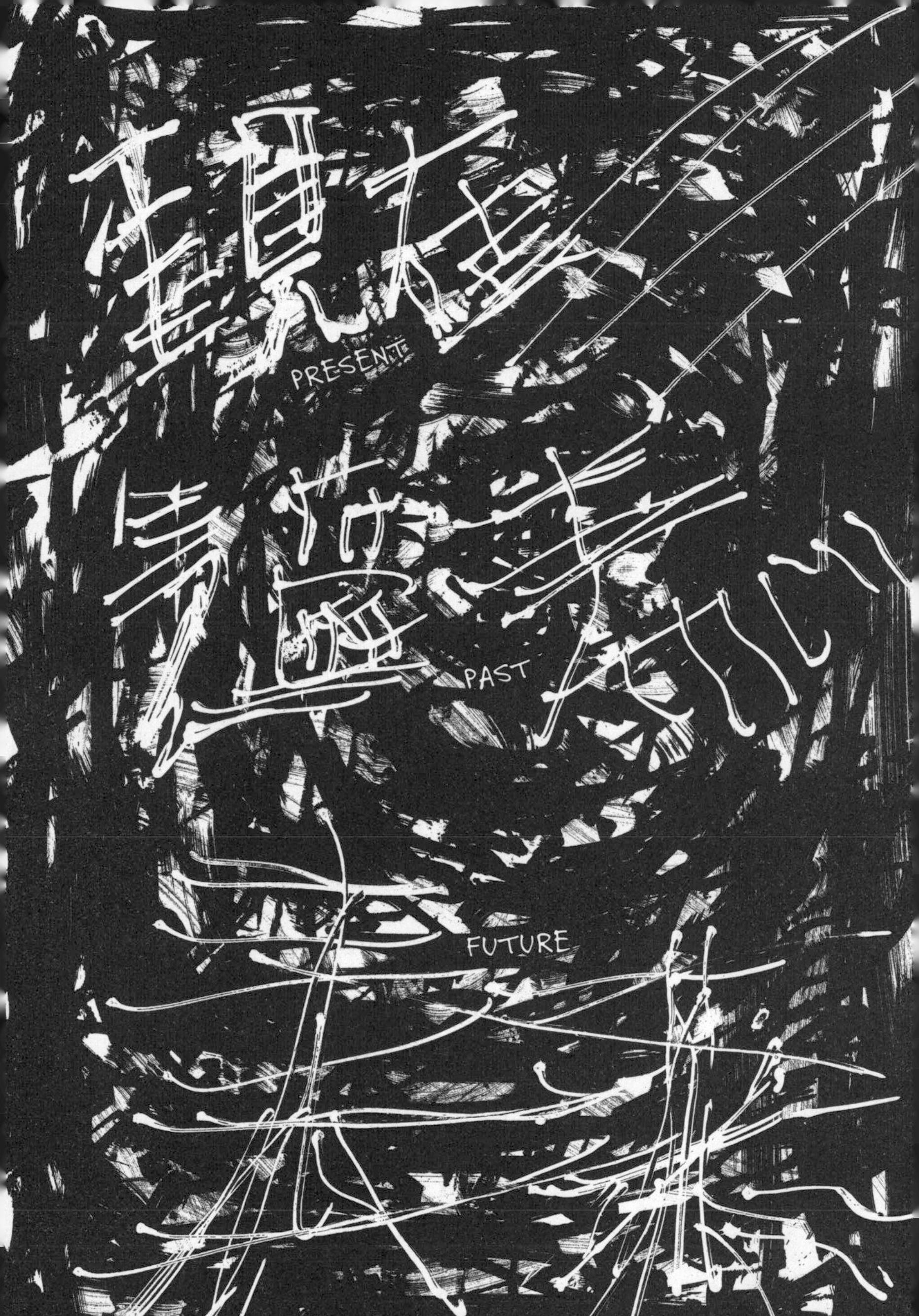
PRESENT
PAST
FUTURE

CHAPTER CCXVII: SELF-UNAWARE

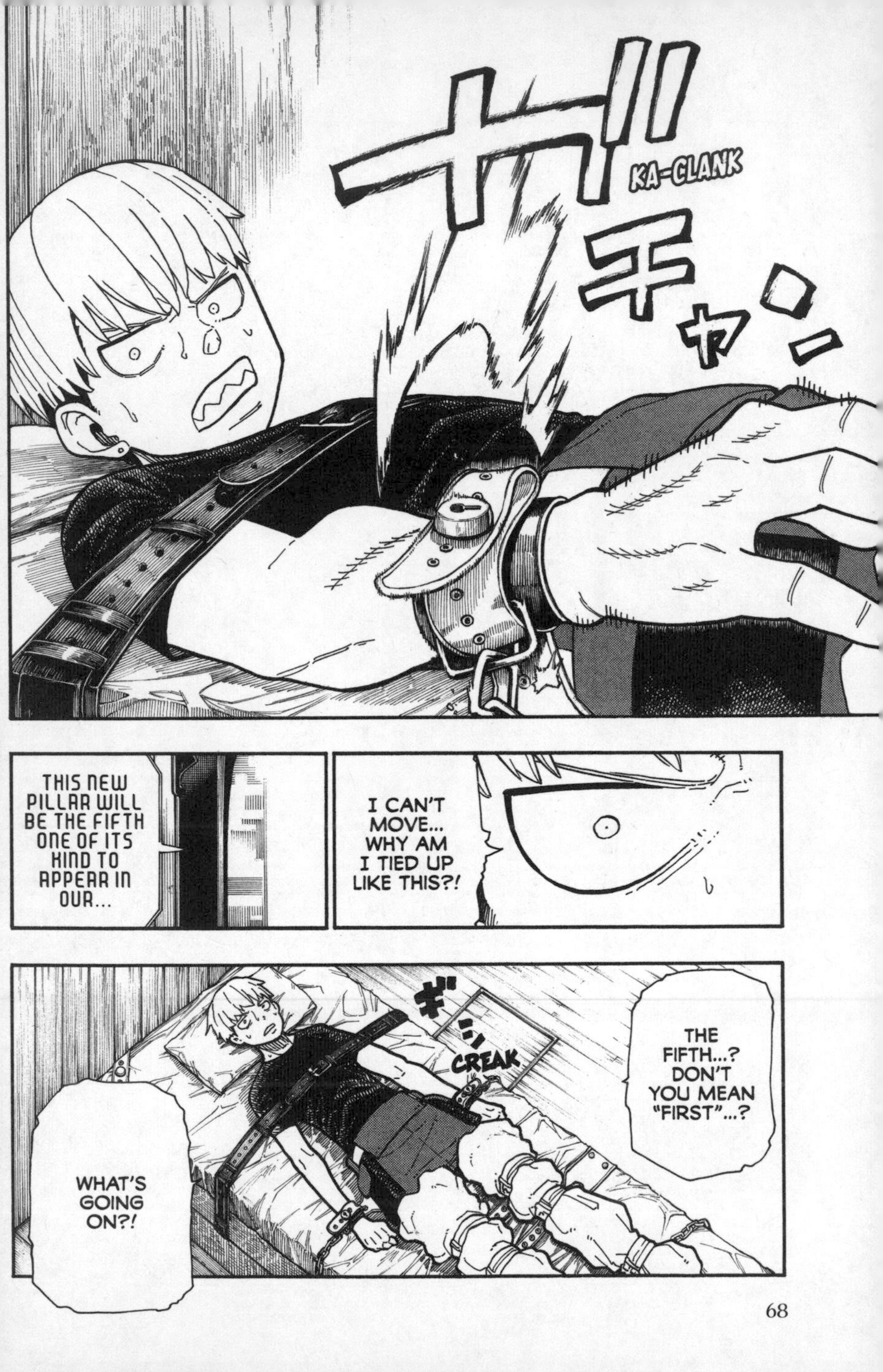
KA-CLANK
I CAN'T MOVE... WHY AM I TIED UP LIKE THIS?!
THIS NEW PILLAR WILL BE THE FIFTH ONE OF ITS KIND TO APPEAR IN OUR...
THE FIFTH...? DON'T YOU MEAN "FIRST"...?
CREAK
WHAT'S GOING ON?!

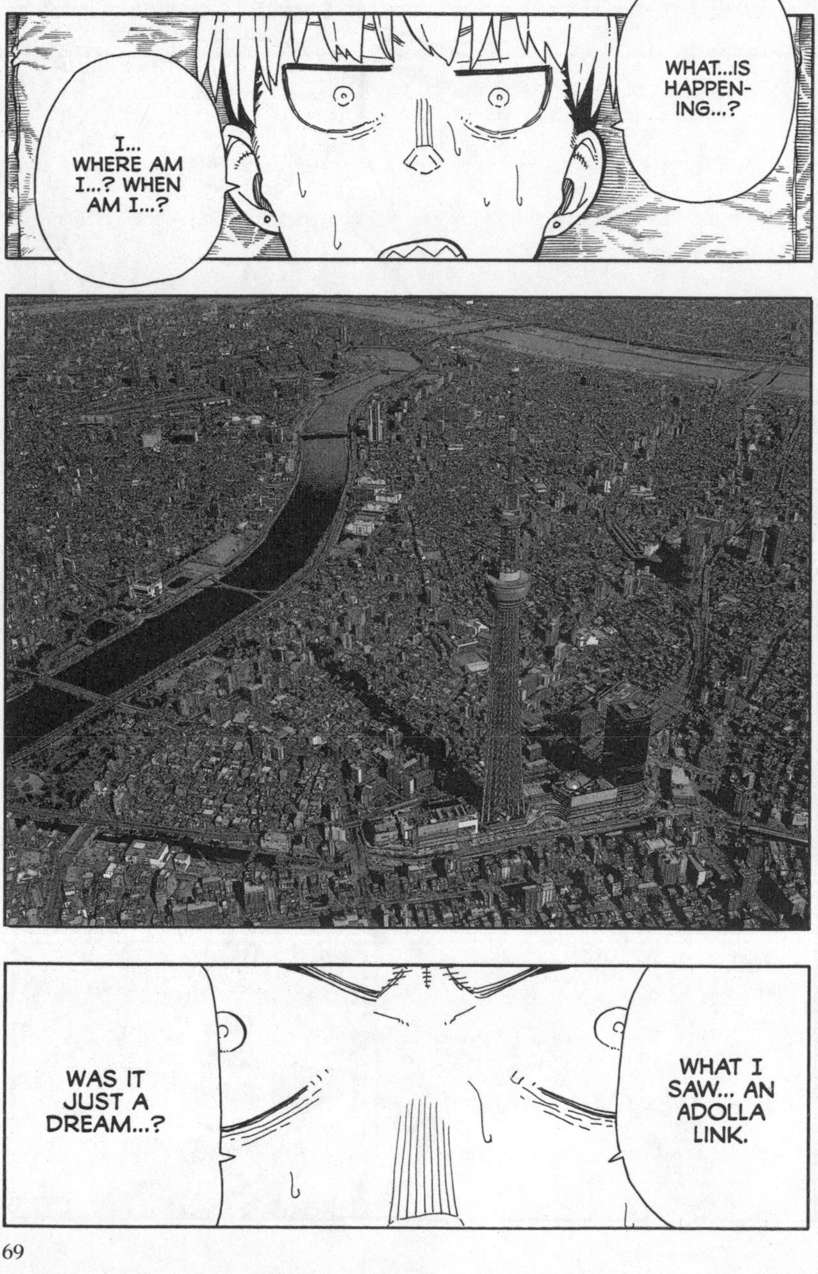
WHAT...IS HAPPEN-ING...?
I... WHERE AM I...? WHEN AM I...?
WHAT I SAW... AN ADOLLA LINK.
WAS IT JUST A DREAM...?

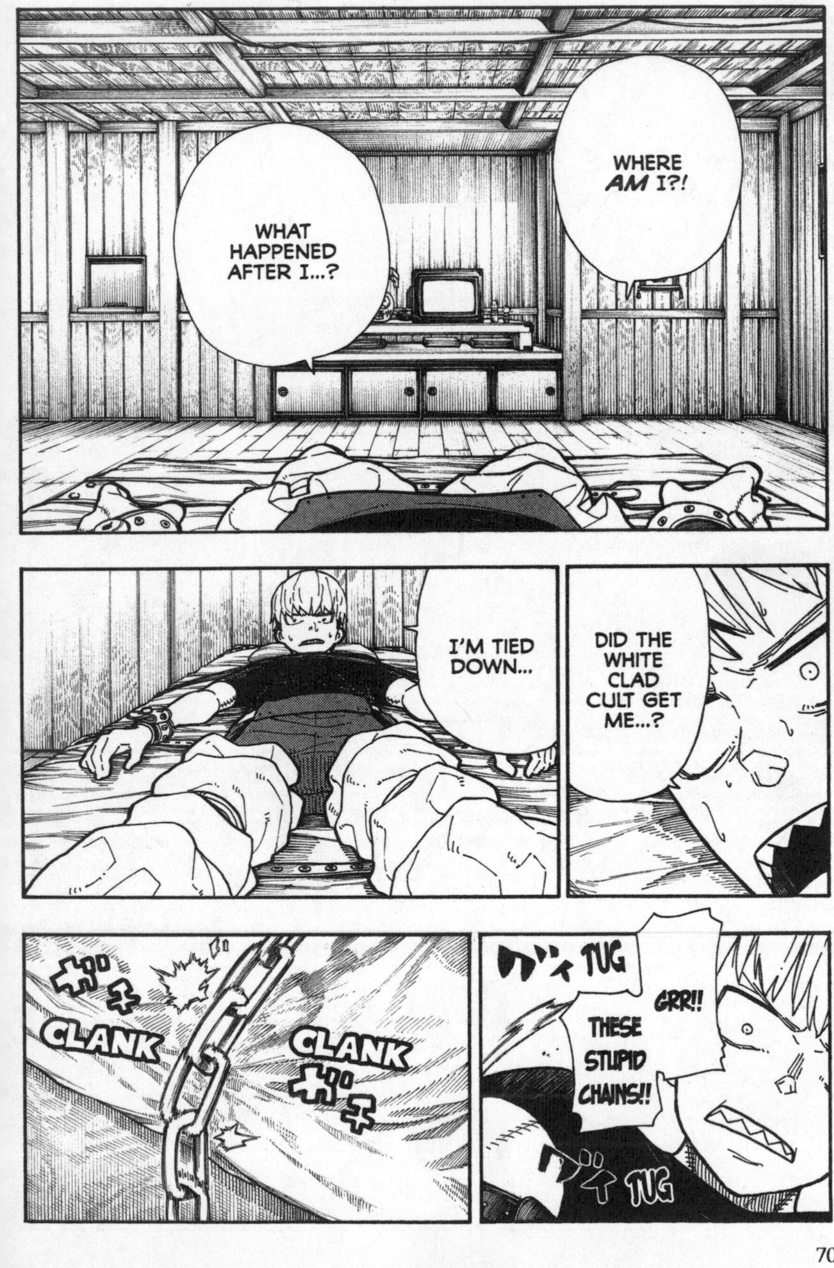
WHERE AM I?!
WHAT HAPPENED AFTER I...?
DID THE WHITE CLAD CULT GET ME...?
I'M TIED DOWN...
TUG
GRR!!
THESE STUPID CHAINS!!
TUG
CLANK
CLANK

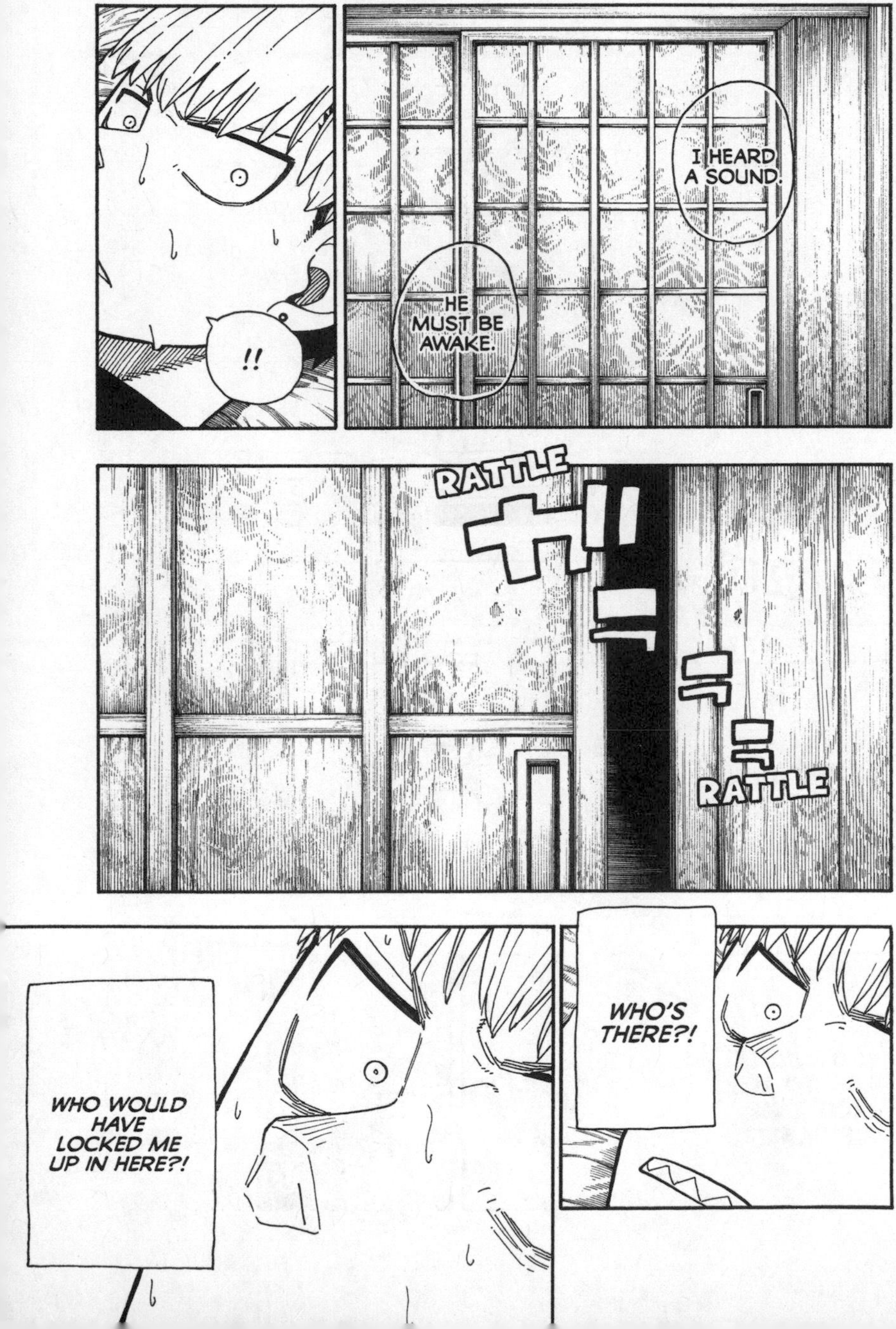
I HEARD A SOUND.
HE MUST BE AWAKE.
!!
RATTLE
RATTLE
WHO'S THERE?!
WHO WOULD HAVE LOCKED ME UP IN HERE?!

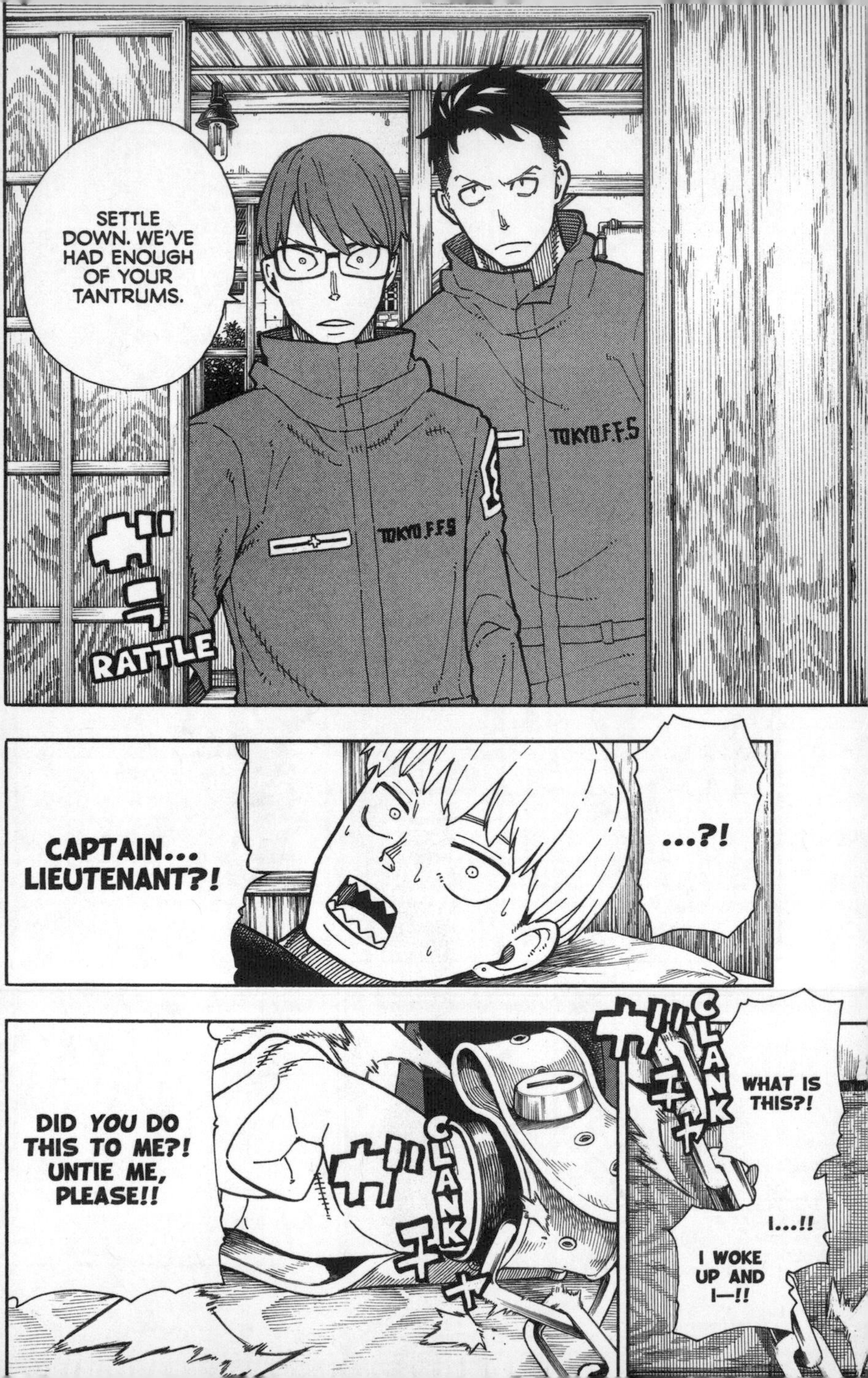
SETTLE DOWN. WE'VE HAD ENOUGH OF YOUR TANTRUMS.
RATTLE
...?!
CAPTAIN... LIEUTENANT?!
WHAT IS THIS?!
CLANK
I...!!
I WOKE UP AND I—!!
CLANK
DID *YOU* DO THIS TO ME?! UNTIE ME, PLEASE!!

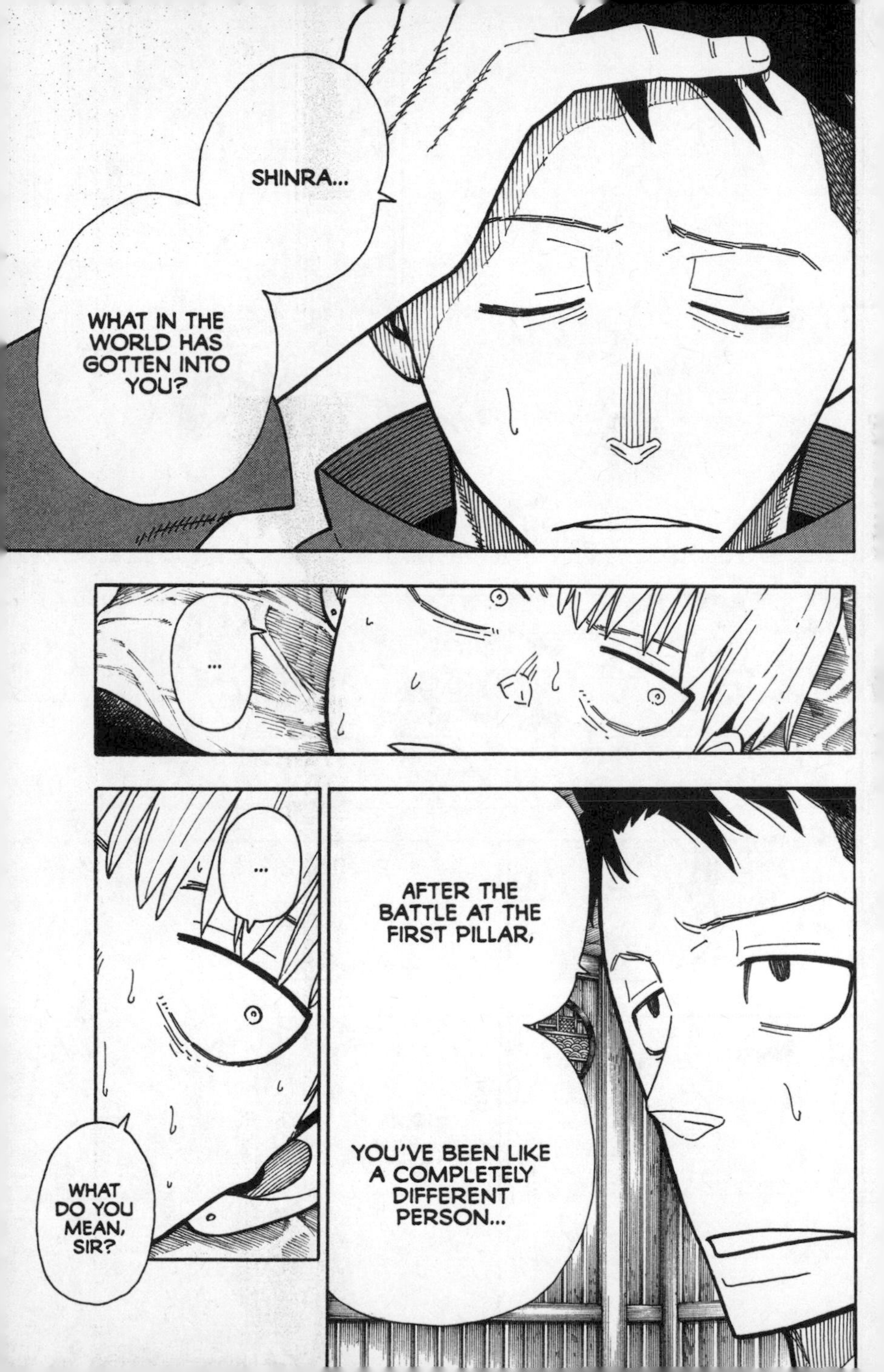
SHINRA...
WHAT IN THE WORLD HAS GOTTEN INTO YOU?
...
AFTER THE BATTLE AT THE FIRST PILLAR,
YOU'VE BEEN LIKE A COMPLETELY DIFFERENT PERSON...
...
WHAT DO YOU MEAN, SIR?

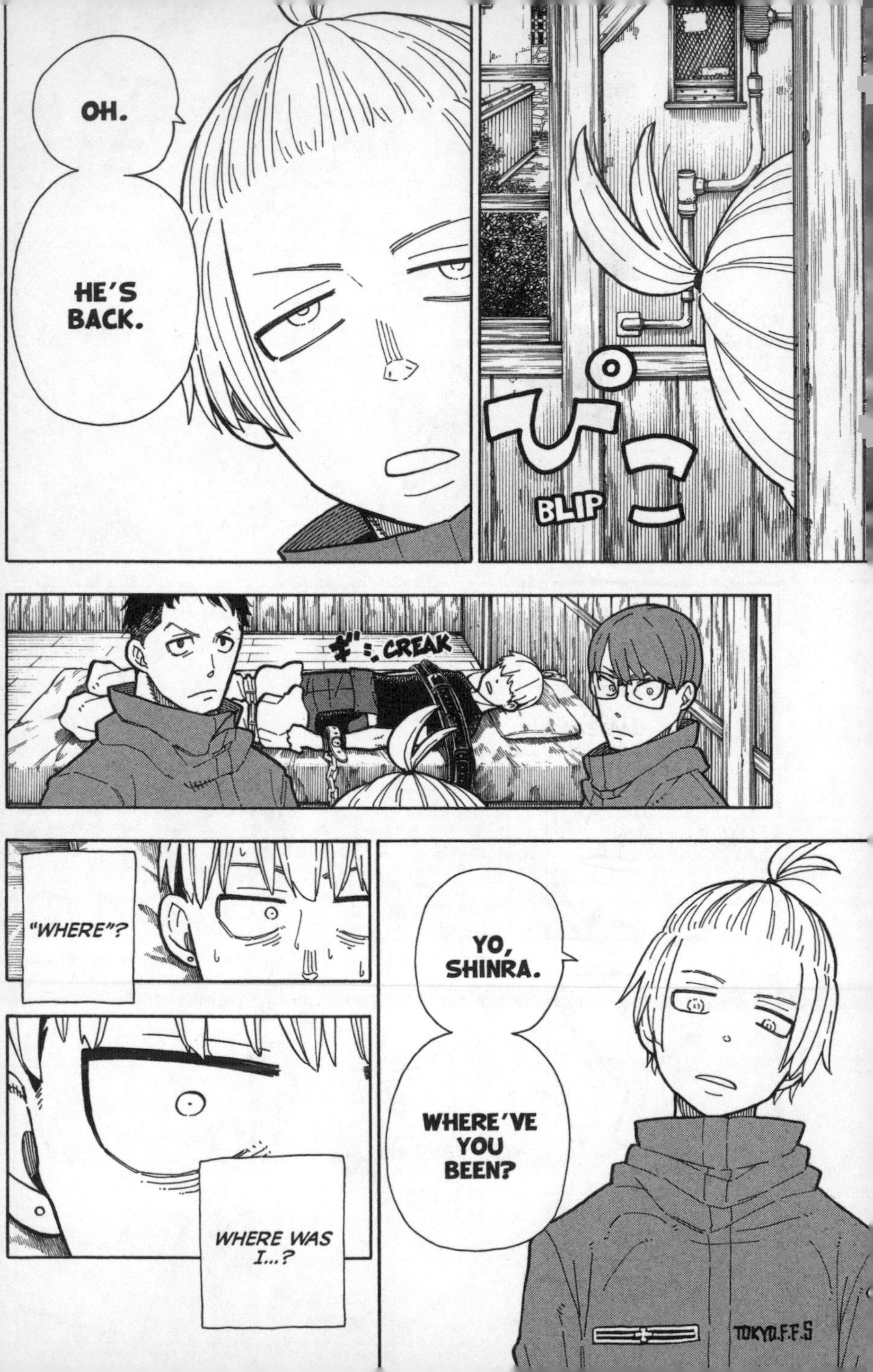
ぴこ
BLIP
OH.
HE'S BACK.
ギ
CREAK
YO, SHINRA.
WHERE'VE YOU BEEN?
TOKYO.F.F.S
"WHERE"?
WHERE WAS I...?

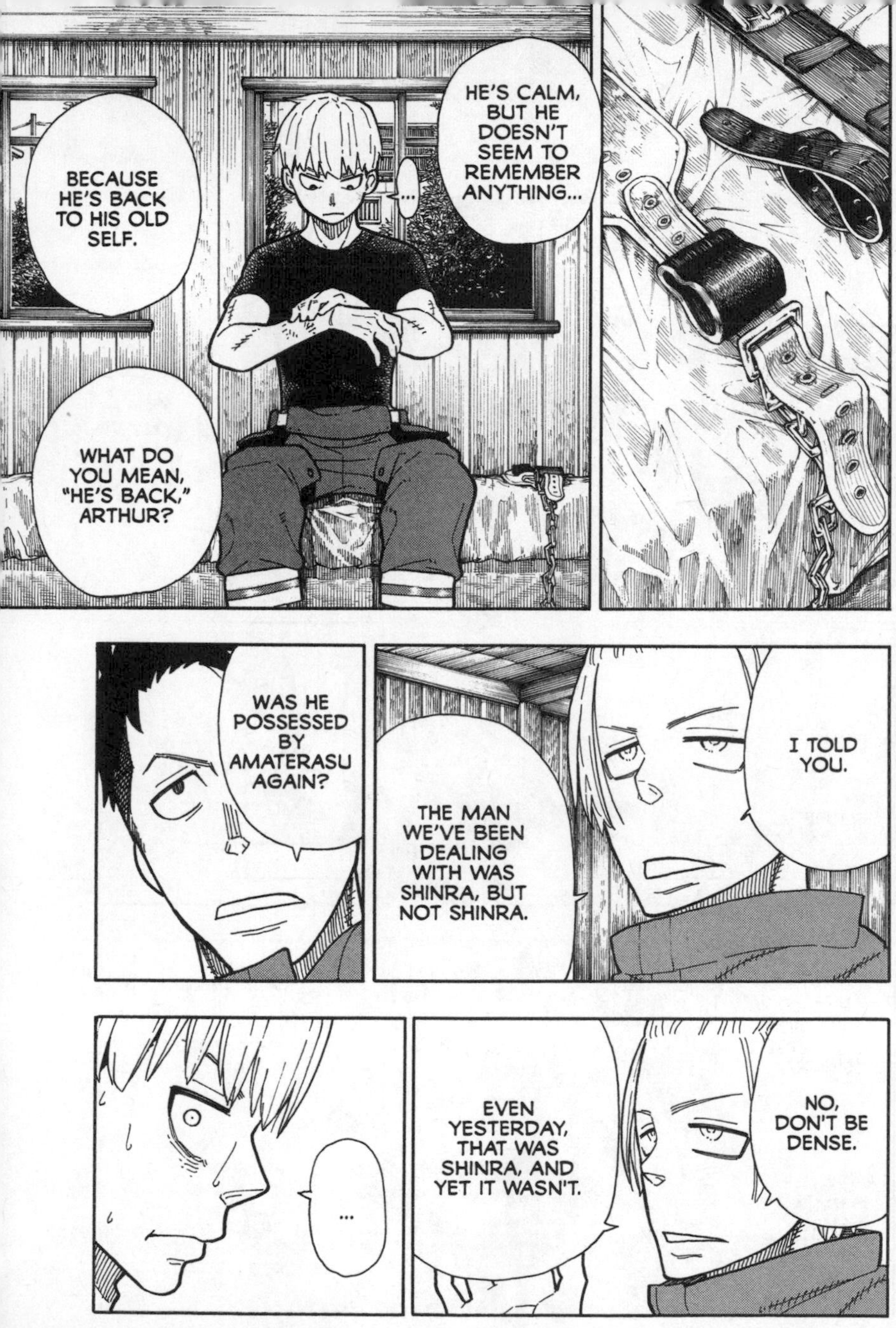
HE'S CALM, BUT HE DOESN'T SEEM TO REMEMBER ANYTHING...
...
BECAUSE HE'S BACK TO HIS OLD SELF.
WHAT DO YOU MEAN, "HE'S BACK," ARTHUR?
I TOLD YOU.
THE MAN WE'VE BEEN DEALING WITH WAS SHINRA, BUT NOT SHINRA.
WAS HE POSSESSED BY AMATERASU AGAIN?
NO, DON'T BE DENSE.
EVEN YESTERDAY, THAT WAS SHINRA, AND YET IT WASN'T.
...

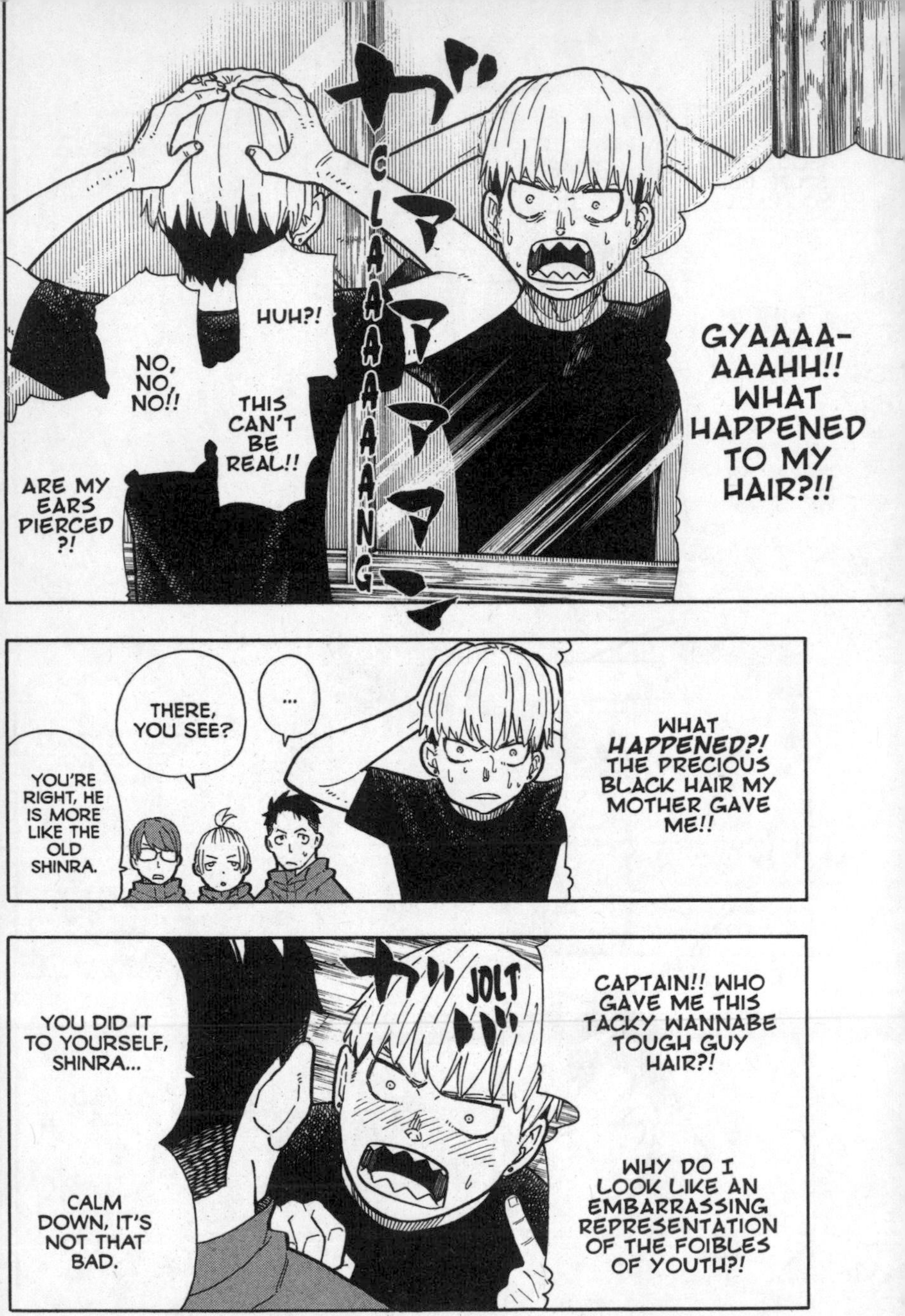
GYAAAA-AAAHH!! WHAT HAPPENED TO MY HAIR?!!
CLAAAAAAANG
HUH?!
THIS CAN'T BE REAL!!
NO, NO, NO!!
ARE MY EARS PIERCED?!
WHAT *HAPPENED*?! THE PRECIOUS BLACK HAIR MY MOTHER GAVE ME!!
...
THERE, YOU SEE?
YOU'RE RIGHT, HE IS MORE LIKE THE OLD SHINRA.
CAPTAIN!! WHO GAVE ME THIS TACKY WANNABE TOUGH GUY HAIR?!
JOLT
WHY DO I LOOK LIKE AN EMBARRASSING REPRESENTATION OF THE FOIBLES OF YOUTH?!
YOU DID IT TO YOURSELF, SHINRA...
CALM DOWN, IT'S NOT THAT BAD.

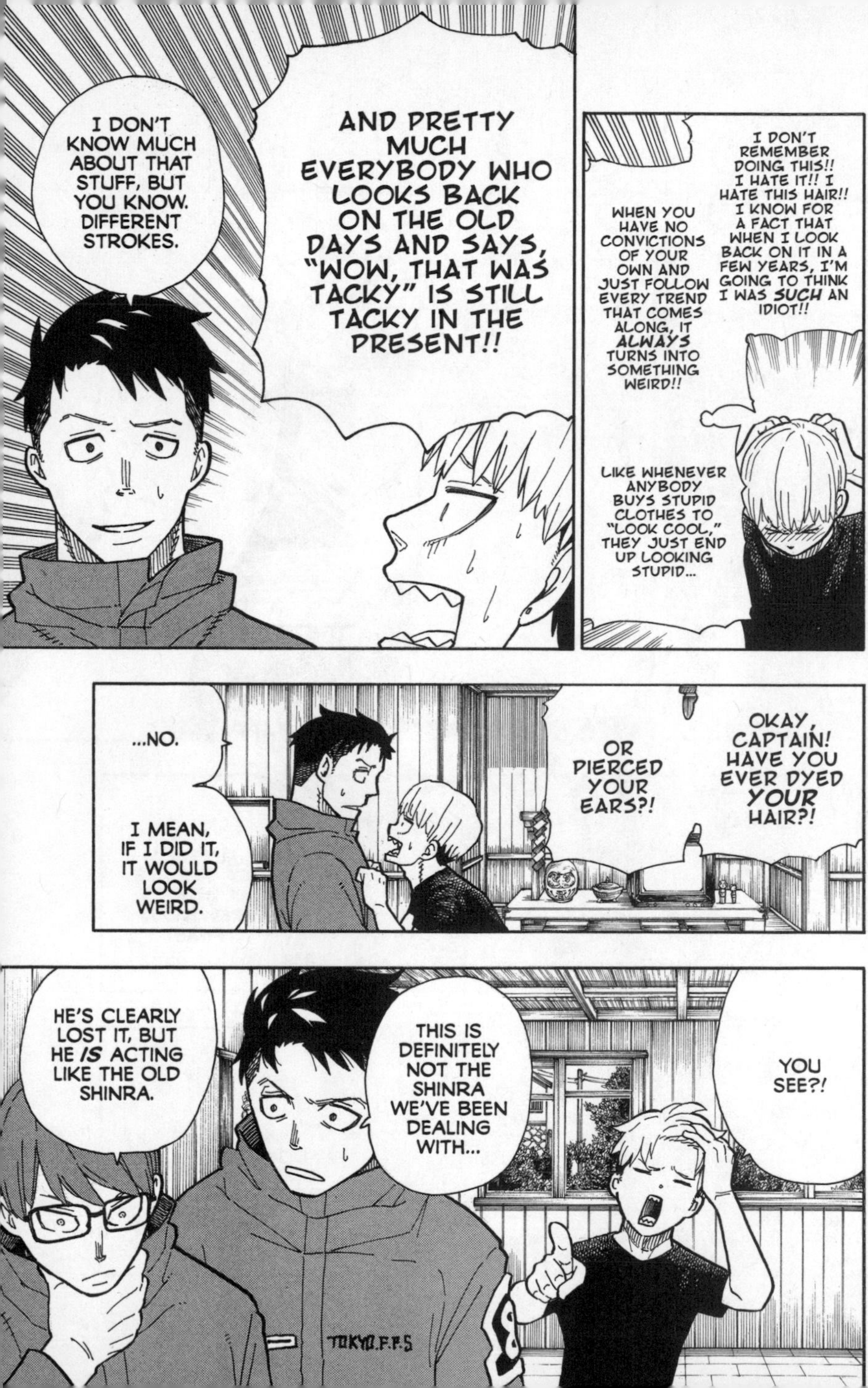
I DON'T REMEMBER DOING THIS!! I HATE IT!! I HATE THIS HAIR!! I KNOW FOR A FACT THAT WHEN I LOOK BACK ON IT IN A FEW YEARS, I'M GOING TO THINK I WAS SUCH AN IDIOT!!
WHEN YOU HAVE NO CONVICTIONS OF YOUR OWN AND JUST FOLLOW EVERY TREND THAT COMES ALONG, IT ALWAYS TURNS INTO SOMETHING WEIRD!!
LIKE WHENEVER ANYBODY BUYS STUPID CLOTHES TO "LOOK COOL," THEY JUST END UP LOOKING STUPID...
AND PRETTY MUCH EVERYBODY WHO LOOKS BACK ON THE OLD DAYS AND SAYS, "WOW, THAT WAS TACKY" IS STILL TACKY IN THE PRESENT!!
I DON'T KNOW MUCH ABOUT THAT STUFF, BUT YOU KNOW. DIFFERENT STROKES.
OKAY, CAPTAIN! HAVE YOU EVER DYED YOUR HAIR?!
OR PIERCED YOUR EARS?!
...NO.
I MEAN, IF I DID IT, IT WOULD LOOK WEIRD.
YOU SEE?!
THIS IS DEFINITELY NOT THE SHINRA WE'VE BEEN DEALING WITH...
HE'S CLEARLY LOST IT, BUT HE IS ACTING LIKE THE OLD SHINRA.
TOKYO.F.F.S

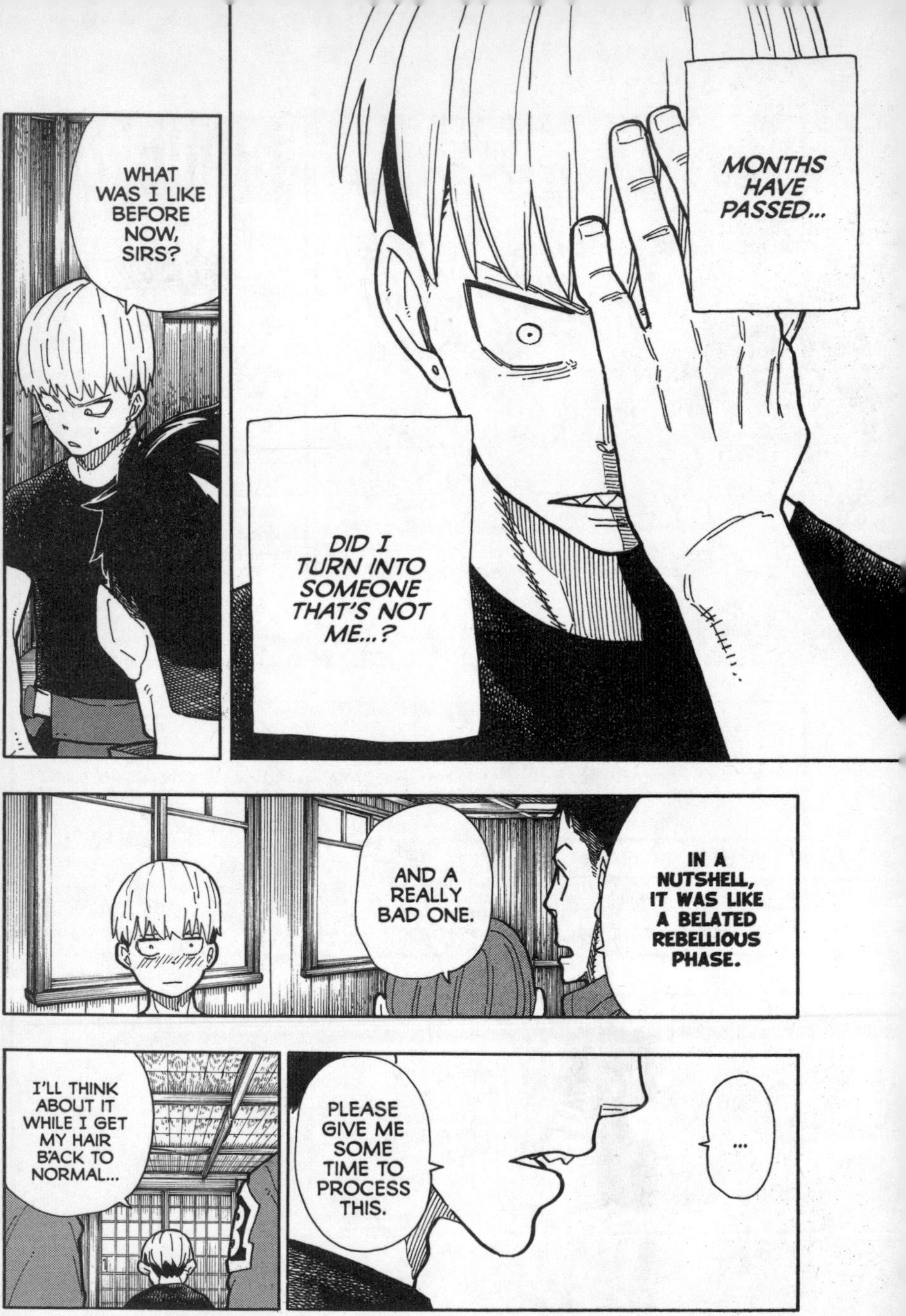
MONTHS HAVE PASSED...
DID I TURN INTO SOMEONE THAT'S NOT ME...?
WHAT WAS I LIKE BEFORE NOW, SIRS?
IN A NUTSHELL, IT WAS LIKE A BELATED REBELLIOUS PHASE.
AND A REALLY BAD ONE.
...
PLEASE GIVE ME SOME TIME TO PROCESS THIS.
I'LL THINK ABOUT IT WHILE I GET MY HAIR BACK TO NORMAL...

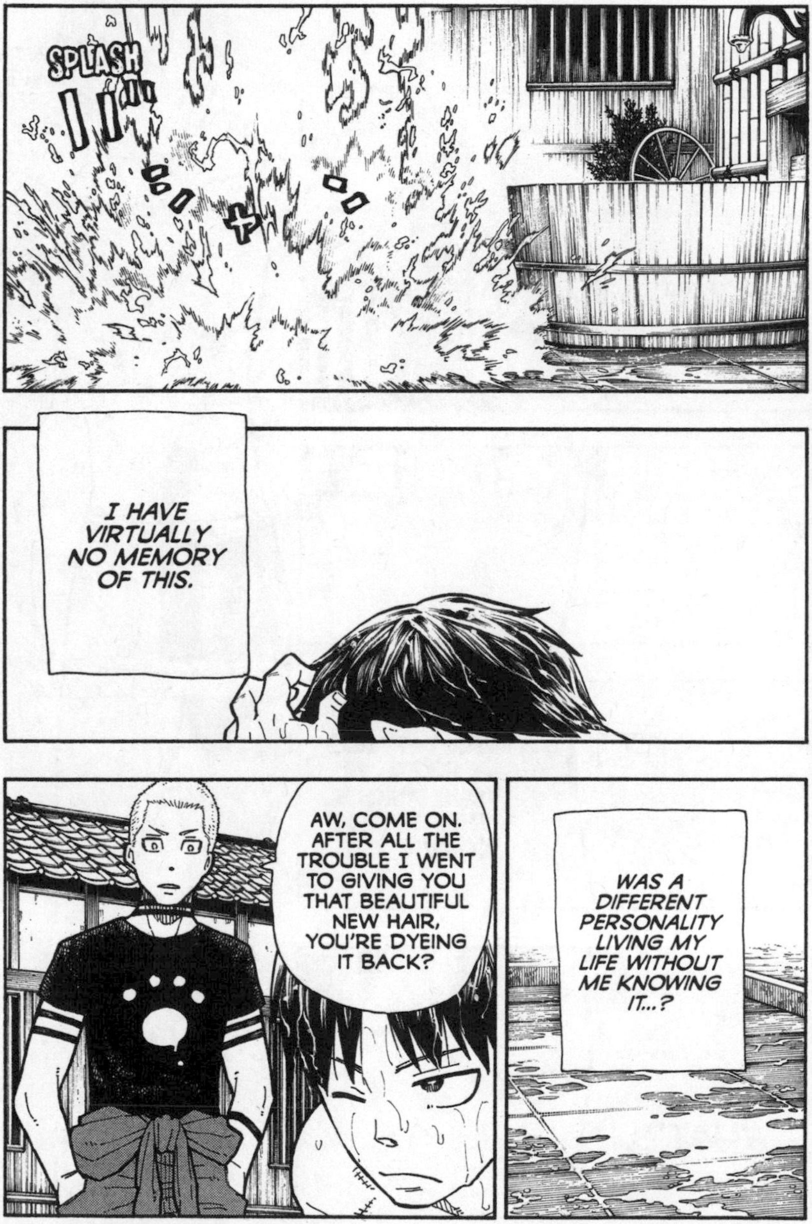
SPLASH
I HAVE VIRTUALLY NO MEMORY OF THIS.
WAS A DIFFERENT PERSONALITY LIVING MY LIFE WITHOUT ME KNOWING IT...?
AW, COME ON. AFTER ALL THE TROUBLE I WENT TO GIVING YOU THAT BEAUTIFUL NEW HAIR, YOU'RE DYEING IT BACK?

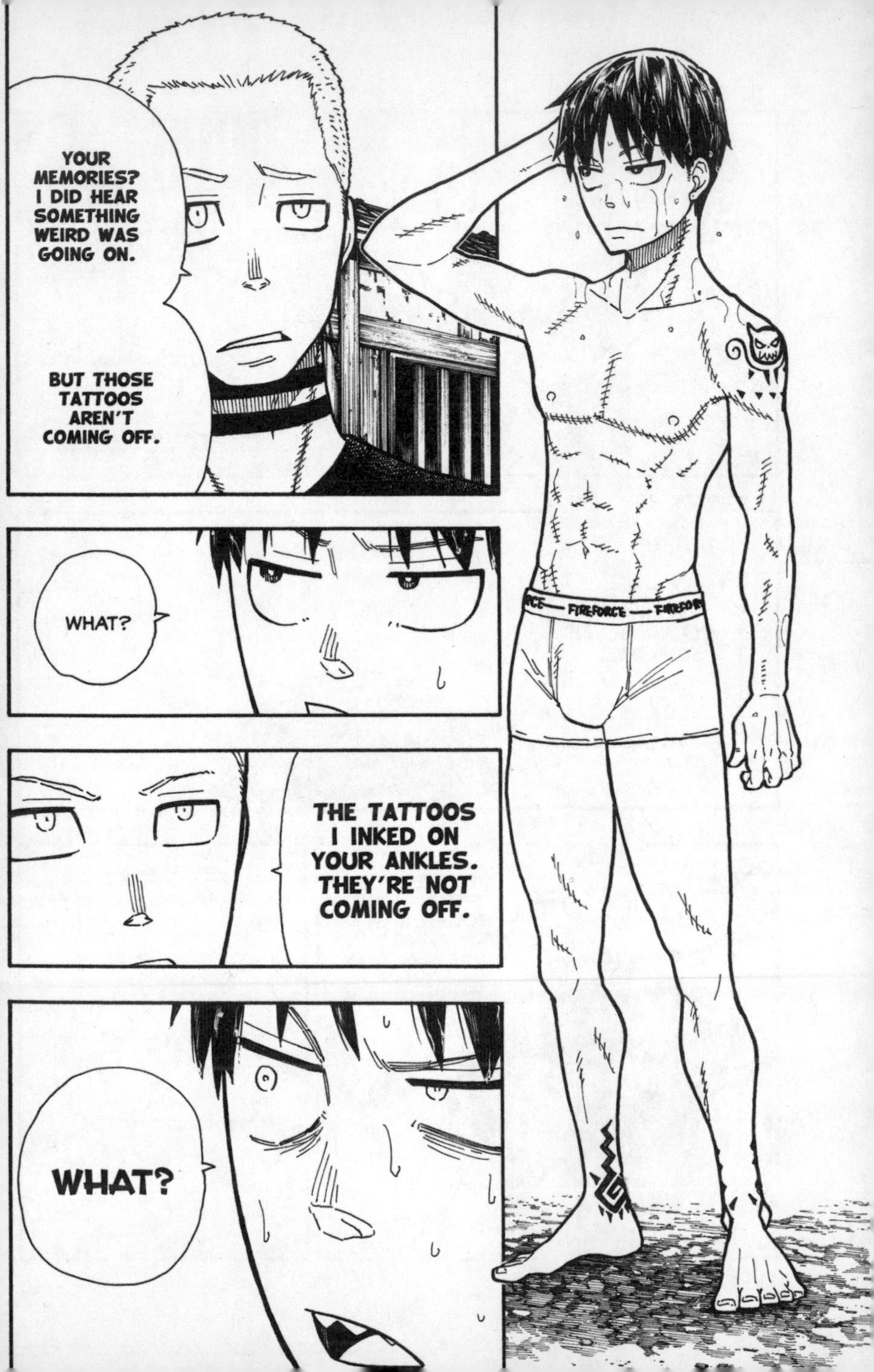
FIREFORCE
YOUR MEMORIES? I DID HEAR SOMETHING WEIRD WAS GOING ON.
BUT THOSE TATTOOS AREN'T COMING OFF.
WHAT?
THE TATTOOS I INKED ON YOUR ANKLES. THEY'RE NOT COMING OFF.
WHAT?

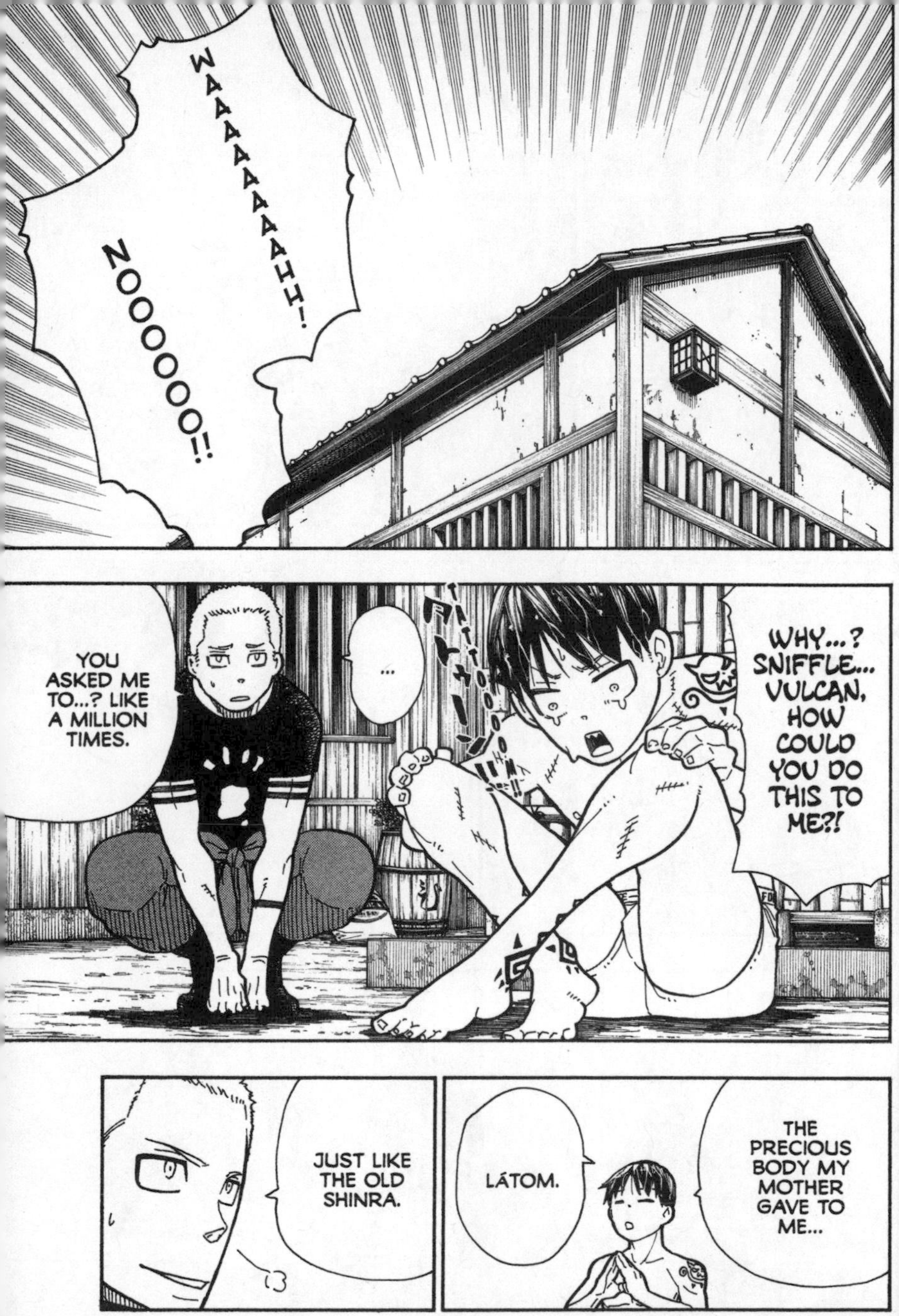
WAAAAAAAAHH!
NOOOOOO!!
WHY...? SNIFFLE... VULCAN, HOW COULD YOU DO THIS TO ME?!
TATTOOOOOM!!
...
YOU ASKED ME TO...? LIKE A MILLION TIMES.
THE PRECIOUS BODY MY MOTHER GAVE TO ME...
LÁTOM.
JUST LIKE THE OLD SHINRA.

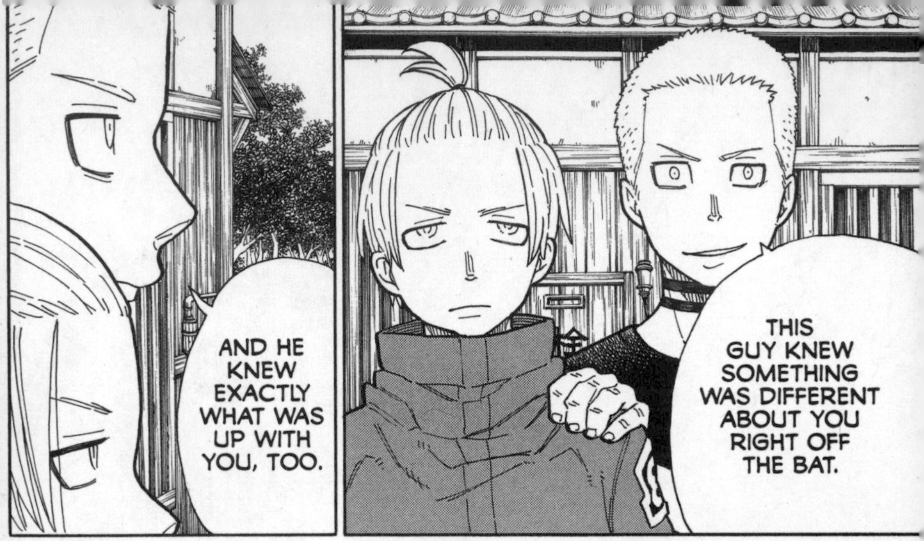
THIS GUY KNEW SOMETHING WAS DIFFERENT ABOUT YOU RIGHT OFF THE BAT.
AND HE KNEW EXACTLY WHAT WAS UP WITH YOU, TOO.

Sign: Hydrant

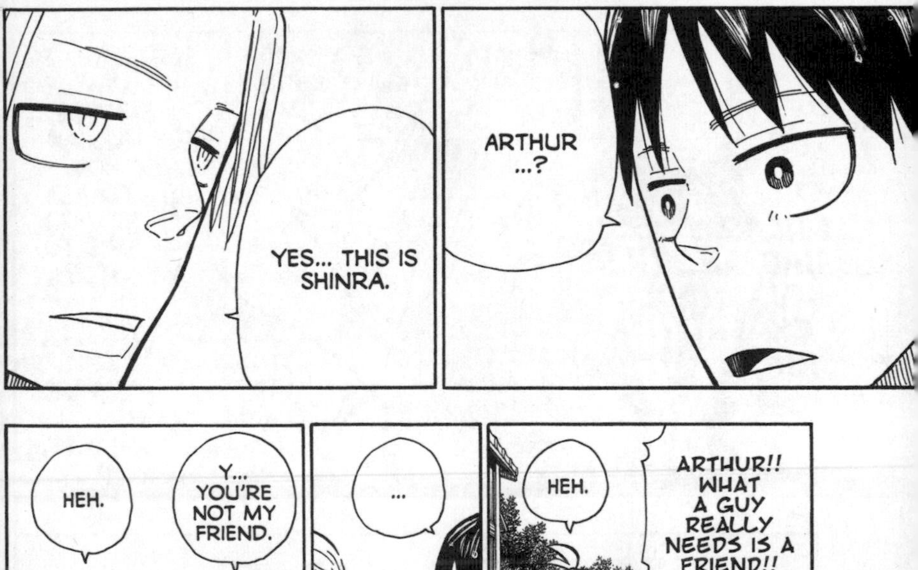
ARTHUR ...?
YES... THIS IS SHINRA.
ARTHUR!! WHAT A GUY REALLY NEEDS IS A FRIEND!!
HEH.
...
Y... YOU'RE NOT MY FRIEND.
HEH.

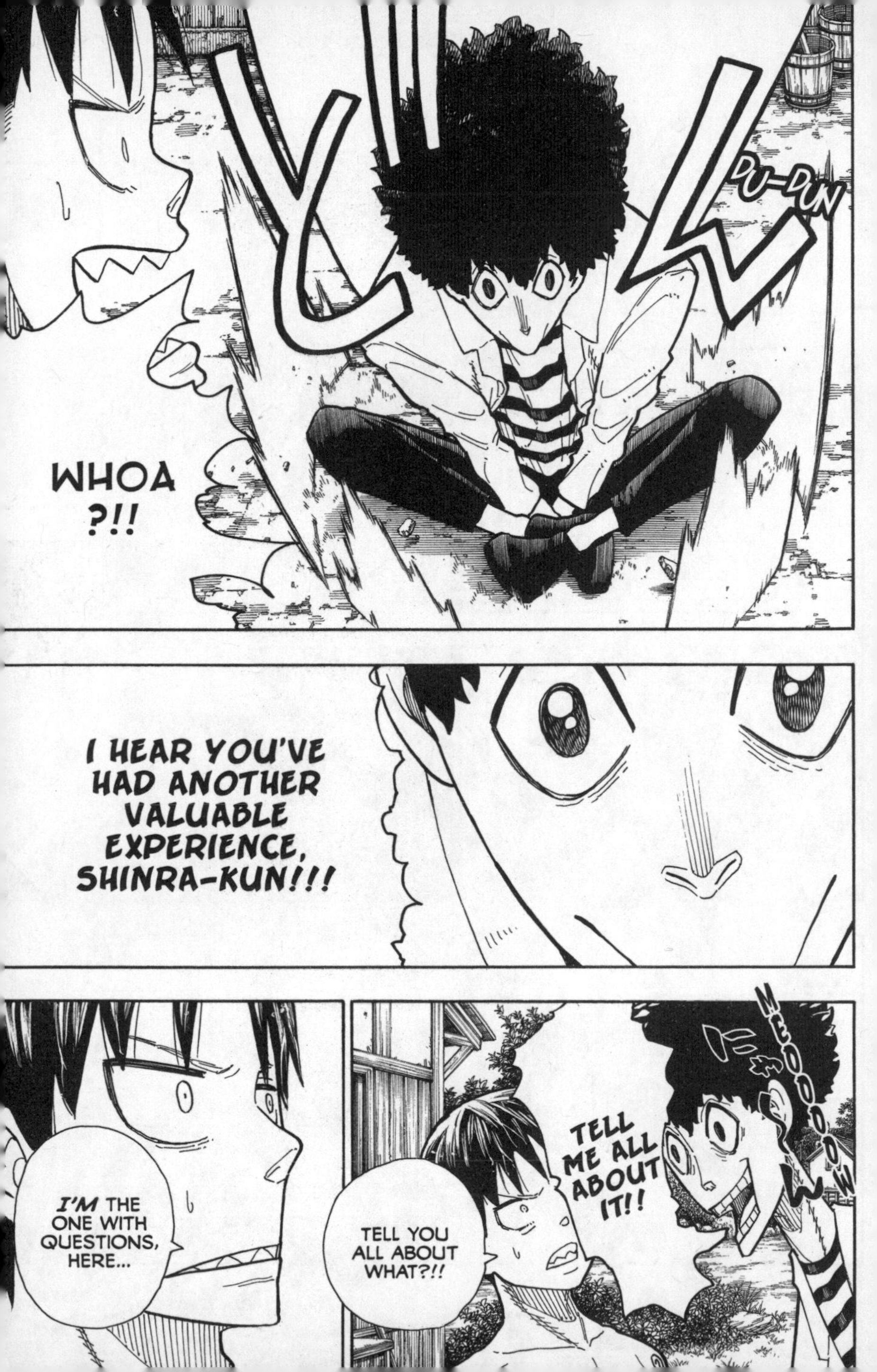
DU-DUN
WHOA ?!!
I HEAR YOU'VE HAD ANOTHER VALUABLE EXPERIENCE, SHINRA-KUN!!!
MEOOOOOW
TELL ME ALL ABOUT IT!!
TELL YOU ALL ABOUT WHAT?!!
I'M THE ONE WITH QUESTIONS, HERE...

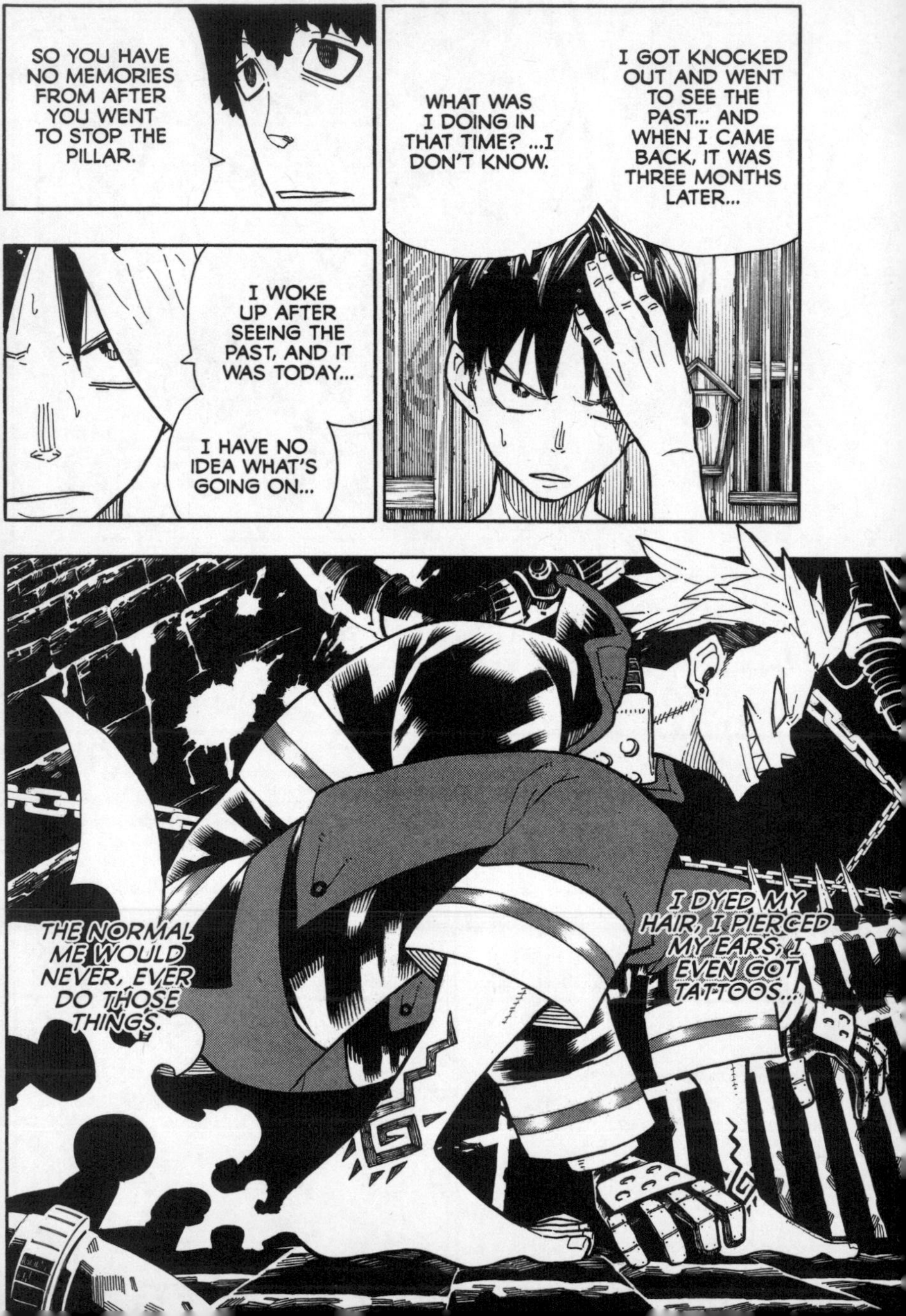
I GOT KNOCKED OUT AND WENT TO SEE THE PAST... AND WHEN I CAME BACK, IT WAS THREE MONTHS LATER...
WHAT WAS I DOING IN THAT TIME? ...I DON'T KNOW.
SO YOU HAVE NO MEMORIES FROM AFTER YOU WENT TO STOP THE PILLAR.
I WOKE UP AFTER SEEING THE PAST, AND IT WAS TODAY...
I HAVE NO IDEA WHAT'S GOING ON...
I DYED MY HAIR, I PIERCED MY EARS, I EVEN GOT TATTOOS...
THE NORMAL ME WOULD NEVER, EVER DO THOSE THINGS.

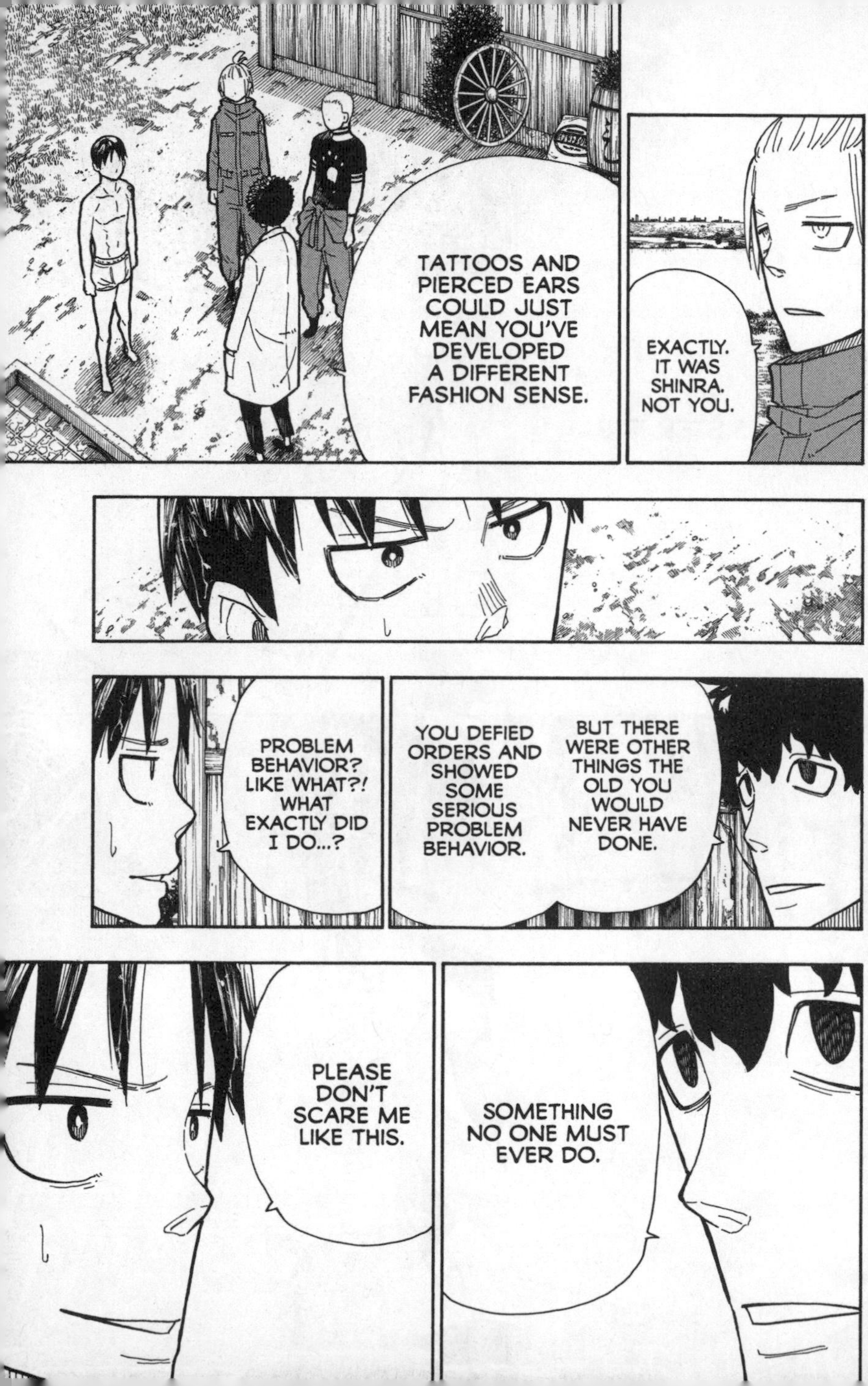
EXACTLY. IT WAS SHINRA. NOT YOU.
TATTOOS AND PIERCED EARS COULD JUST MEAN YOU'VE DEVELOPED A DIFFERENT FASHION SENSE.
YOU DEFIED ORDERS AND SHOWED SOME SERIOUS PROBLEM BEHAVIOR.
BUT THERE WERE OTHER THINGS THE OLD YOU WOULD NEVER HAVE DONE.
PROBLEM BEHAVIOR? LIKE WHAT?! WHAT EXACTLY DID I DO...?
SOMETHING NO ONE MUST EVER DO.
PLEASE DON'T SCARE ME LIKE THIS.

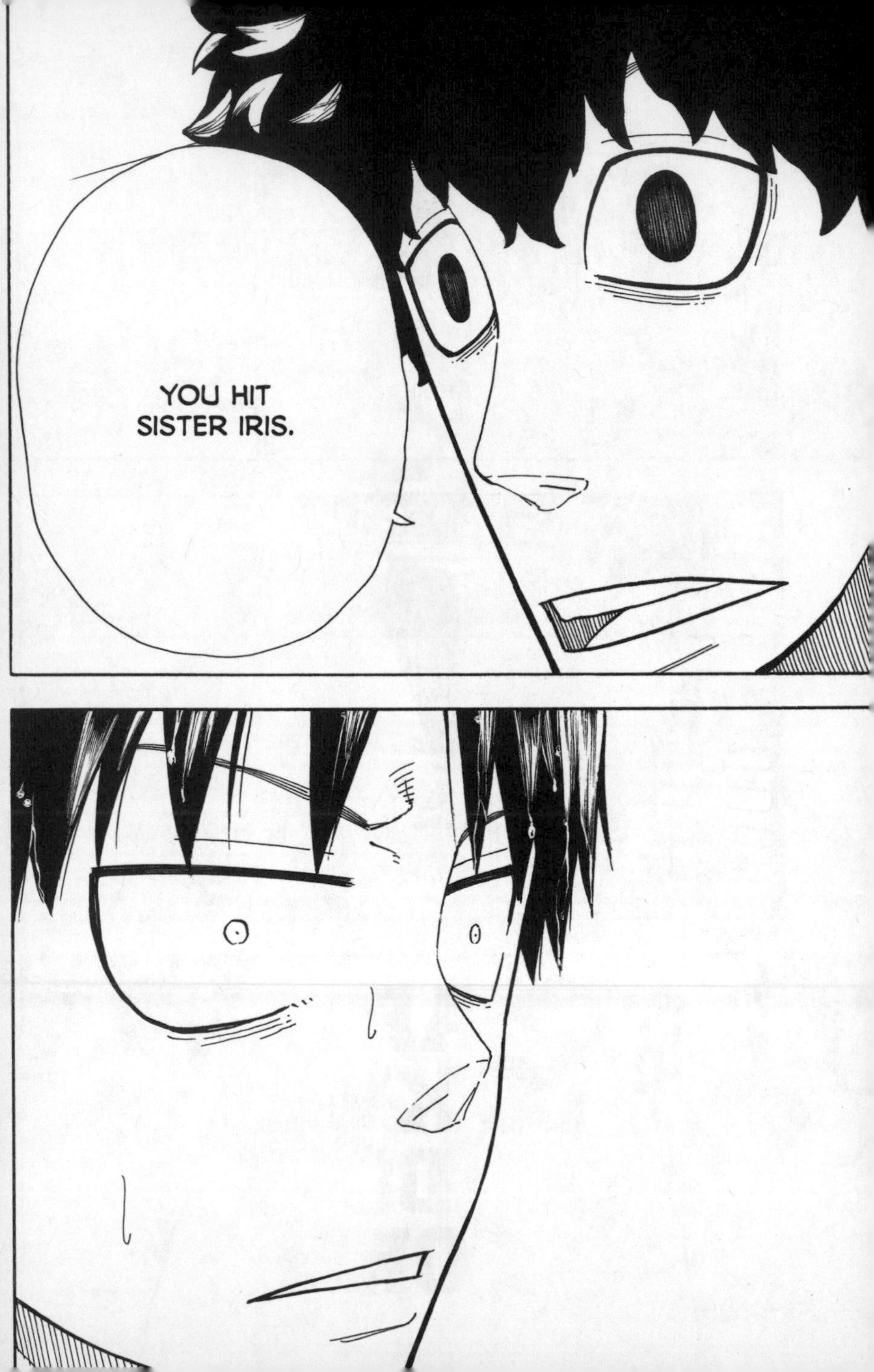
YOU HIT SISTER IRIS.

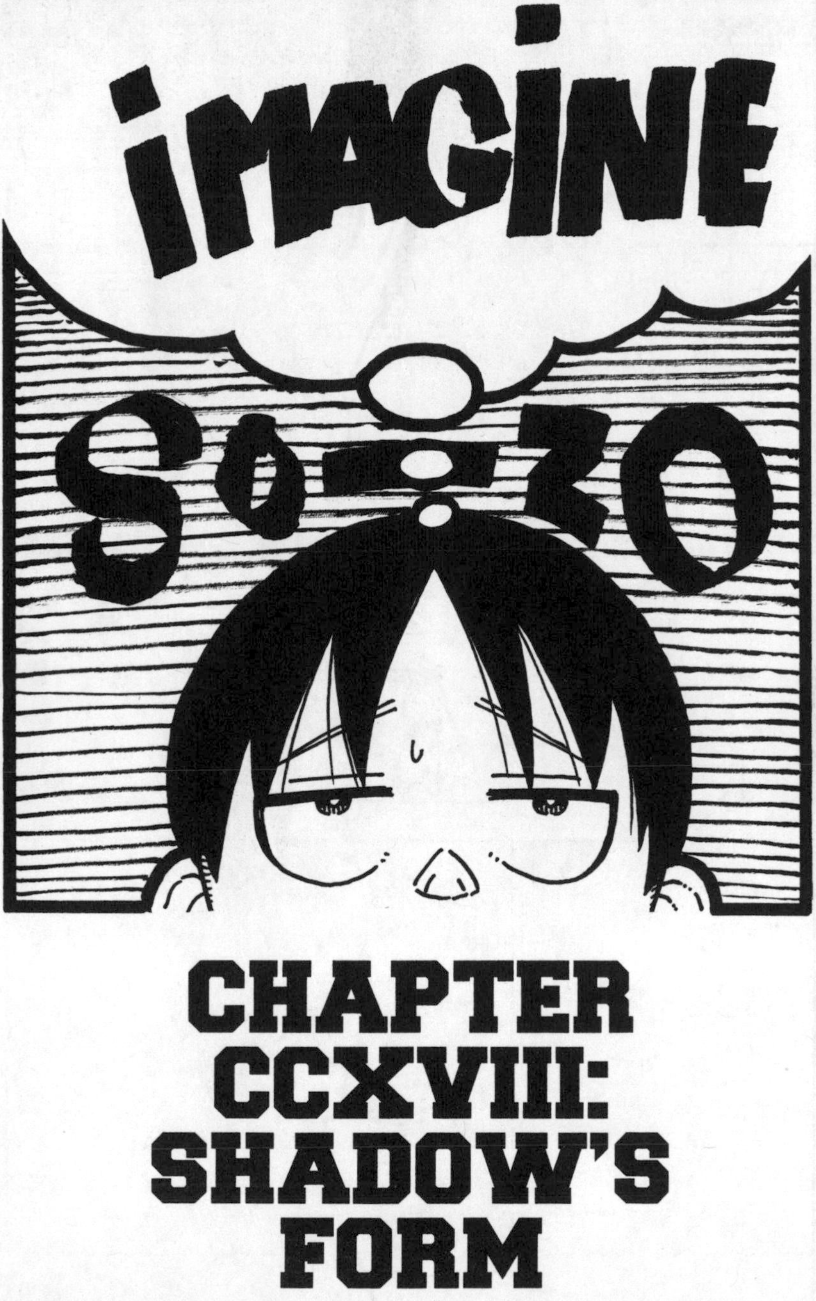
IMAGINE
SO-ZO

CHAPTER CCXVIII: SHADOW'S FORM

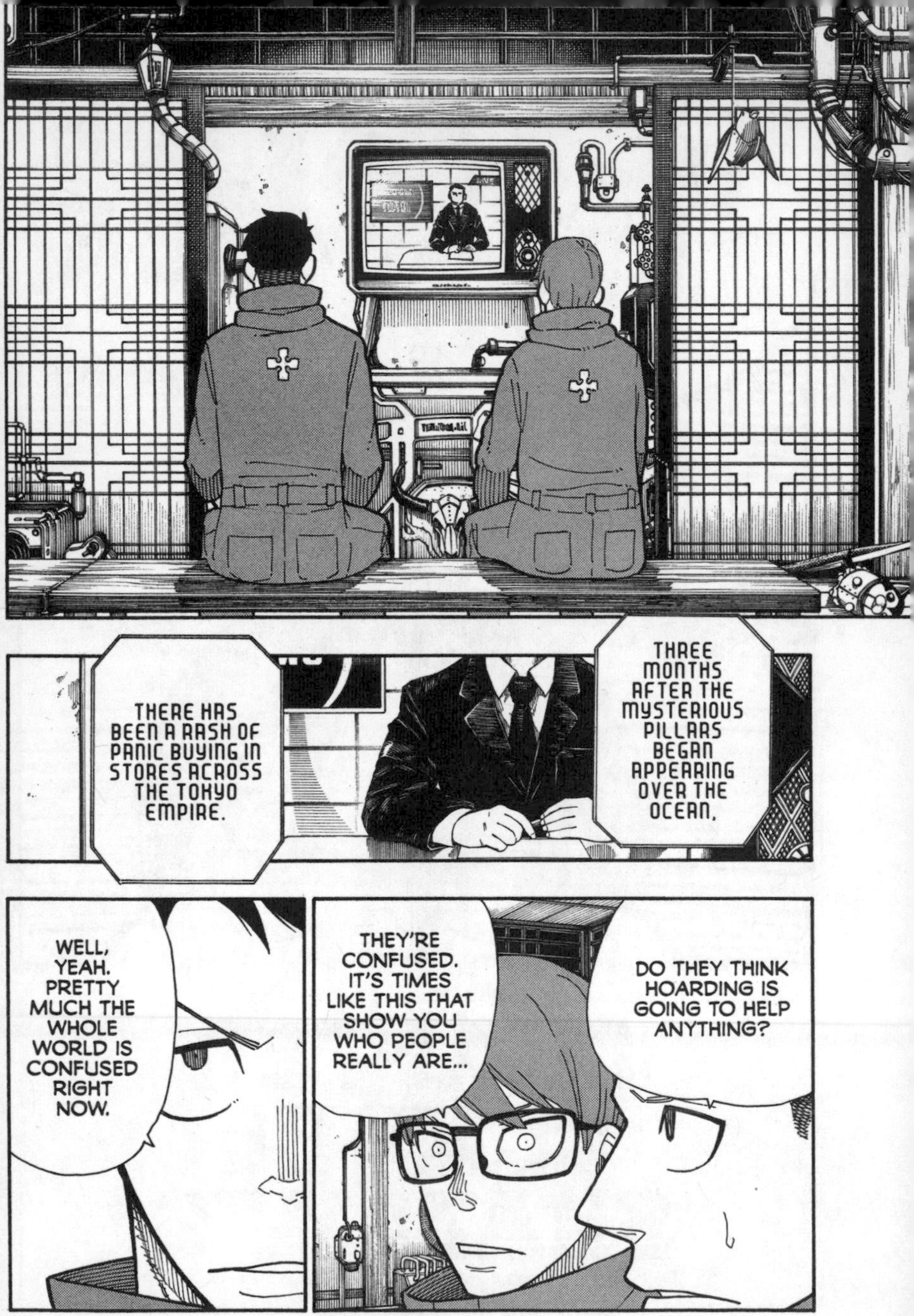
THREE MONTHS AFTER THE MYSTERIOUS PILLARS BEGAN APPEARING OVER THE OCEAN,
THERE HAS BEEN A RASH OF PANIC BUYING IN STORES ACROSS THE TOKYO EMPIRE.
DO THEY THINK HOARDING IS GOING TO HELP ANYTHING?
THEY'RE CONFUSED. IT'S TIMES LIKE THIS THAT SHOW YOU WHO PEOPLE REALLY ARE...
WELL, YEAH. PRETTY MUCH THE WHOLE WORLD IS CONFUSED RIGHT NOW.

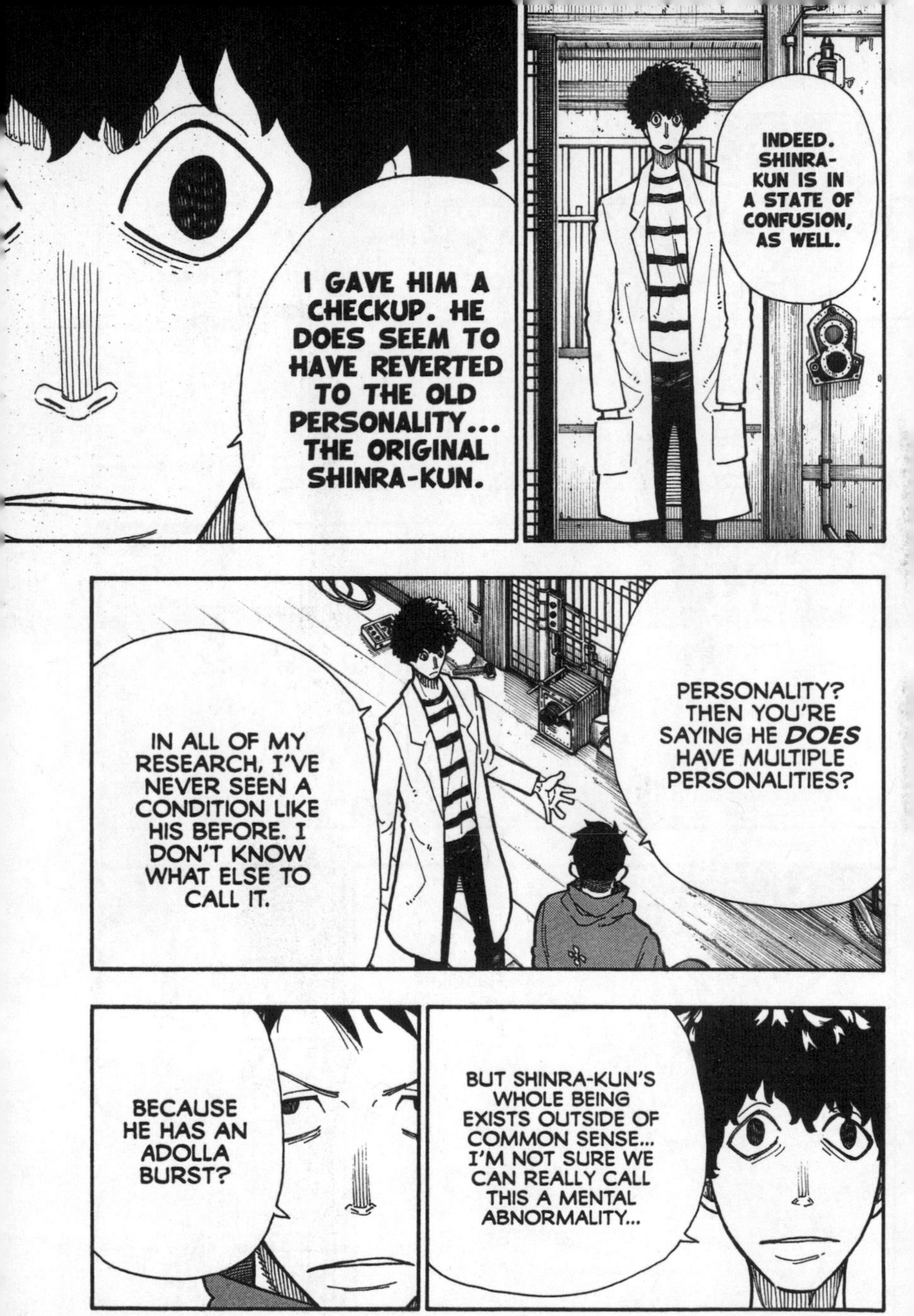
INDEED. SHINRA-KUN IS IN A STATE OF CONFUSION, AS WELL.
I GAVE HIM A CHECKUP. HE DOES SEEM TO HAVE REVERTED TO THE OLD PERSONALITY... THE ORIGINAL SHINRA-KUN.
PERSONALITY? THEN YOU'RE SAYING HE *DOES* HAVE MULTIPLE PERSONALITIES?
IN ALL OF MY RESEARCH, I'VE NEVER SEEN A CONDITION LIKE HIS BEFORE. I DON'T KNOW WHAT ELSE TO CALL IT.
BUT SHINRA-KUN'S WHOLE BEING EXISTS OUTSIDE OF COMMON SENSE... I'M NOT SURE WE CAN REALLY CALL THIS A MENTAL ABNORMALITY...
BECAUSE HE HAS AN ADOLLA BURST?

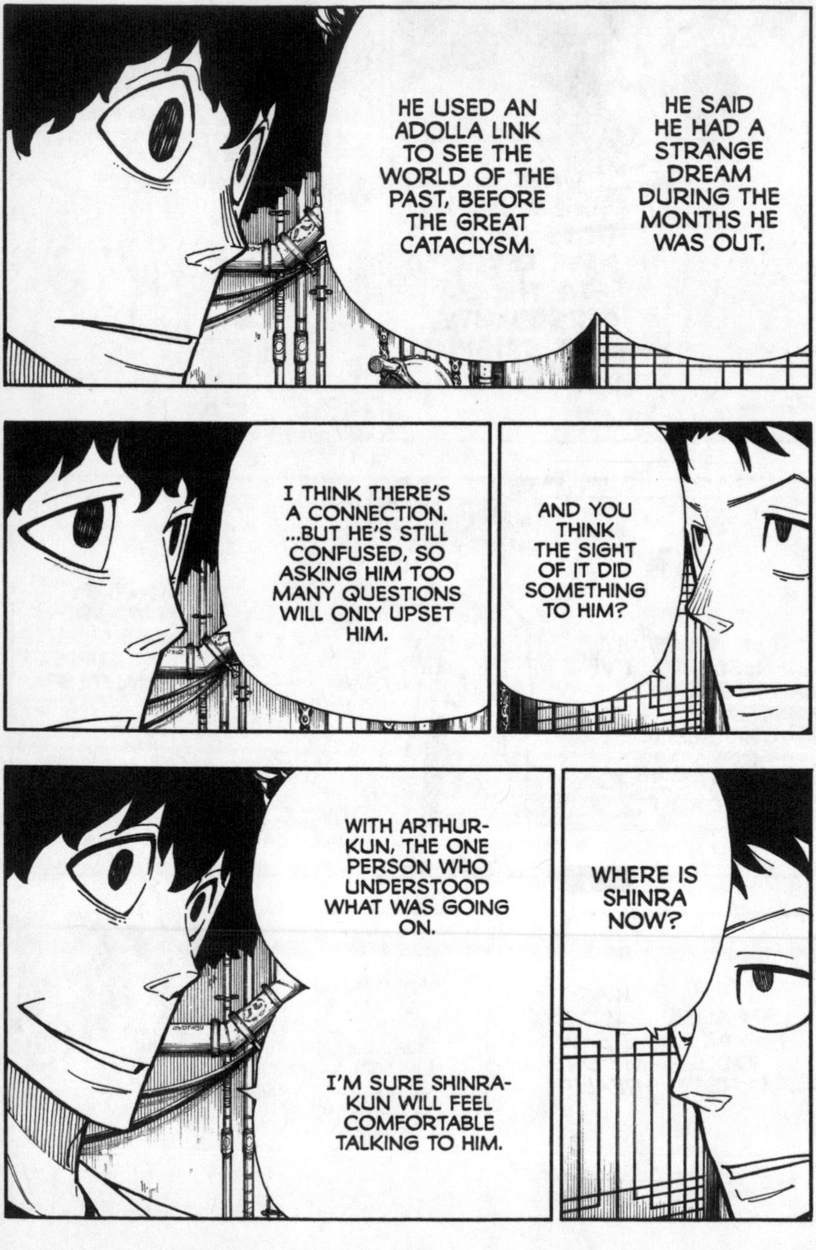
HE SAID HE HAD A STRANGE DREAM DURING THE MONTHS HE WAS OUT.
HE USED AN ADOLLA LINK TO SEE THE WORLD OF THE PAST, BEFORE THE GREAT CATACLYSM.
AND YOU THINK THE SIGHT OF IT DID SOMETHING TO HIM?
I THINK THERE'S A CONNECTION. ...BUT HE'S STILL CONFUSED, SO ASKING HIM TOO MANY QUESTIONS WILL ONLY UPSET HIM.
WHERE IS SHINRA NOW?
WITH ARTHUR-KUN, THE ONE PERSON WHO UNDERSTOOD WHAT WAS GOING ON.
I'M SURE SHINRA-KUN WILL FEEL COMFORTABLE TALKING TO HIM.

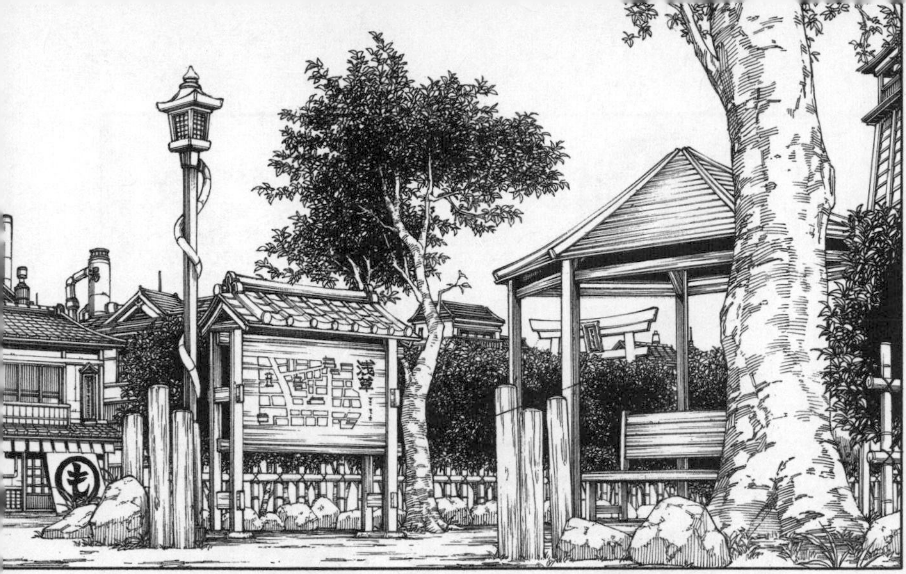

Sign: Asakusa

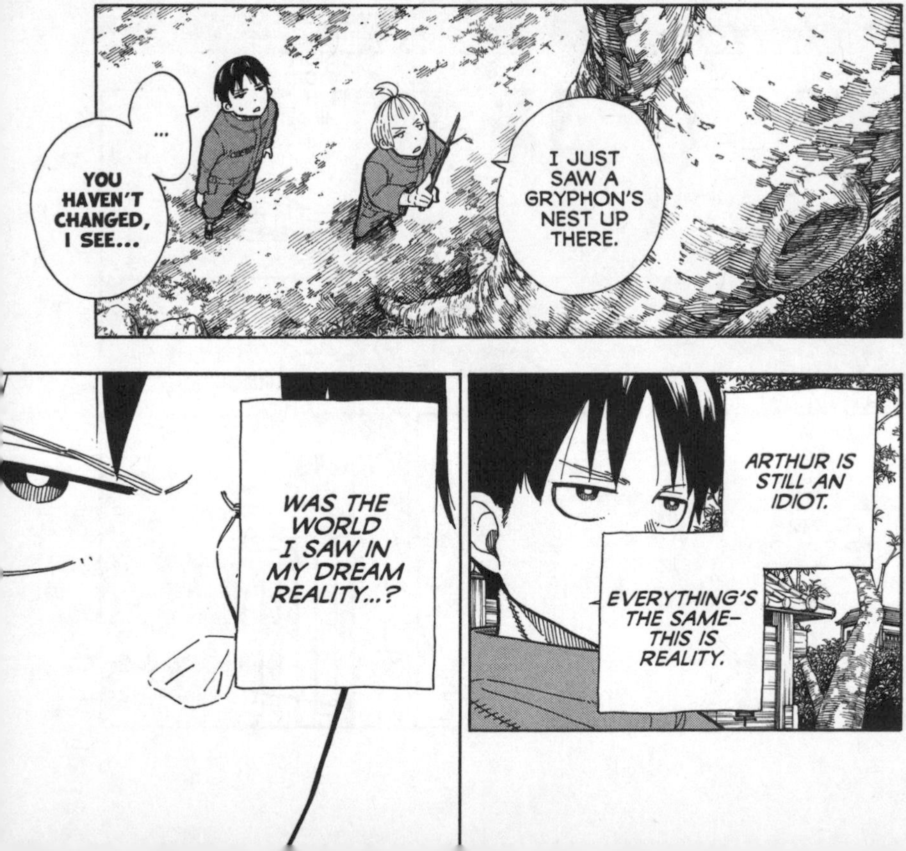
I JUST SAW A GRYPHON'S NEST UP THERE.
...
YOU HAVEN'T CHANGED, I SEE...
ARTHUR IS STILL AN IDIOT.
EVERYTHING'S THE SAME— THIS IS REALITY.
WAS THE WORLD I SAW IN MY DREAM REALITY...?

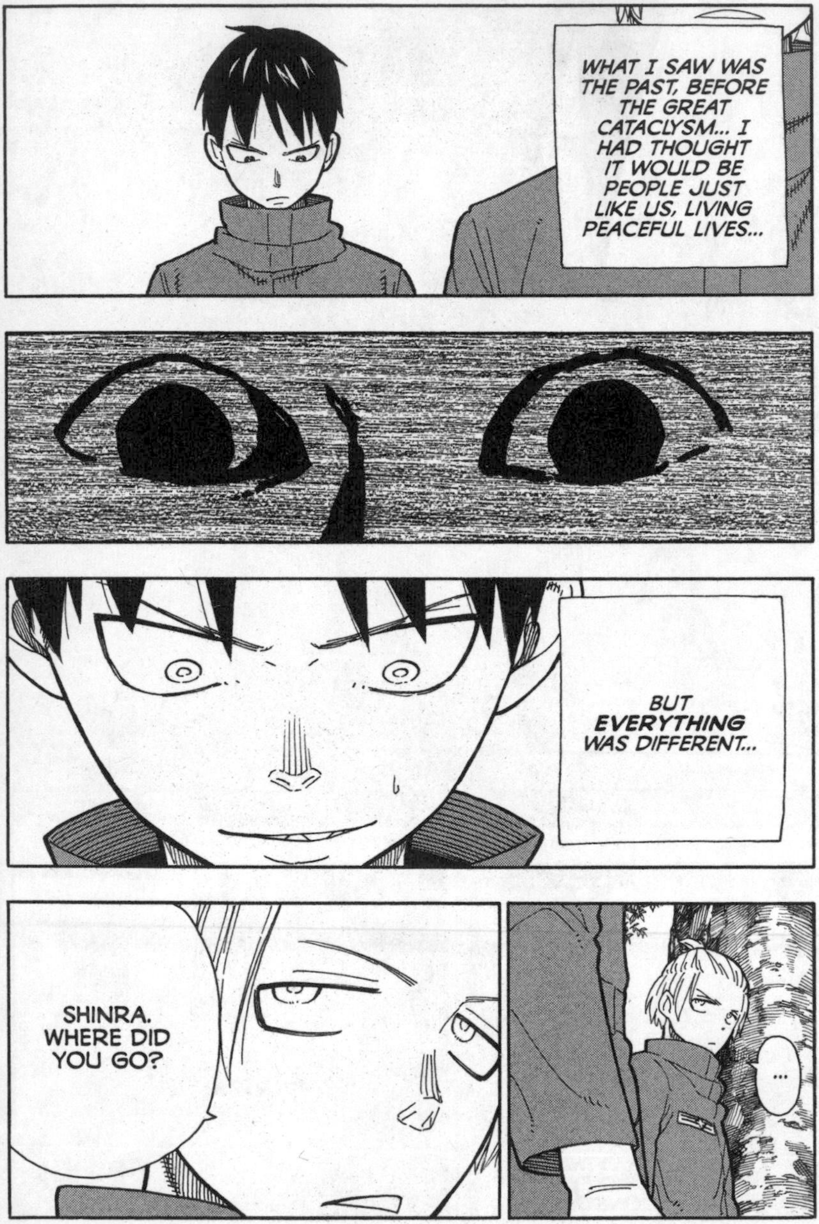
WHAT I SAW WAS THE PAST, BEFORE THE GREAT CATACLYSM... I HAD THOUGHT IT WOULD BE PEOPLE JUST LIKE US, LIVING PEACEFUL LIVES...
BUT EVERYTHING WAS DIFFERENT...
...
SHINRA. WHERE DID YOU GO?

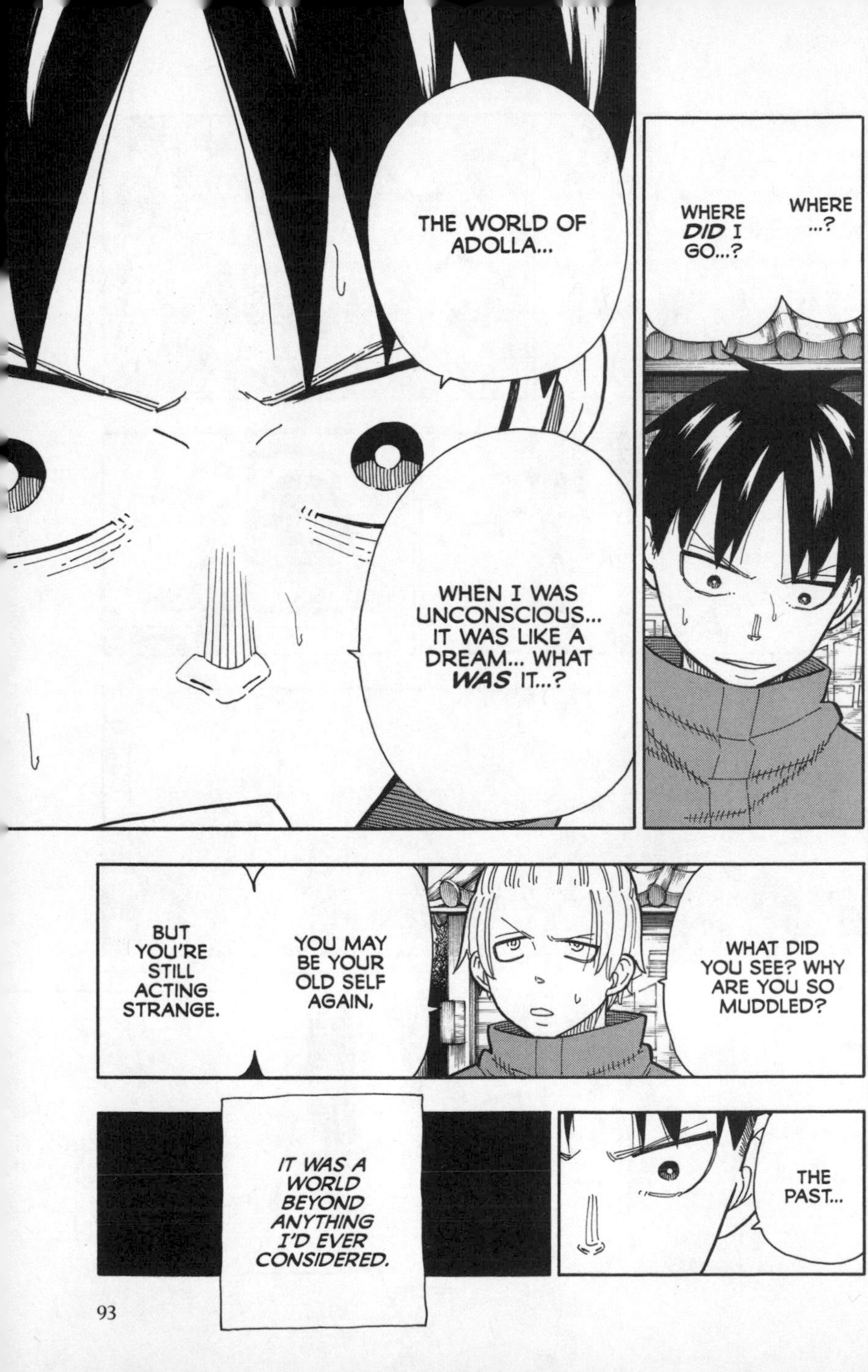
WHERE ...?
WHERE *DID* I GO...?
THE WORLD OF ADOLLA...
WHEN I WAS UNCONSCIOUS... IT WAS LIKE A DREAM... WHAT *WAS* IT...?
WHAT DID YOU SEE? WHY ARE YOU SO MUDDLED?
YOU MAY BE YOUR OLD SELF AGAIN,
BUT YOU'RE STILL ACTING STRANGE.
THE PAST...
IT WAS A WORLD BEYOND ANYTHING I'D EVER CONSIDERED.

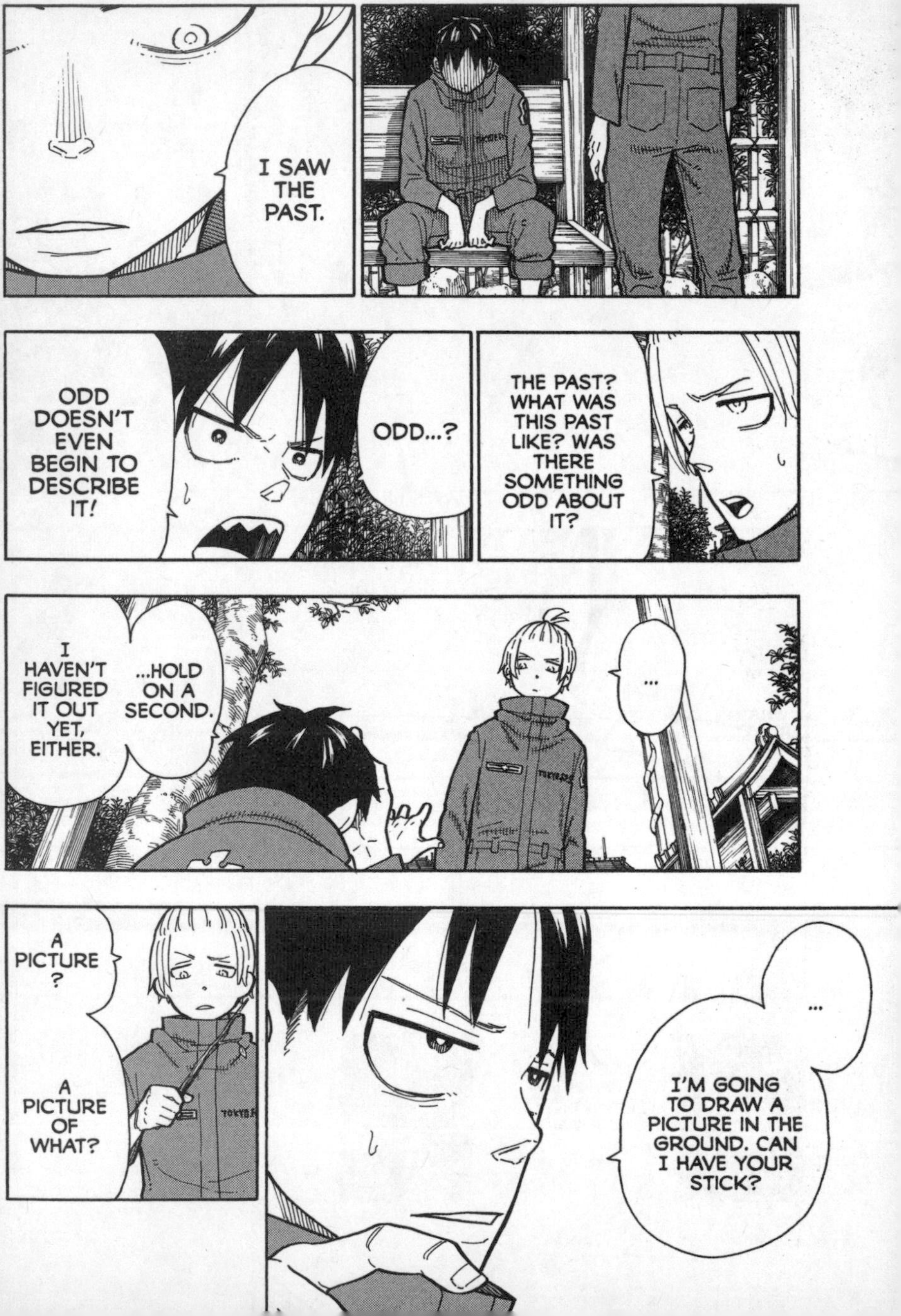
I SAW THE PAST.
THE PAST? WHAT WAS THIS PAST LIKE? WAS THERE SOMETHING ODD ABOUT IT?
ODD...?
ODD DOESN'T EVEN BEGIN TO DESCRIBE IT!
...
...HOLD ON A SECOND.
I HAVEN'T FIGURED IT OUT YET, EITHER.
...
I'M GOING TO DRAW A PICTURE IN THE GROUND. CAN I HAVE YOUR STICK?
A PICTURE?
A PICTURE OF WHAT?

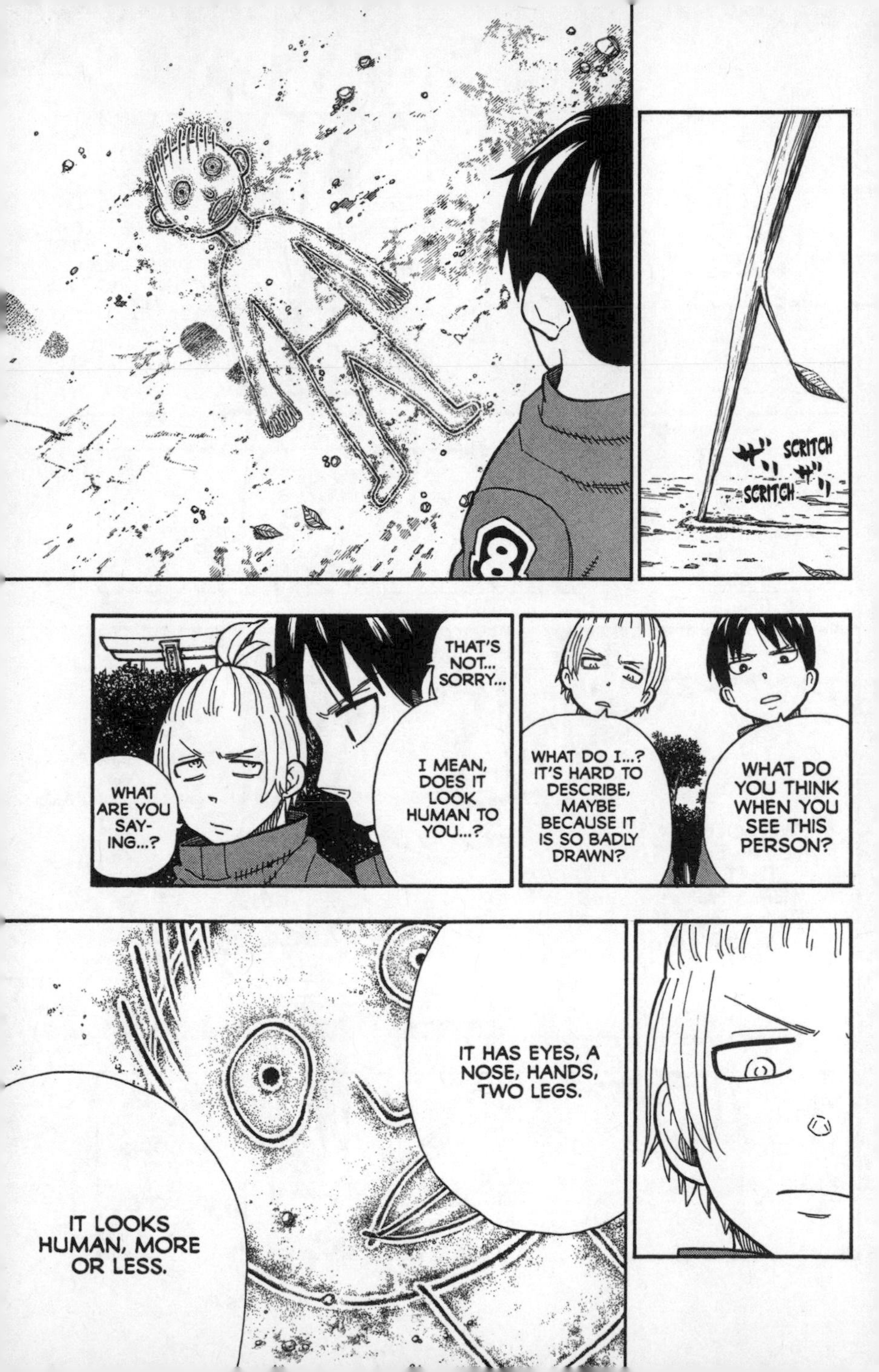

ザッ SCRITCH
SCRITCH ザッ
WHAT DO YOU THINK WHEN YOU SEE THIS PERSON?
WHAT DO I...? IT'S HARD TO DESCRIBE, MAYBE BECAUSE IT IS SO BADLY DRAWN?
THAT'S NOT... SORRY...
I MEAN, DOES IT LOOK HUMAN TO YOU...?
WHAT ARE YOU SAYING...?
IT HAS EYES, A NOSE, HANDS, TWO LEGS.
IT LOOKS HUMAN, MORE OR LESS.

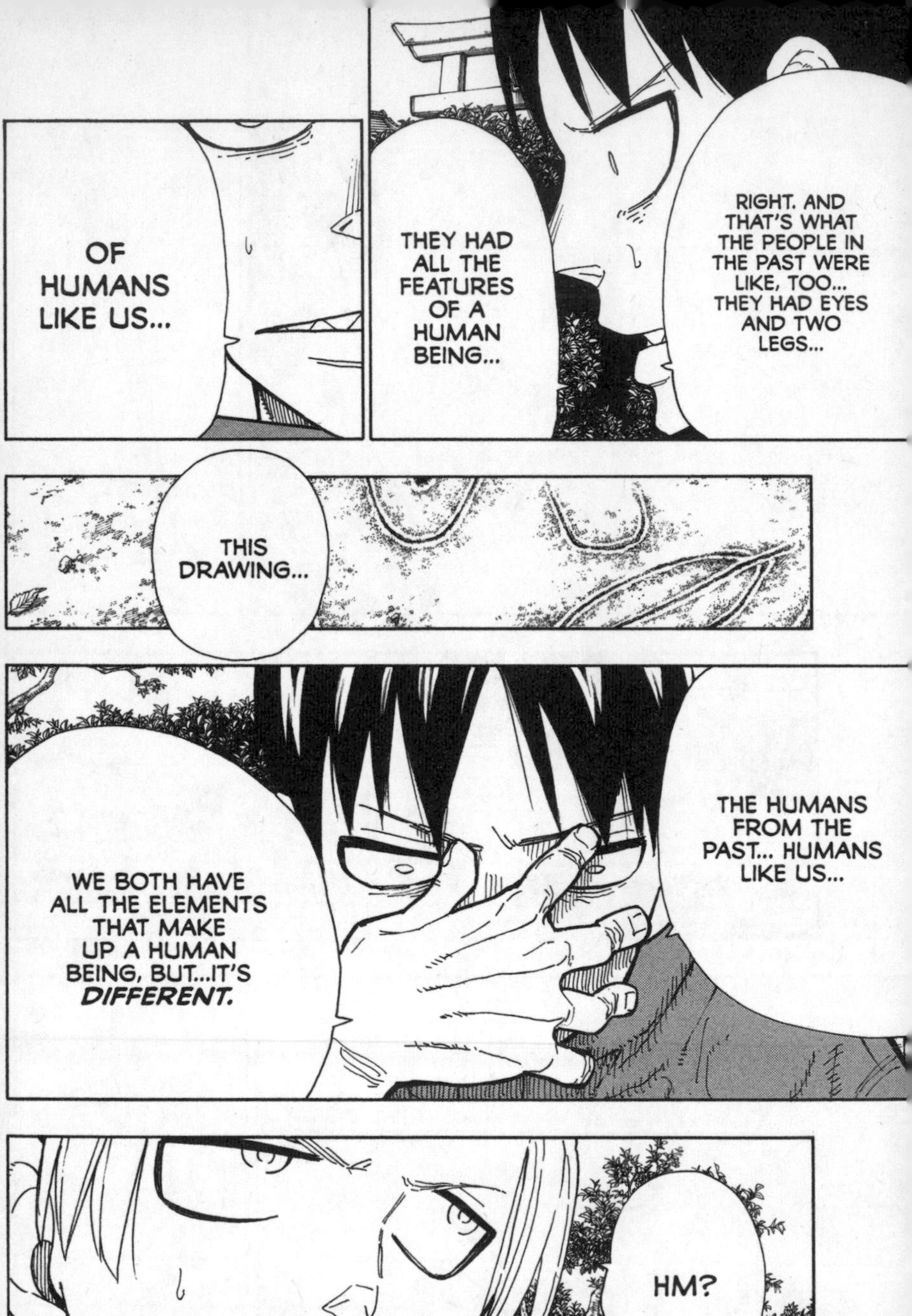
RIGHT. AND THAT'S WHAT THE PEOPLE IN THE PAST WERE LIKE, TOO... THEY HAD EYES AND TWO LEGS...
THEY HAD ALL THE FEATURES OF A HUMAN BEING...
OF HUMANS LIKE US...
THIS DRAWING...
THE HUMANS FROM THE PAST... HUMANS LIKE US...
WE BOTH HAVE ALL THE ELEMENTS THAT MAKE UP A HUMAN BEING, BUT...IT'S *DIFFERENT.*
HM?

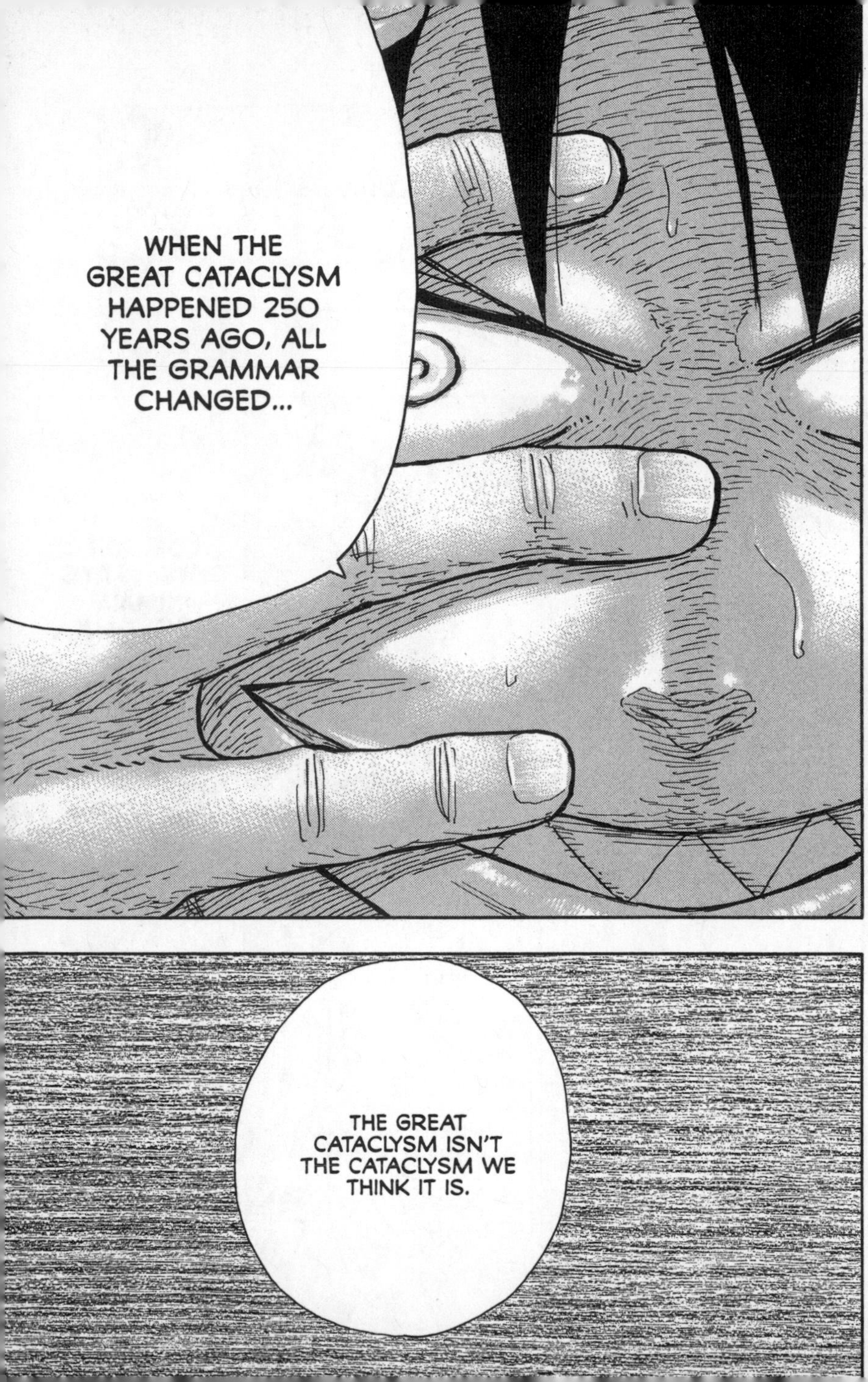
WHEN THE GREAT CATACLYSM HAPPENED 250 YEARS AGO, ALL THE GRAMMAR CHANGED...
THE GREAT CATACLYSM ISN'T THE CATACLYSM WE THINK IT IS.

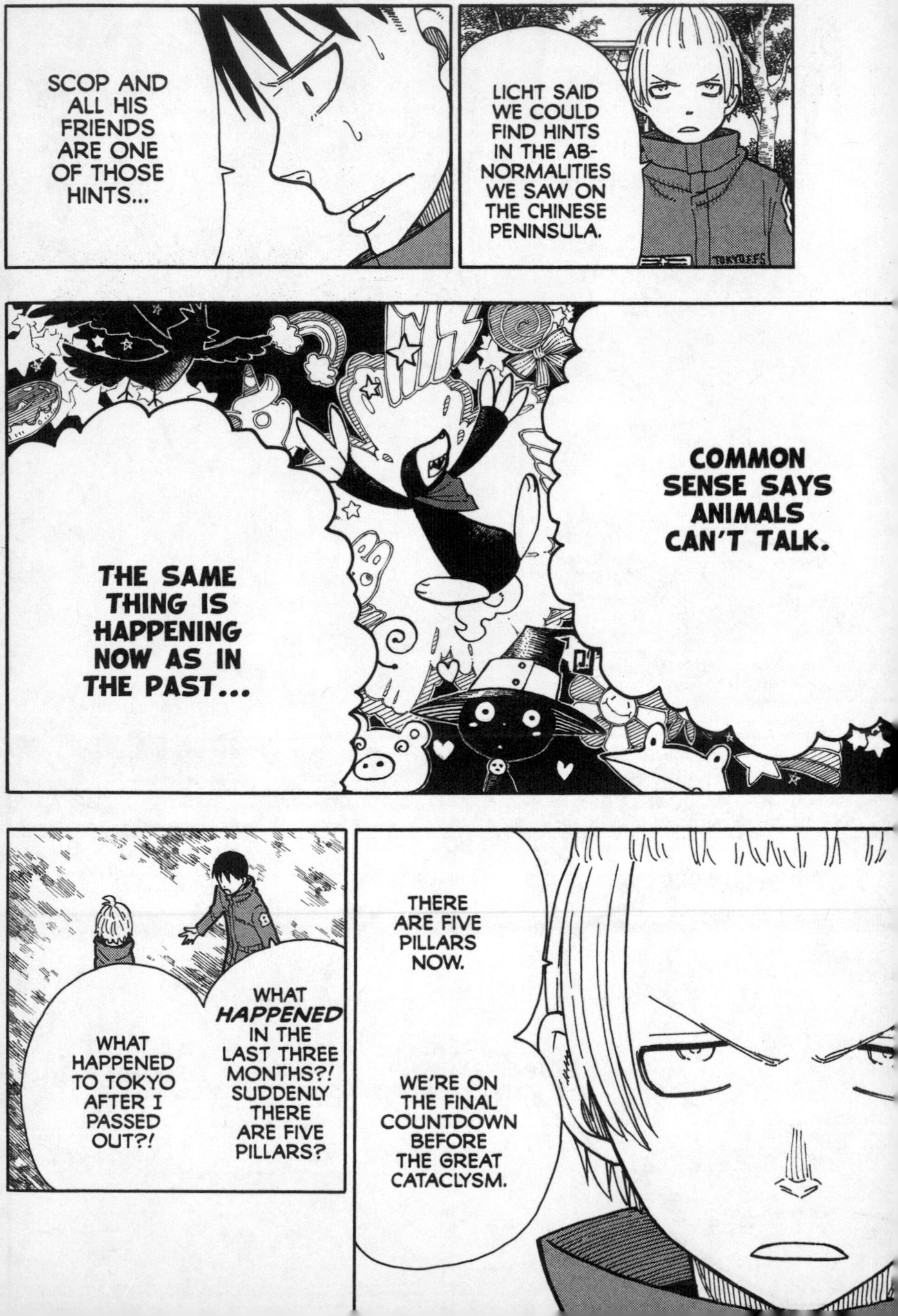
LICHT SAID WE COULD FIND HINTS IN THE AB-NORMALITIES WE SAW ON THE CHINESE PENINSULA.
SCOP AND ALL HIS FRIENDS ARE ONE OF THOSE HINTS...
COMMON SENSE SAYS ANIMALS CAN'T TALK.
THE SAME THING IS HAPPENING NOW AS IN THE PAST...
THERE ARE FIVE PILLARS NOW.
WE'RE ON THE FINAL COUNTDOWN BEFORE THE GREAT CATACLYSM.
WHAT *HAPPENED* IN THE LAST THREE MONTHS?! SUDDENLY THERE ARE FIVE PILLARS?
WHAT HAPPENED TO TOKYO AFTER I PASSED OUT?!

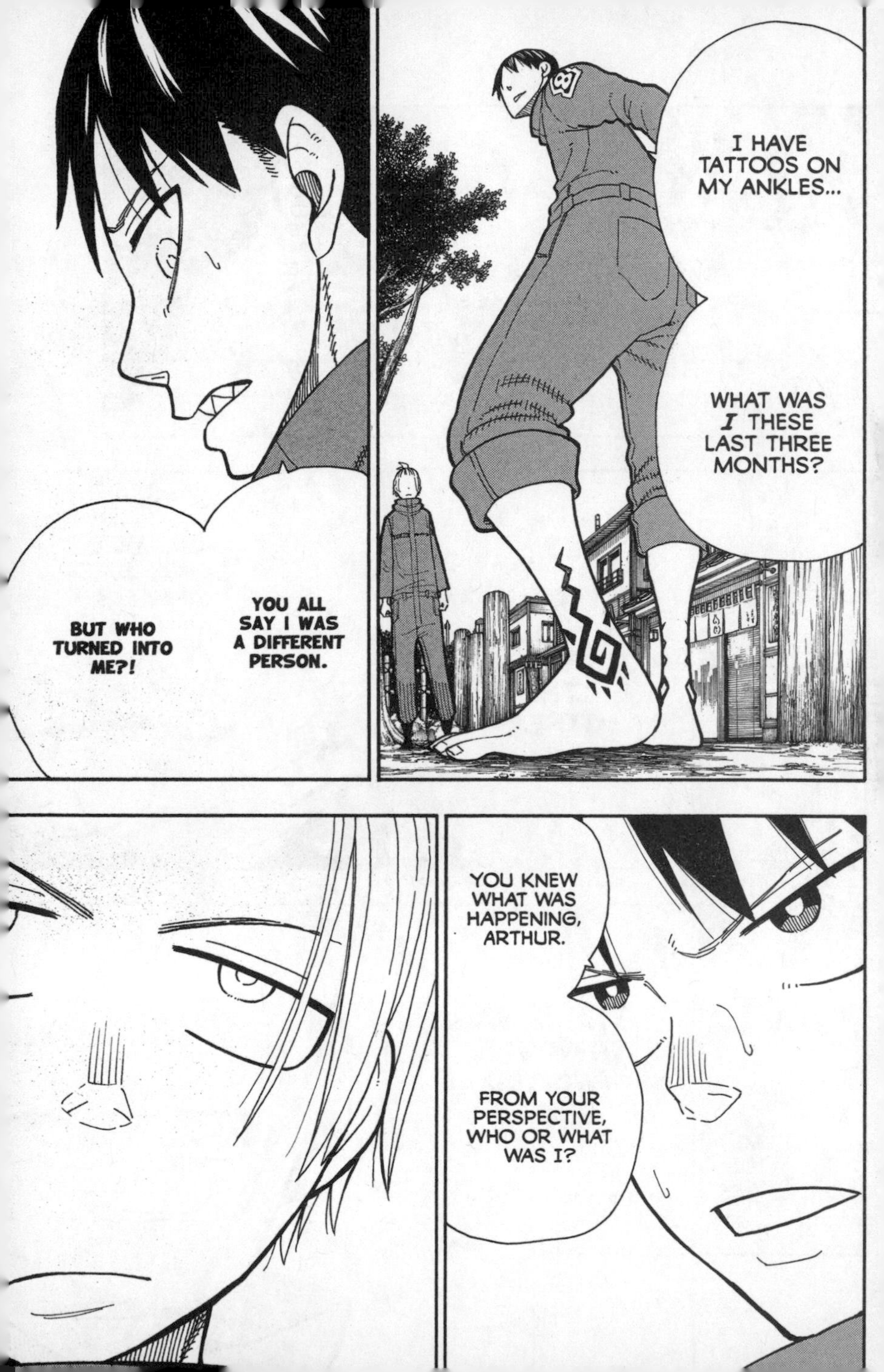
I HAVE TATTOOS ON MY ANKLES...
WHAT WAS *I* THESE LAST THREE MONTHS?
YOU ALL SAY I WAS A DIFFERENT PERSON.
BUT WHO TURNED INTO ME?!
YOU KNEW WHAT WAS HAPPENING, ARTHUR.
FROM YOUR PERSPECTIVE, WHO OR WHAT WAS I?

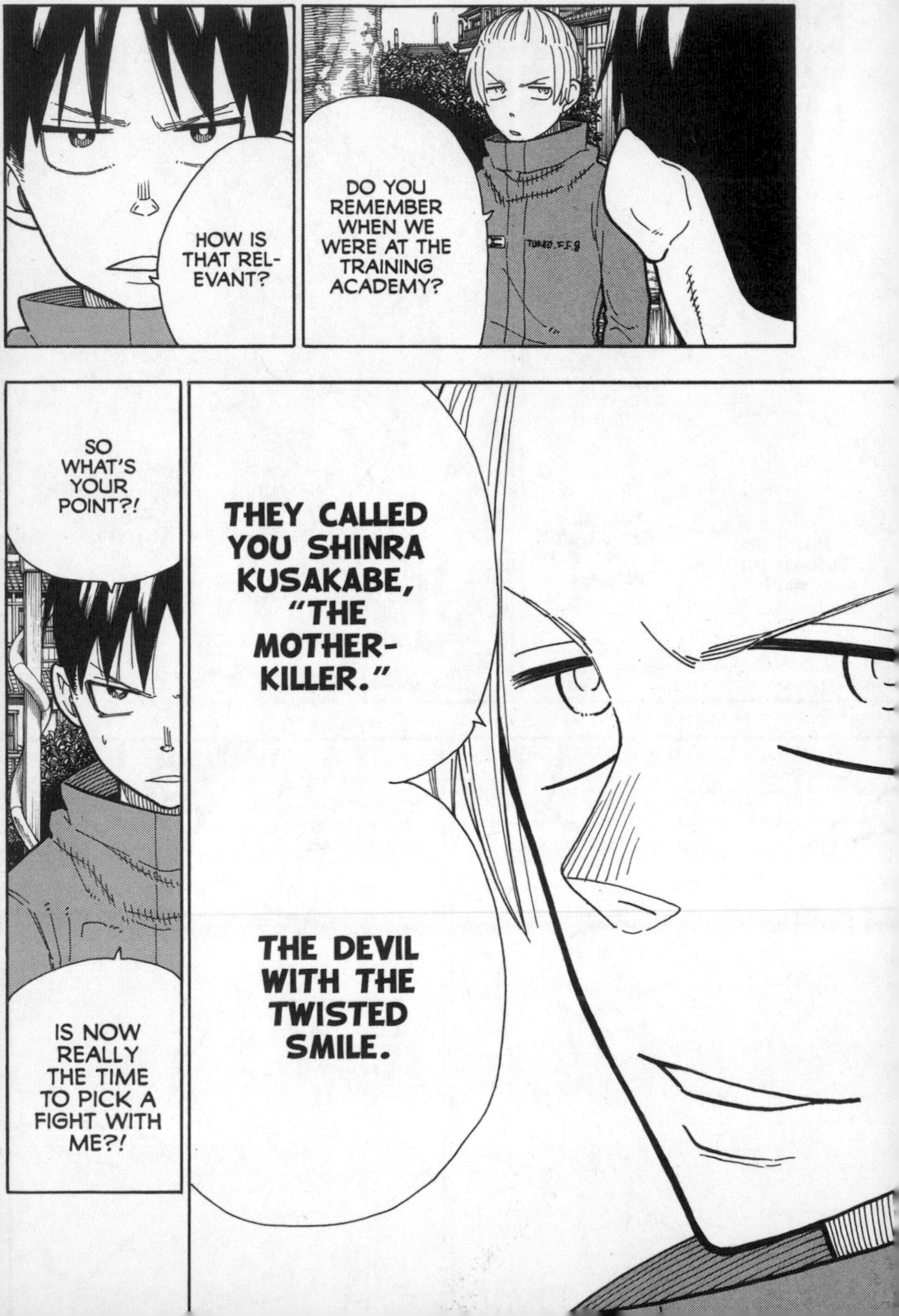
DO YOU REMEMBER WHEN WE WERE AT THE TRAINING ACADEMY?
TOKYO F.F.S
HOW IS THAT REL-EVANT?
THEY CALLED YOU SHINRA KUSAKABE, "THE MOTHER-KILLER."
THE DEVIL WITH THE TWISTED SMILE.
SO WHAT'S YOUR POINT?!
IS NOW REALLY THE TIME TO PICK A FIGHT WITH ME?!

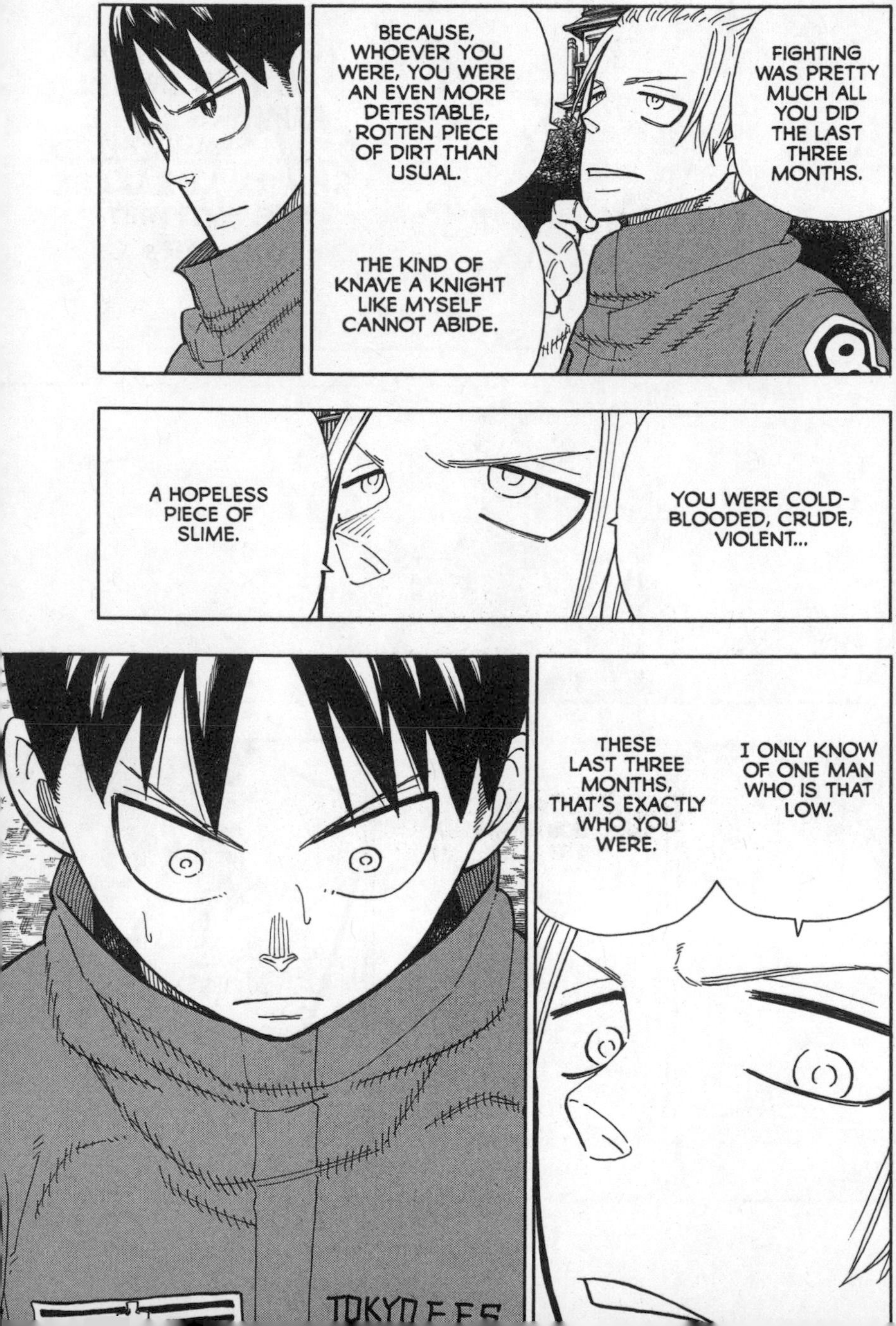
FIGHTING WAS PRETTY MUCH ALL YOU DID THE LAST THREE MONTHS.
BECAUSE, WHOEVER YOU WERE, YOU WERE AN EVEN MORE DETESTABLE, ROTTEN PIECE OF DIRT THAN USUAL.
THE KIND OF KNAVE A KNIGHT LIKE MYSELF CANNOT ABIDE.
YOU WERE COLD-BLOODED, CRUDE, VIOLENT...
A HOPELESS PIECE OF SLIME.
I ONLY KNOW OF ONE MAN WHO IS THAT LOW.
THESE LAST THREE MONTHS, THAT'S EXACTLY WHO YOU WERE.

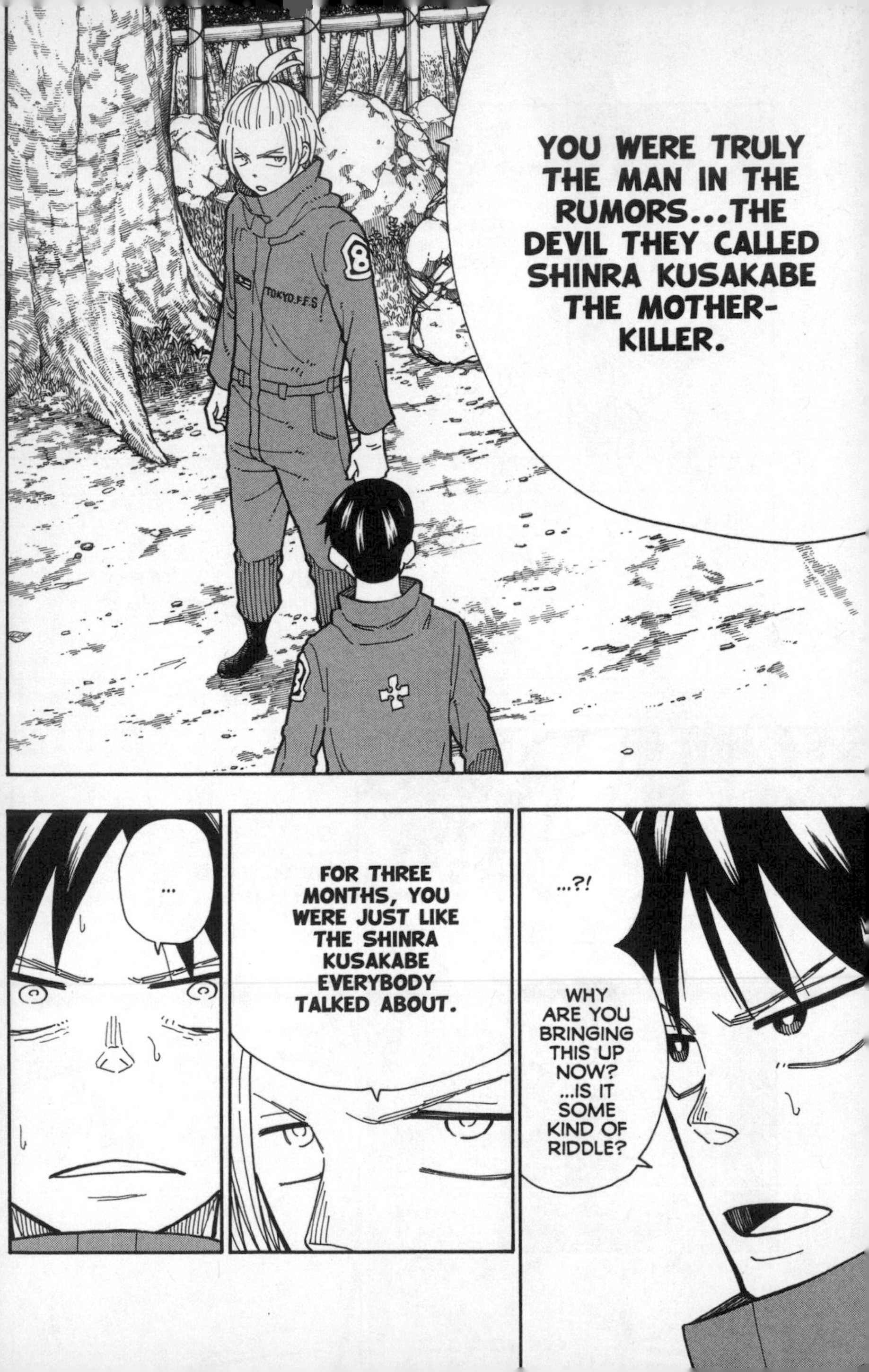
YOU WERE TRULY THE MAN IN THE RUMORS...THE DEVIL THEY CALLED SHINRA KUSAKABE THE MOTHER-KILLER.
...?!
WHY ARE YOU BRINGING THIS UP NOW? ...IS IT SOME KIND OF RIDDLE?
FOR THREE MONTHS, YOU WERE JUST LIKE THE SHINRA KUSAKABE EVERYBODY TALKED ABOUT.
...

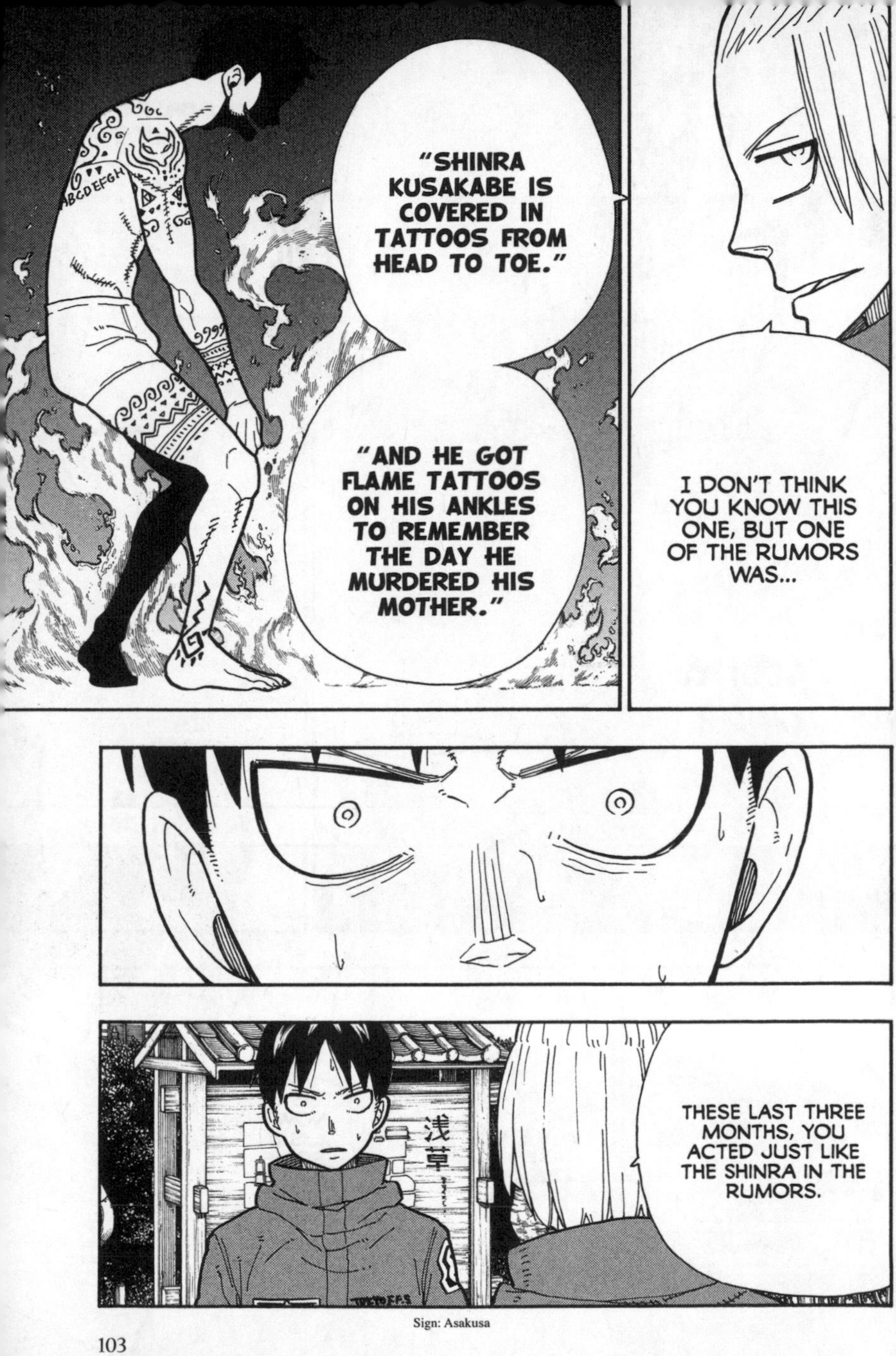
I DON'T THINK YOU KNOW THIS ONE, BUT ONE OF THE RUMORS WAS...
"SHINRA KUSAKABE IS COVERED IN TATTOOS FROM HEAD TO TOE."
"AND HE GOT FLAME TATTOOS ON HIS ANKLES TO REMEMBER THE DAY HE MURDERED HIS MOTHER."
THESE LAST THREE MONTHS, YOU ACTED JUST LIKE THE SHINRA IN THE RUMORS.
浅草
Sign: Asakusa

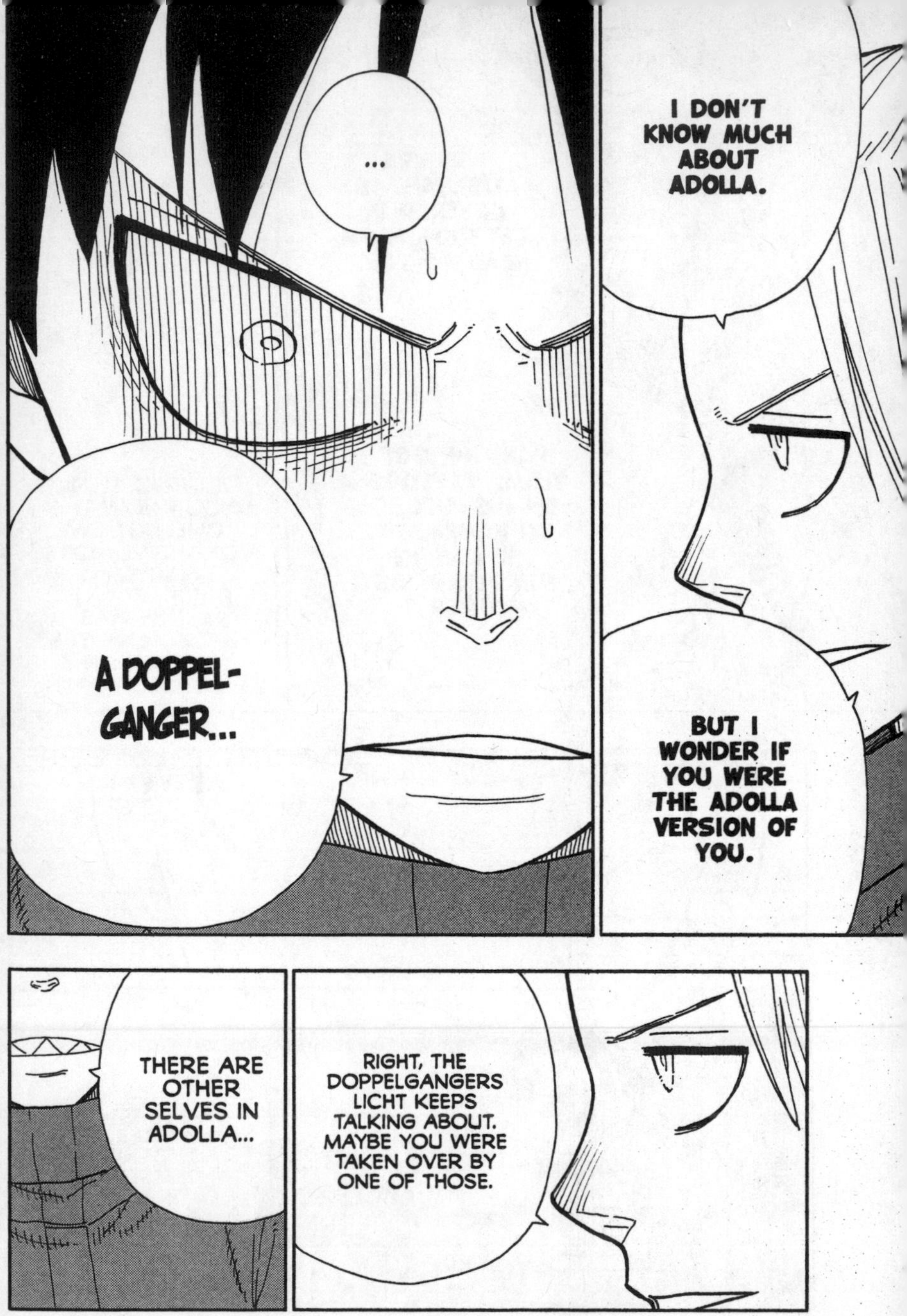
I DON'T KNOW MUCH ABOUT ADOLLA.
BUT I WONDER IF YOU WERE THE ADOLLA VERSION OF YOU.
...
A DOPPEL-GANGER...
RIGHT, THE DOPPELGANGERS LICHT KEEPS TALKING ABOUT. MAYBE YOU WERE TAKEN OVER BY ONE OF THOSE.
THERE ARE OTHER SELVES IN ADOLLA...

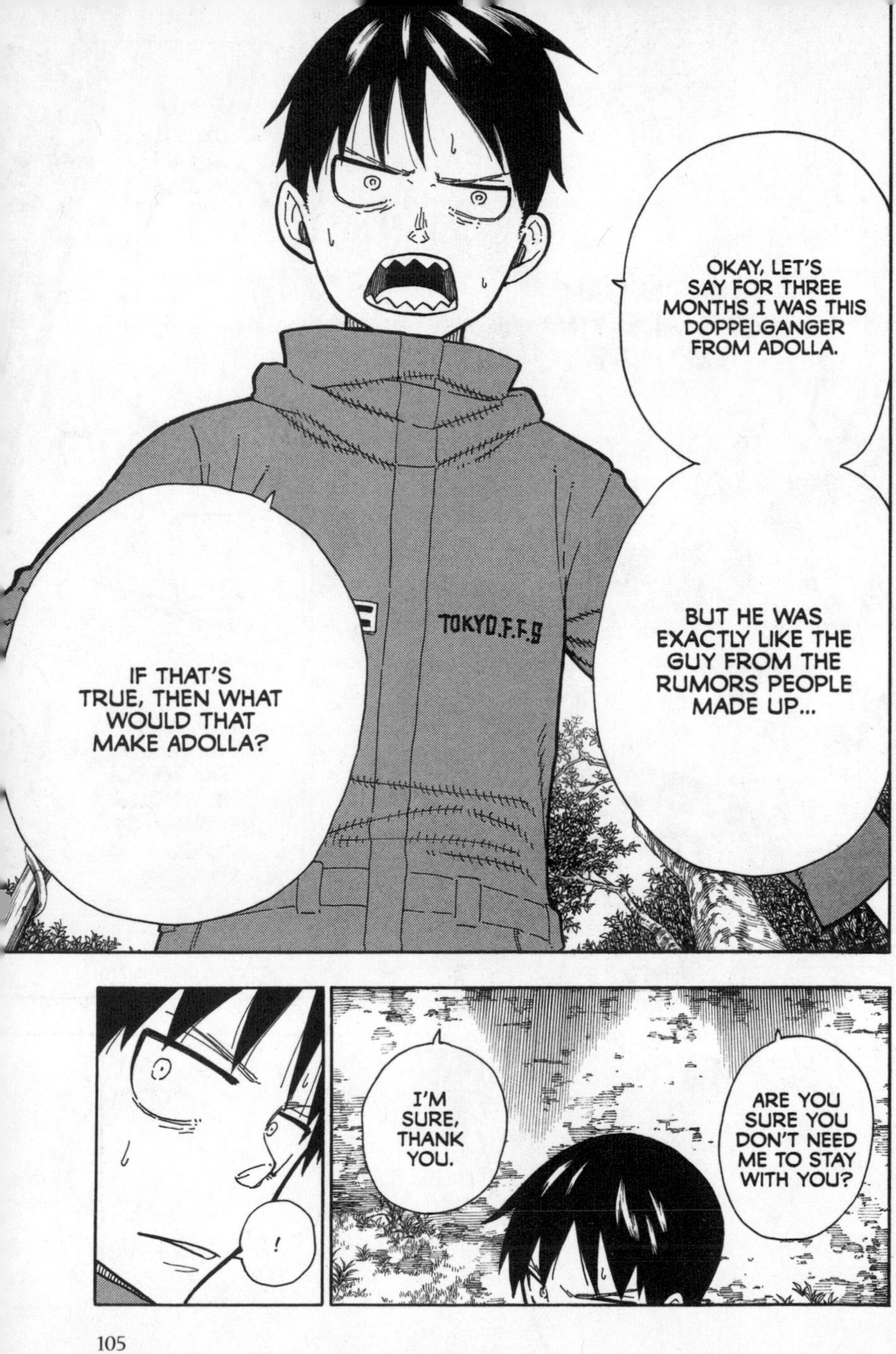
OKAY, LET'S SAY FOR THREE MONTHS I WAS THIS DOPPELGANGER FROM ADOLLA.
BUT HE WAS EXACTLY LIKE THE GUY FROM THE RUMORS PEOPLE MADE UP...
TOKYO.F.F.8
IF THAT'S TRUE, THEN WHAT WOULD THAT MAKE ADOLLA?
ARE YOU SURE YOU DON'T NEED ME TO STAY WITH YOU?
I'M SURE, THANK YOU.
!

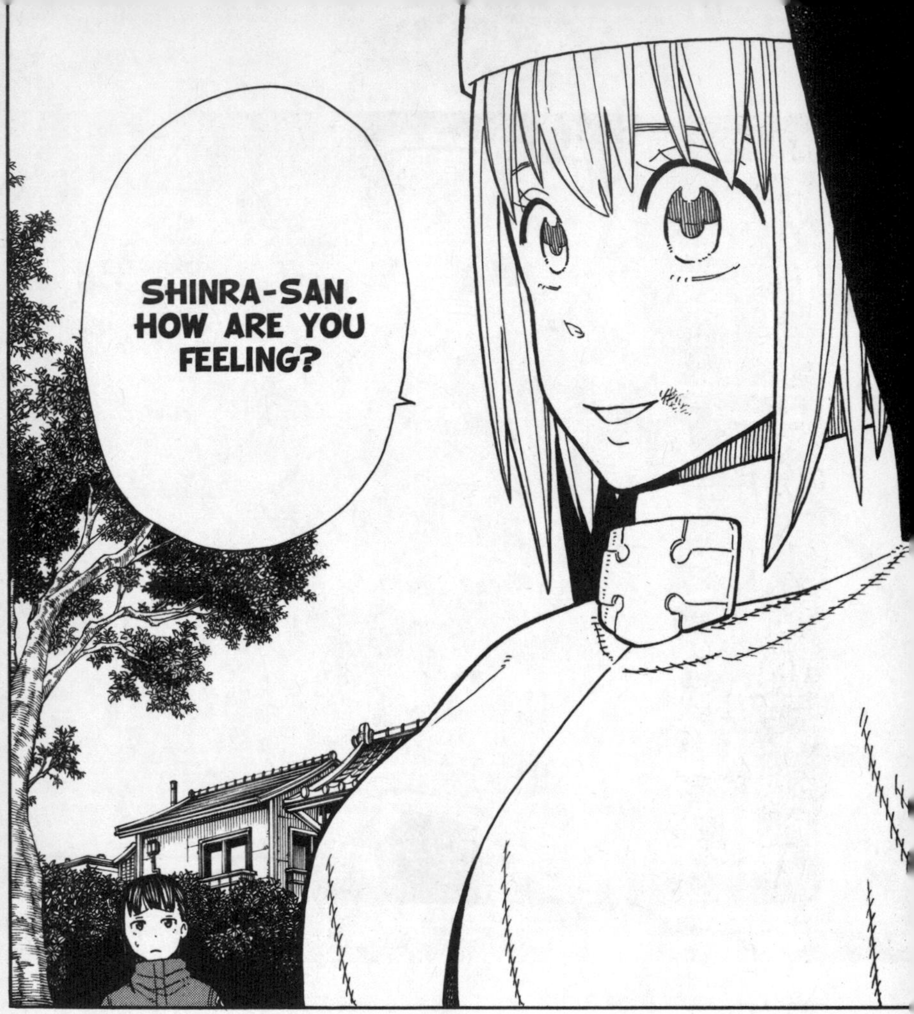
SHINRA-SAN. HOW ARE YOU FEELING?

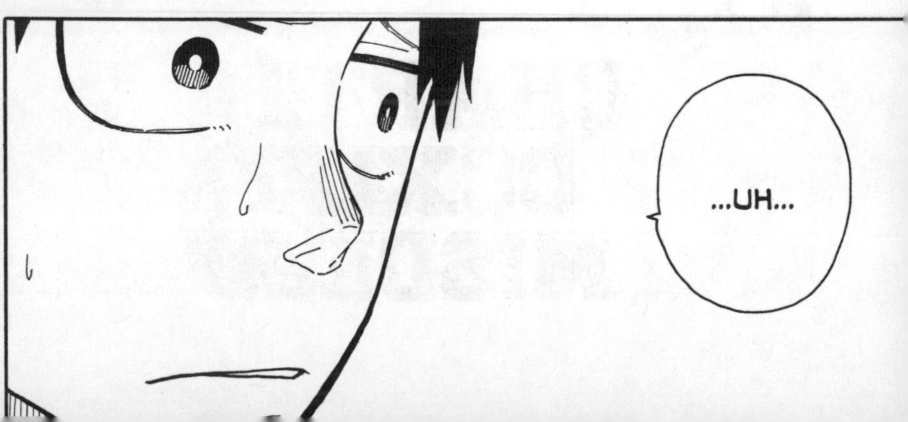
...UH...

CHAPTER
CCXIX:
MISDEED

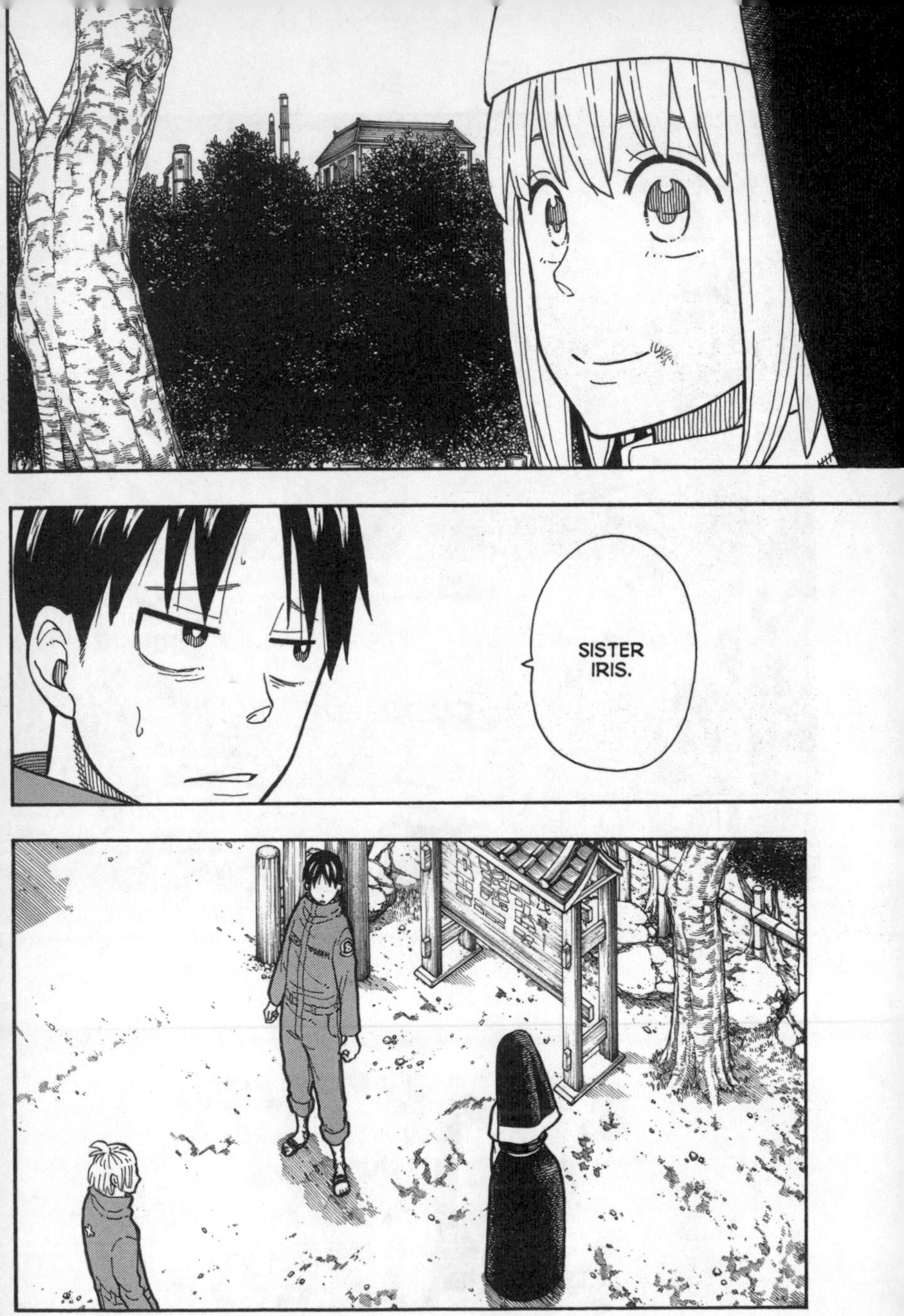
SISTER IRIS.

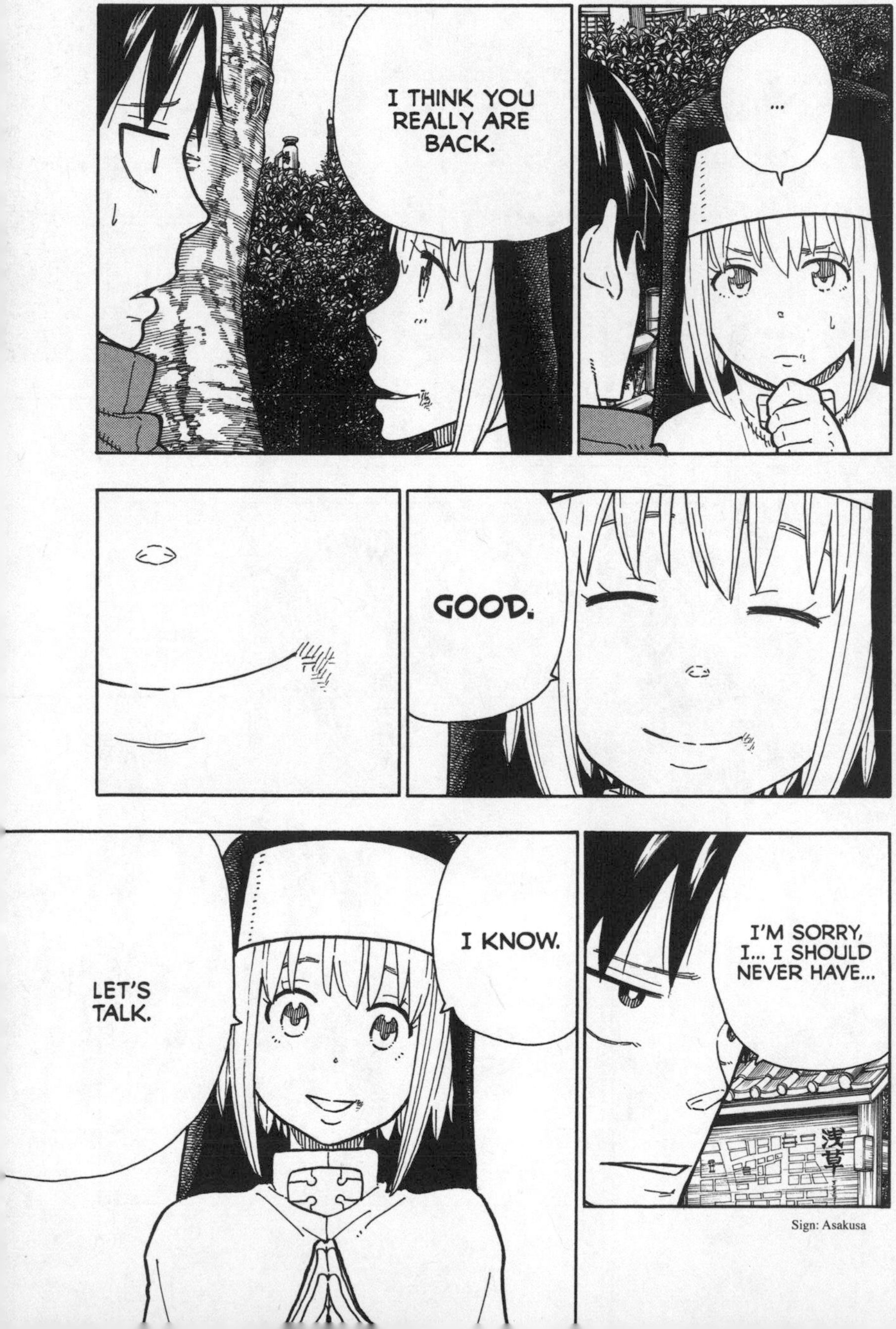
...
I THINK YOU REALLY ARE BACK.
GOOD.
I'M SORRY, I... I SHOULD NEVER HAVE...
I KNOW.
LET'S TALK.
Sign: Asakusa

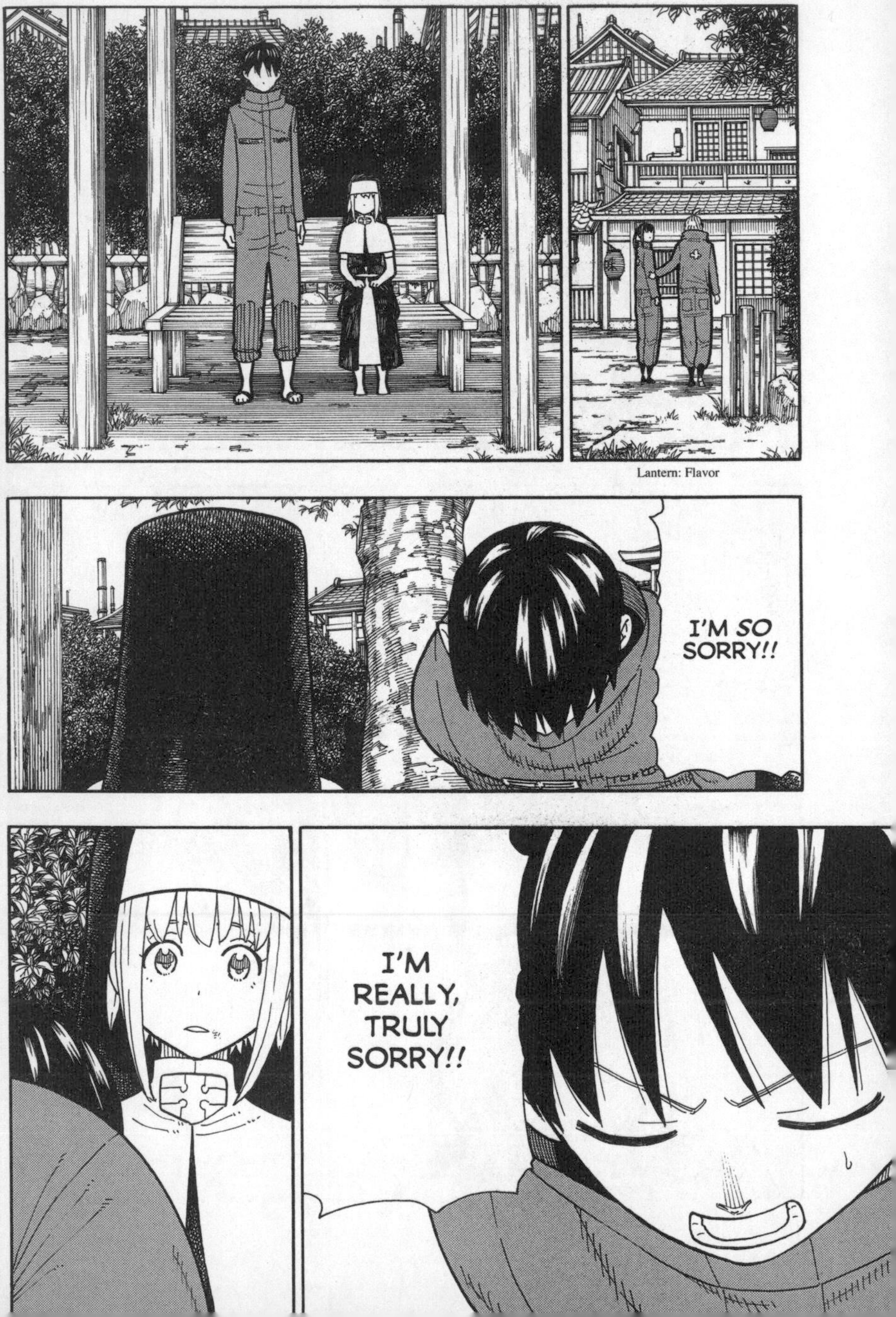
Lantern: Flavor
I'M SO SORRY!!
I'M REALLY, TRULY SORRY!!

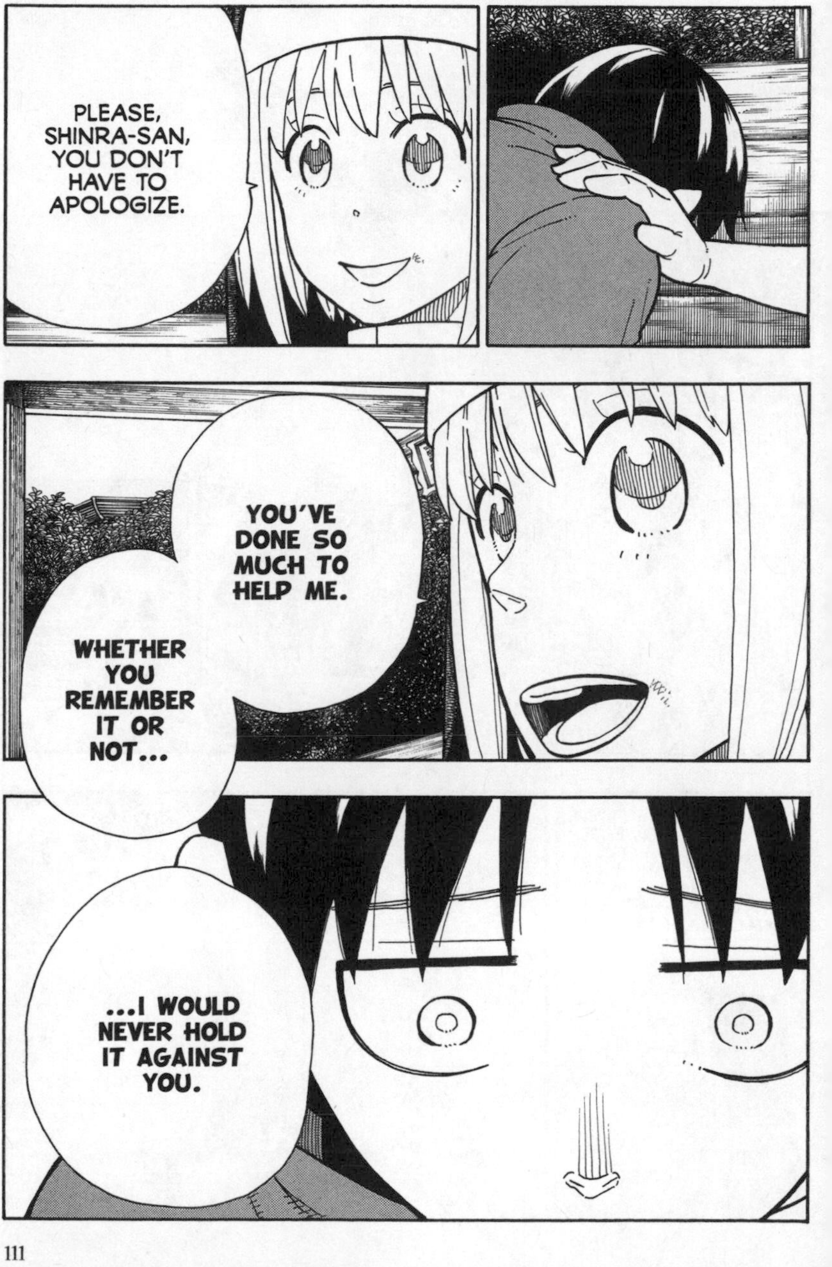
PLEASE, SHINRA-SAN, YOU DON'T HAVE TO APOLOGIZE.
YOU'VE DONE SO MUCH TO HELP ME.
WHETHER YOU REMEMBER IT OR NOT...
...I WOULD NEVER HOLD IT AGAINST YOU.

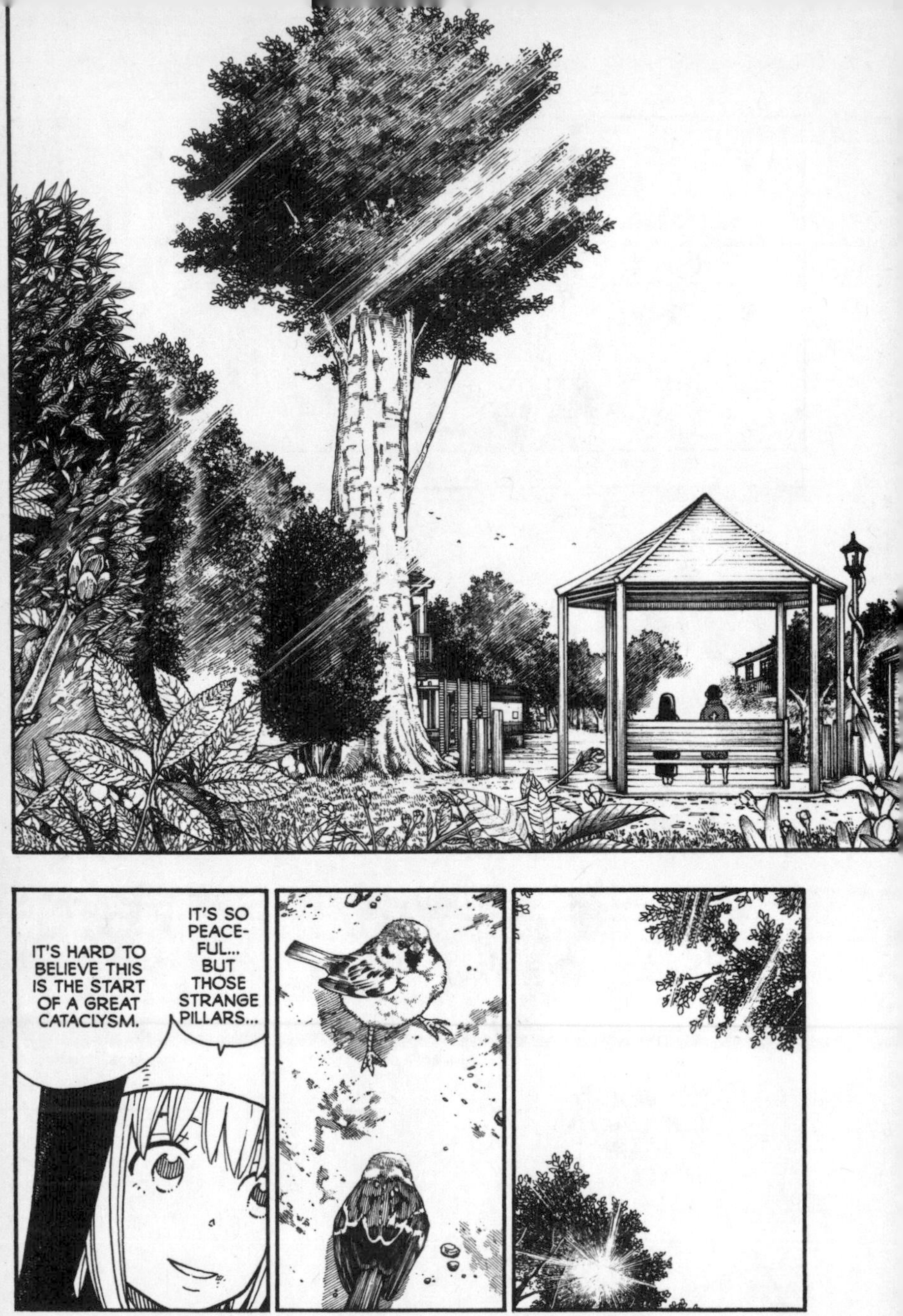
IT'S SO PEACE-FUL... BUT THOSE STRANGE PILLARS...
IT'S HARD TO BELIEVE THIS IS THE START OF A GREAT CATACLYSM.

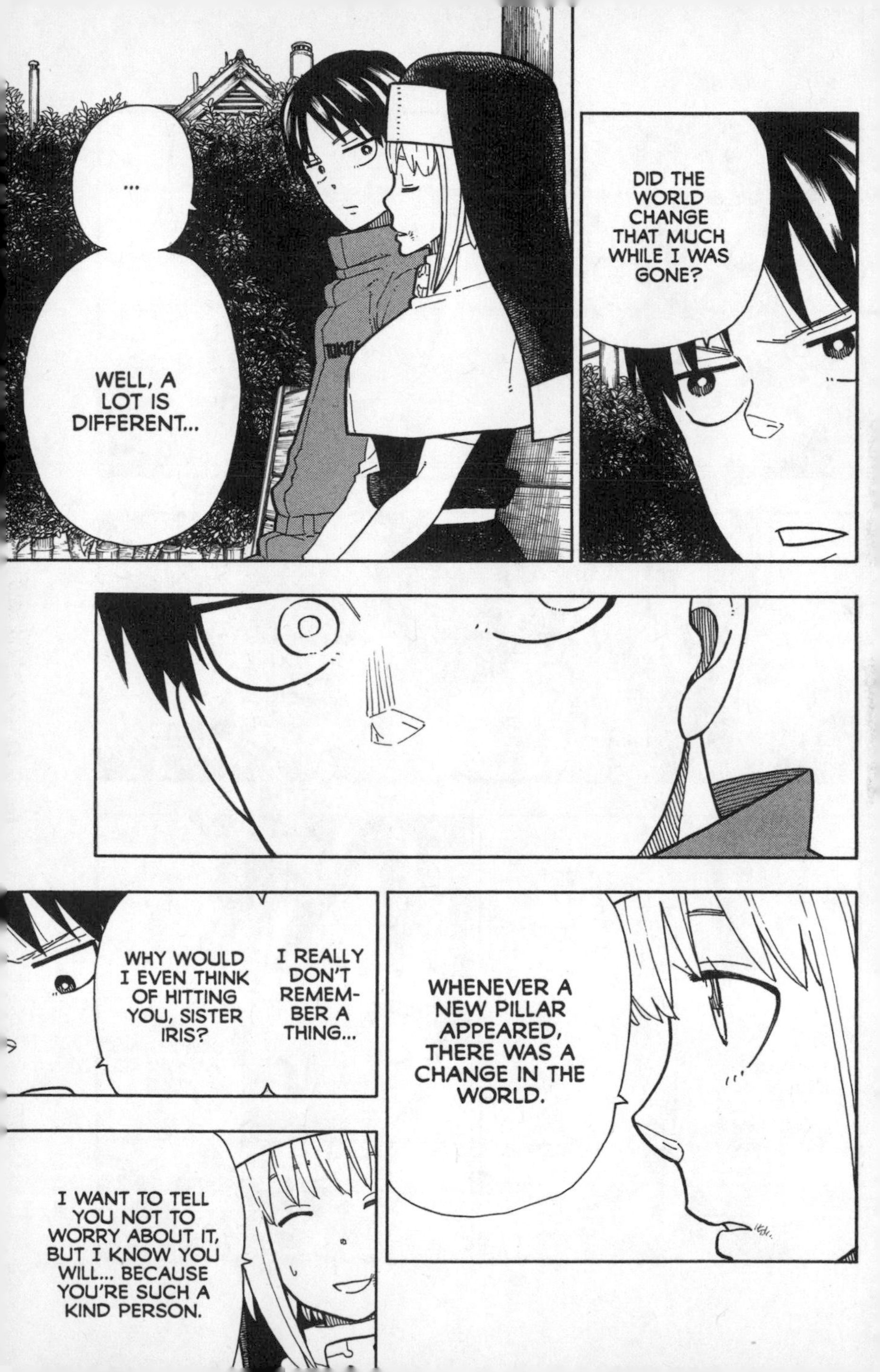
DID THE WORLD CHANGE THAT MUCH WHILE I WAS GONE?
...
WELL, A LOT IS DIFFERENT...
WHENEVER A NEW PILLAR APPEARED, THERE WAS A CHANGE IN THE WORLD.
I REALLY DON'T REMEMBER A THING...
WHY WOULD I EVEN THINK OF HITTING YOU, SISTER IRIS?
I WANT TO TELL YOU NOT TO WORRY ABOUT IT, BUT I KNOW YOU WILL... BECAUSE YOU'RE SUCH A KIND PERSON.

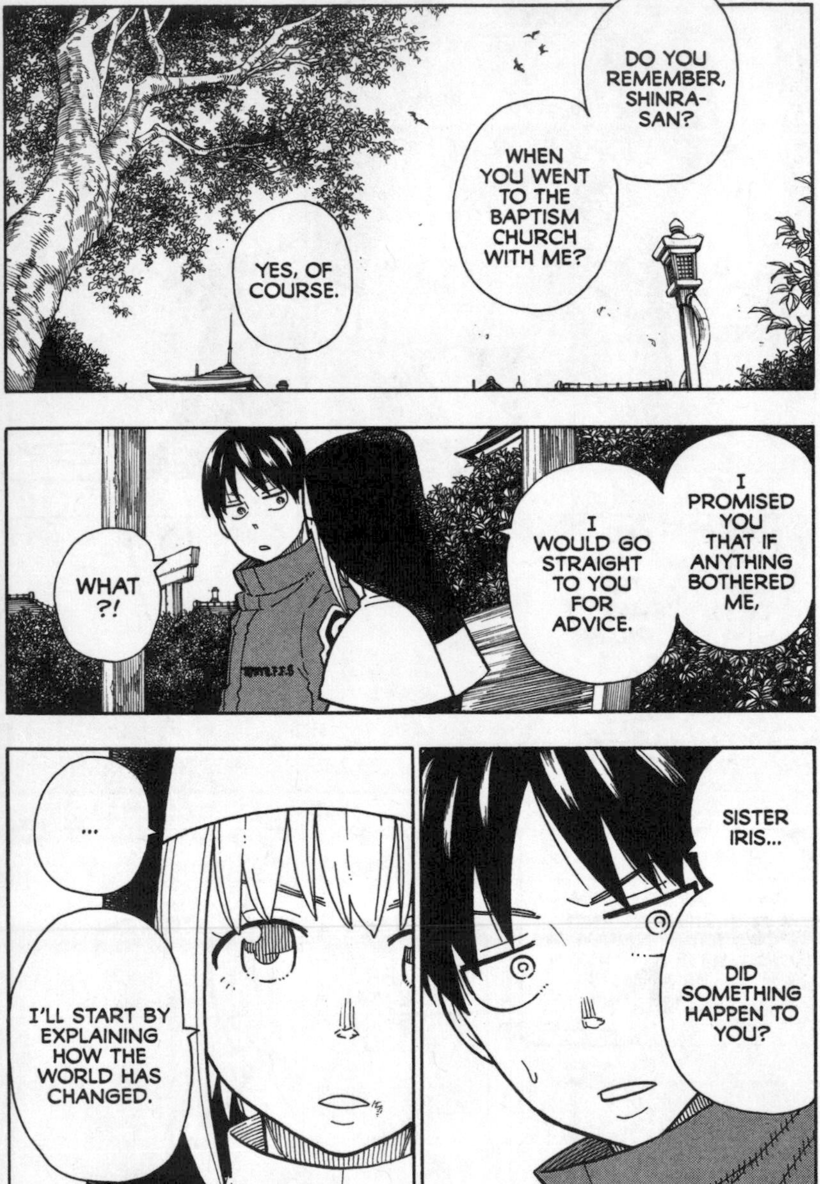
DO YOU REMEMBER, SHINRA-SAN?
WHEN YOU WENT TO THE BAPTISM CHURCH WITH ME?
YES, OF COURSE.
I PROMISED YOU THAT IF ANYTHING BOTHERED ME,
I WOULD GO STRAIGHT TO YOU FOR ADVICE.
WHAT?!
SISTER IRIS...
DID SOMETHING HAPPEN TO YOU?
...
I'LL START BY EXPLAINING HOW THE WORLD HAS CHANGED.

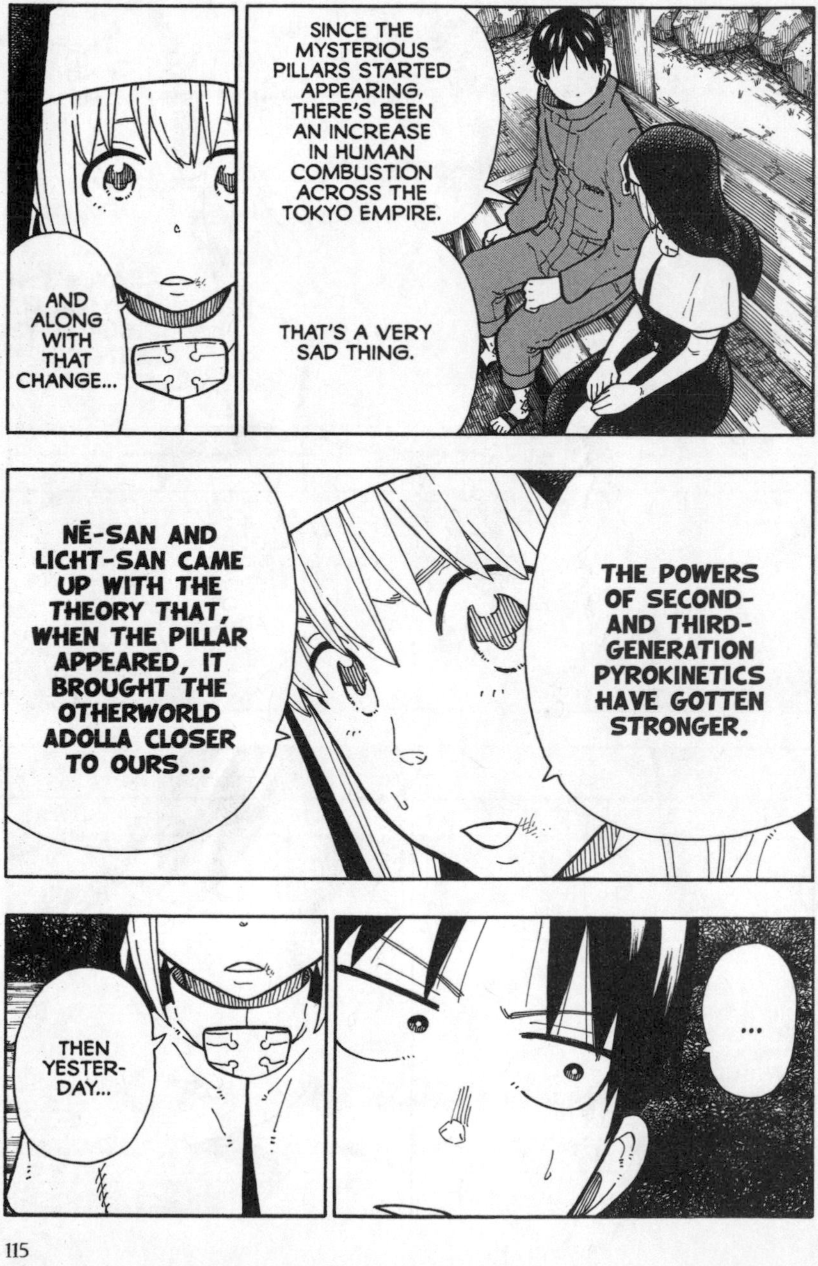
SINCE THE MYSTERIOUS PILLARS STARTED APPEARING, THERE'S BEEN AN INCREASE IN HUMAN COMBUSTION ACROSS THE TOKYO EMPIRE.
THAT'S A VERY SAD THING.
AND ALONG WITH THAT CHANGE...
THE POWERS OF SECOND- AND THIRD-GENERATION PYROKINETICS HAVE GOTTEN STRONGER.
NĒ-SAN AND LICHT-SAN CAME UP WITH THE THEORY THAT, WHEN THE PILLAR APPEARED, IT BROUGHT THE OTHERWORLD ADOLLA CLOSER TO OURS...
...
THEN YESTER-DAY...

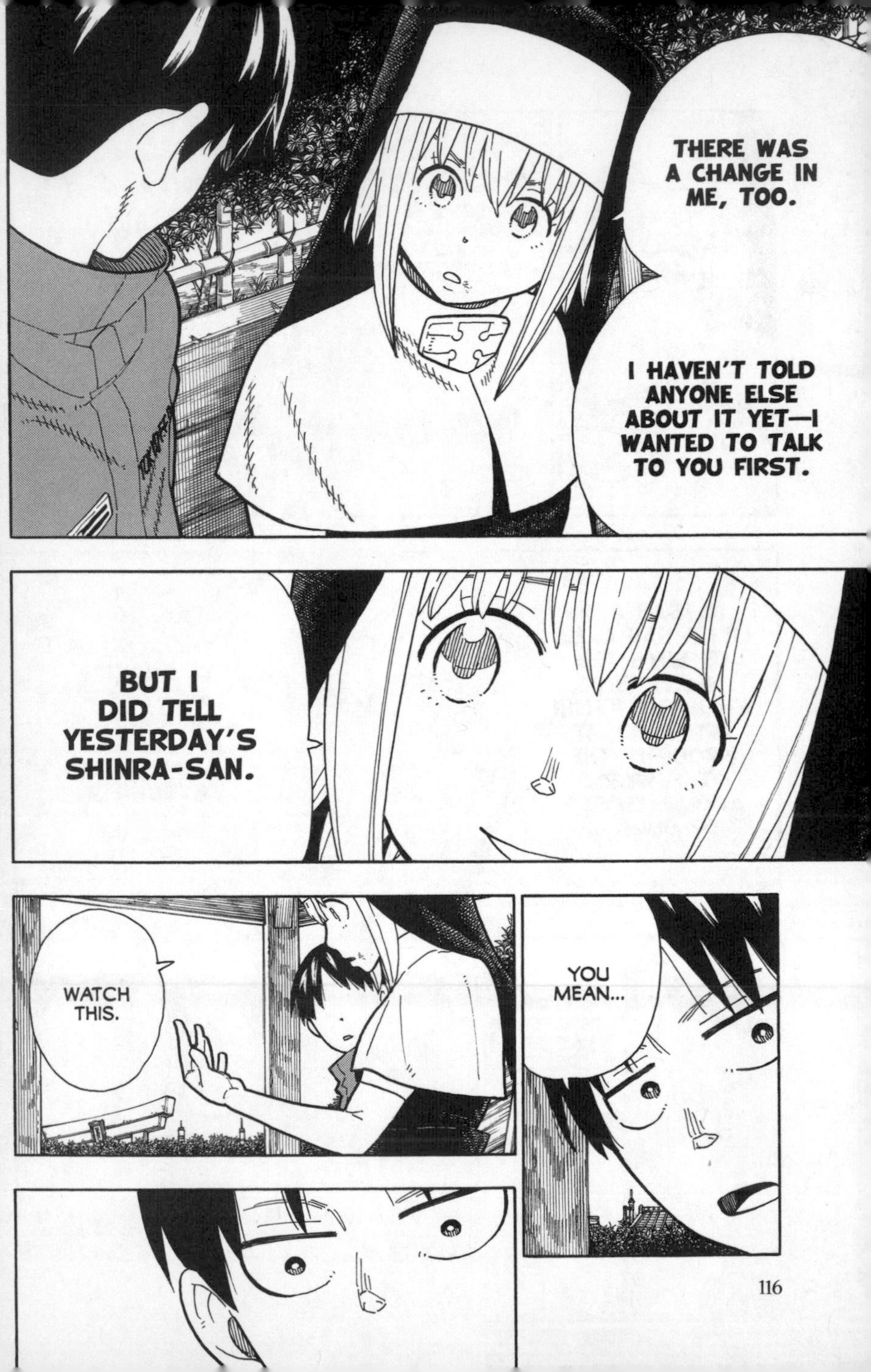
THERE WAS A CHANGE IN ME, TOO.
I HAVEN'T TOLD ANYONE ELSE ABOUT IT YET—I WANTED TO TALK TO YOU FIRST.
BUT I DID TELL YESTERDAY'S SHINRA-SAN.
YOU MEAN...
WATCH THIS.

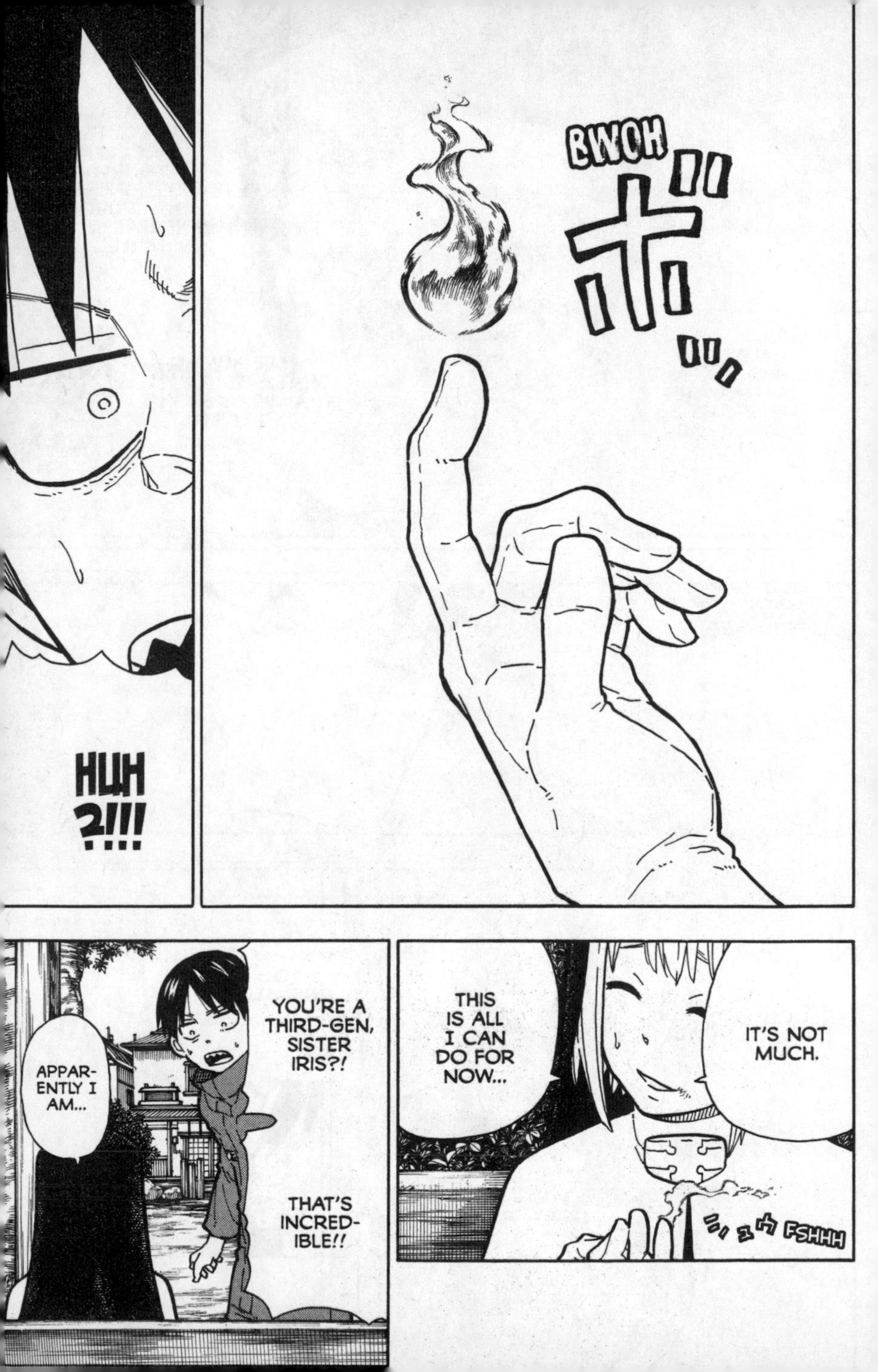
BWOH
HUH ?!!!
IT'S NOT MUCH.
THIS IS ALL I CAN DO FOR NOW...
FSHHH
YOU'RE A THIRD-GEN, SISTER IRIS?!
THAT'S INCREDIBLE!!
APPARENTLY I AM...

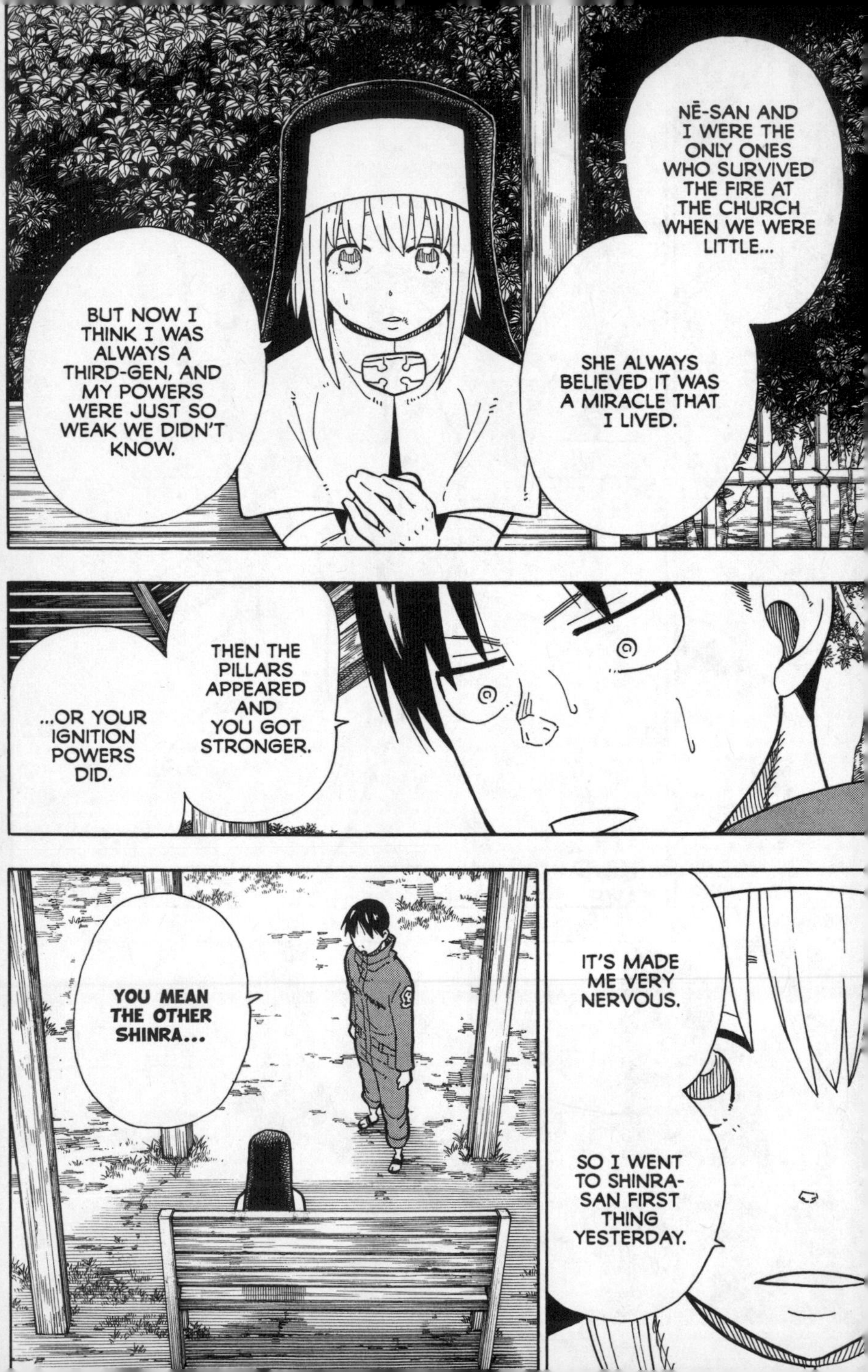
NĒ-SAN AND I WERE THE ONLY ONES WHO SURVIVED THE FIRE AT THE CHURCH WHEN WE WERE LITTLE...
SHE ALWAYS BELIEVED IT WAS A MIRACLE THAT I LIVED.
BUT NOW I THINK I WAS ALWAYS A THIRD-GEN, AND MY POWERS WERE JUST SO WEAK WE DIDN'T KNOW.
THEN THE PILLARS APPEARED AND YOU GOT STRONGER.
...OR YOUR IGNITION POWERS DID.
IT'S MADE ME VERY NERVOUS.
SO I WENT TO SHINRA-SAN FIRST THING YESTERDAY.
YOU MEAN THE OTHER SHINRA...

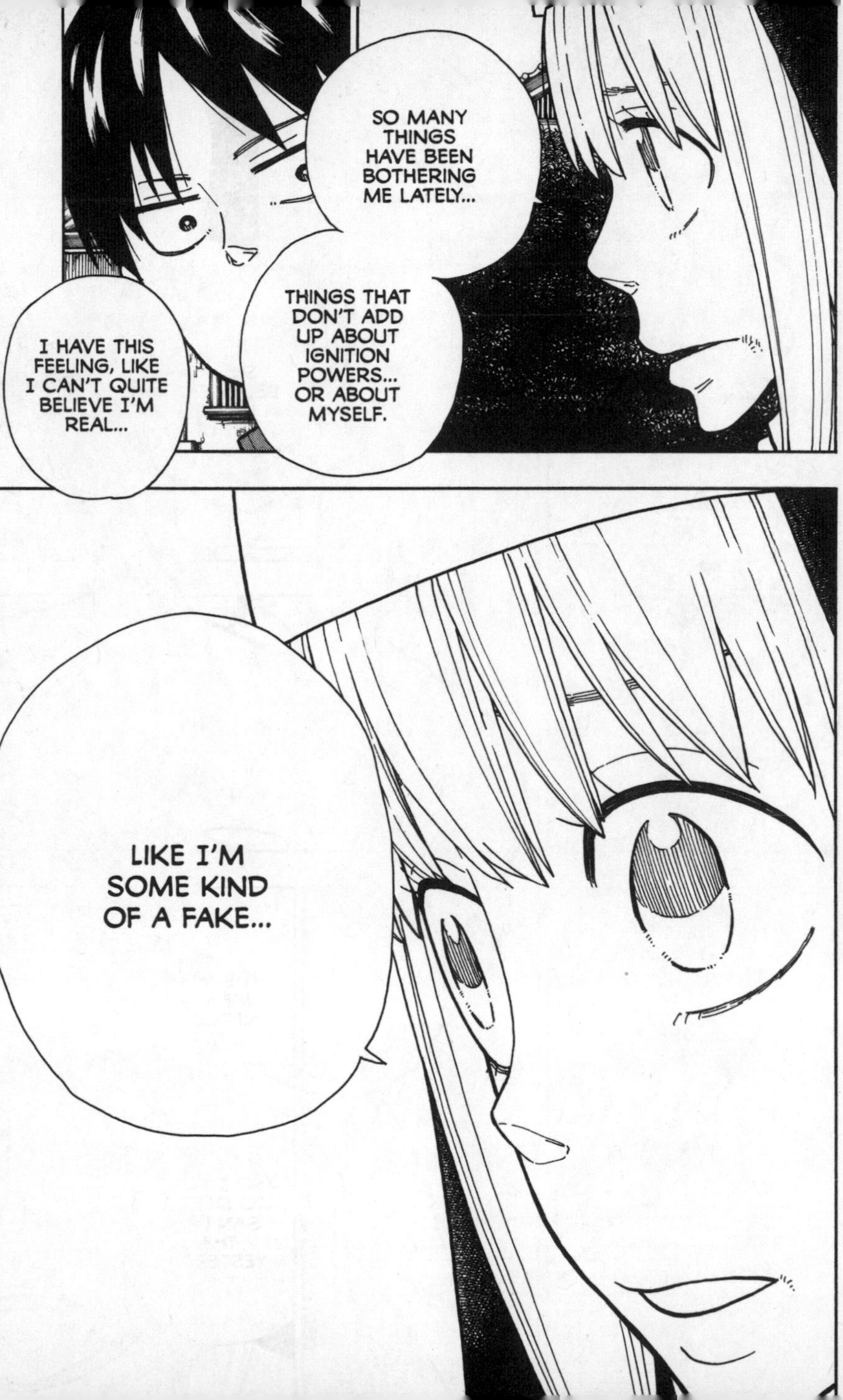
SO MANY THINGS HAVE BEEN BOTHERING ME LATELY...
THINGS THAT DON'T ADD UP ABOUT IGNITION POWERS... OR ABOUT MYSELF.
I HAVE THIS FEELING, LIKE I CAN'T QUITE BELIEVE I'M REAL...
LIKE I'M SOME KIND OF A FAKE...

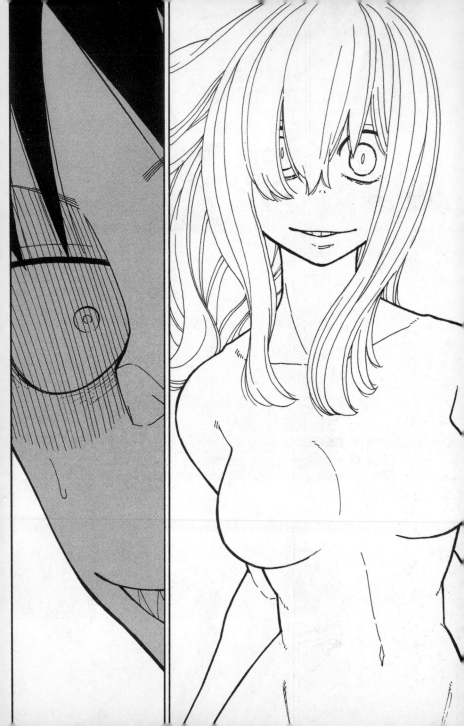

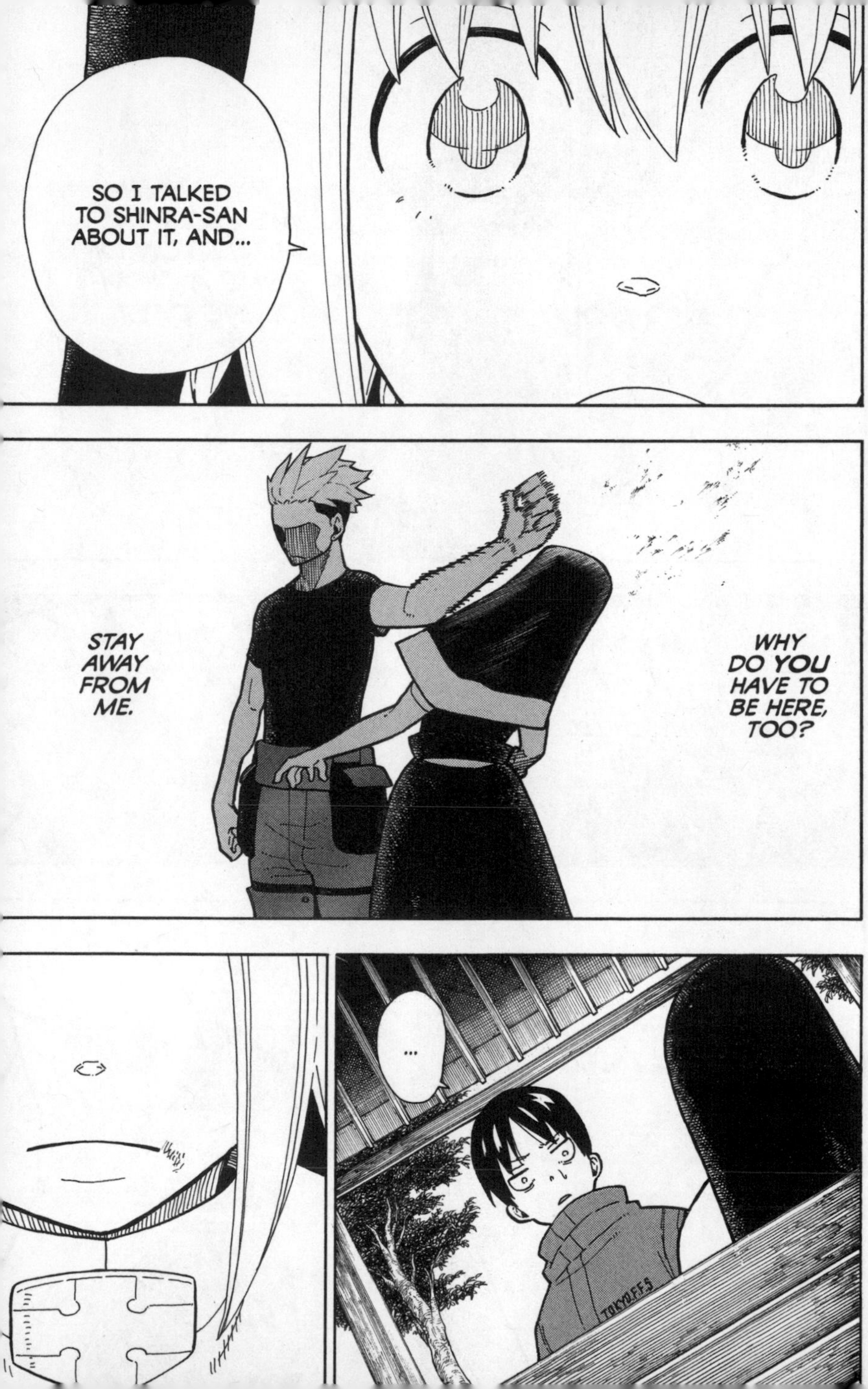
SO I TALKED TO SHINRA-SAN ABOUT IT, AND...
WHY DO YOU HAVE TO BE HERE, TOO?
STAY AWAY FROM ME.
...

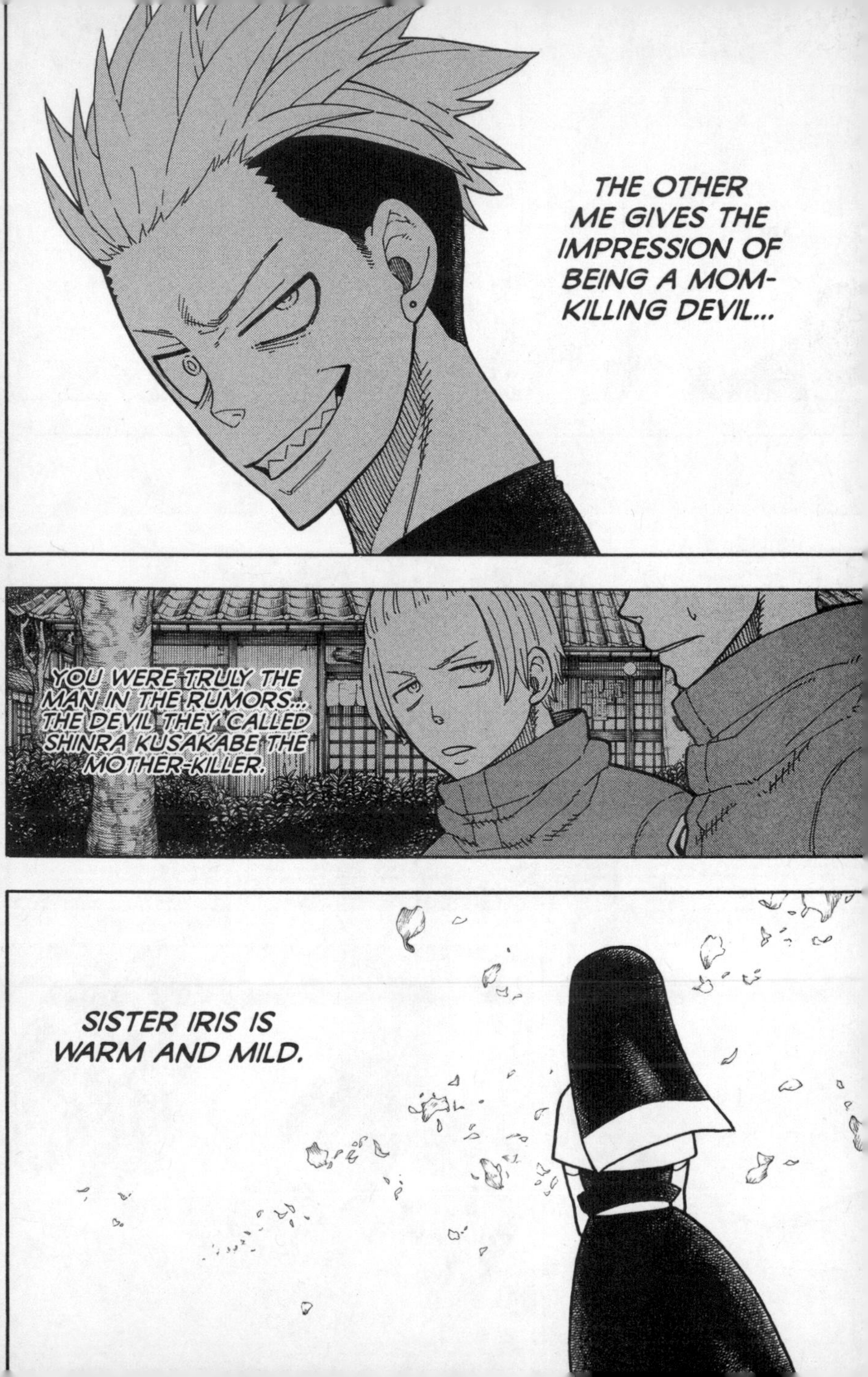
THE OTHER ME GIVES THE IMPRESSION OF BEING A MOM-KILLING DEVIL...
YOU WERE TRULY THE MAN IN THE RUMORS... THE DEVIL THEY CALLED SHINRA KUSAKABE THE MOTHER-KILLER.
SISTER IRIS IS WARM AND MILD.

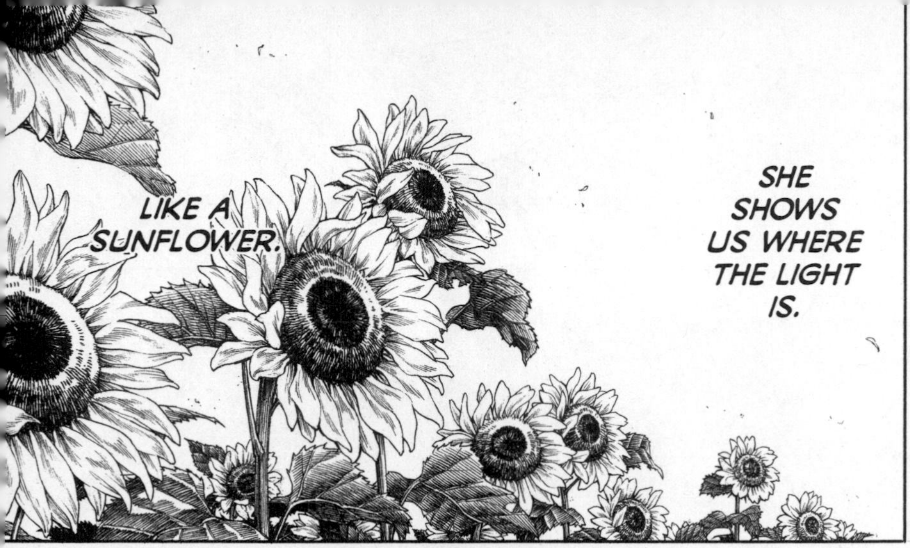
SHE SHOWS US WHERE THE LIGHT IS.
LIKE A SUNFLOWER.
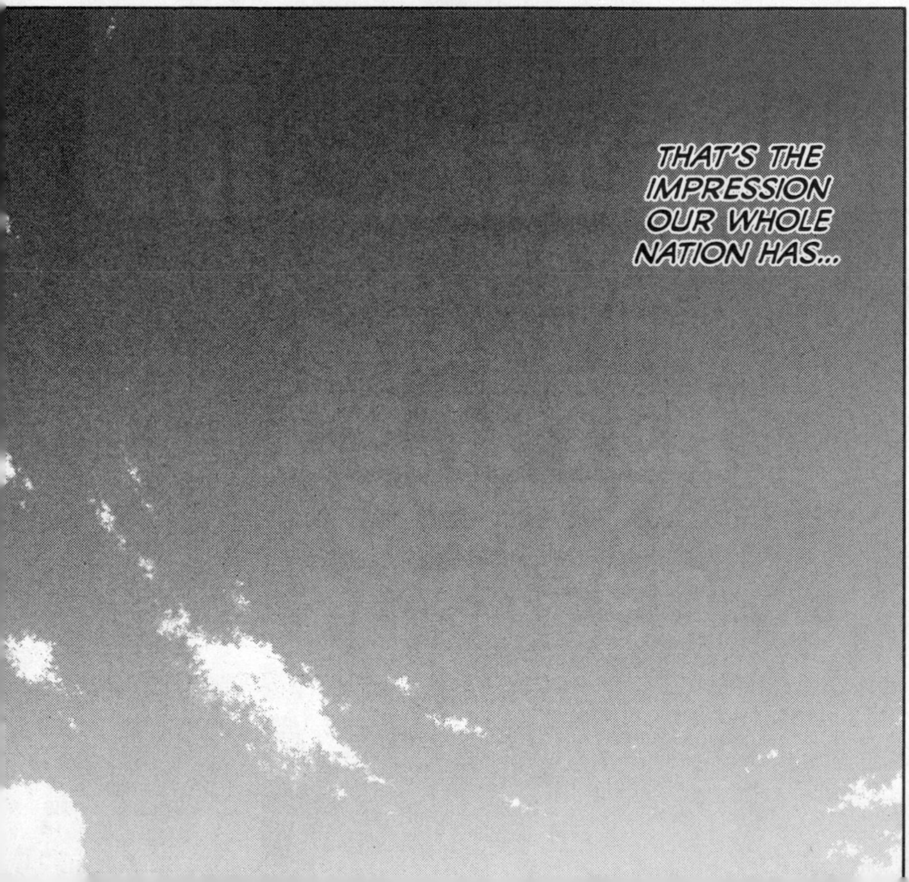
THAT'S THE IMPRESSION OUR WHOLE NATION HAS...

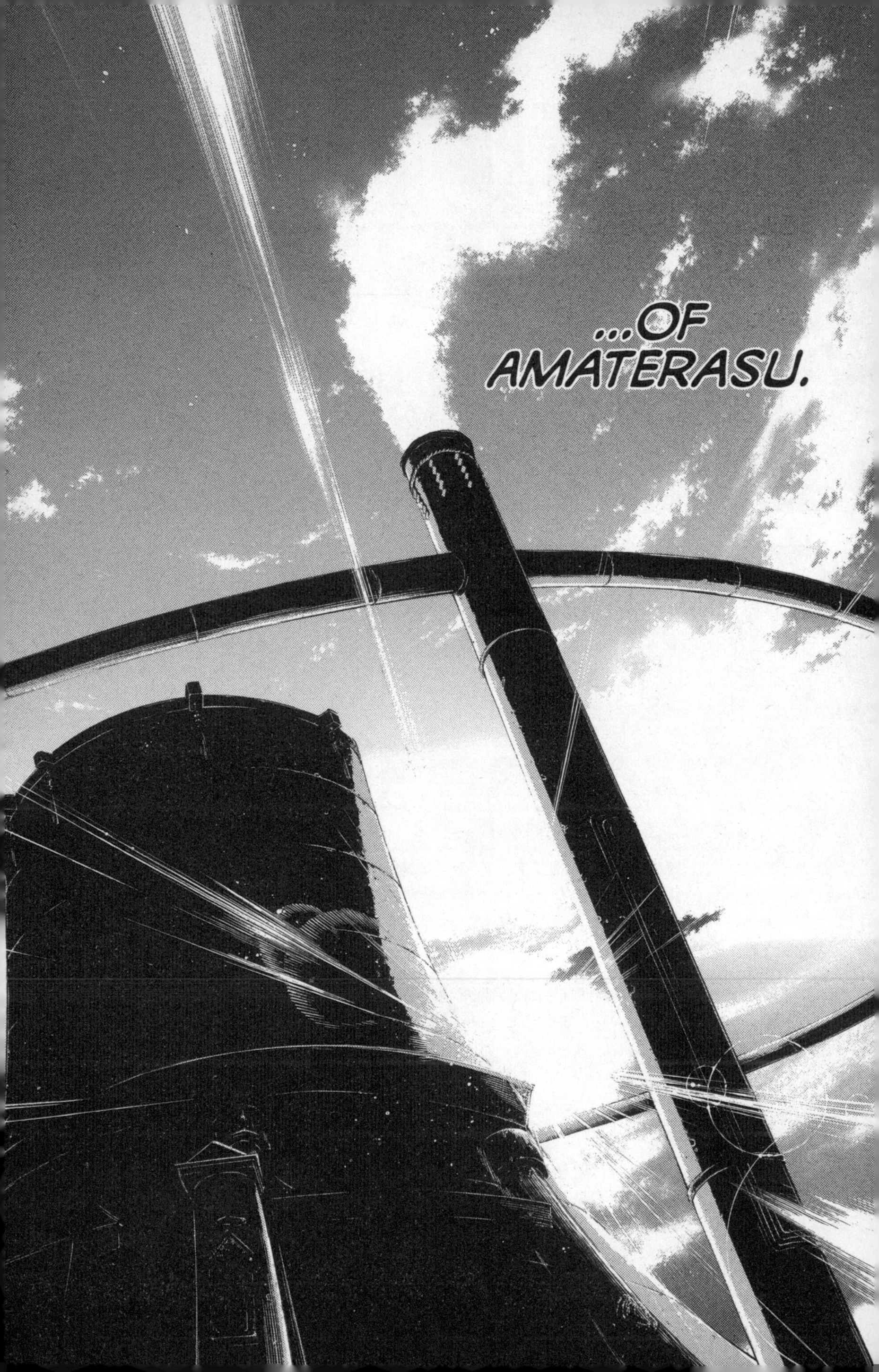
...OF AMATERASU.

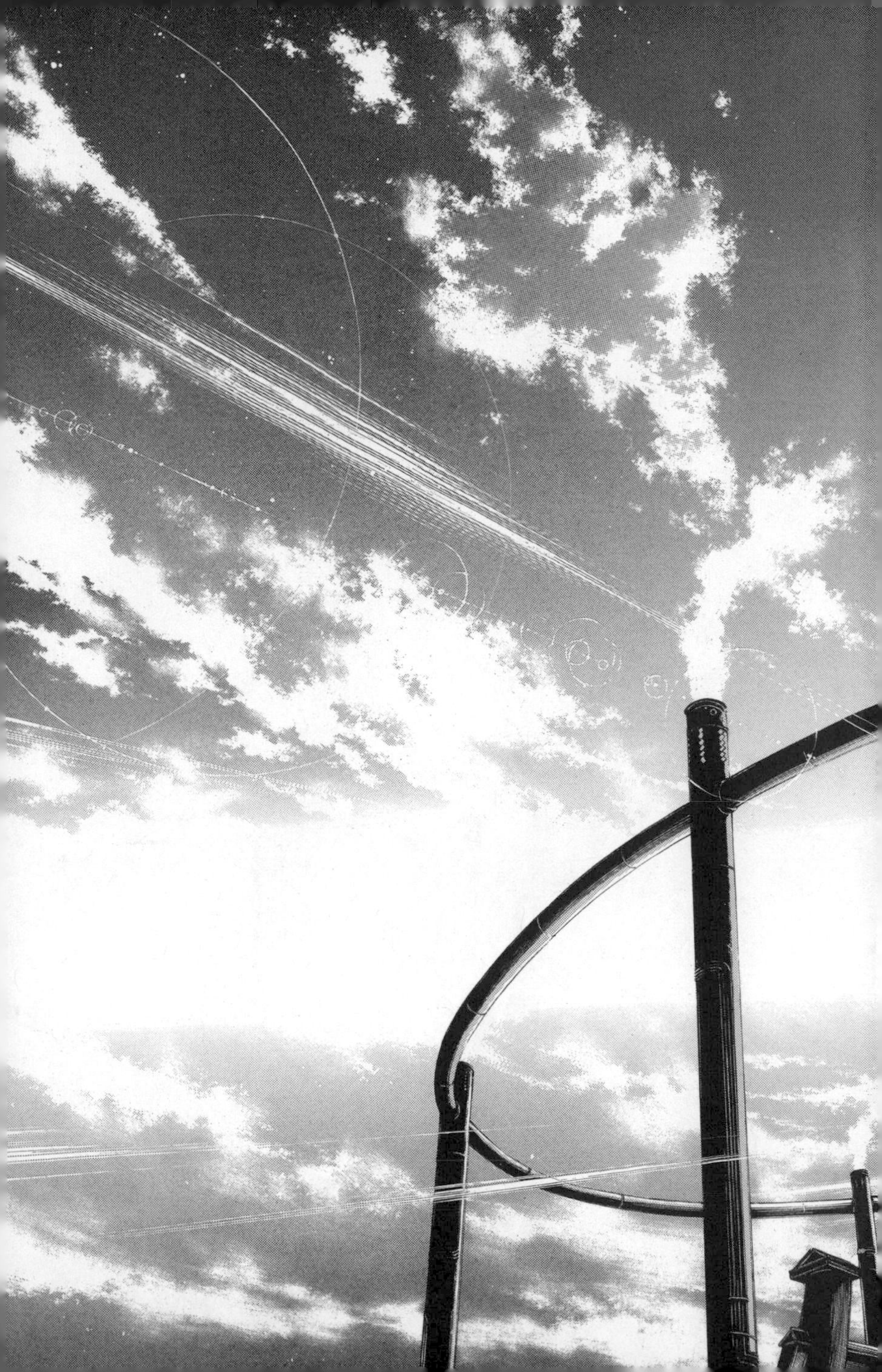

FIRE FORCE

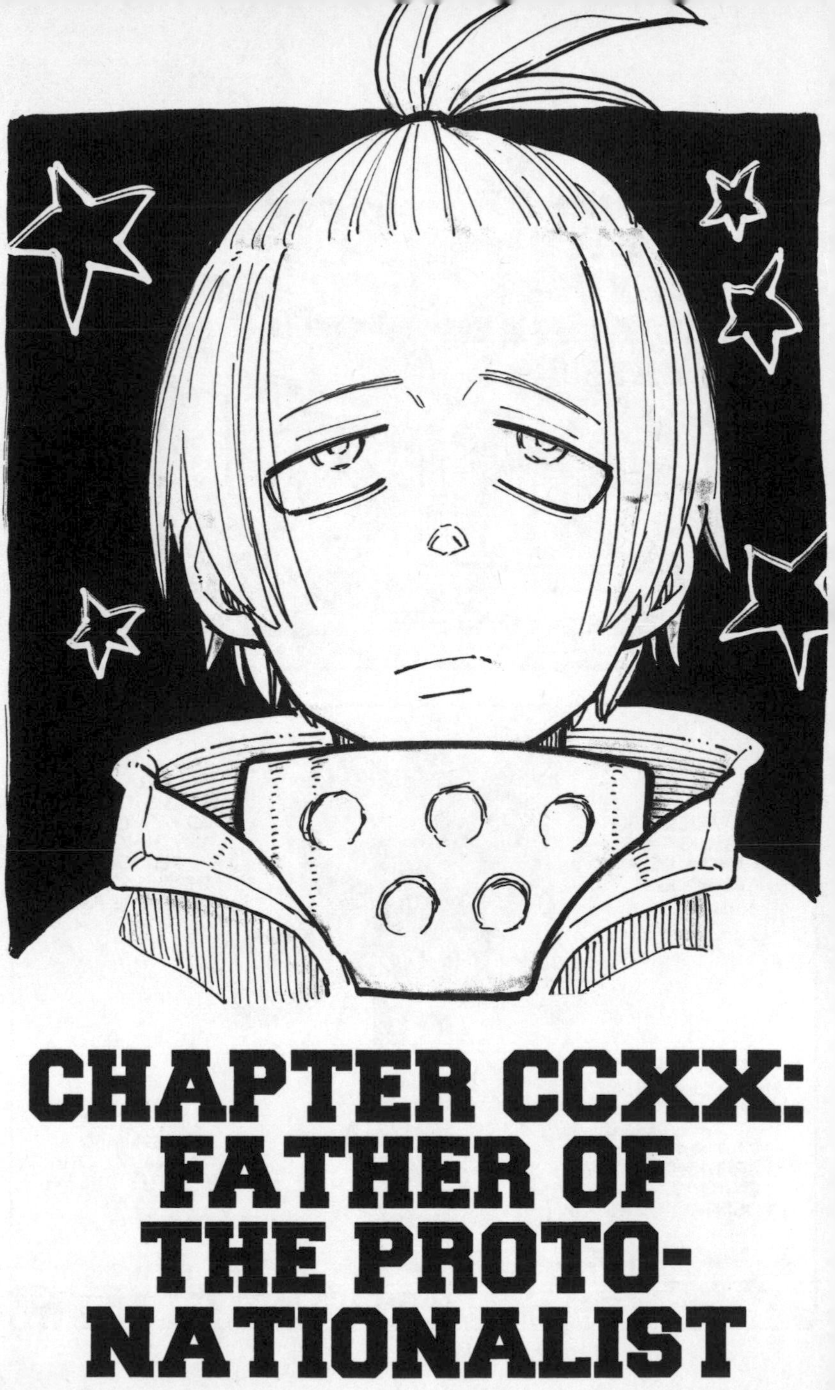

CHAPTER CCXX: FATHER OF THE PROTO-NATIONALIST

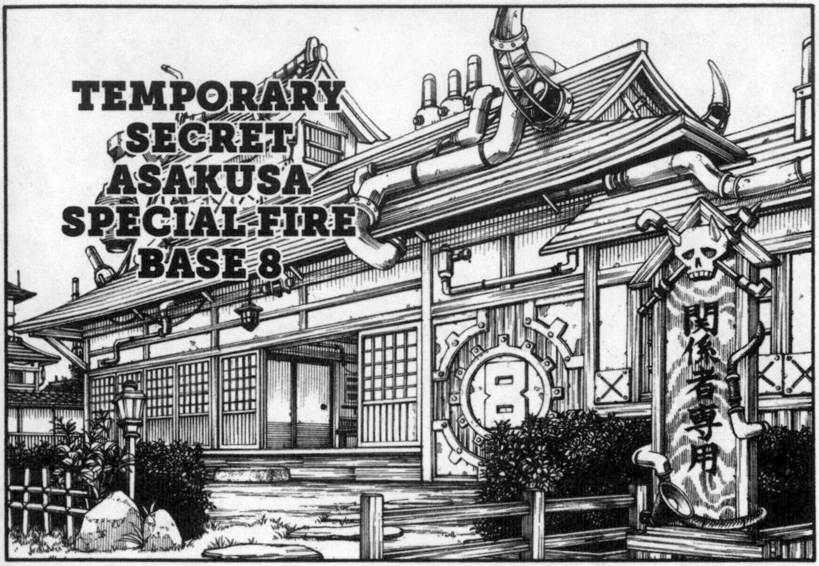
TEMPORARY SECRET ASAKUSA SPECIAL FIRE BASE 8
関係者専用

Sign: Authorized Personnel Only

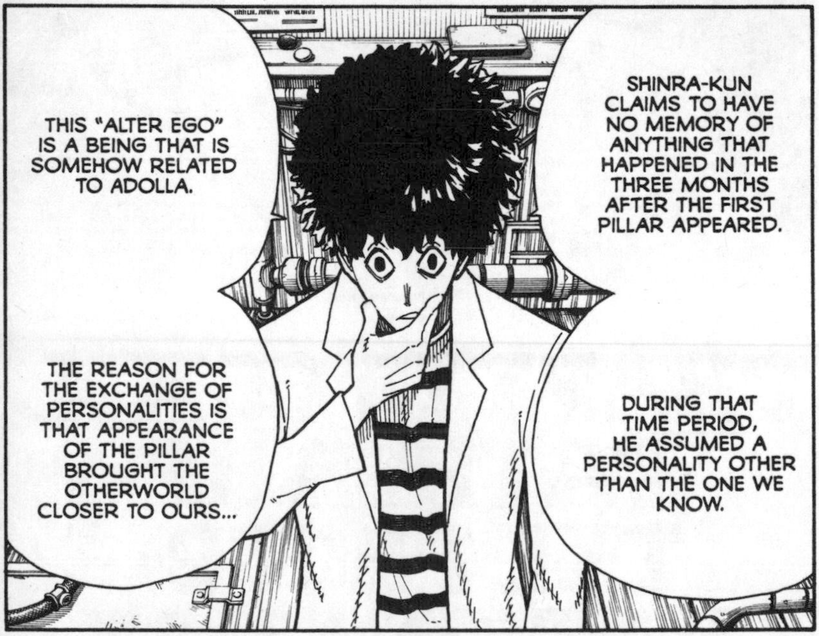
SHINRA-KUN CLAIMS TO HAVE NO MEMORY OF ANYTHING THAT HAPPENED IN THE THREE MONTHS AFTER THE FIRST PILLAR APPEARED.
DURING THAT TIME PERIOD, HE ASSUMED A PERSONALITY OTHER THAN THE ONE WE KNOW.
THIS "ALTER EGO" IS A BEING THAT IS SOMEHOW RELATED TO ADOLLA.
THE REASON FOR THE EXCHANGE OF PERSONALITIES IS THAT APPEARANCE OF THE PILLAR BROUGHT THE OTHERWORLD CLOSER TO OURS...

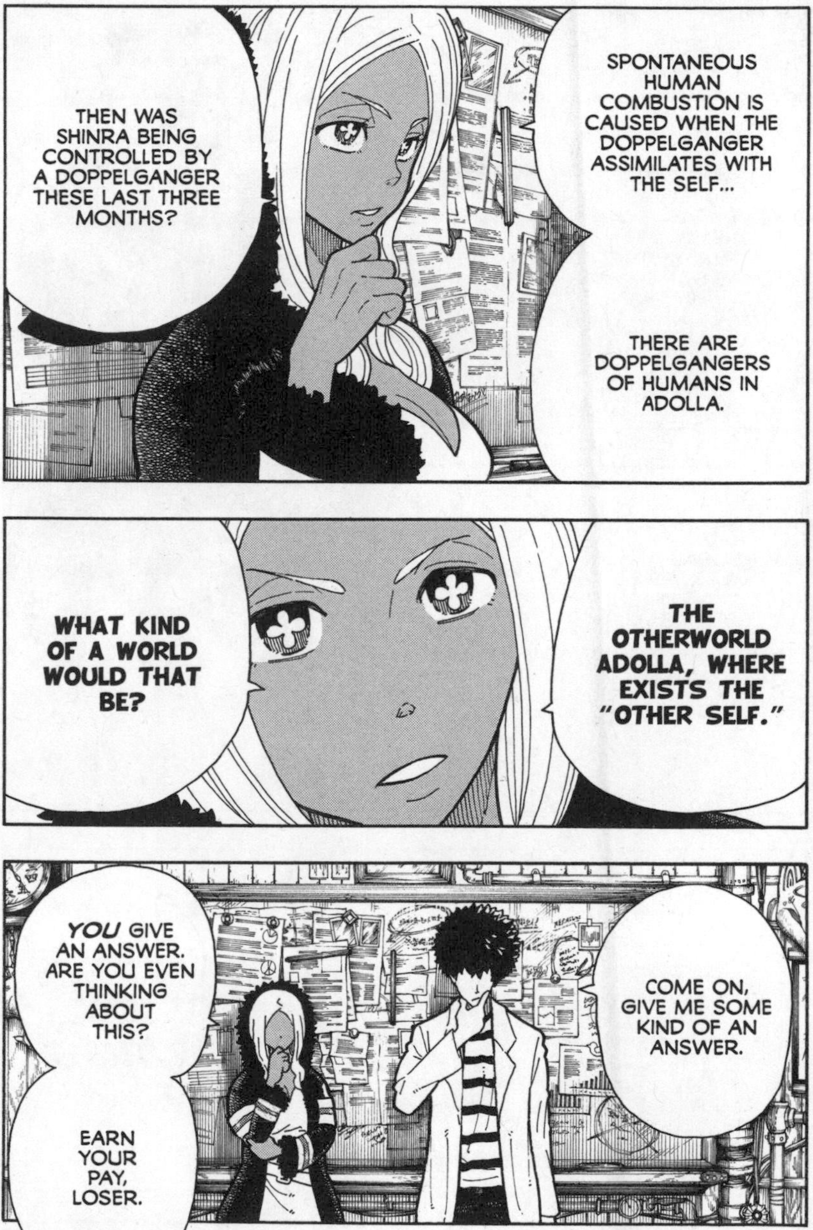
SPONTANEOUS HUMAN COMBUSTION IS CAUSED WHEN THE DOPPELGANGER ASSIMILATES WITH THE SELF...
THERE ARE DOPPELGANGERS OF HUMANS IN ADOLLA.
THEN WAS SHINRA BEING CONTROLLED BY A DOPPELGANGER THESE LAST THREE MONTHS?
THE OTHERWORLD ADOLLA, WHERE EXISTS THE "OTHER SELF."
WHAT KIND OF A WORLD WOULD THAT BE?
COME ON, GIVE ME SOME KIND OF AN ANSWER.
YOU GIVE AN ANSWER. ARE YOU EVEN THINKING ABOUT THIS?
EARN YOUR PAY, LOSER.

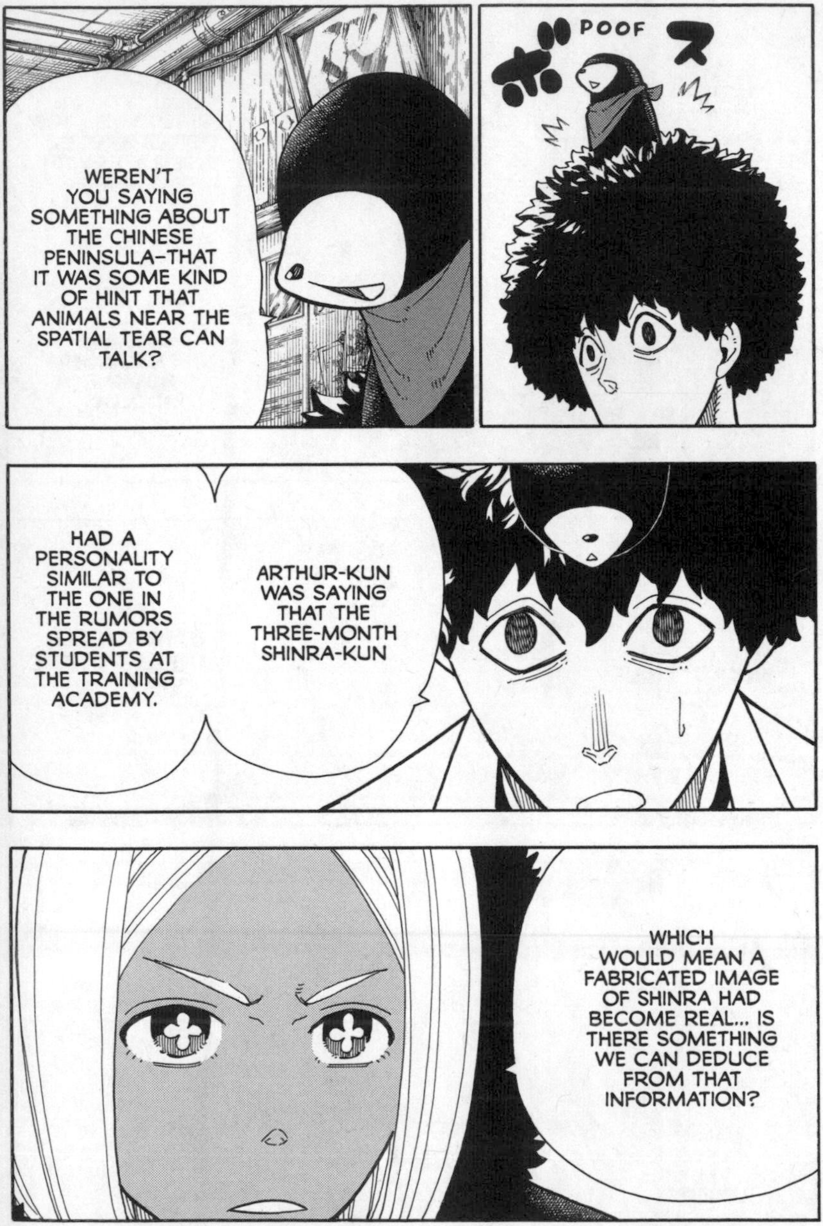
POOF
WEREN'T YOU SAYING SOMETHING ABOUT THE CHINESE PENINSULA–THAT IT WAS SOME KIND OF HINT THAT ANIMALS NEAR THE SPATIAL TEAR CAN TALK?
ARTHUR-KUN WAS SAYING THAT THE THREE-MONTH SHINRA-KUN
HAD A PERSONALITY SIMILAR TO THE ONE IN THE RUMORS SPREAD BY STUDENTS AT THE TRAINING ACADEMY.
WHICH WOULD MEAN A FABRICATED IMAGE OF SHINRA HAD BECOME REAL... IS THERE SOMETHING WE CAN DEDUCE FROM THAT INFORMATION?

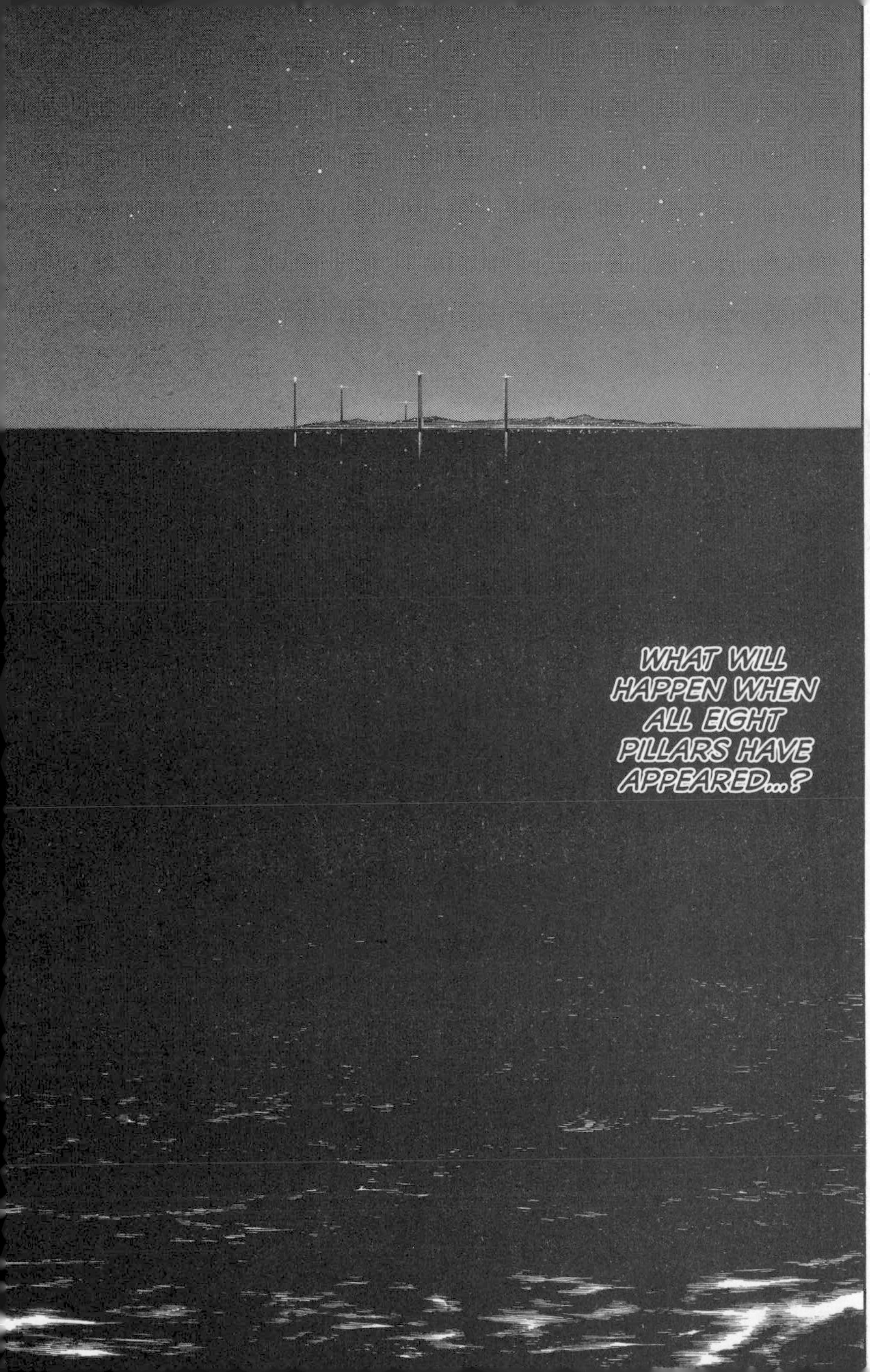
WHAT WILL HAPPEN WHEN ALL EIGHT PILLARS HAVE APPEARED...?

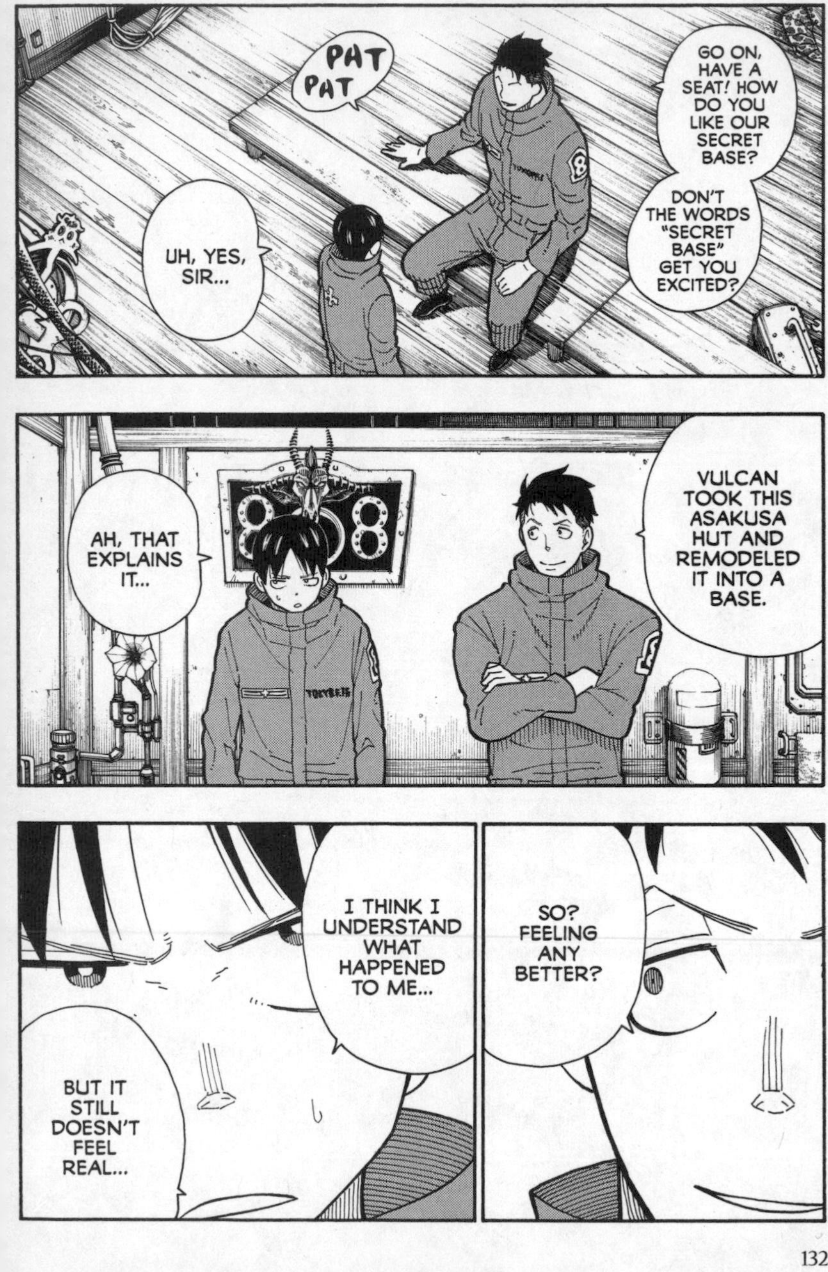
GO ON, HAVE A SEAT! HOW DO YOU LIKE OUR SECRET BASE?
DON'T THE WORDS "SECRET BASE" GET YOU EXCITED?
PAT PAT
UH, YES, SIR...
VULCAN TOOK THIS ASAKUSA HUT AND REMODELED IT INTO A BASE.
AH, THAT EXPLAINS IT...
SO? FEELING ANY BETTER?
I THINK I UNDERSTAND WHAT HAPPENED TO ME...
BUT IT STILL DOESN'T FEEL REAL...

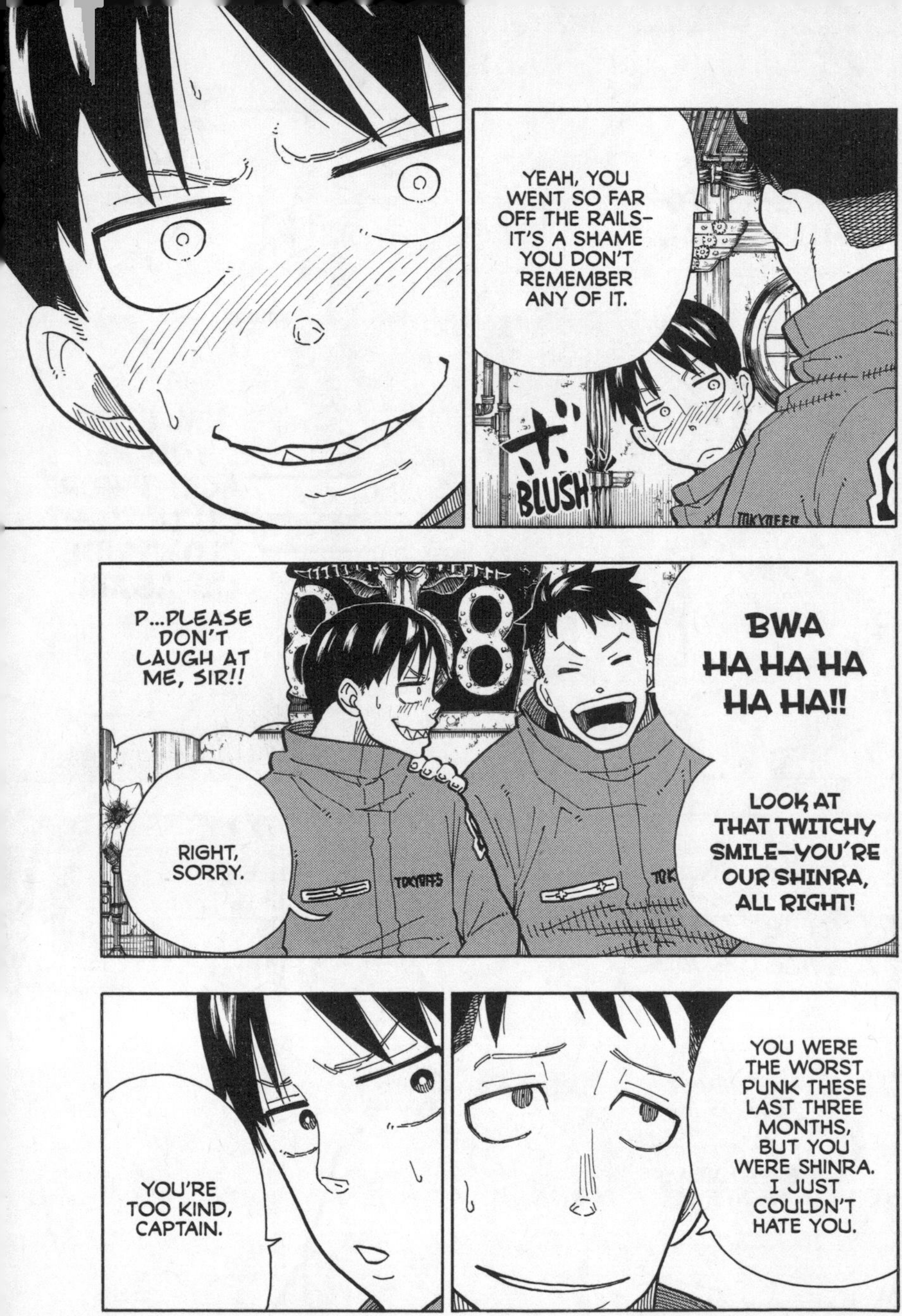
YEAH, YOU WENT SO FAR OFF THE RAILS—IT'S A SHAME YOU DON'T REMEMBER ANY OF IT.
ボ
BLUSH
BWA HA HA HA HA HA!!
LOOK AT THAT TWITCHY SMILE—YOU'RE OUR SHINRA, ALL RIGHT!
P...PLEASE DON'T LAUGH AT ME, SIR!!
RIGHT, SORRY.
YOU WERE THE WORST PUNK THESE LAST THREE MONTHS, BUT YOU WERE SHINRA. I JUST COULDN'T HATE YOU.
YOU'RE TOO KIND, CAPTAIN.

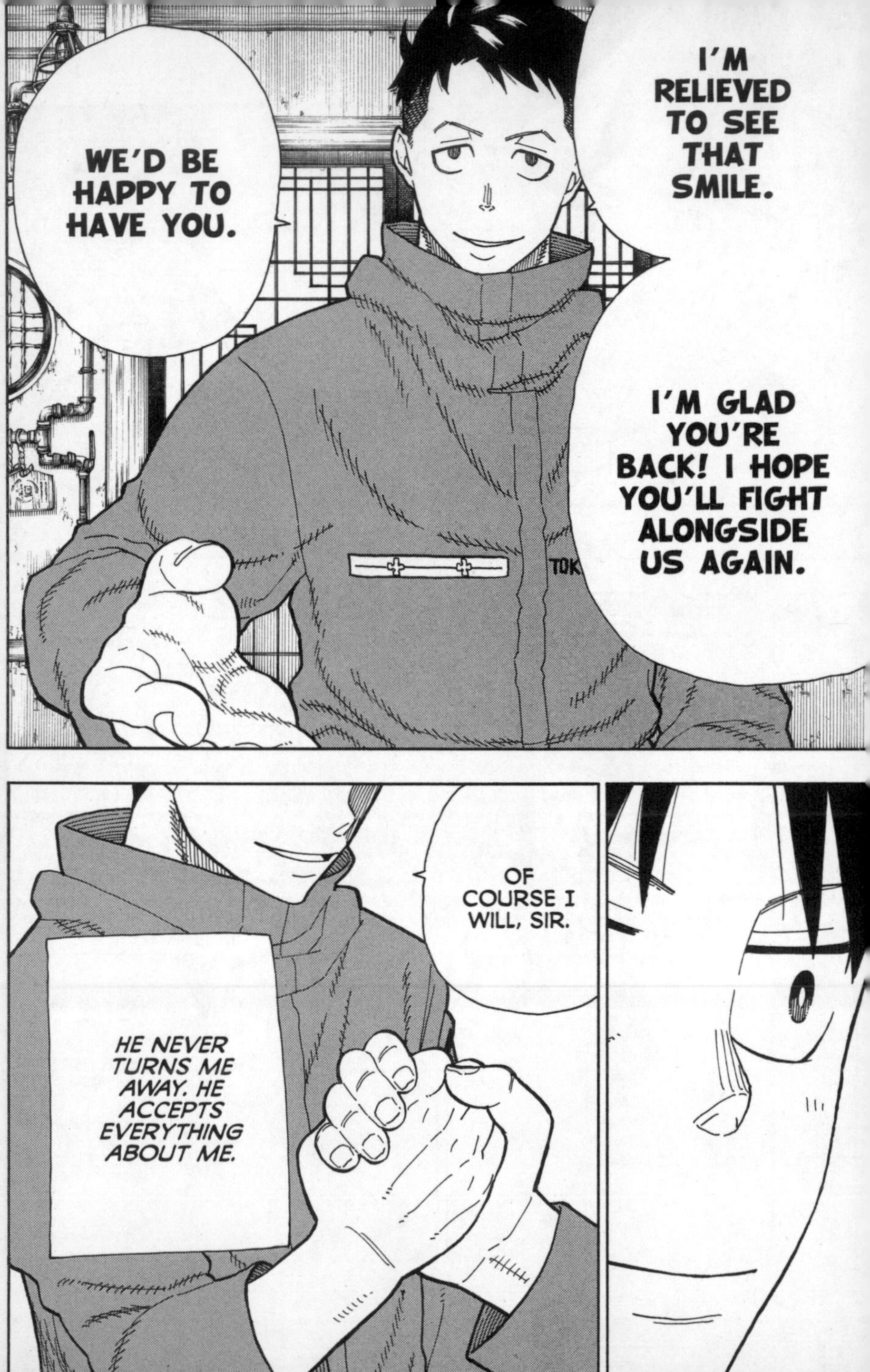
I'M RELIEVED TO SEE THAT SMILE.
WE'D BE HAPPY TO HAVE YOU.
I'M GLAD YOU'RE BACK! I HOPE YOU'LL FIGHT ALONGSIDE US AGAIN.
OF COURSE I WILL, SIR.
HE NEVER TURNS ME AWAY. HE ACCEPTS EVERYTHING ABOUT ME.

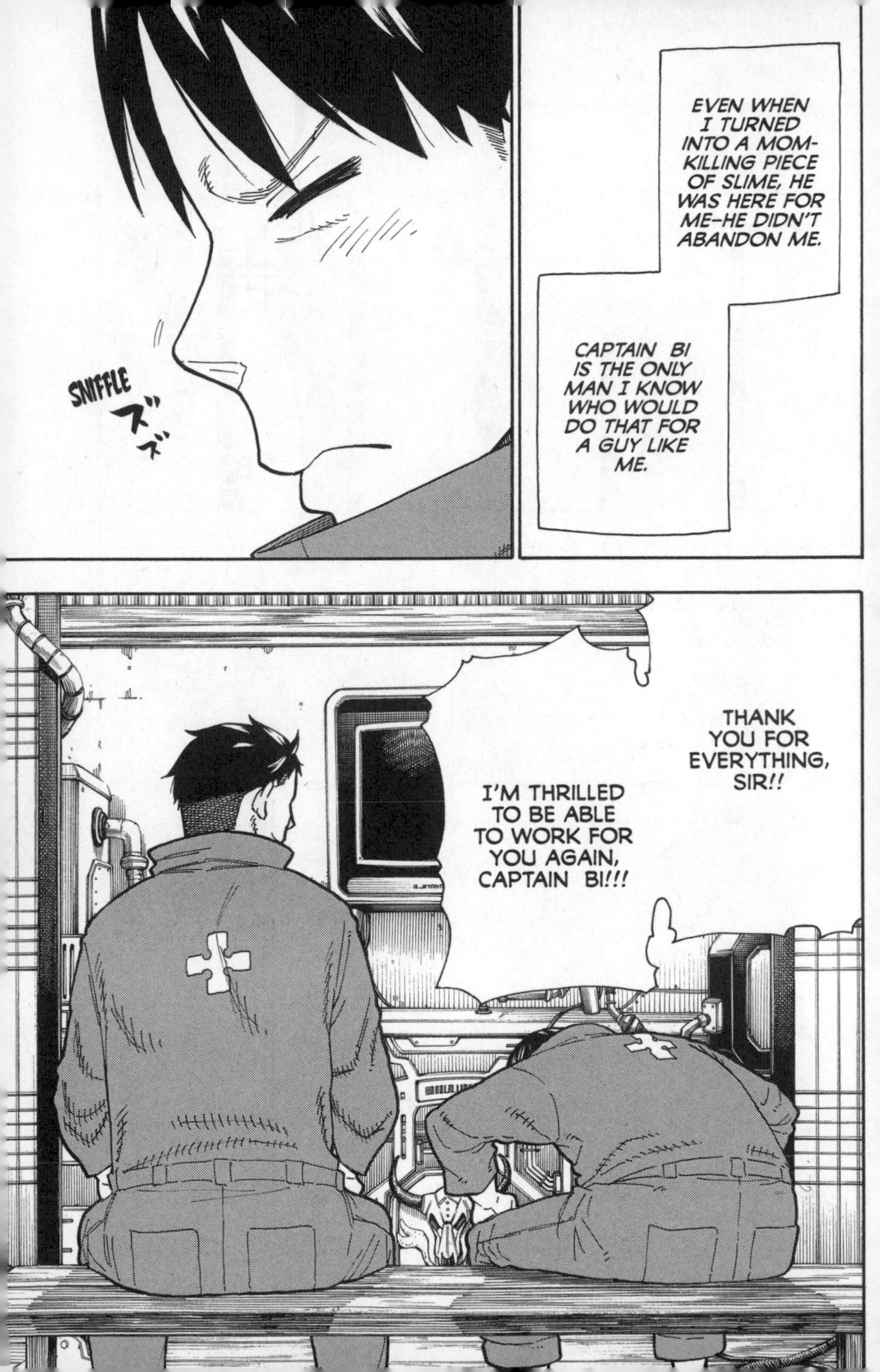
EVEN WHEN I TURNED INTO A MOM-KILLING PIECE OF SLIME, HE WAS HERE FOR ME—HE DIDN'T ABANDON ME.
CAPTAIN BI IS THE ONLY MAN I KNOW WHO WOULD DO THAT FOR A GUY LIKE ME.
SNIFFLE
ズズ
THANK YOU FOR EVERYTHING, SIR!!
I'M THRILLED TO BE ABLE TO WORK FOR YOU AGAIN, CAPTAIN BI!!!

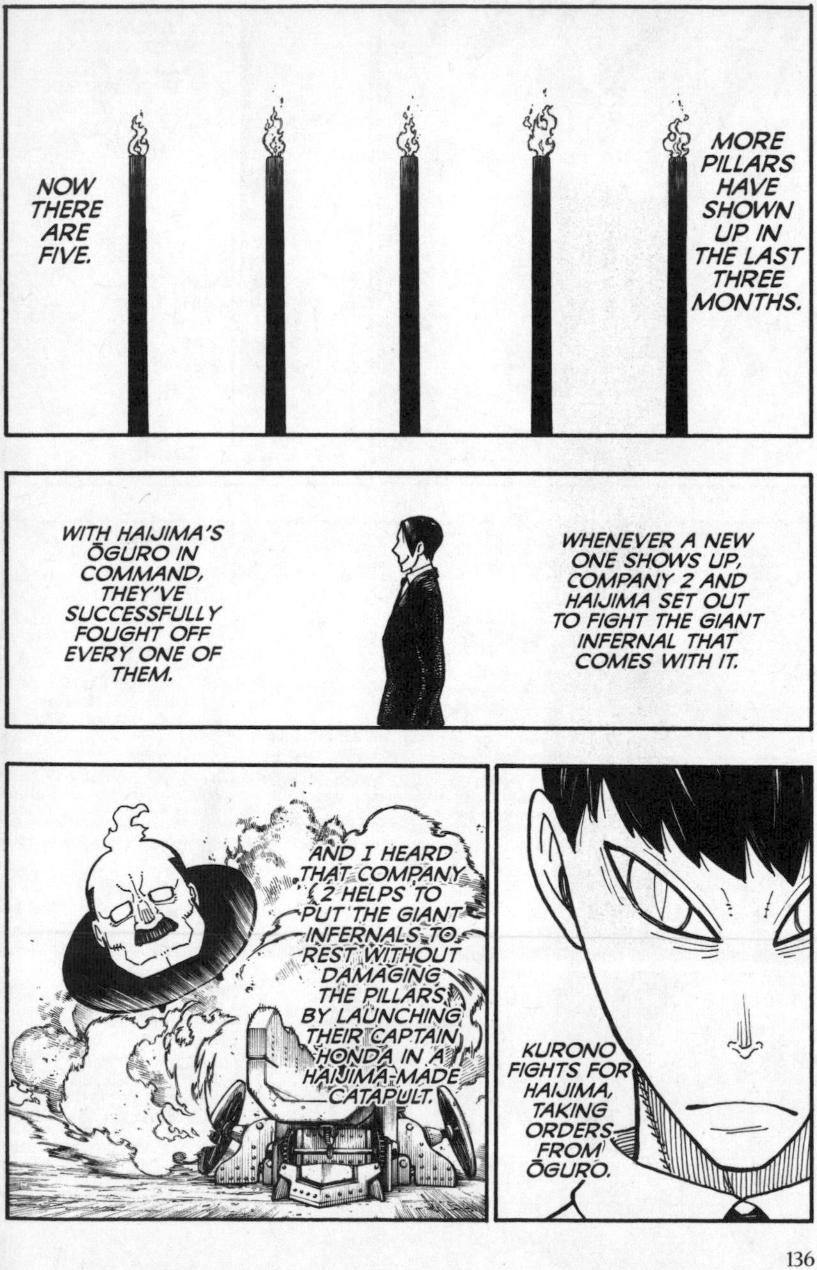
MORE PILLARS HAVE SHOWN UP IN THE LAST THREE MONTHS.
NOW THERE ARE FIVE.
WHENEVER A NEW ONE SHOWS UP, COMPANY 2 AND HAIJIMA SET OUT TO FIGHT THE GIANT INFERNAL THAT COMES WITH IT.
WITH HAIJIMA'S ŌGURO IN COMMAND, THEY'VE SUCCESSFULLY FOUGHT OFF EVERY ONE OF THEM.
KURONO FIGHTS FOR HAIJIMA, TAKING ORDERS FROM ŌGURO.
AND I HEARD THAT COMPANY 2 HELPS TO PUT THE GIANT INFERNALS TO REST WITHOUT DAMAGING THE PILLARS BY LAUNCHING THEIR CAPTAIN HONDA IN A HAIJIMA-MADE CATAPULT.

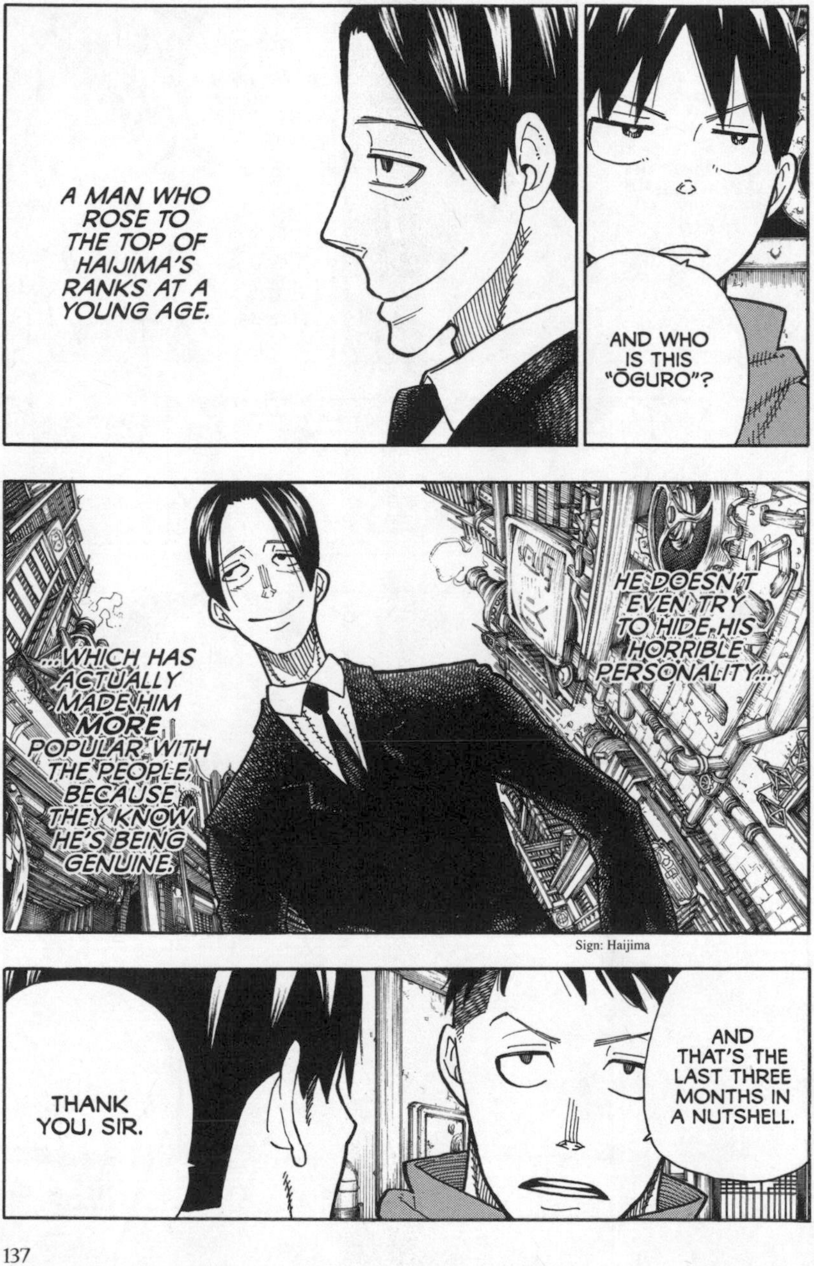
AND WHO IS THIS "ŌGURO"?
A MAN WHO ROSE TO THE TOP OF HAIJIMA'S RANKS AT A YOUNG AGE.
HE DOESN'T EVEN TRY TO HIDE HIS HORRIBLE PERSONALITY...
...WHICH HAS ACTUALLY MADE HIM MORE POPULAR WITH THE PEOPLE BECAUSE THEY KNOW HE'S BEING GENUINE.
AND THAT'S THE LAST THREE MONTHS IN A NUTSHELL.
THANK YOU, SIR.

Sign: Haijima

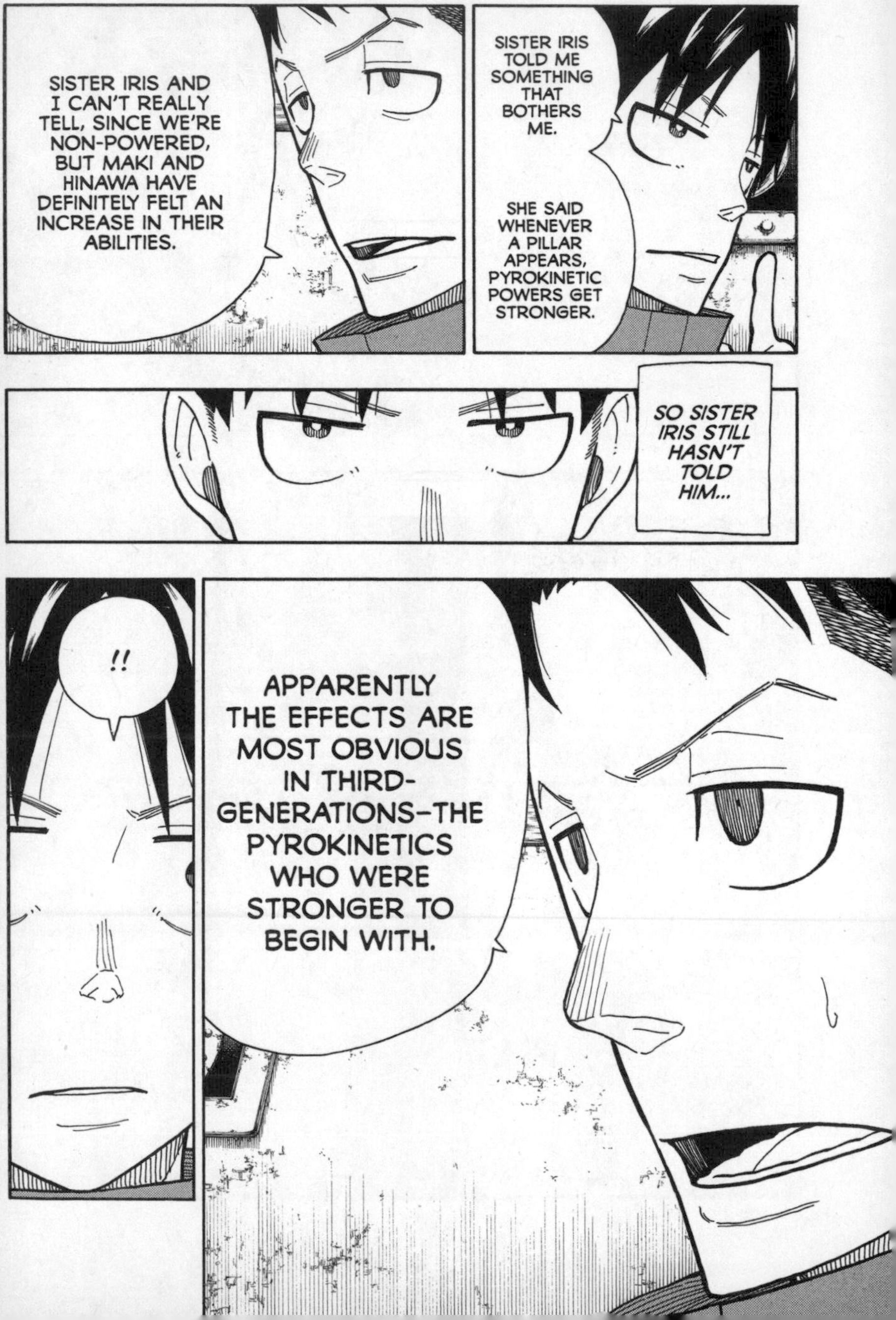
SISTER IRIS TOLD ME SOMETHING THAT BOTHERS ME.
SHE SAID WHENEVER A PILLAR APPEARS, PYROKINETIC POWERS GET STRONGER.
SISTER IRIS AND I CAN'T REALLY TELL, SINCE WE'RE NON-POWERED, BUT MAKI AND HINAWA HAVE DEFINITELY FELT AN INCREASE IN THEIR ABILITIES.
SO SISTER IRIS STILL HASN'T TOLD HIM...
APPARENTLY THE EFFECTS ARE MOST OBVIOUS IN THIRD-GENERATIONS—THE PYROKINETICS WHO WERE STRONGER TO BEGIN WITH.
!!

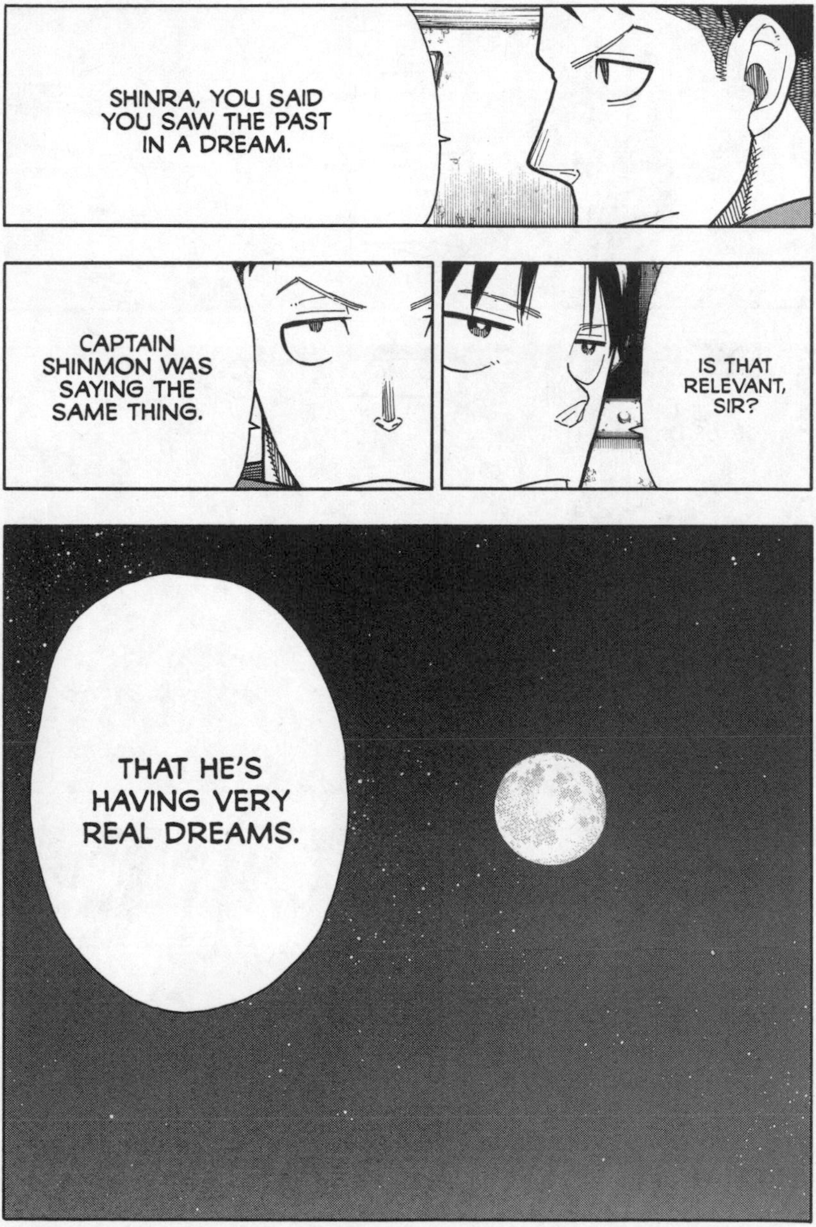
SHINRA, YOU SAID YOU SAW THE PAST IN A DREAM.
IS THAT RELEVANT, SIR?
CAPTAIN SHINMON WAS SAYING THE SAME THING.
THAT HE'S HAVING VERY REAL DREAMS.

Label: Mizuno Three Rivers Subterranean River Water
Beloved, Nakamoto Brewery, Made from finest Wakamizu rice

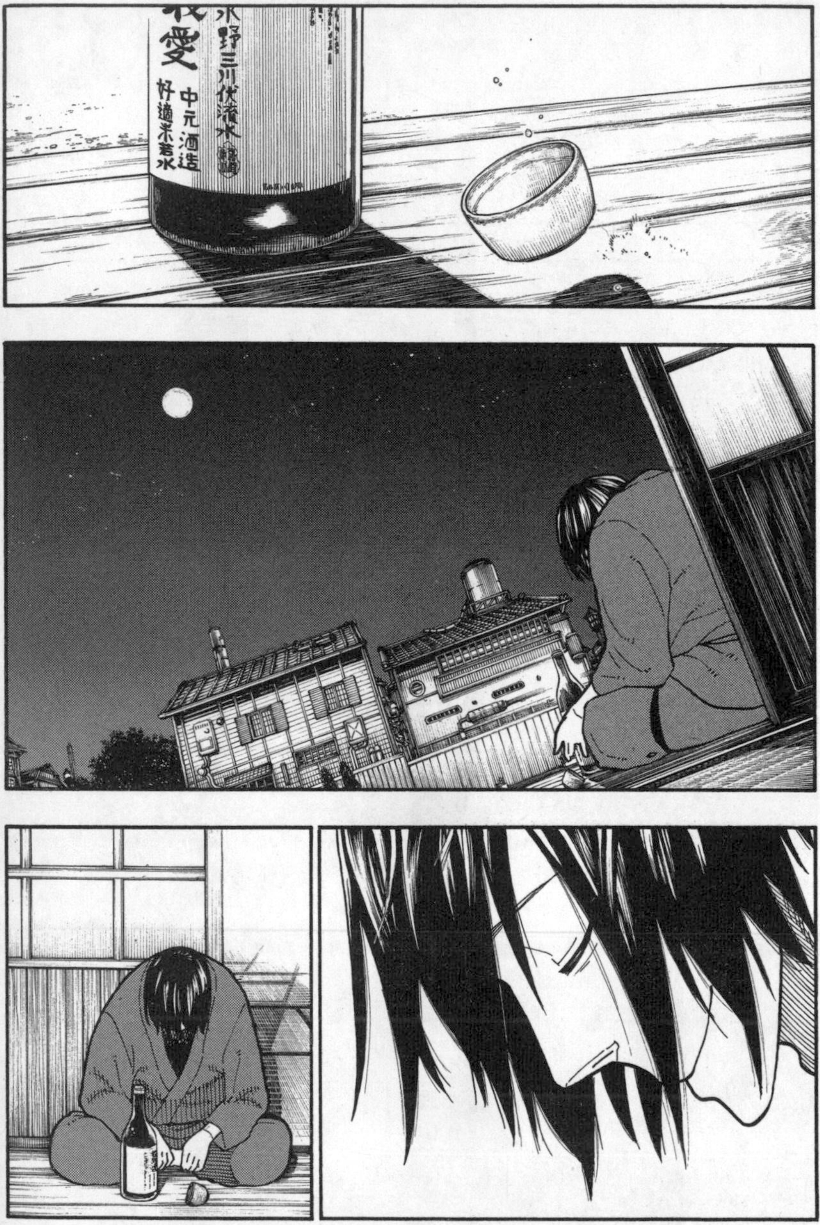
中元酒造
好適米若水

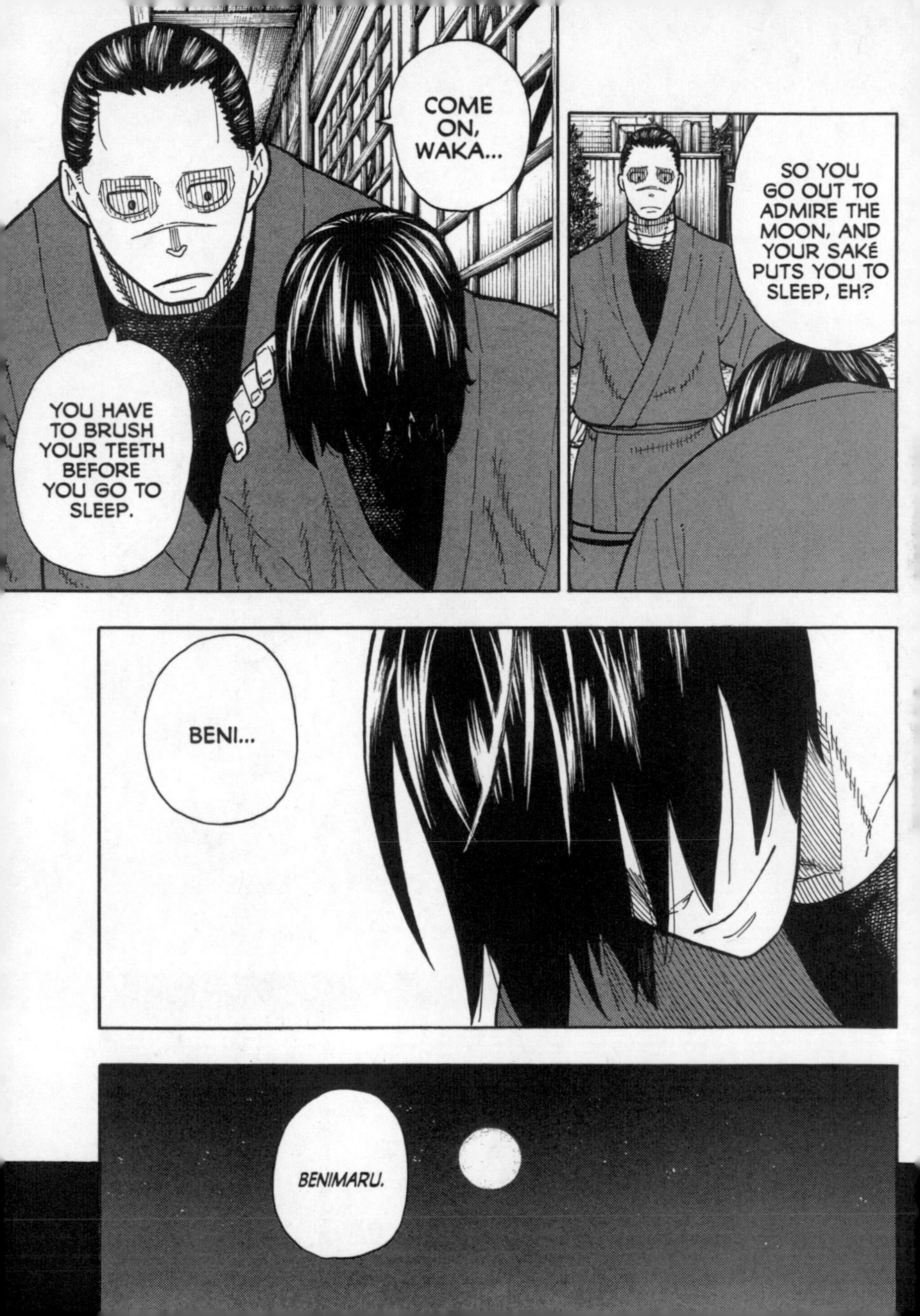
SO YOU GO OUT TO ADMIRE THE MOON, AND YOUR SAKÉ PUTS YOU TO SLEEP, EH?
COME ON, WAKA...
YOU HAVE TO BRUSH YOUR TEETH BEFORE YOU GO TO SLEEP.
BENI...
BENIMARU.

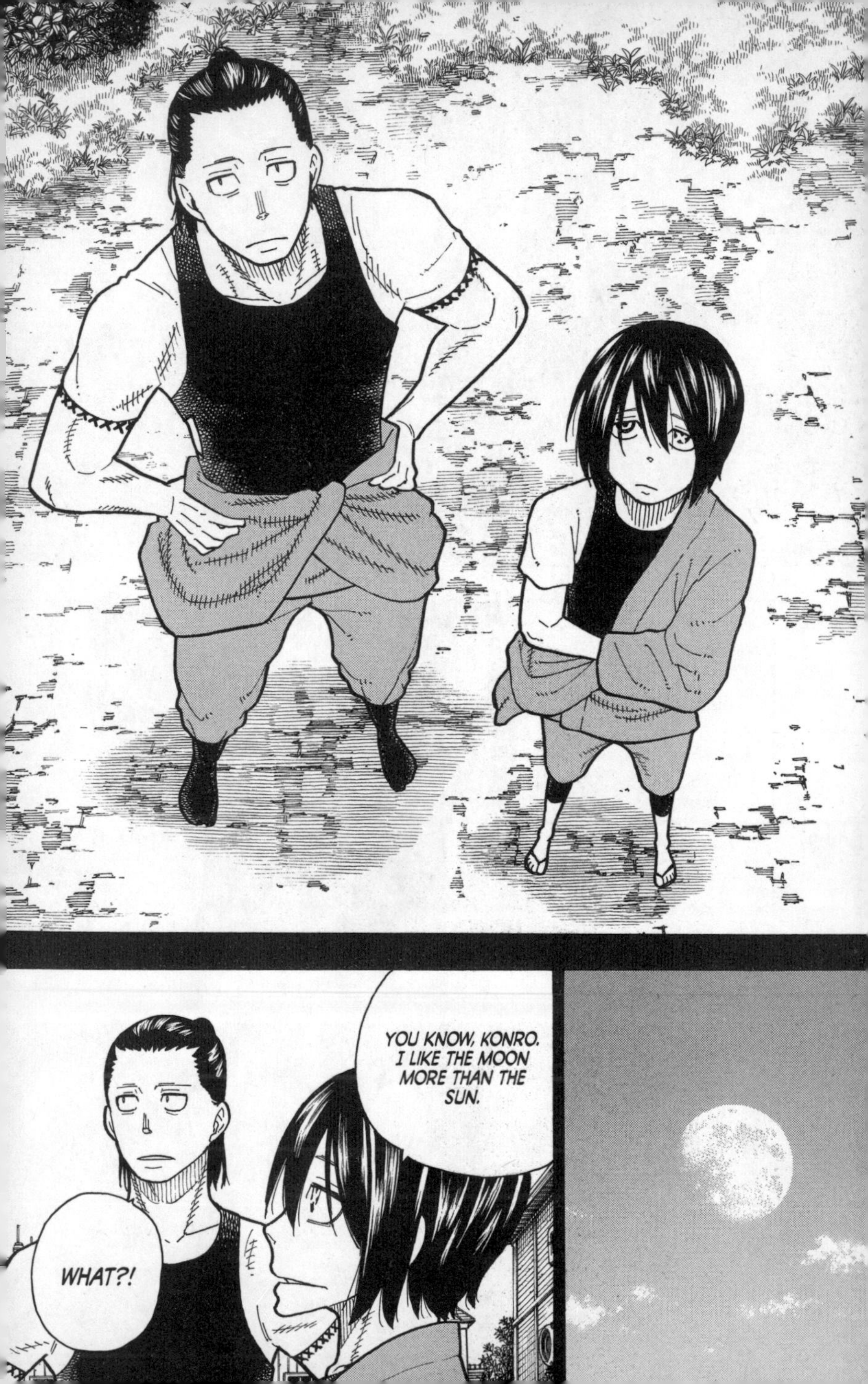
YOU KNOW, KONRO. I LIKE THE MOON MORE THAN THE SUN.
WHAT?!

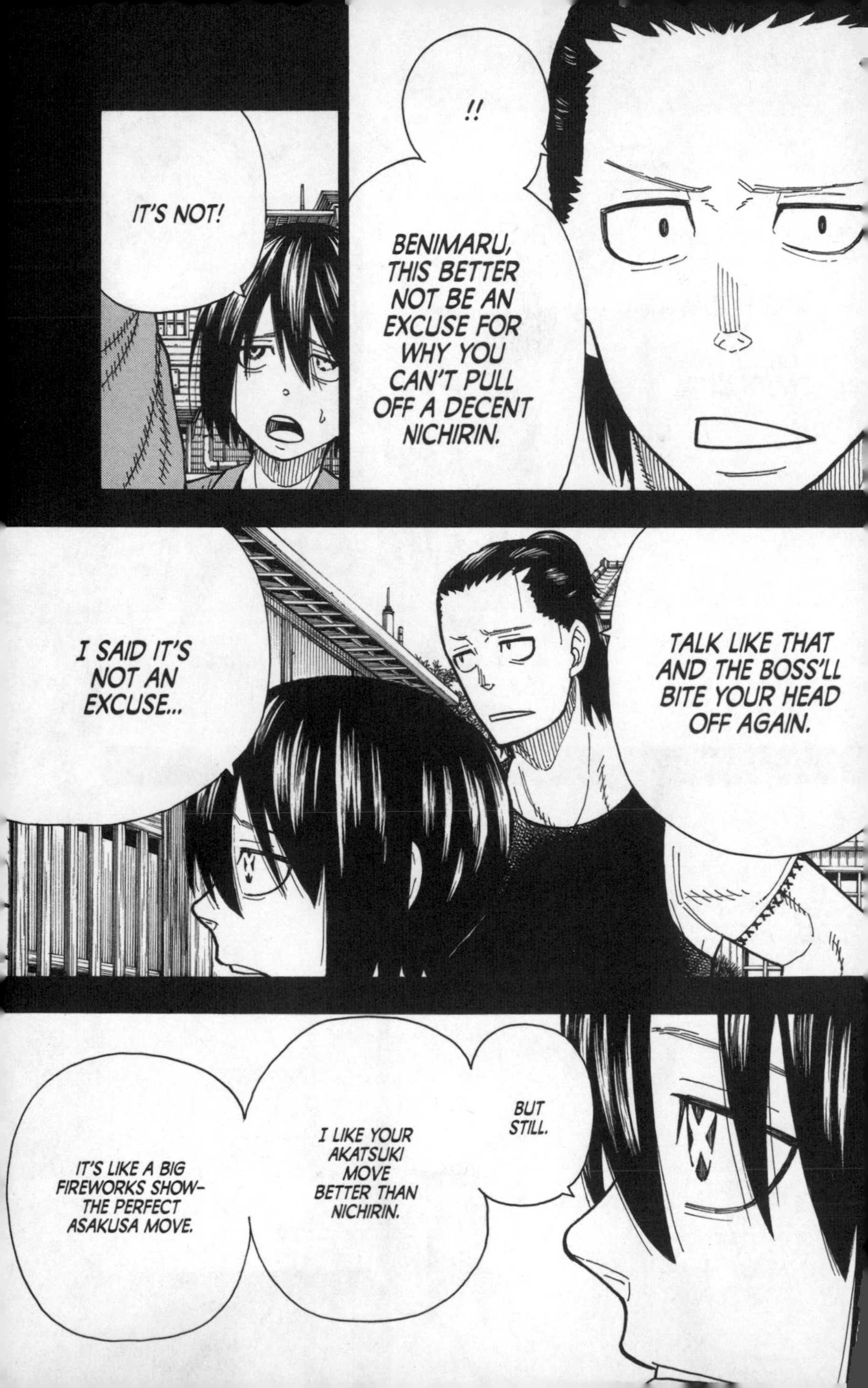
!!
BENIMARU, THIS BETTER NOT BE AN EXCUSE FOR WHY YOU CAN'T PULL OFF A DECENT NICHIRIN.
IT'S NOT!
TALK LIKE THAT AND THE BOSS'LL BITE YOUR HEAD OFF AGAIN.
I SAID IT'S NOT AN EXCUSE...
BUT STILL.
I LIKE YOUR AKATSUKI MOVE BETTER THAN NICHIRIN.
IT'S LIKE A BIG FIREWORKS SHOW– THE PERFECT ASAKUSA MOVE.

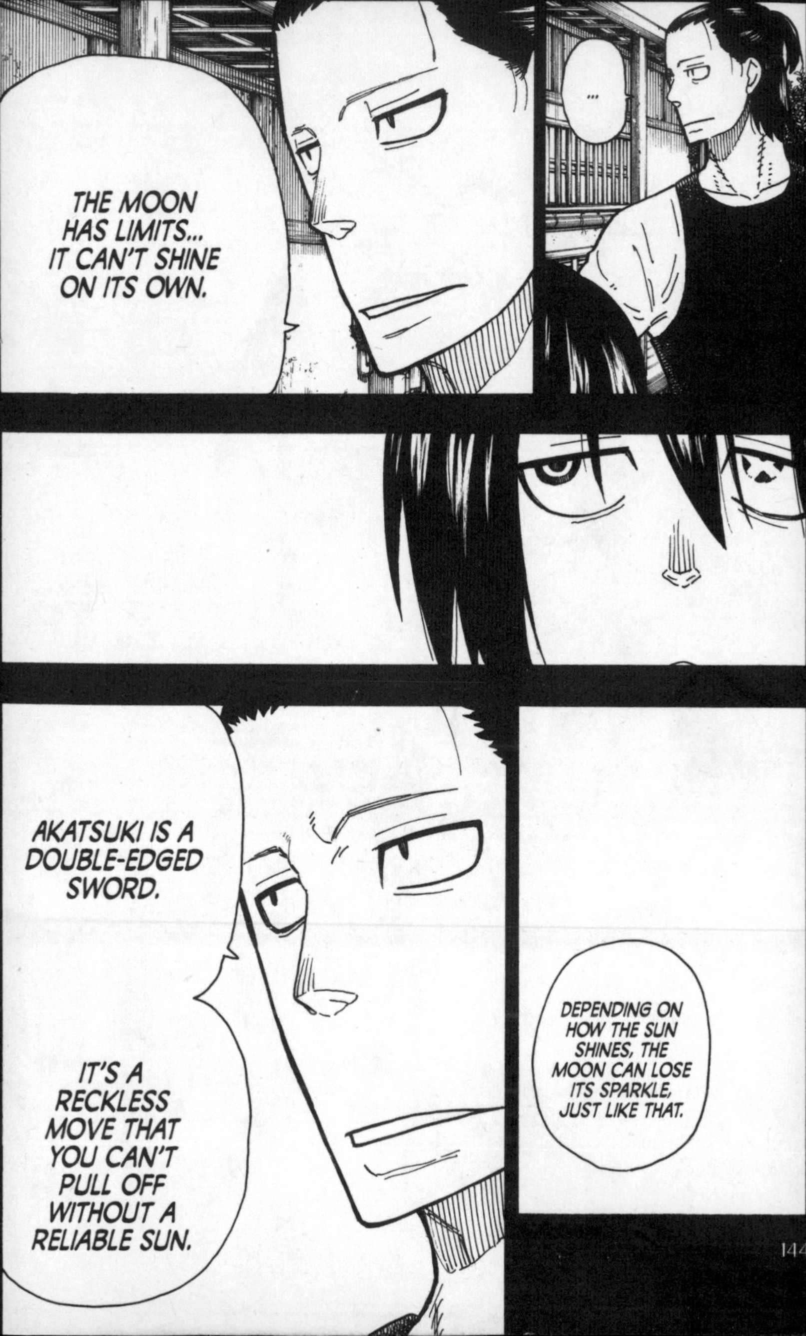
...
THE MOON HAS LIMITS... IT CAN'T SHINE ON ITS OWN.
DEPENDING ON HOW THE SUN SHINES, THE MOON CAN LOSE ITS SPARKLE, JUST LIKE THAT.
AKATSUKI IS A DOUBLE-EDGED SWORD.
IT'S A RECKLESS MOVE THAT YOU CAN'T PULL OFF WITHOUT A RELIABLE SUN.

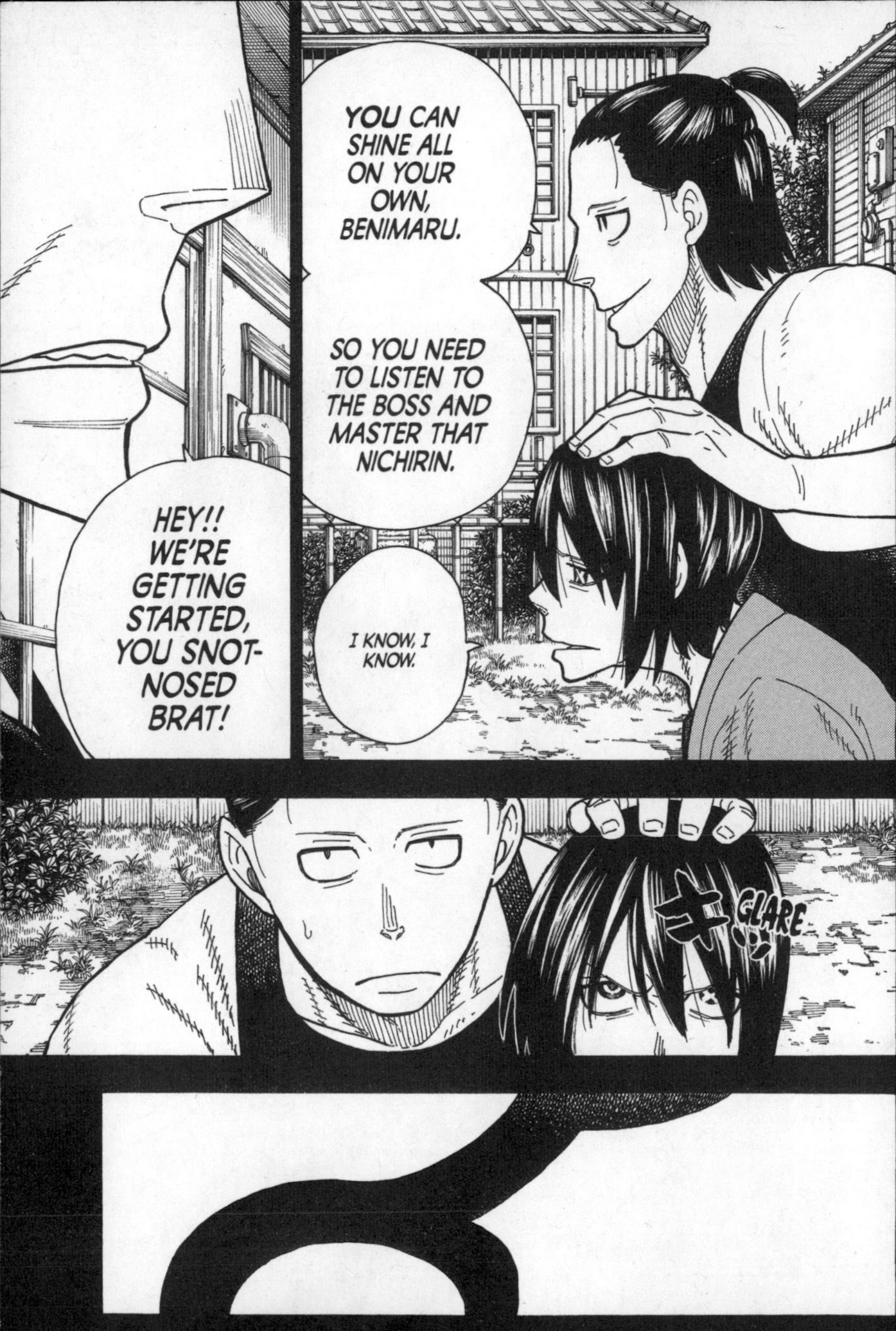
YOU CAN SHINE ALL ON YOUR OWN, BENIMARU.
SO YOU NEED TO LISTEN TO THE BOSS AND MASTER THAT NICHIRIN.
I KNOW, I KNOW.
HEY!! WE'RE GETTING STARTED, YOU SNOT-NOSED BRAT!
GLARE

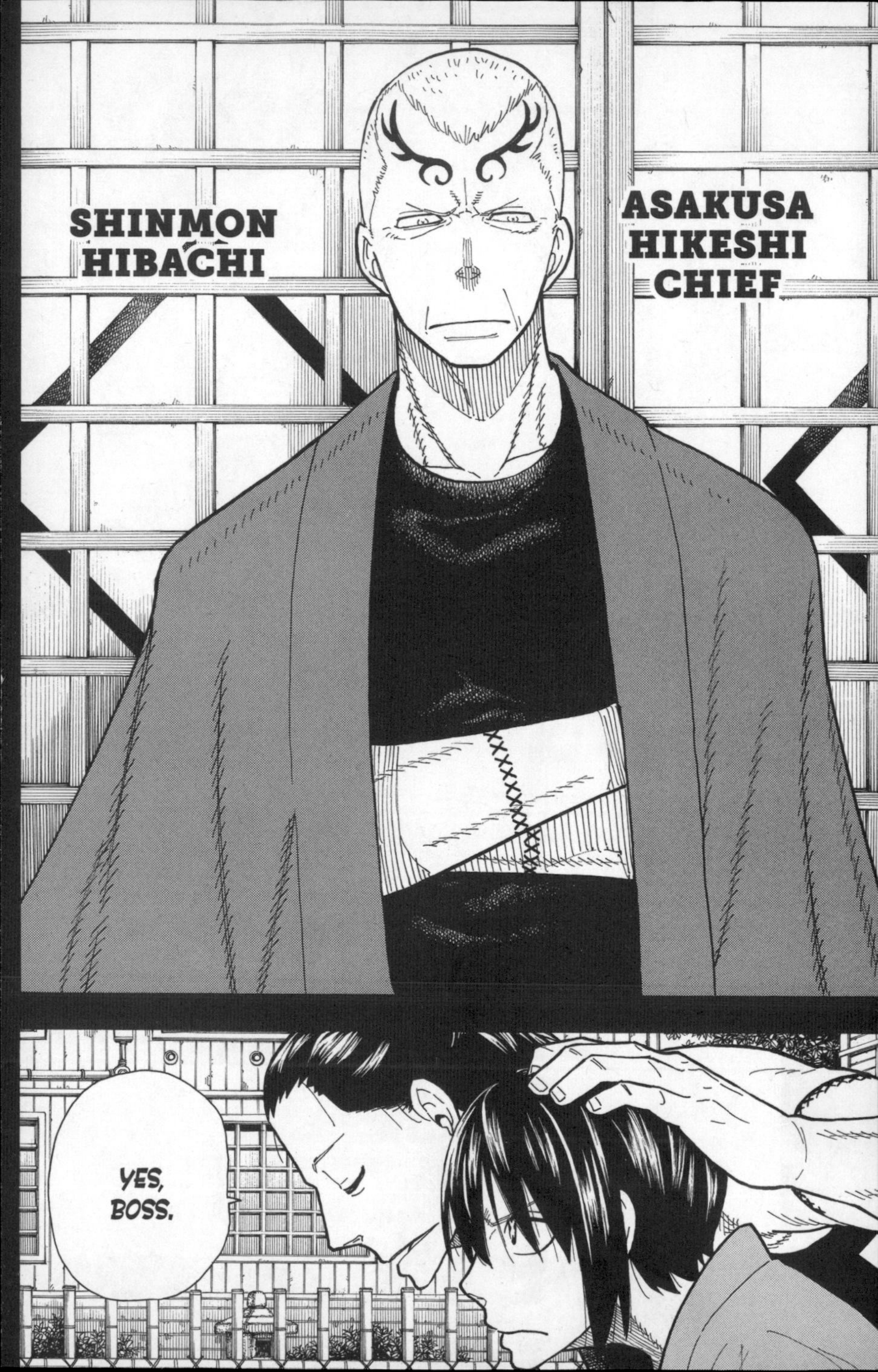
SHINMON HIBACHI
ASAKUSA HIKESHI CHIEF
YES, BOSS.

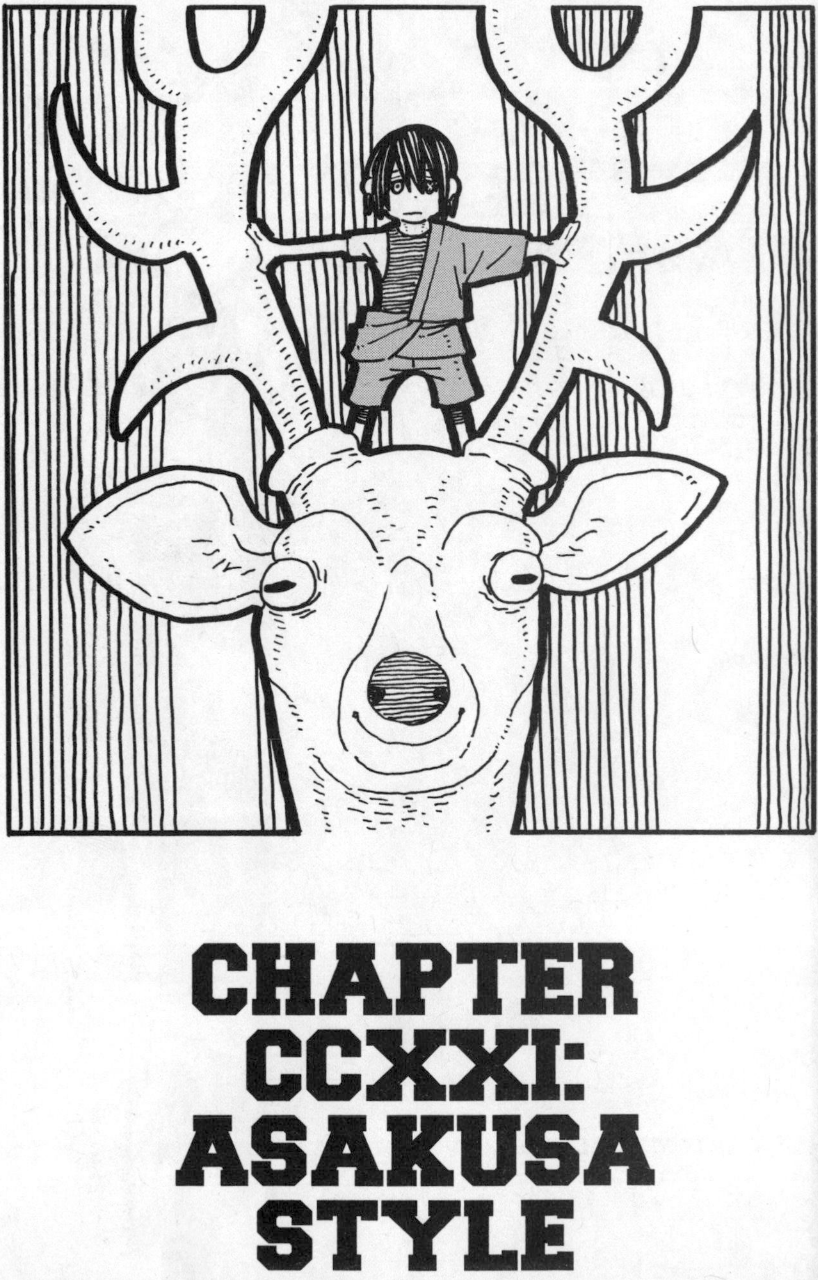

CHAPTER CCXXI: ASAKUSA STYLE

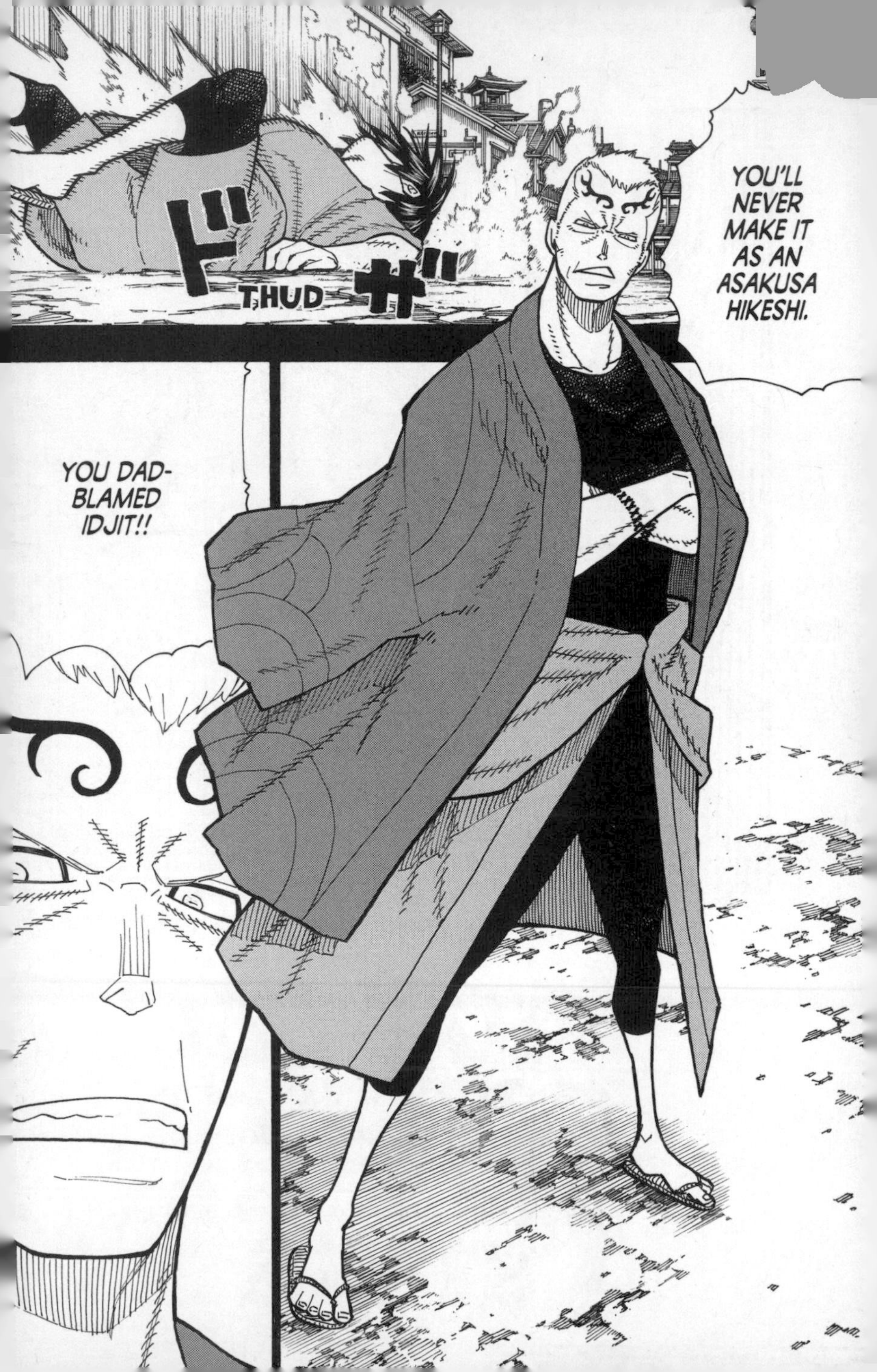
ドザッ
THUD
YOU'LL NEVER MAKE IT AS AN ASAKUSA HIKESHI.
YOU DAD-BLAMED IDJIT!!

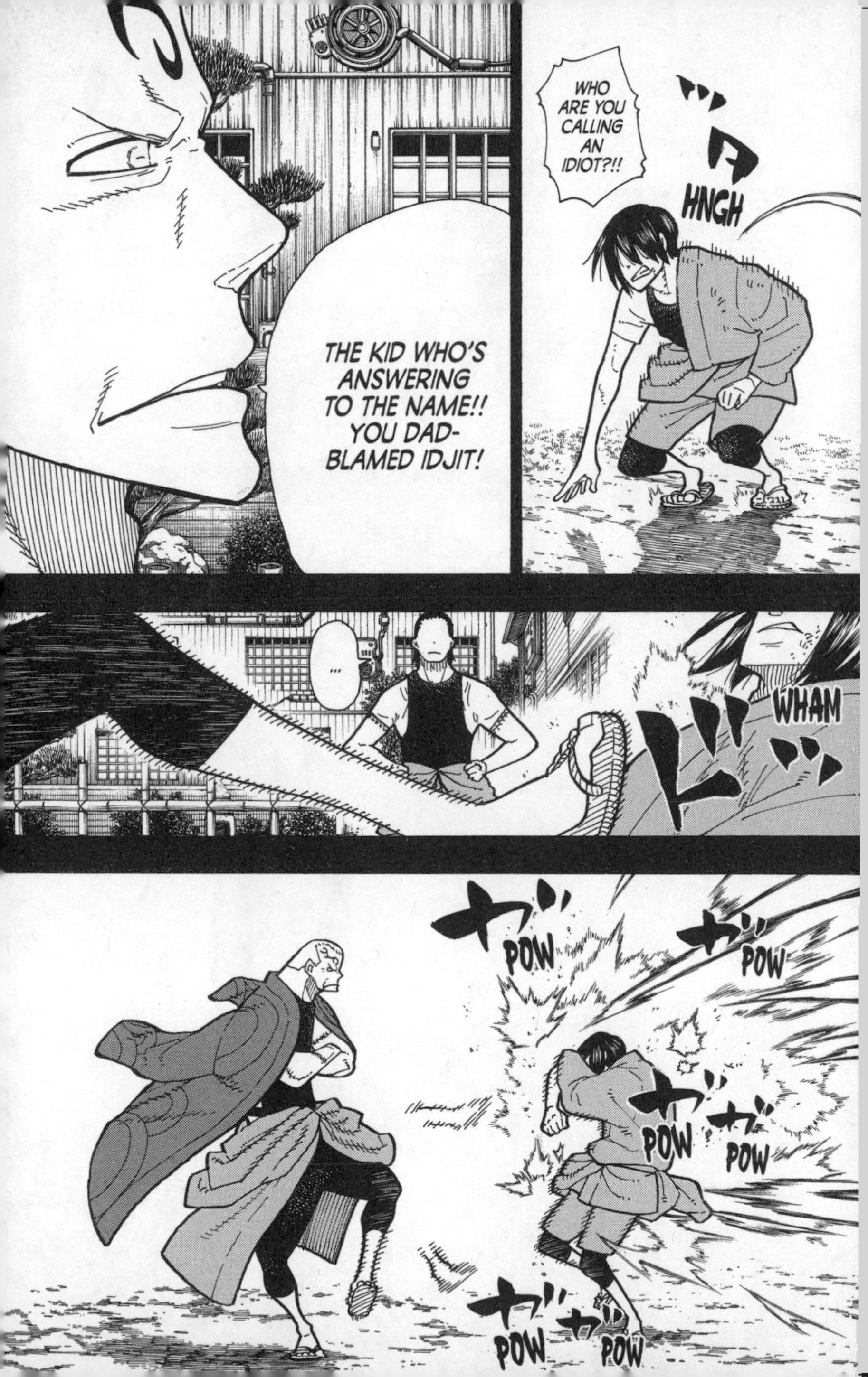
WHO ARE YOU CALLING AN IDIOT?!!
HNGH
THE KID WHO'S ANSWERING TO THE NAME!! YOU DAD-BLAMED IDJIT!
WHAM
...
POW
POW
POW
POW
POW
POW

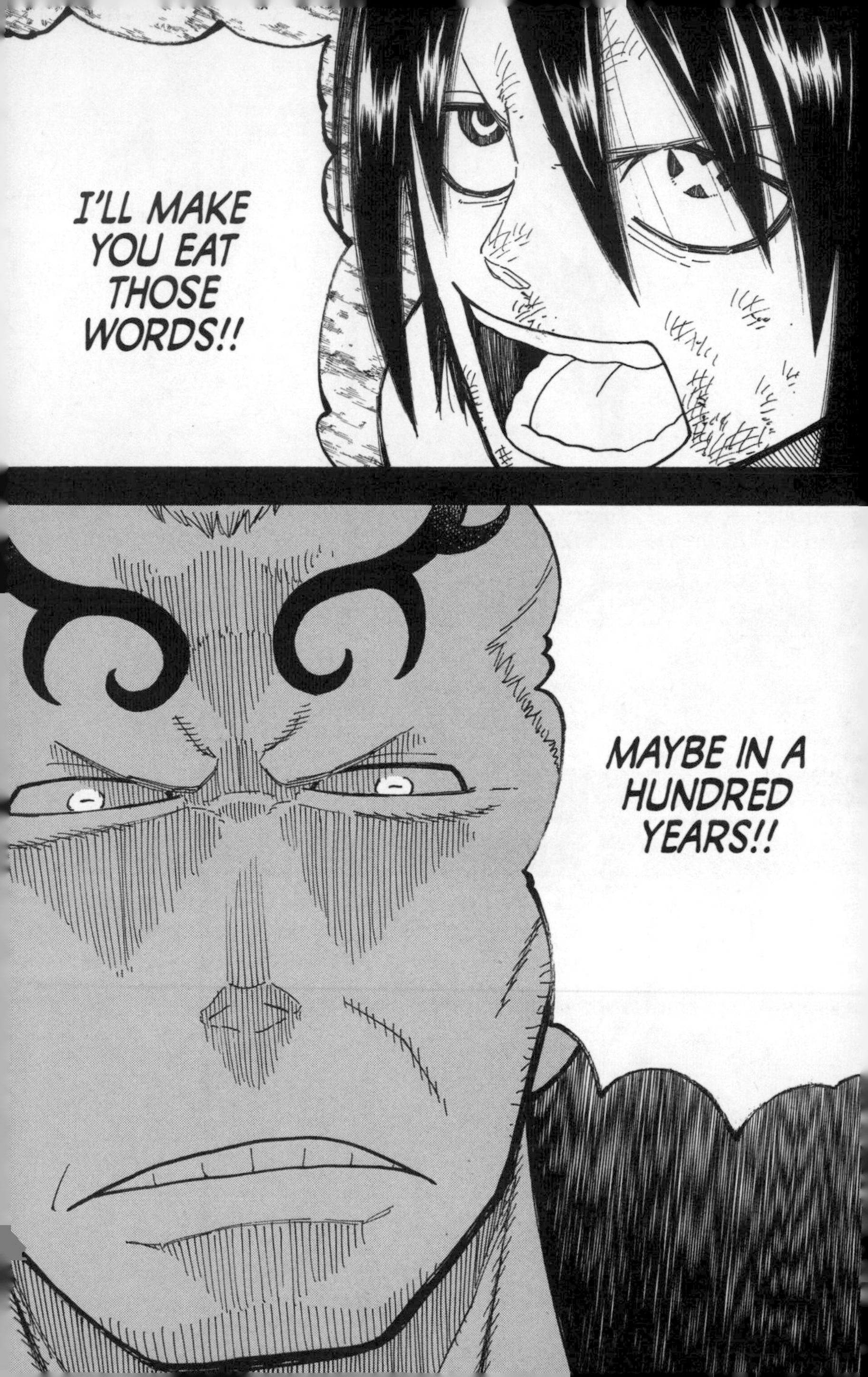
I'LL MAKE YOU EAT THOSE WORDS!!
MAYBE IN A HUNDRED YEARS!!

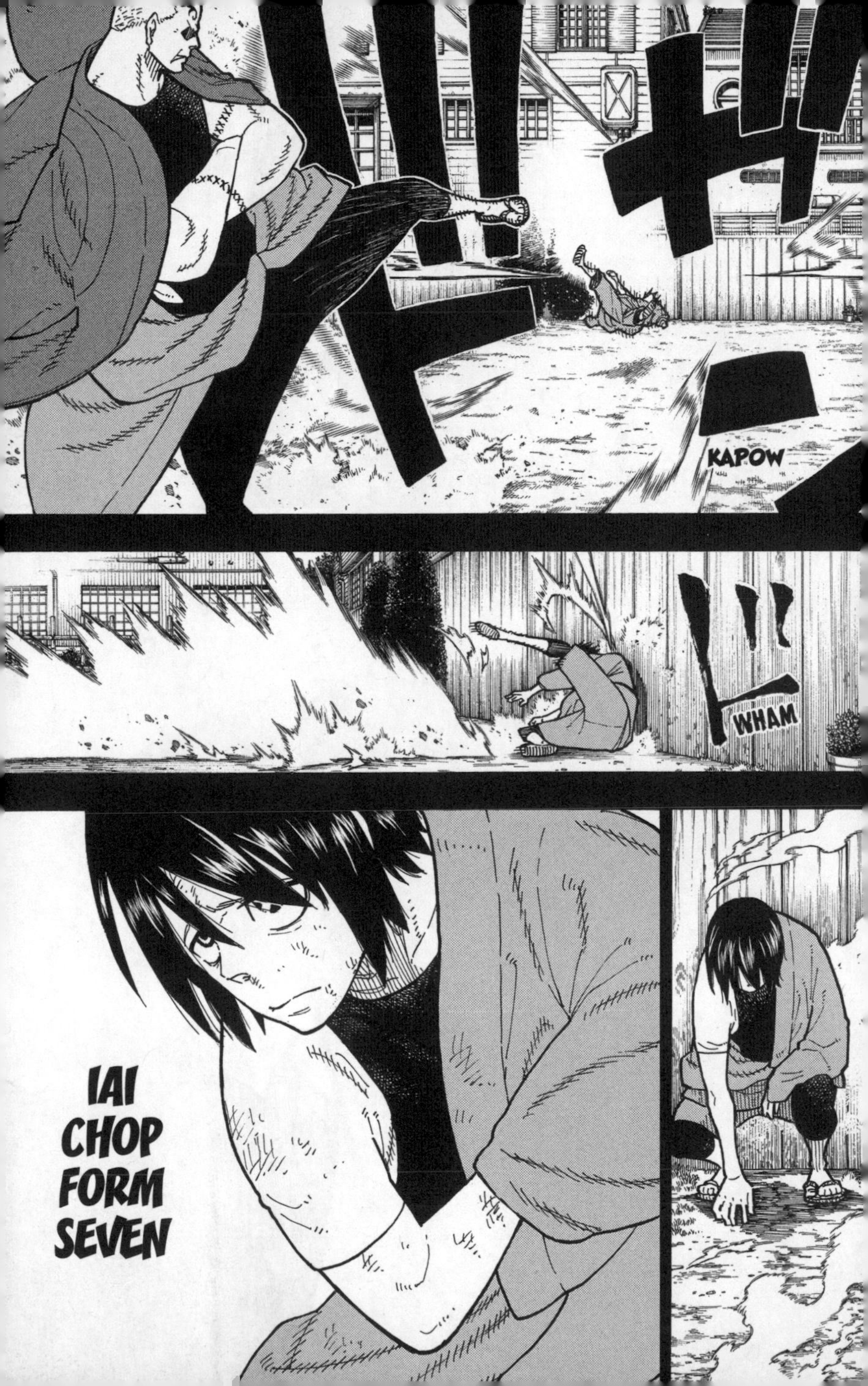
KAPOW
WHAM
IAI CHOP FORM SEVEN

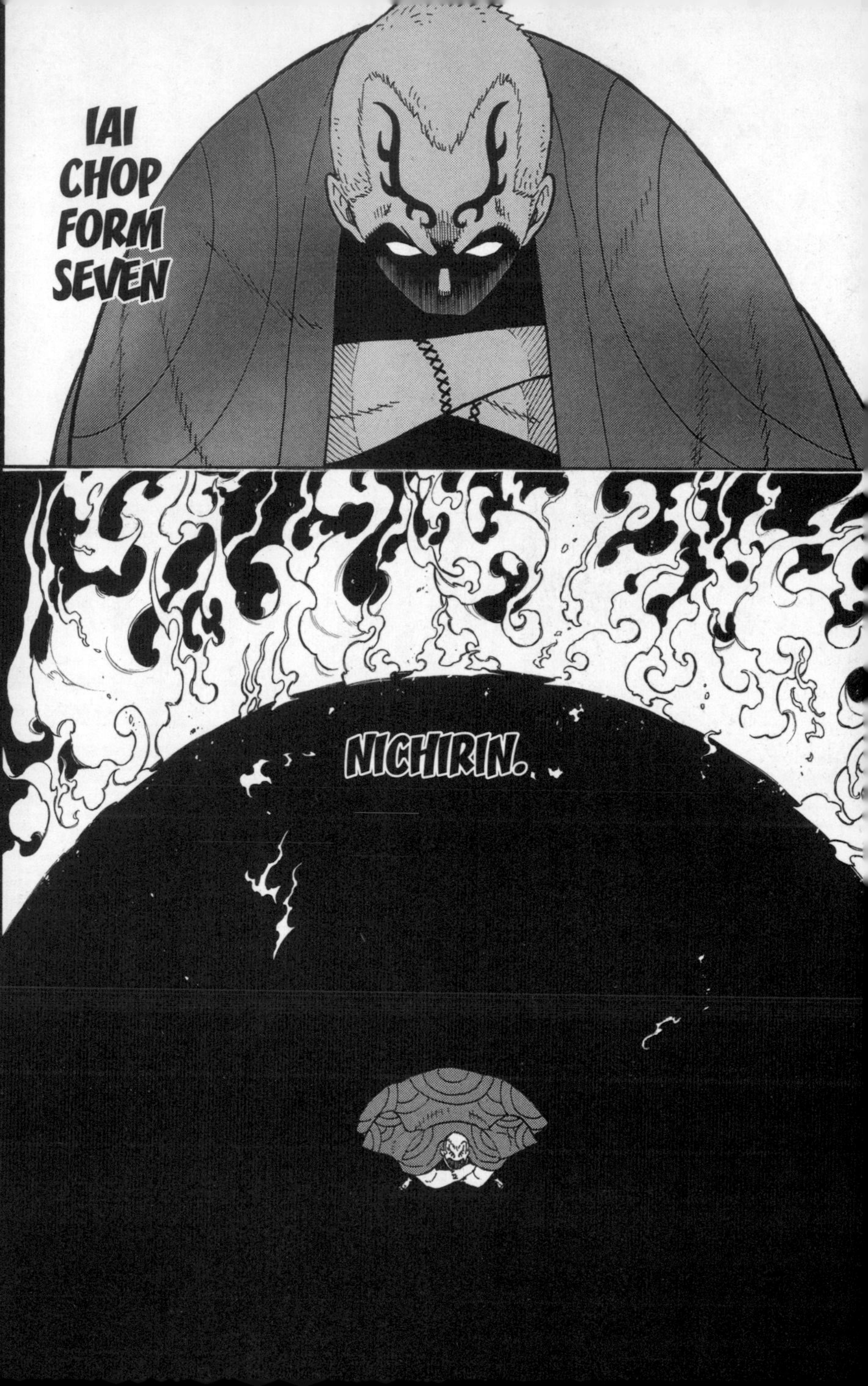
IAI CHOP FORM SEVEN
NICHIRIN.

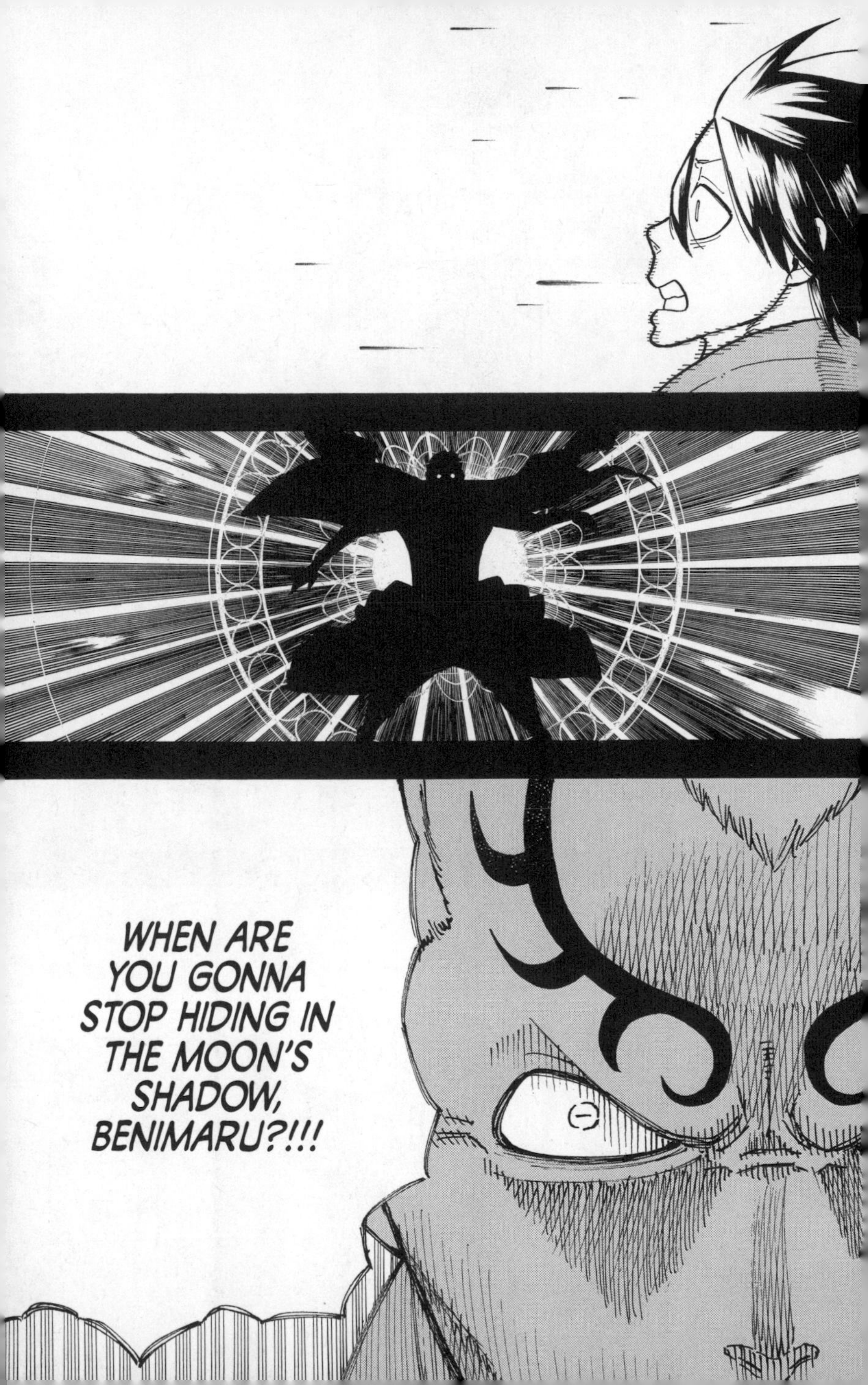
WHEN ARE YOU GONNA STOP HIDING IN THE MOON'S SHADOW, BENIMARU?!!!

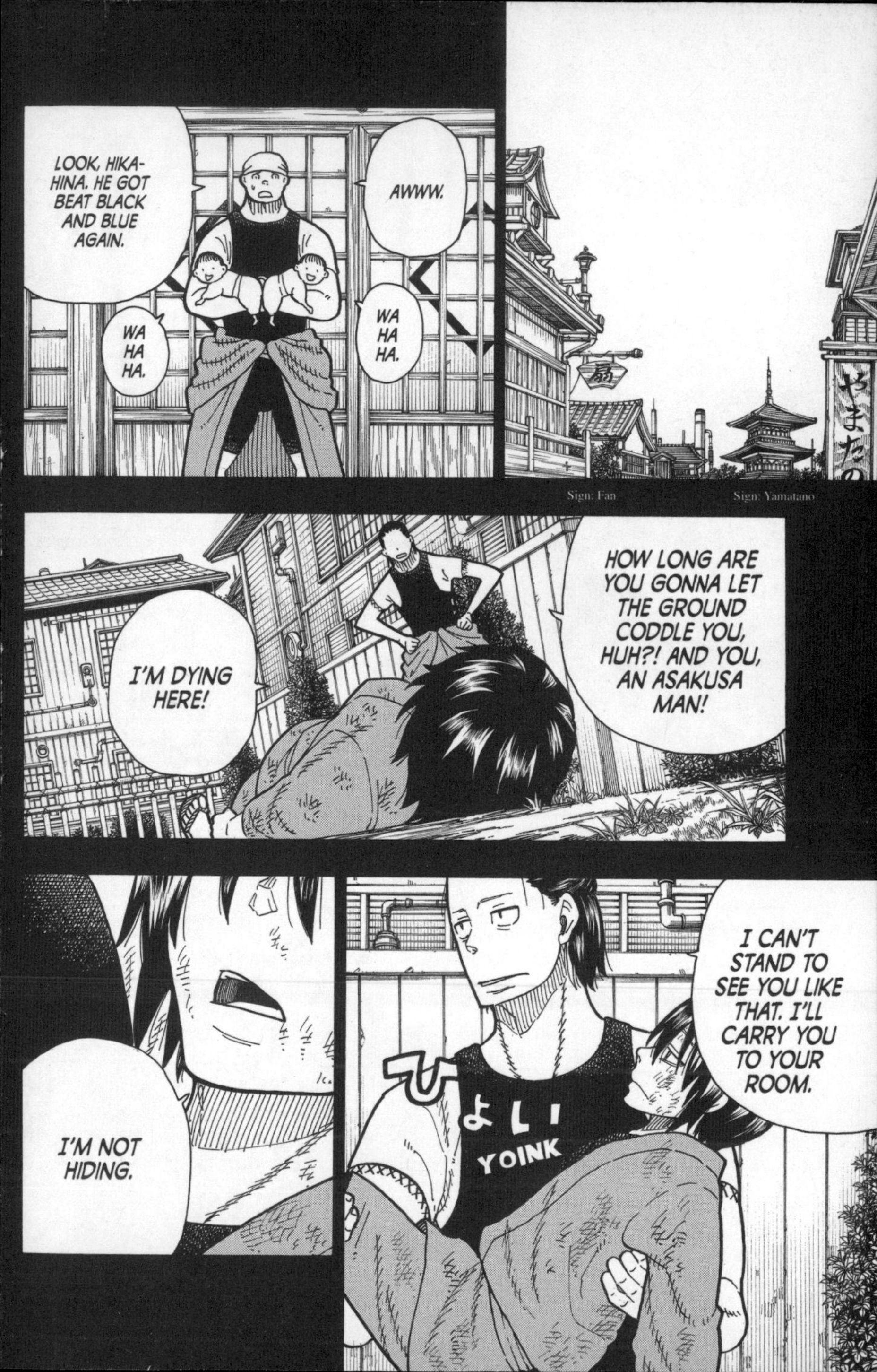
扇
やまたの
Sign: Fan
Sign: Yamatano
LOOK, HIKA-HINA. HE GOT BEAT BLACK AND BLUE AGAIN.
AWWW.
WA HA HA.
WA HA HA.
HOW LONG ARE YOU GONNA LET THE GROUND CODDLE YOU, HUH?! AND YOU, AN ASAKUSA MAN!
I'M DYING HERE!
I CAN'T STAND TO SEE YOU LIKE THAT. I'LL CARRY YOU TO YOUR ROOM.
ひょい
YOINK
I'M NOT HIDING.

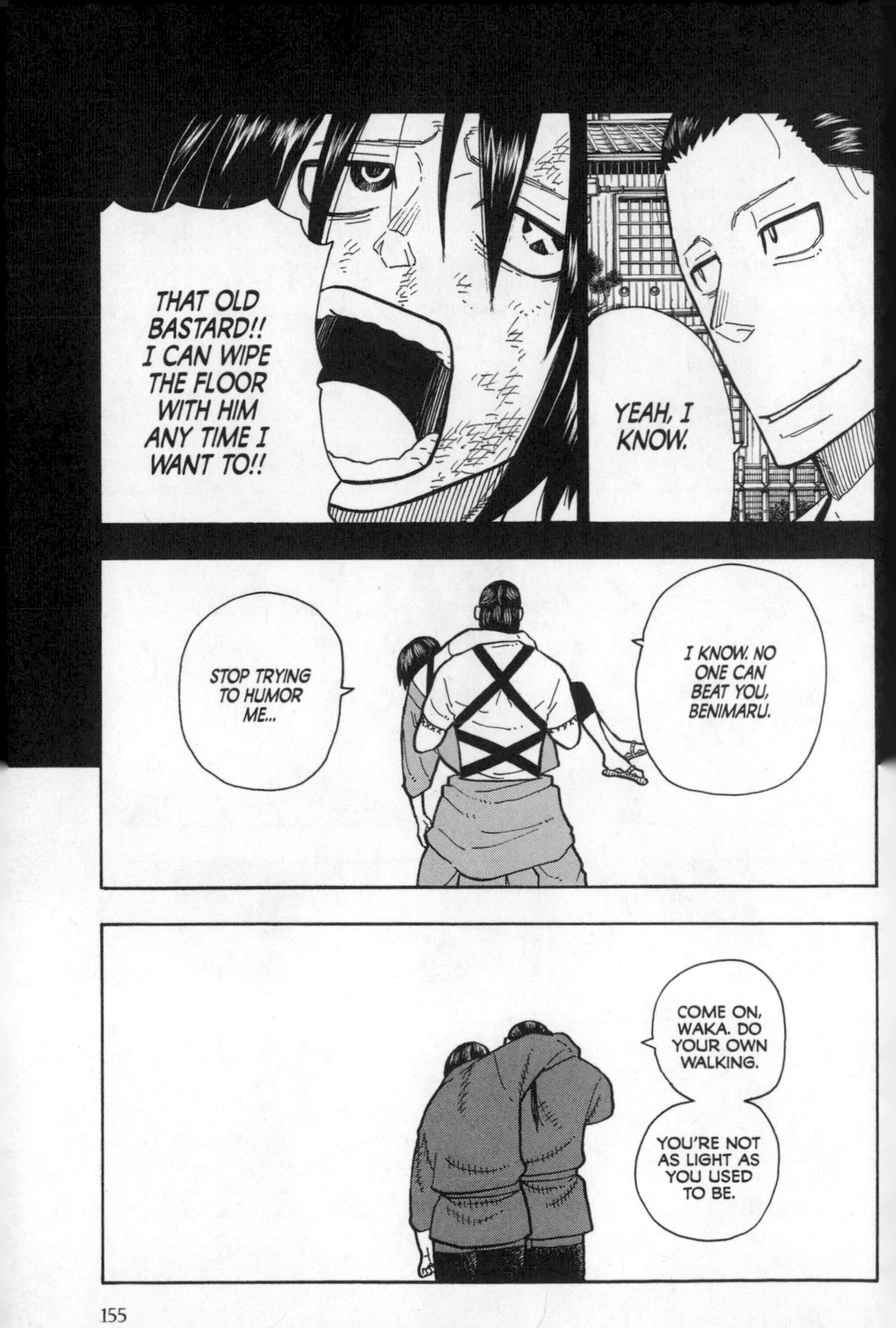
YEAH, I KNOW.
THAT OLD BASTARD!! I CAN WIPE THE FLOOR WITH HIM ANY TIME I WANT TO!!
I KNOW. NO ONE CAN BEAT YOU, BENIMARU.
STOP TRYING TO HUMOR ME...
COME ON, WAKA. DO YOUR OWN WALKING.
YOU'RE NOT AS LIGHT AS YOU USED TO BE.

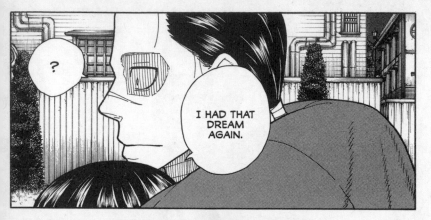

I HAD THAT DREAM AGAIN.
?
THE OLD BOSS WAS THERE, AND YOU, KONRO. AND ME.
TO ME, THOSE MEMORIES ARE FROM A VERY LONG TIME AGO.
I WAS A TINY LITTLE RUNT, BUT YOU WEREN'T ANY DIFFERENT THAN YOU ARE NOW.
MUST SEEM LIKE IT WAS JUST YESTERDAY TO YOU, HUH?
...
YEAH.

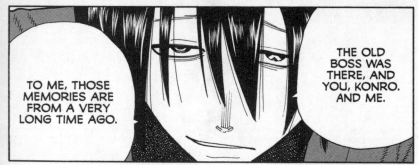

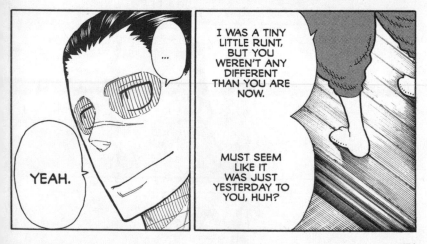

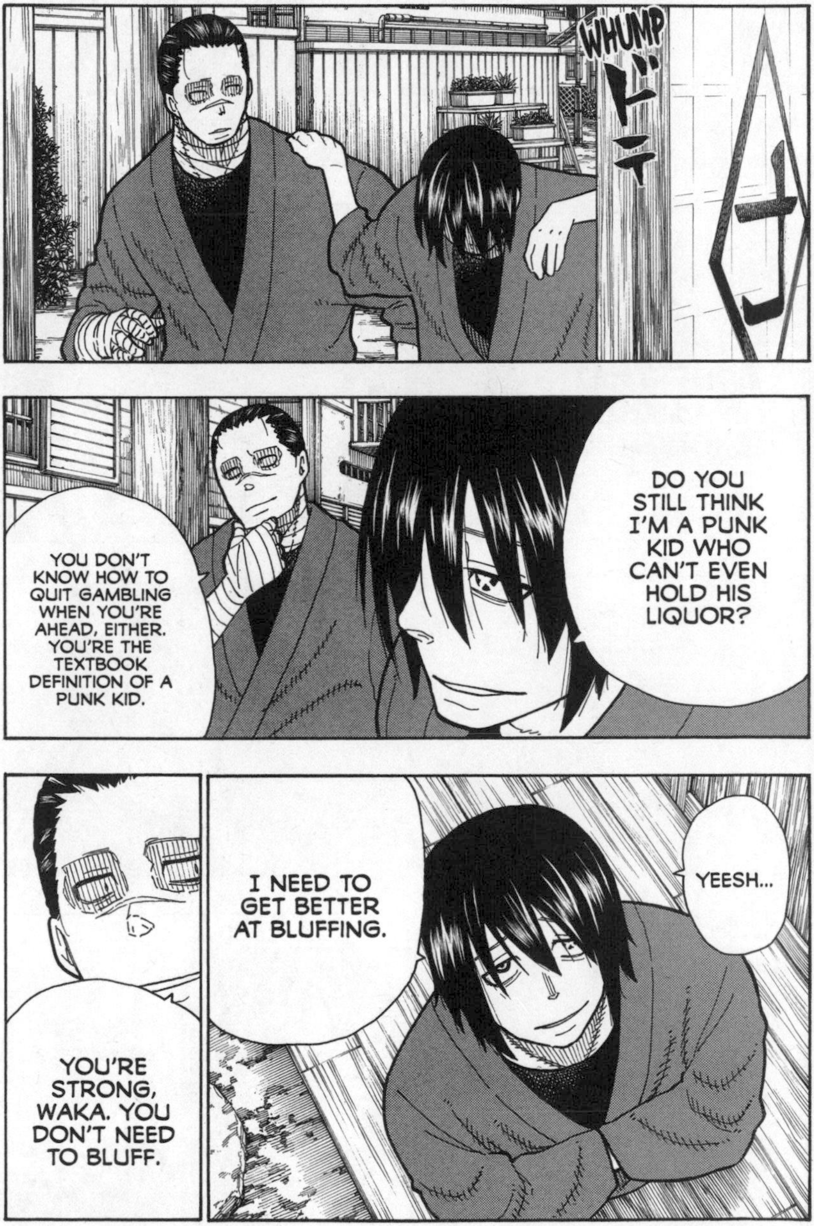
WHUMP
ドテ
DO YOU STILL THINK I'M A PUNK KID WHO CAN'T EVEN HOLD HIS LIQUOR?
YOU DON'T KNOW HOW TO QUIT GAMBLING WHEN YOU'RE AHEAD, EITHER. YOU'RE THE TEXTBOOK DEFINITION OF A PUNK KID.
YEESH...
I NEED TO GET BETTER AT BLUFFING.
YOU'RE STRONG, WAKA. YOU DON'T NEED TO BLUFF.

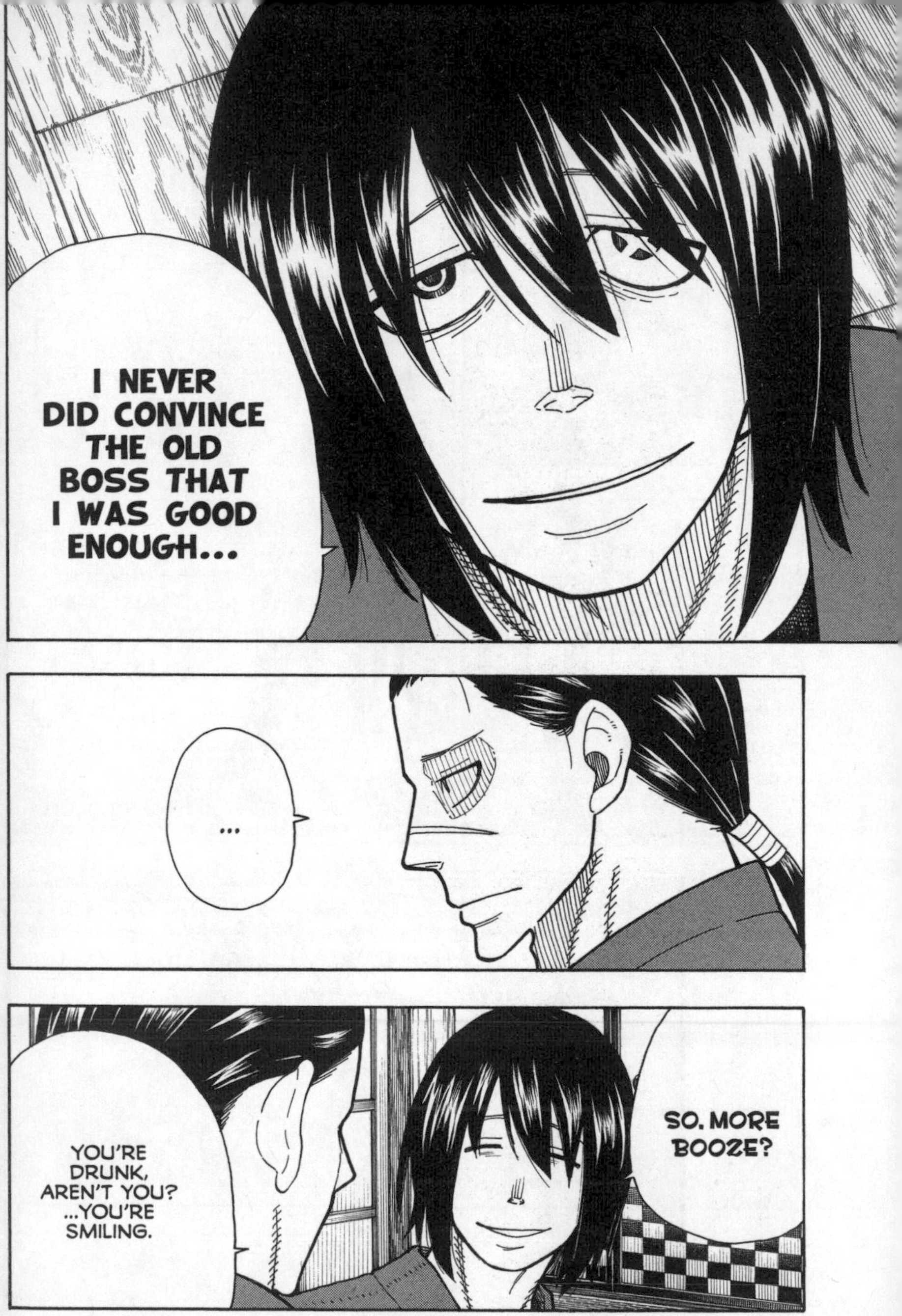
I NEVER DID CONVINCE THE OLD BOSS THAT I WAS GOOD ENOUGH...
...
SO. MORE BOOZE?
YOU'RE DRUNK, AREN'T YOU? ...YOU'RE SMILING.

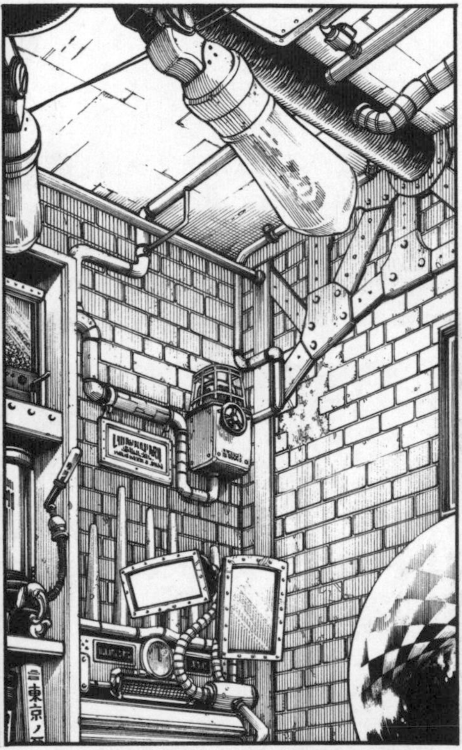
Sign: Tokyo
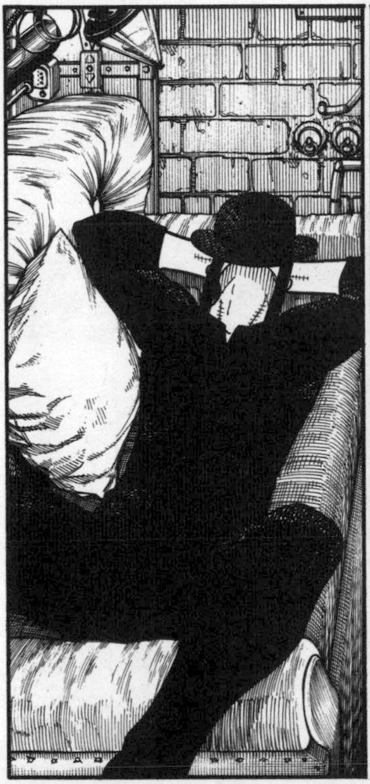
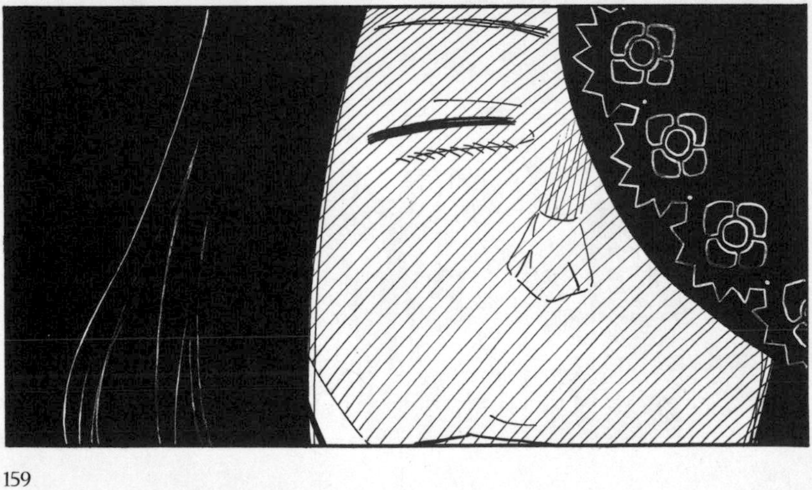

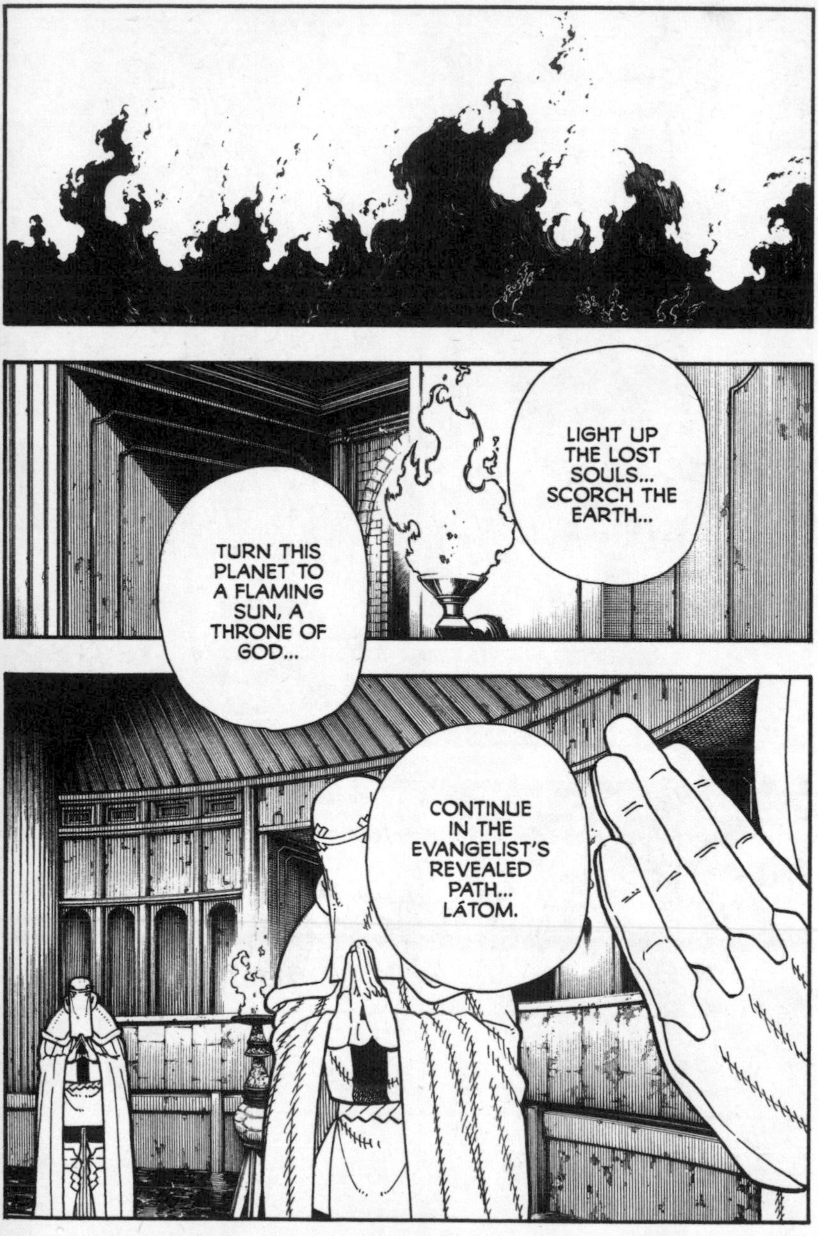
LIGHT UP THE LOST SOULS... SCORCH THE EARTH...
TURN THIS PLANET TO A FLAMING SUN, A THRONE OF GOD...
CONTINUE IN THE EVANGELIST'S REVEALED PATH... LÁTOM.

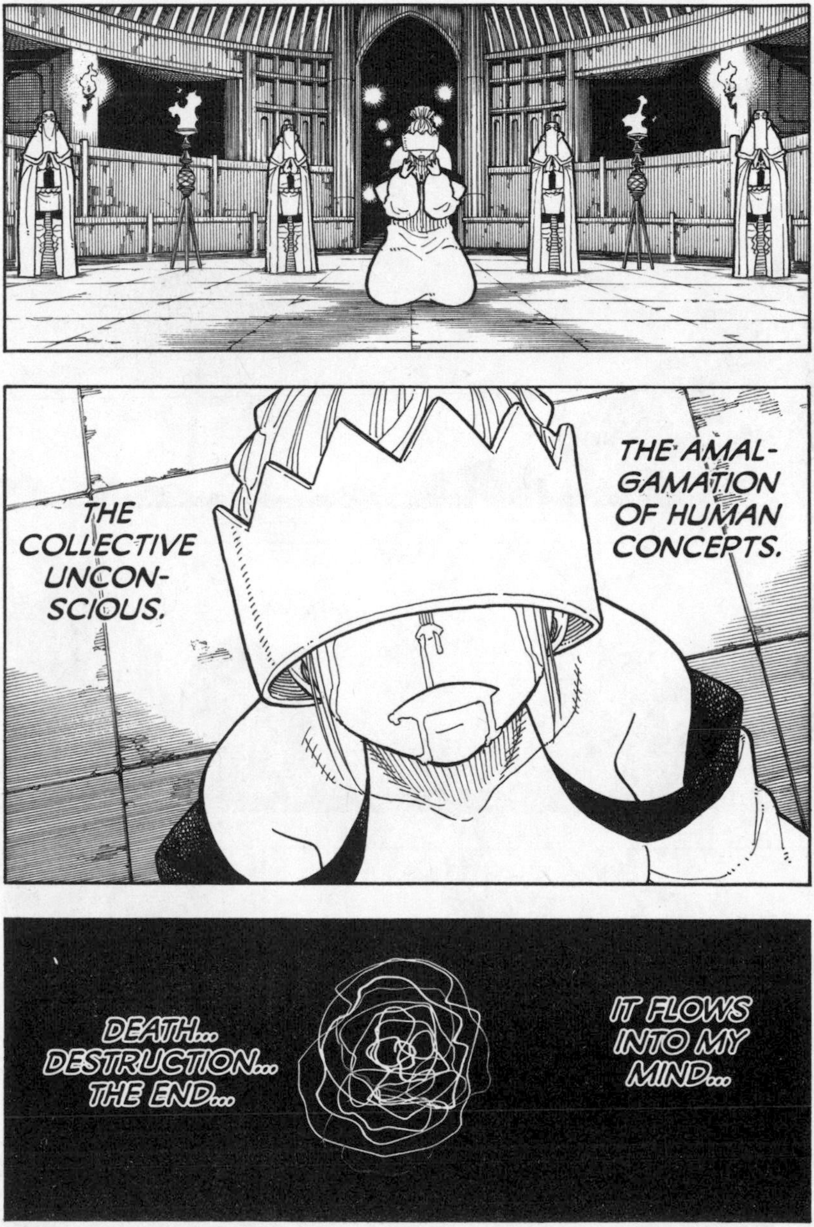
THE AMAL-GAMATION OF HUMAN CONCEPTS.
THE COLLECTIVE UNCON-SCIOUS.
IT FLOWS INTO MY MIND...
DEATH... DESTRUCTION... THE END...

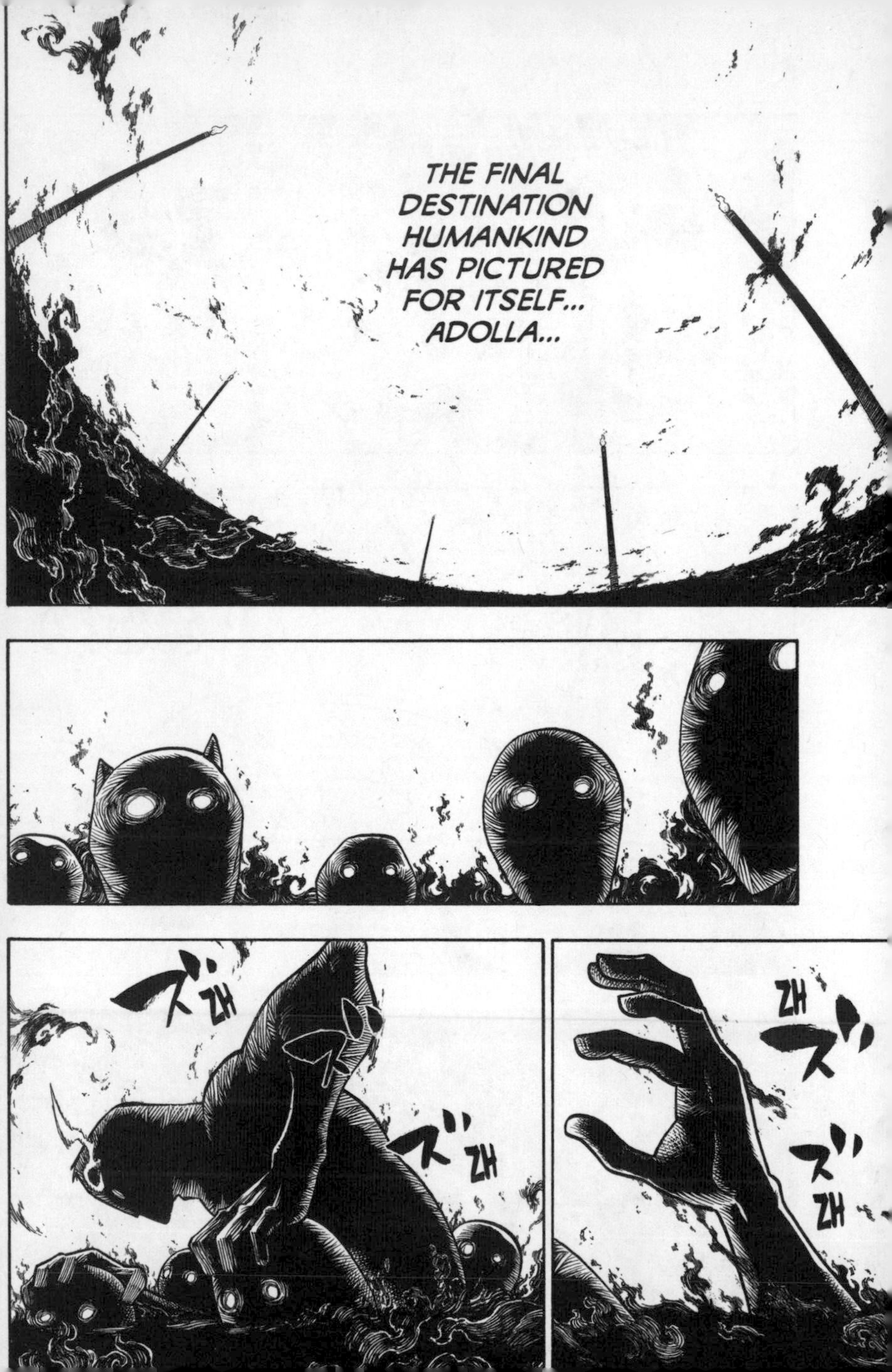
THE FINAL DESTINATION HUMANKIND HAS PICTURED FOR ITSELF... ADOLLA...
ZH ズ
ズ ZH
ズ ZH
ズ ZH

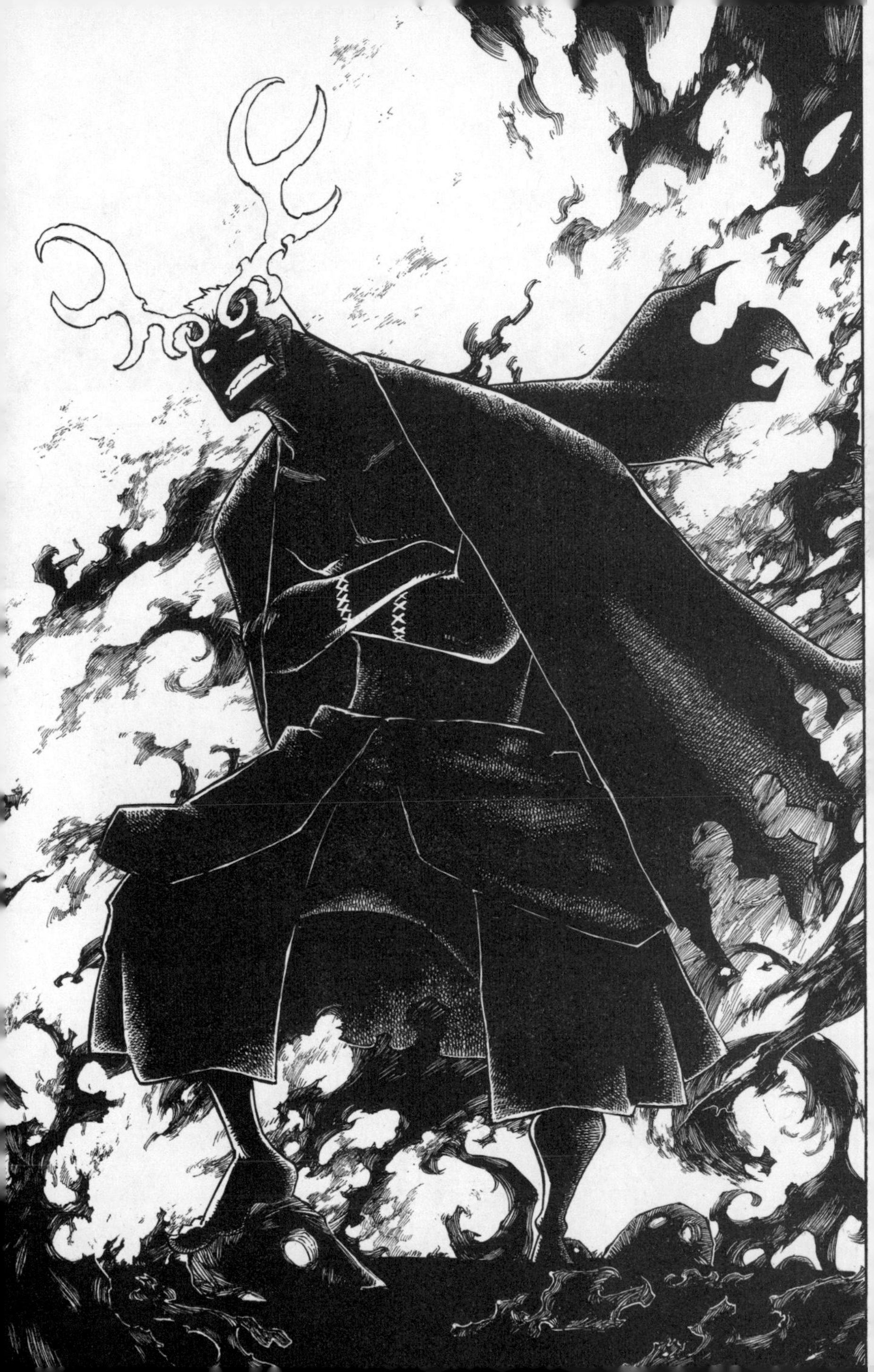

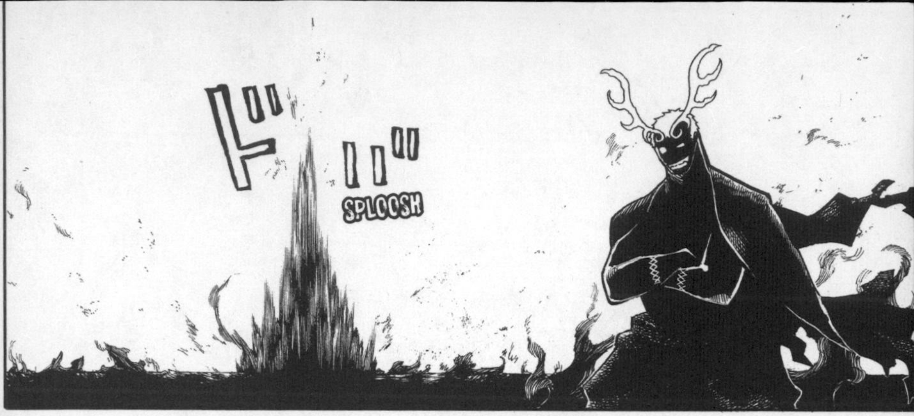
SPLOOSH
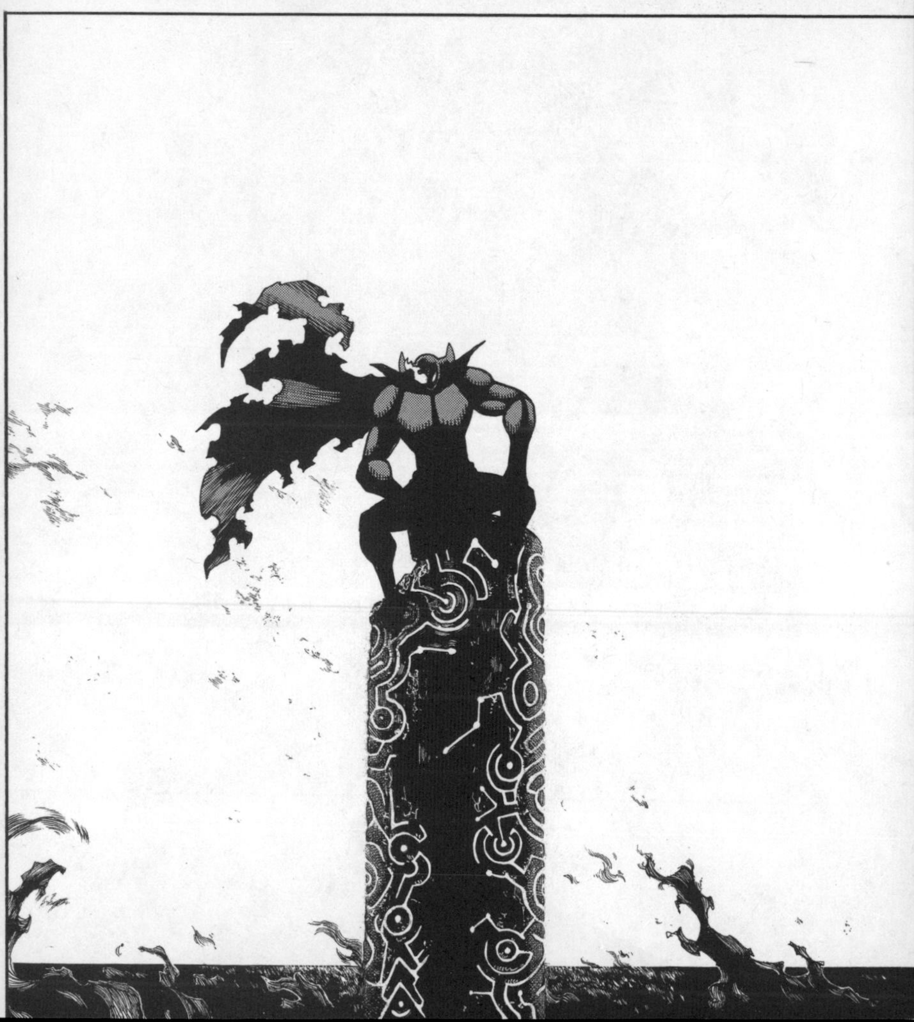

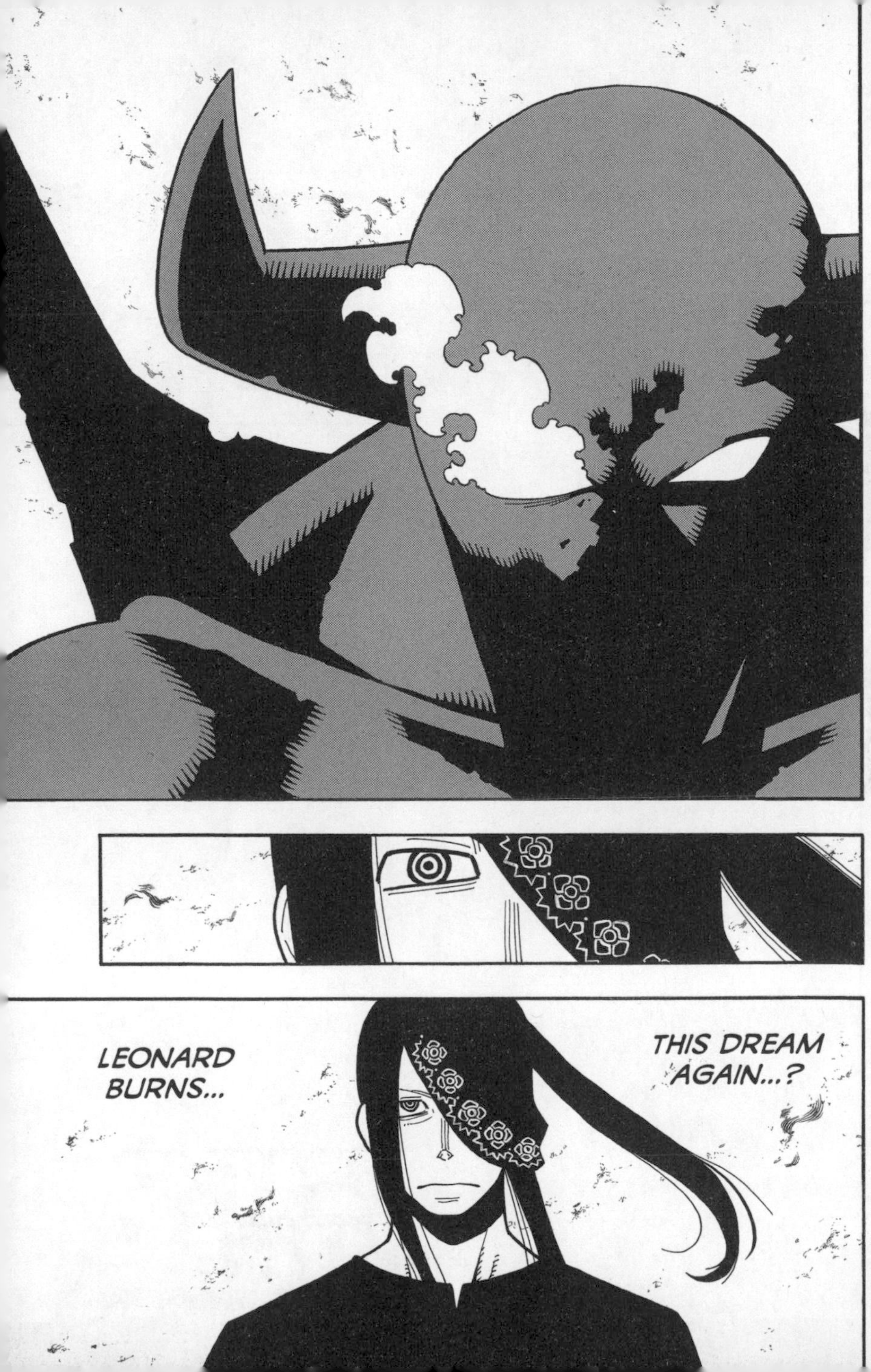
THIS DREAM AGAIN...?
LEONARD BURNS...

FIRE FORCE

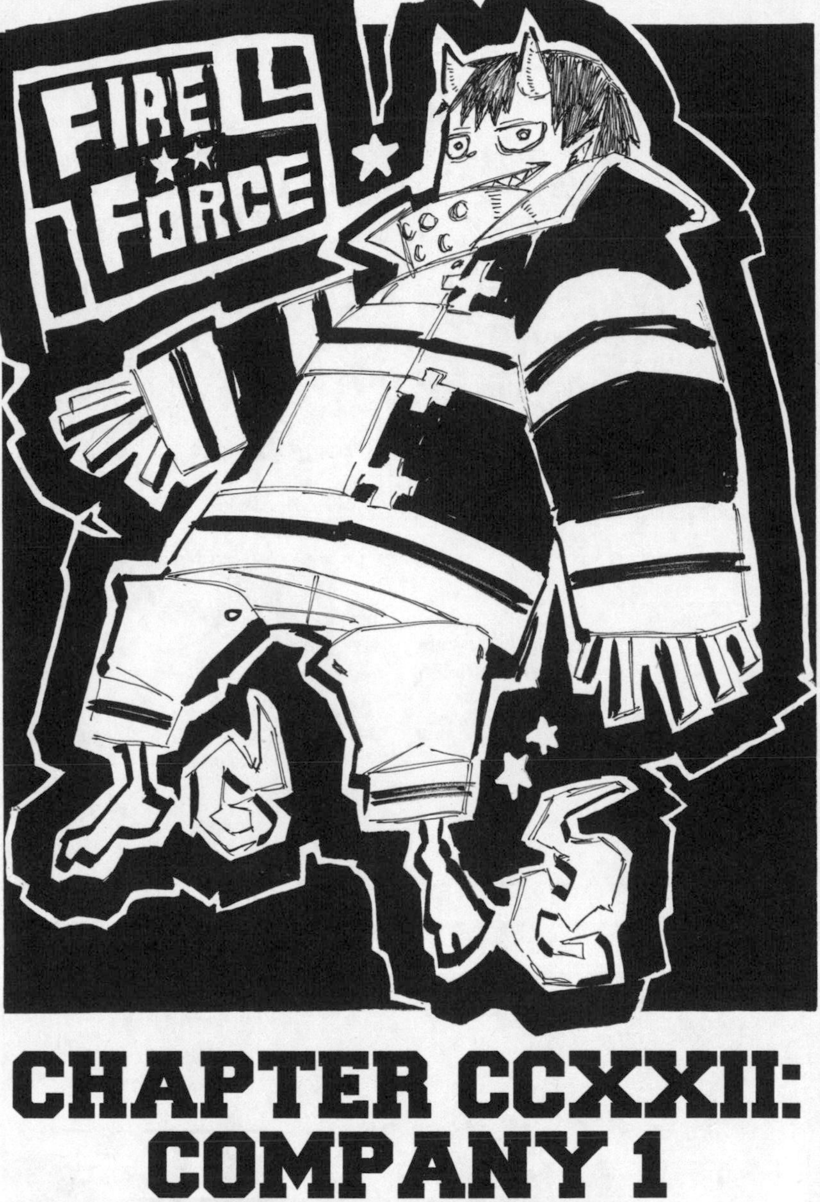
FIRE FORCE

CHAPTER CCXXII: COMPANY 1 RETURNS

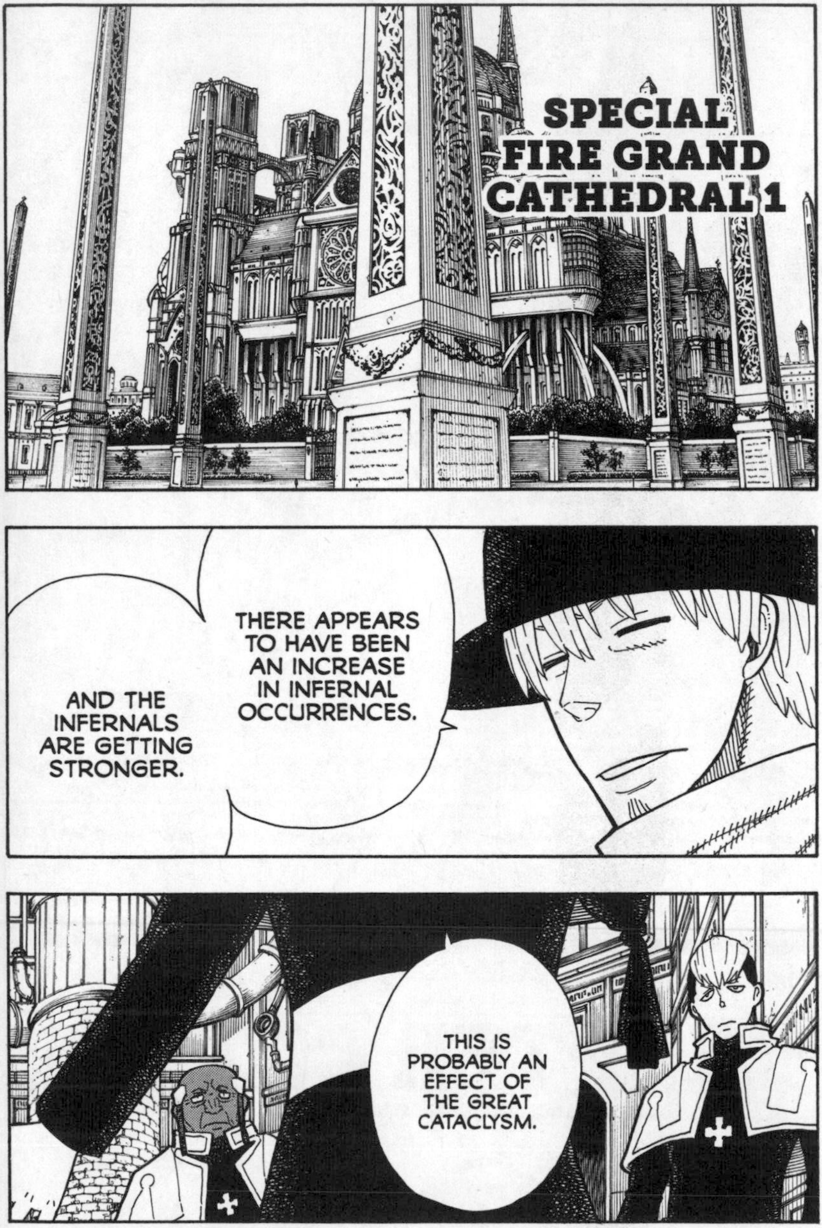
SPECIAL FIRE GRAND CATHEDRAL 1
THERE APPEARS TO HAVE BEEN AN INCREASE IN INFERNAL OCCURRENCES.
AND THE INFERNALS ARE GETTING STRONGER.
THIS IS PROBABLY AN EFFECT OF THE GREAT CATACLYSM.

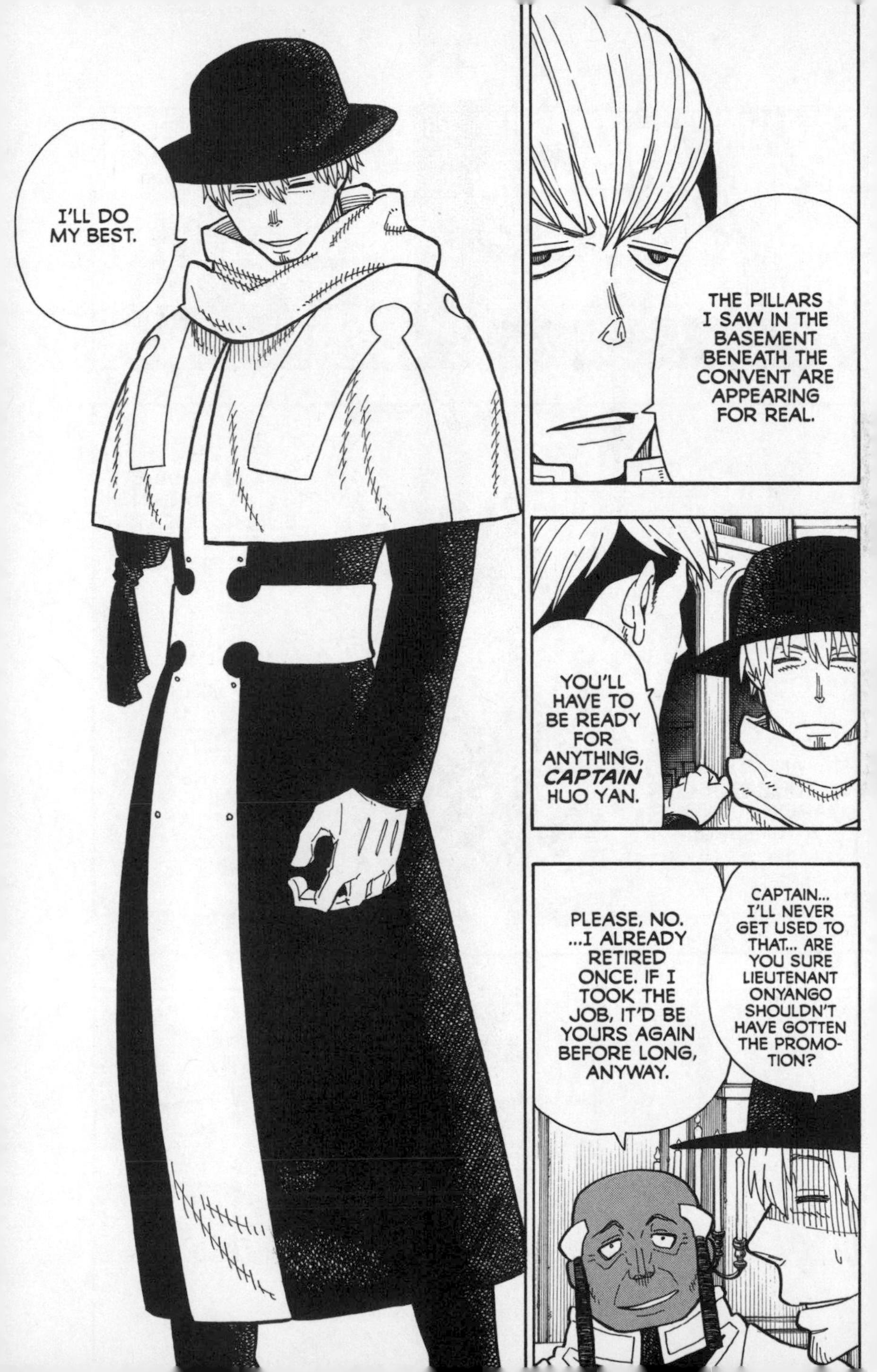
THE PILLARS I SAW IN THE BASEMENT BENEATH THE CONVENT ARE APPEARING FOR REAL.
YOU'LL HAVE TO BE READY FOR ANYTHING, *CAPTAIN* HUO YAN.
CAPTAIN... I'LL NEVER GET USED TO THAT... ARE YOU SURE LIEUTENANT ONYANGO SHOULDN'T HAVE GOTTEN THE PROMOTION?
PLEASE, NO. ...I ALREADY RETIRED ONCE. IF I TOOK THE JOB, IT'D BE YOURS AGAIN BEFORE LONG, ANYWAY.
I'LL DO MY BEST.

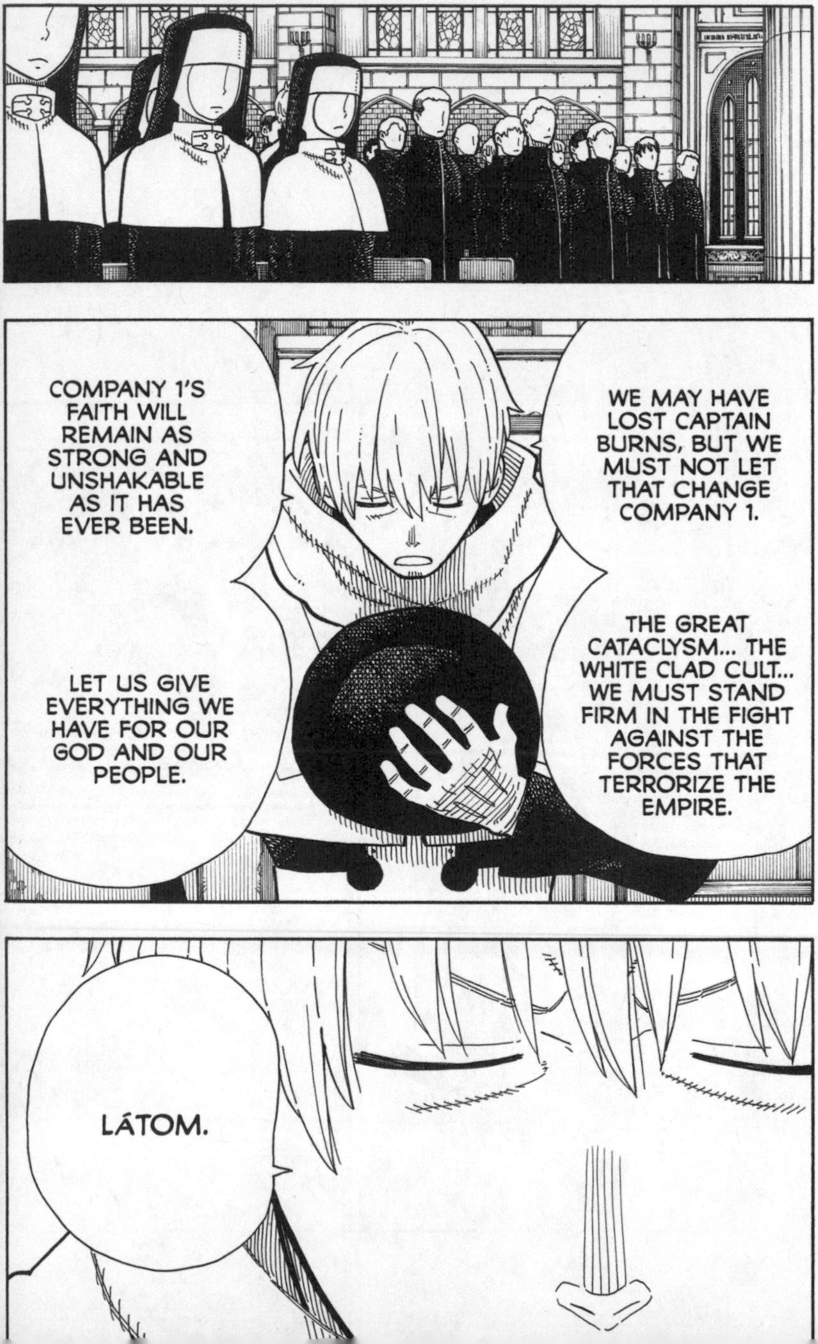
WE MAY HAVE LOST CAPTAIN BURNS, BUT WE MUST NOT LET THAT CHANGE COMPANY 1.
COMPANY 1'S FAITH WILL REMAIN AS STRONG AND UNSHAKABLE AS IT HAS EVER BEEN.
THE GREAT CATACLYSM... THE WHITE CLAD CULT... WE MUST STAND FIRM IN THE FIGHT AGAINST THE FORCES THAT TERRORIZE THE EMPIRE.
LET US GIVE EVERYTHING WE HAVE FOR OUR GOD AND OUR PEOPLE.
LÁTOM.

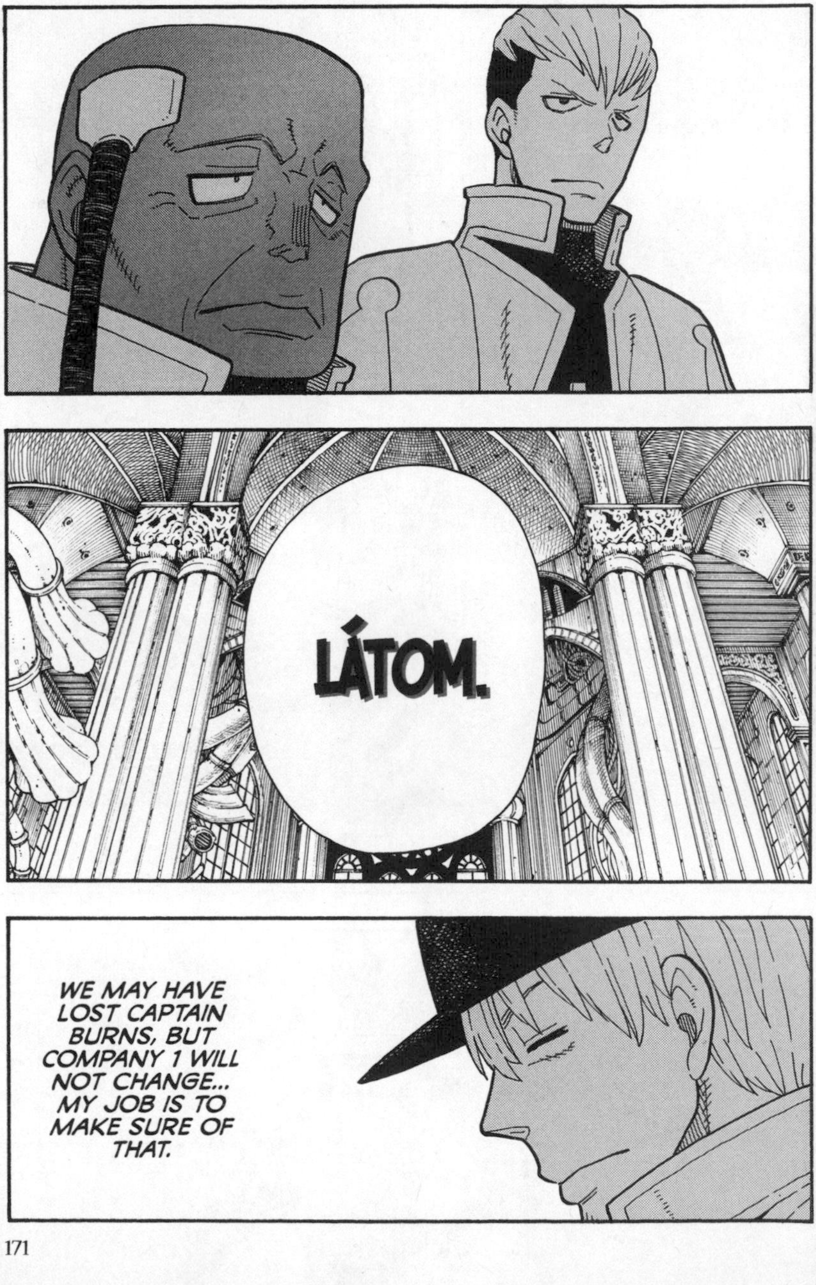
LÁTOM.
WE MAY HAVE LOST CAPTAIN BURNS, BUT COMPANY 1 WILL NOT CHANGE... MY JOB IS TO MAKE SURE OF THAT.

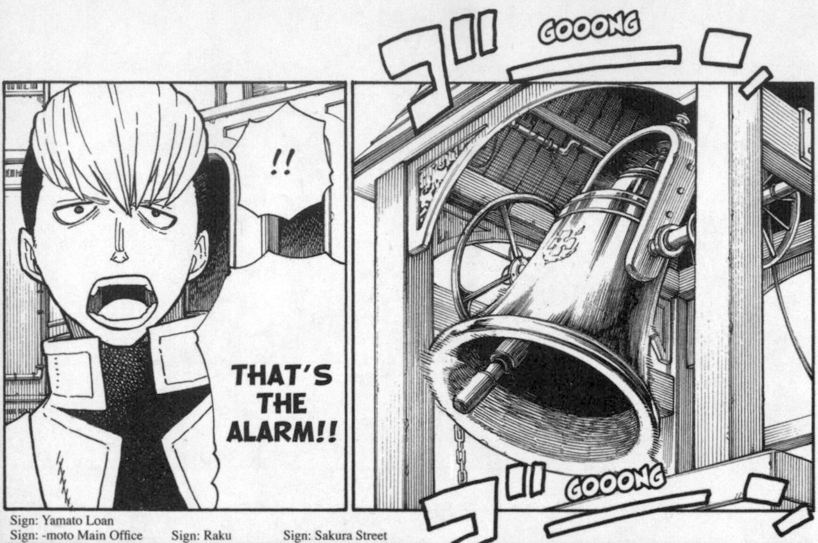
GOOONG
GOOONG
!!
THAT'S THE ALARM!!

Sign: Yamato Loan
Sign: -moto Main Office
Sign: Raku
Sign: Sakura Street

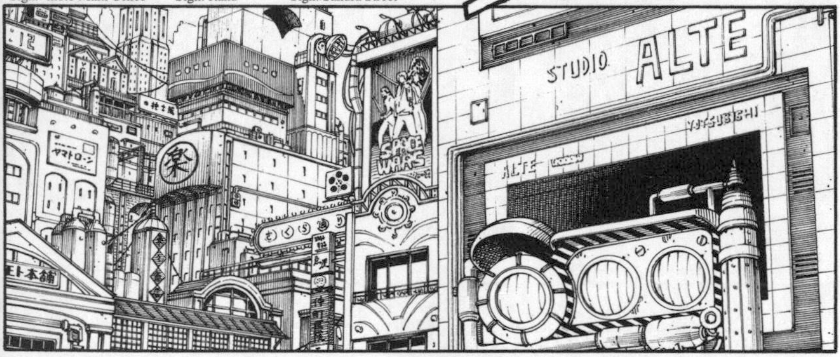
STUDIO ALTE
SPACE WARS

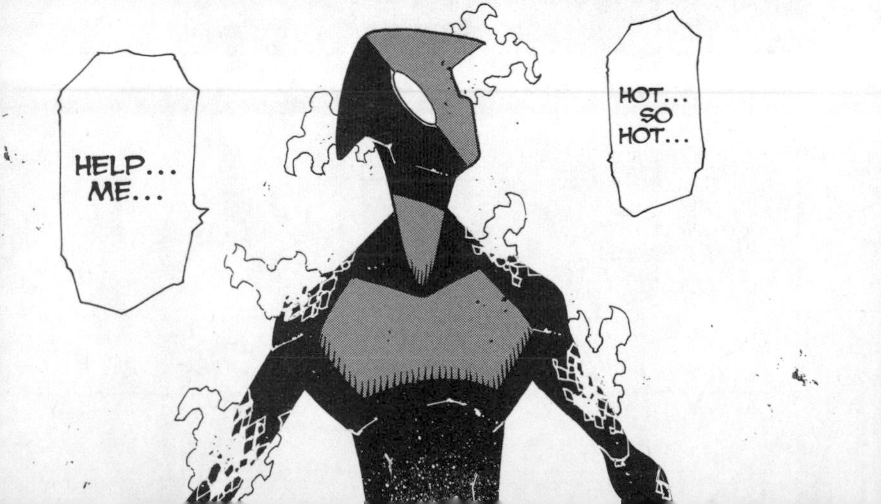
HOT... SO HOT...
HELP... ME...

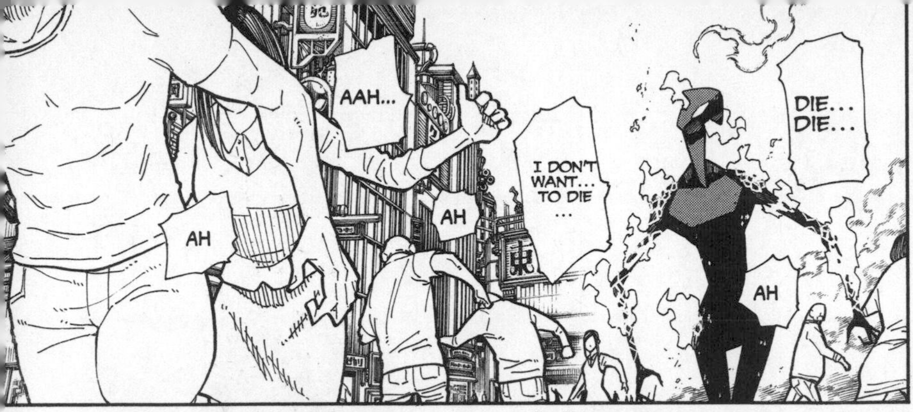
DIE... DIE...
AH
I DON'T WANT... TO DIE ...
AH
AAH...
AH

Sign: Kaen Sign: East

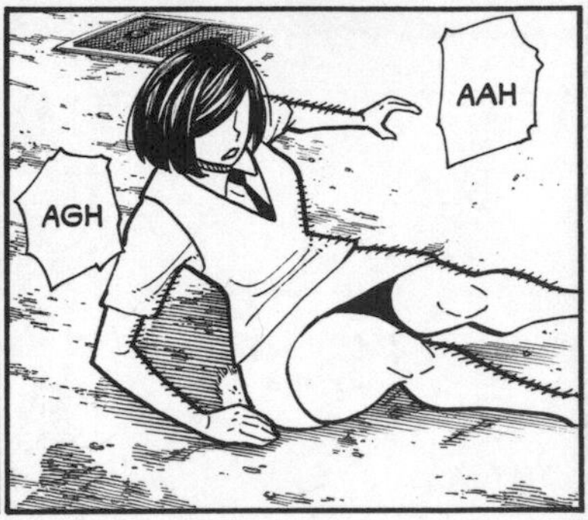
AAH
AGH

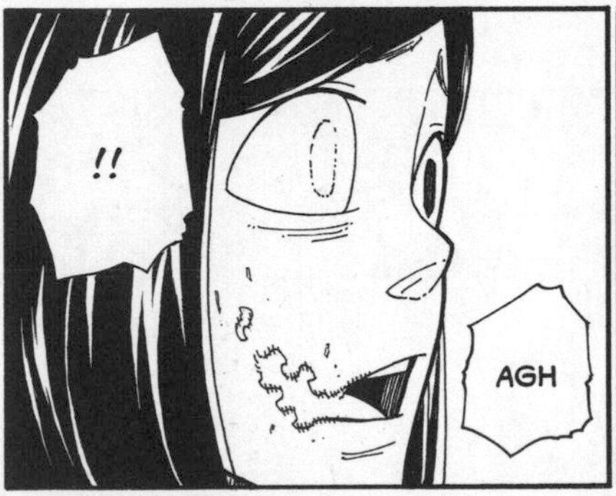
!!
AGH

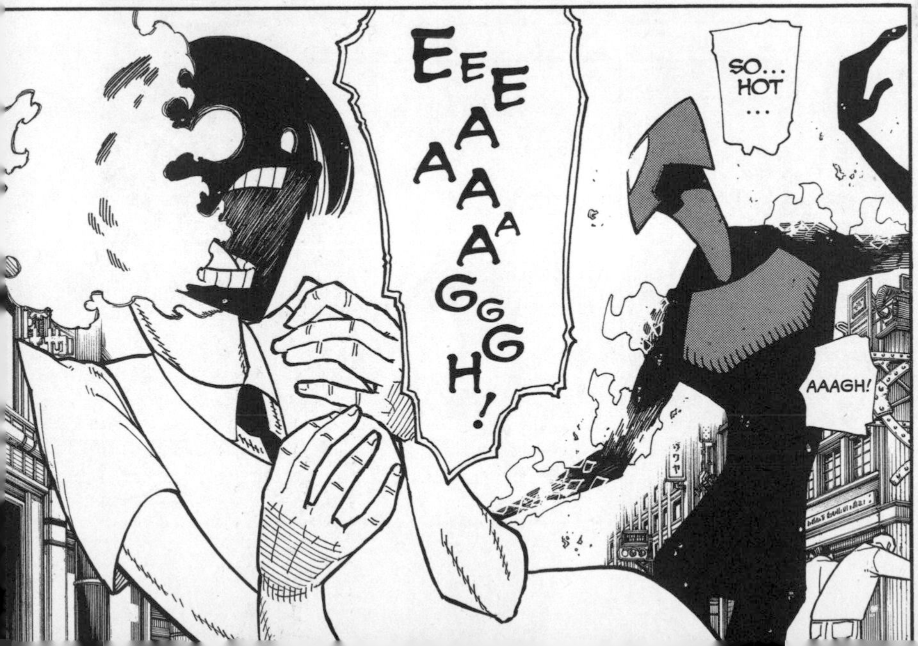
SO... HOT ...
AAAGH!
EEEAAAAAGGGH!

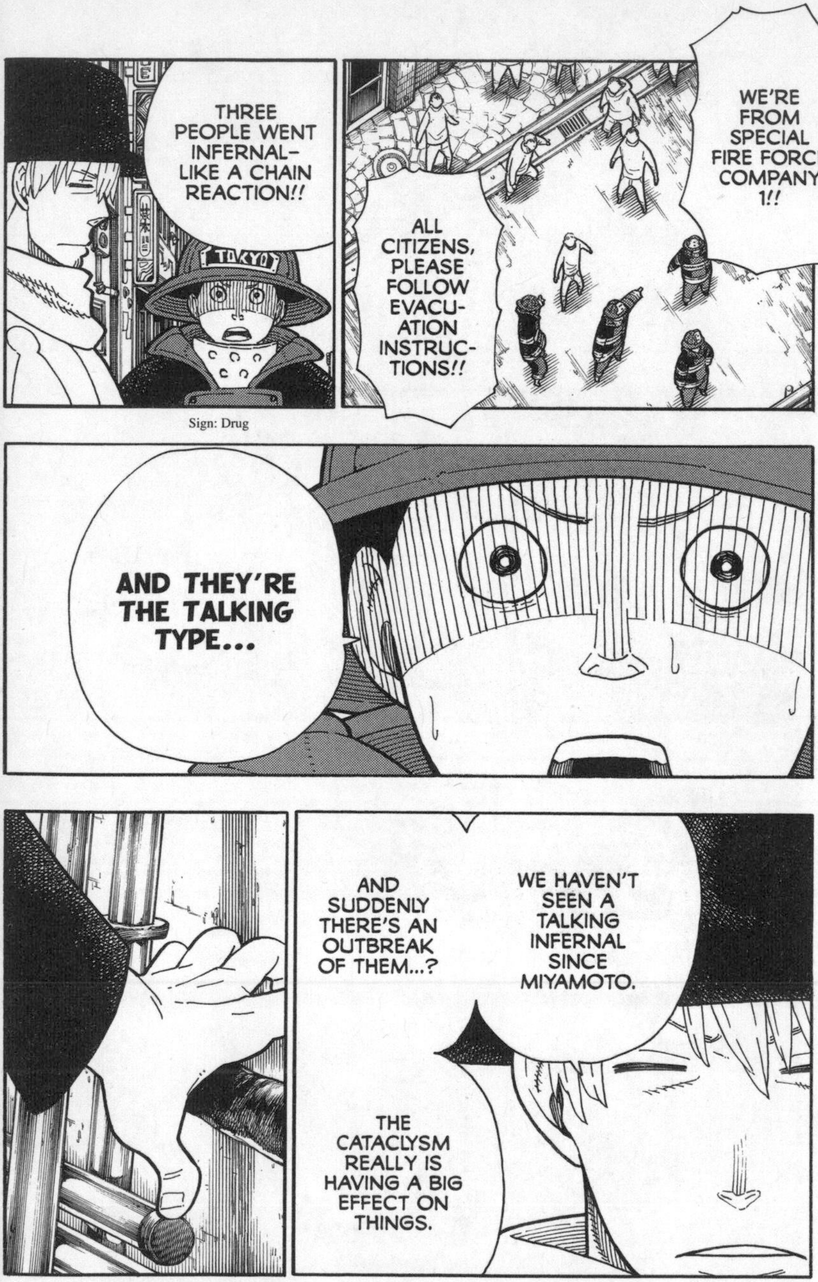
WE'RE FROM SPECIAL FIRE FORCE COMPANY 1!!
ALL CITIZENS, PLEASE FOLLOW EVACUATION INSTRUCTIONS!!
THREE PEOPLE WENT INFERNAL–LIKE A CHAIN REACTION!!
Sign: Drug
AND THEY'RE THE TALKING TYPE...
WE HAVEN'T SEEN A TALKING INFERNAL SINCE MIYAMOTO.
AND SUDDENLY THERE'S AN OUTBREAK OF THEM...?
THE CATACLYSM REALLY IS HAVING A BIG EFFECT ON THINGS.

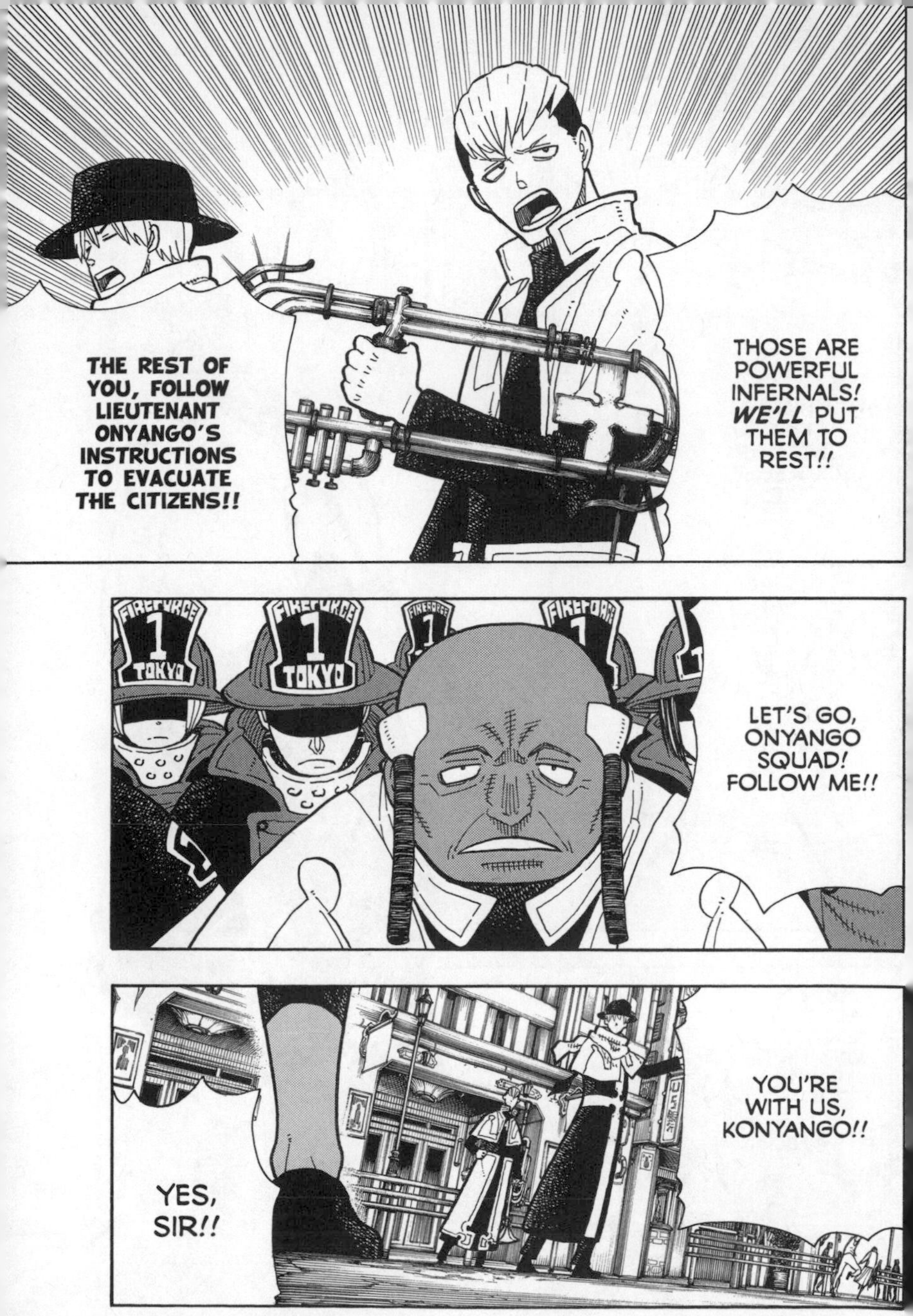
THOSE ARE POWERFUL INFERNALS! *WE'LL* PUT THEM TO REST!!
THE REST OF YOU, FOLLOW LIEUTENANT ONYANGO'S INSTRUCTIONS TO EVACUATE THE CITIZENS!!
FIRE FORCE 1 TOKYO
LET'S GO, ONYANGO SQUAD! FOLLOW ME!!
YOU'RE WITH US, KONYANGO!!
YES, SIR!!

Sign: U5 Bank

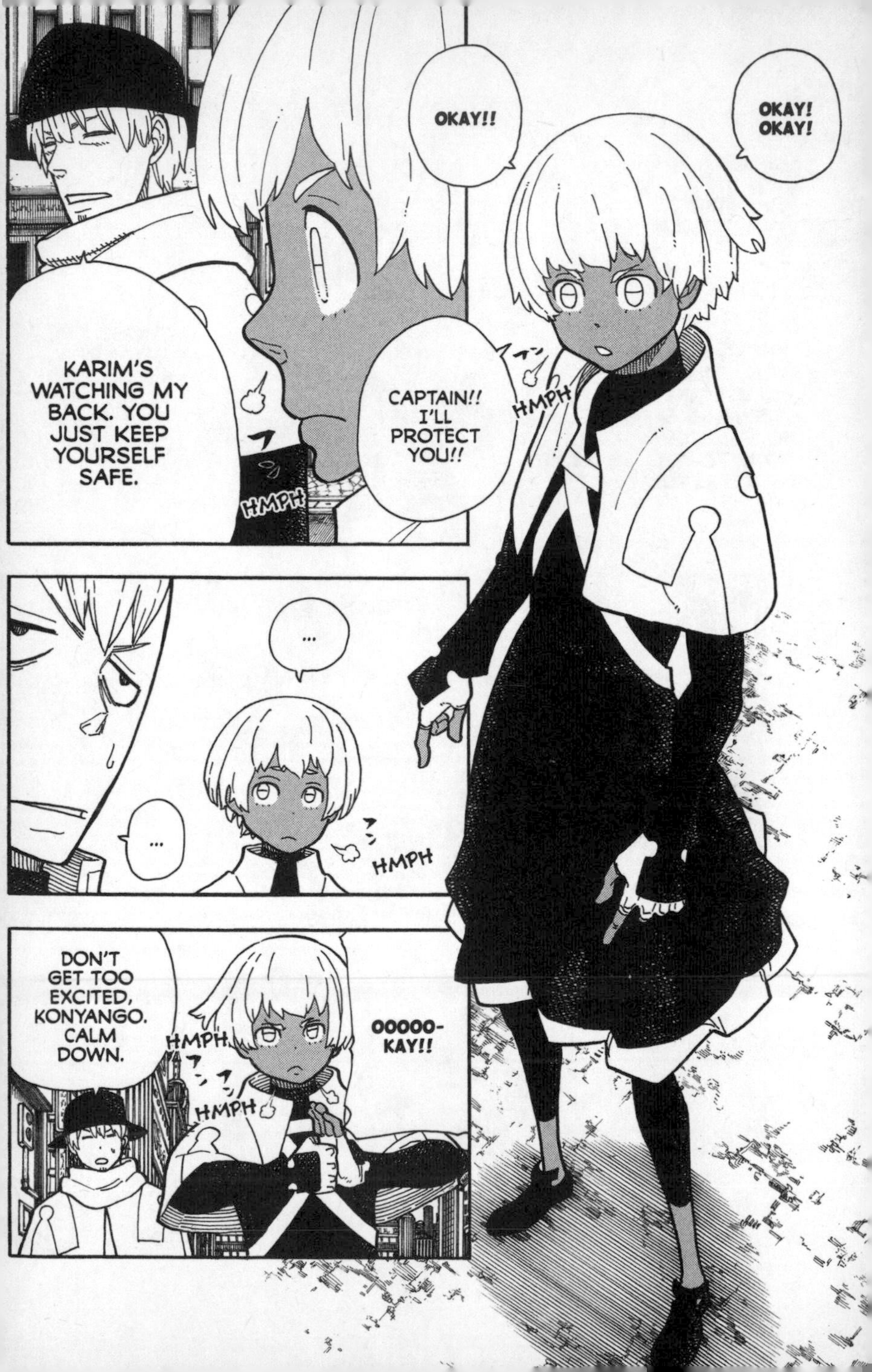
OKAY! OKAY!
OKAY!!
HMPH
CAPTAIN!! I'LL PROTECT YOU!!
KARIM'S WATCHING MY BACK. YOU JUST KEEP YOURSELF SAFE.
HMPH
...
HMPH
...
OOOOO-KAY!!
HMPH
HMPH
DON'T GET TOO EXCITED, KONYANGO. CALM DOWN.

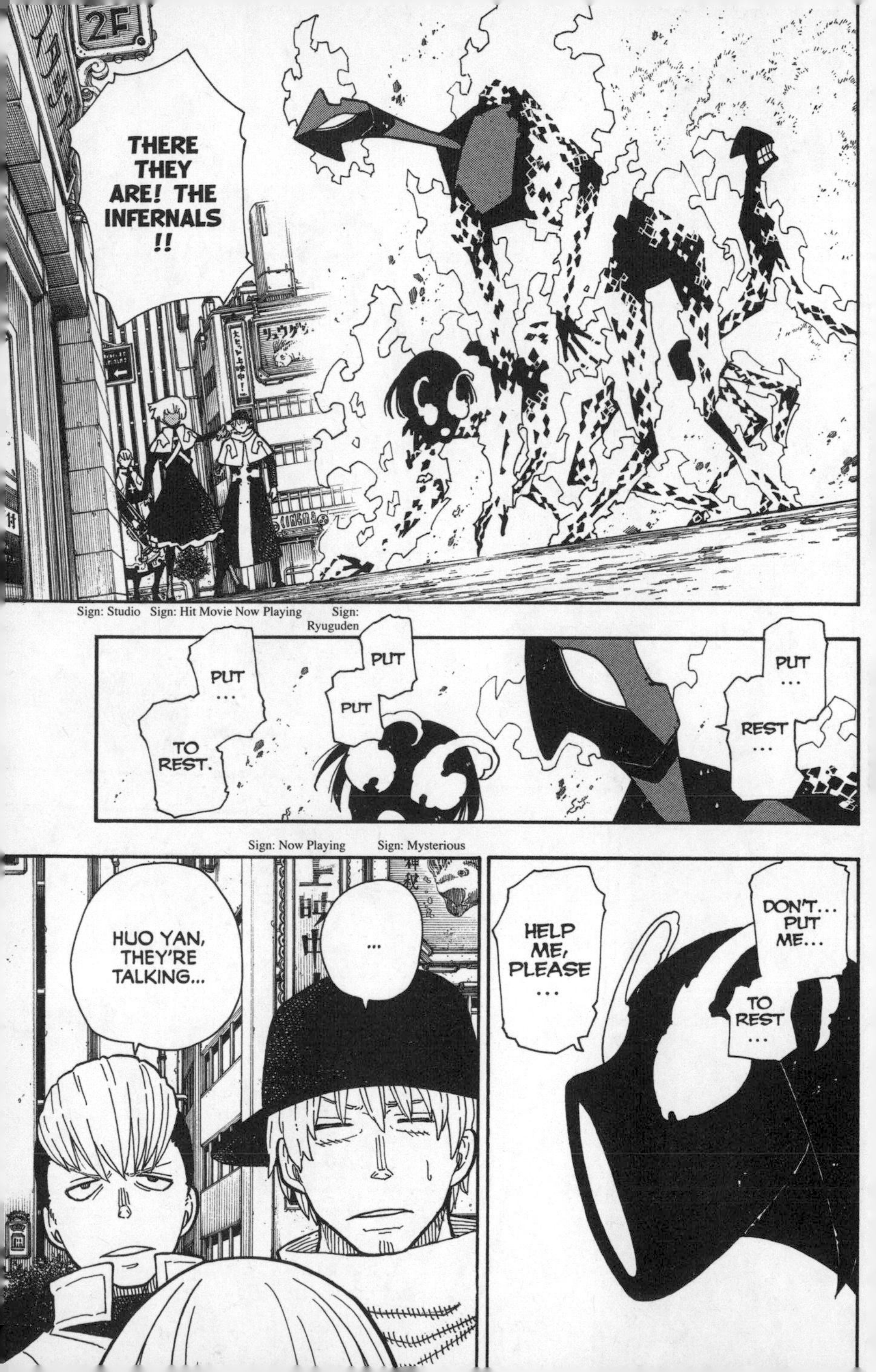
THERE THEY ARE! THE INFERNALS!!
Sign: Studio Sign: Hit Movie Now Playing Sign: Ryuguden
PUT... REST...
PUT PUT
PUT... TO REST.
Sign: Now Playing Sign: Mysterious
DON'T... PUT ME... TO REST...
HELP ME, PLEASE...
HUO YAN, THEY'RE TALKING...
...

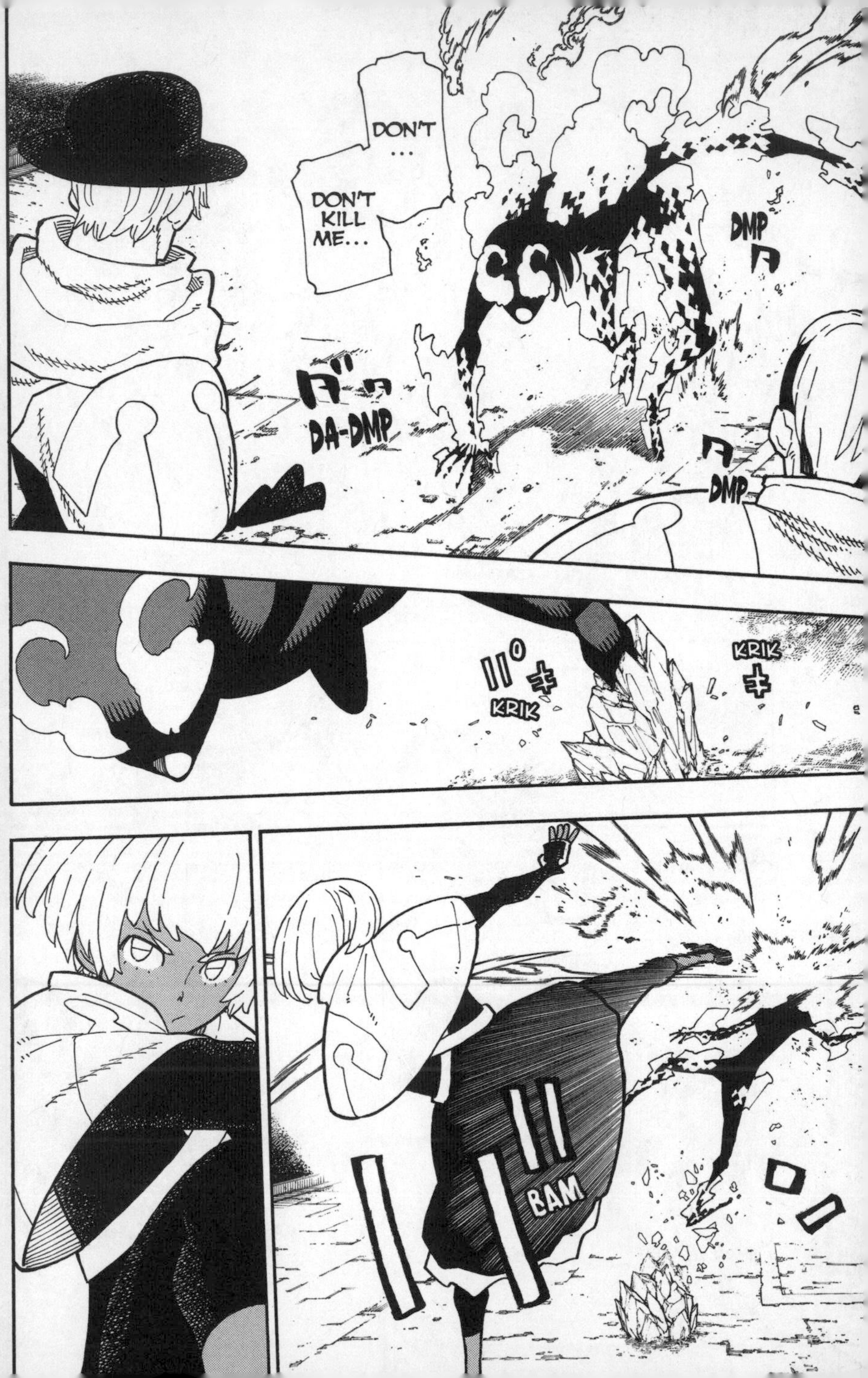
DON'T ...
DON'T KILL ME...
DMP
DA-DMP
DMP
KRIK
KRIK
BAM

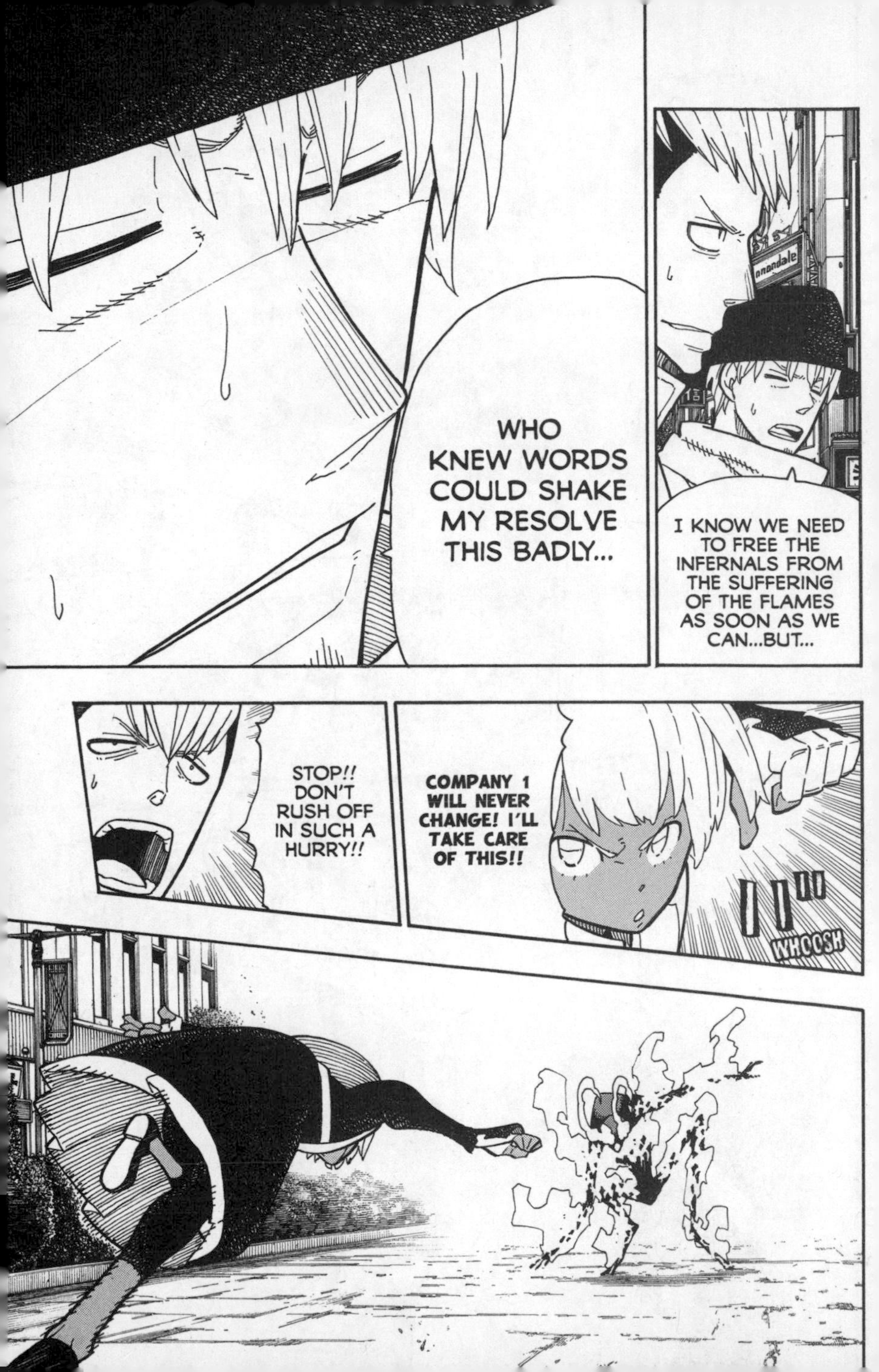
I KNOW WE NEED TO FREE THE INFERNALS FROM THE SUFFERING OF THE FLAMES AS SOON AS WE CAN...BUT...
WHO KNEW WORDS COULD SHAKE MY RESOLVE THIS BADLY...
COMPANY 1 WILL NEVER CHANGE! I'LL TAKE CARE OF THIS!!
WHOOSH
STOP!! DON'T RUSH OFF IN SUCH A HURRY!!

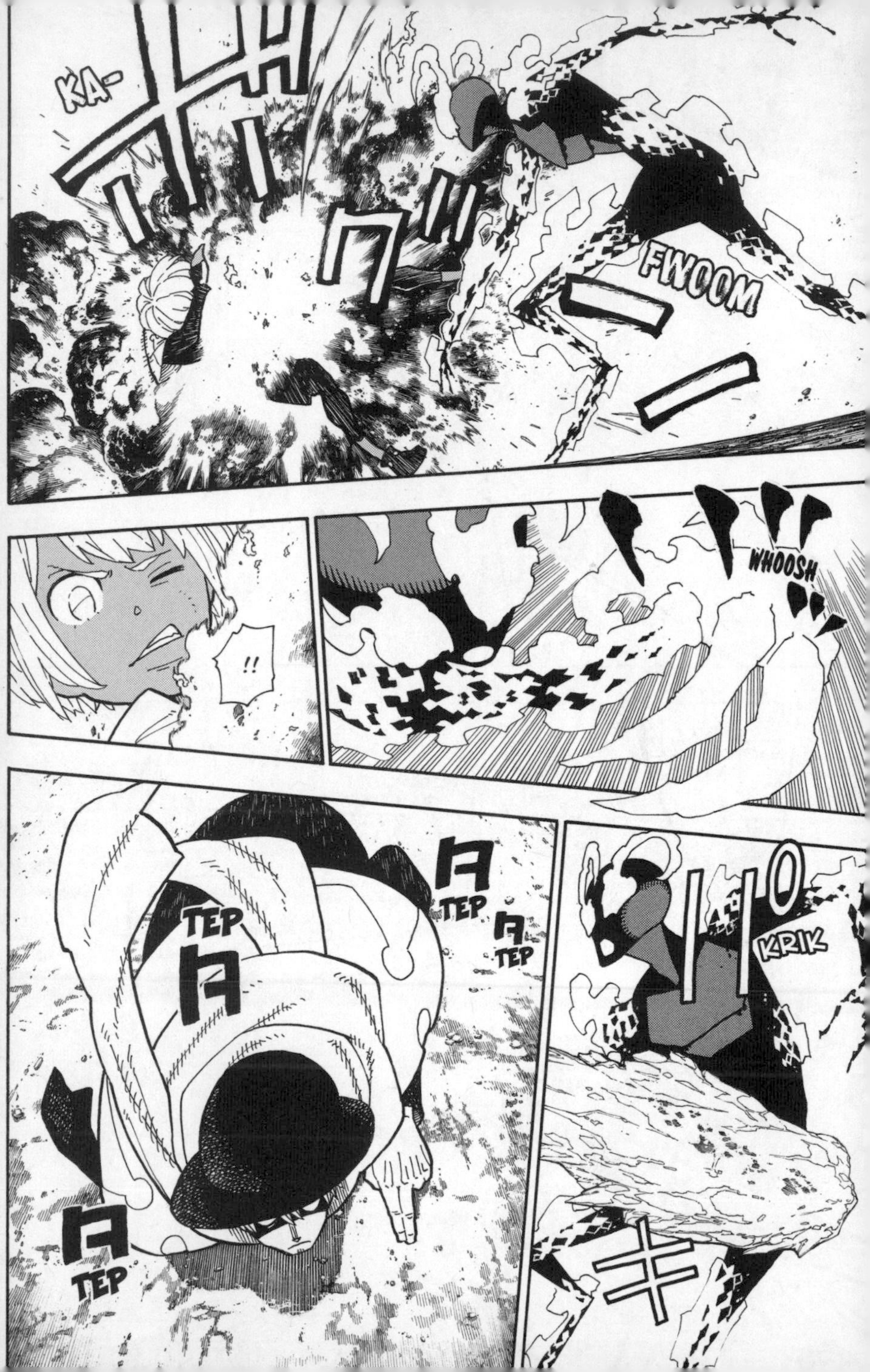
KA-
FWOOM
WHOOSH
!!
KRIK
TEP
TEP
TEP
TEP

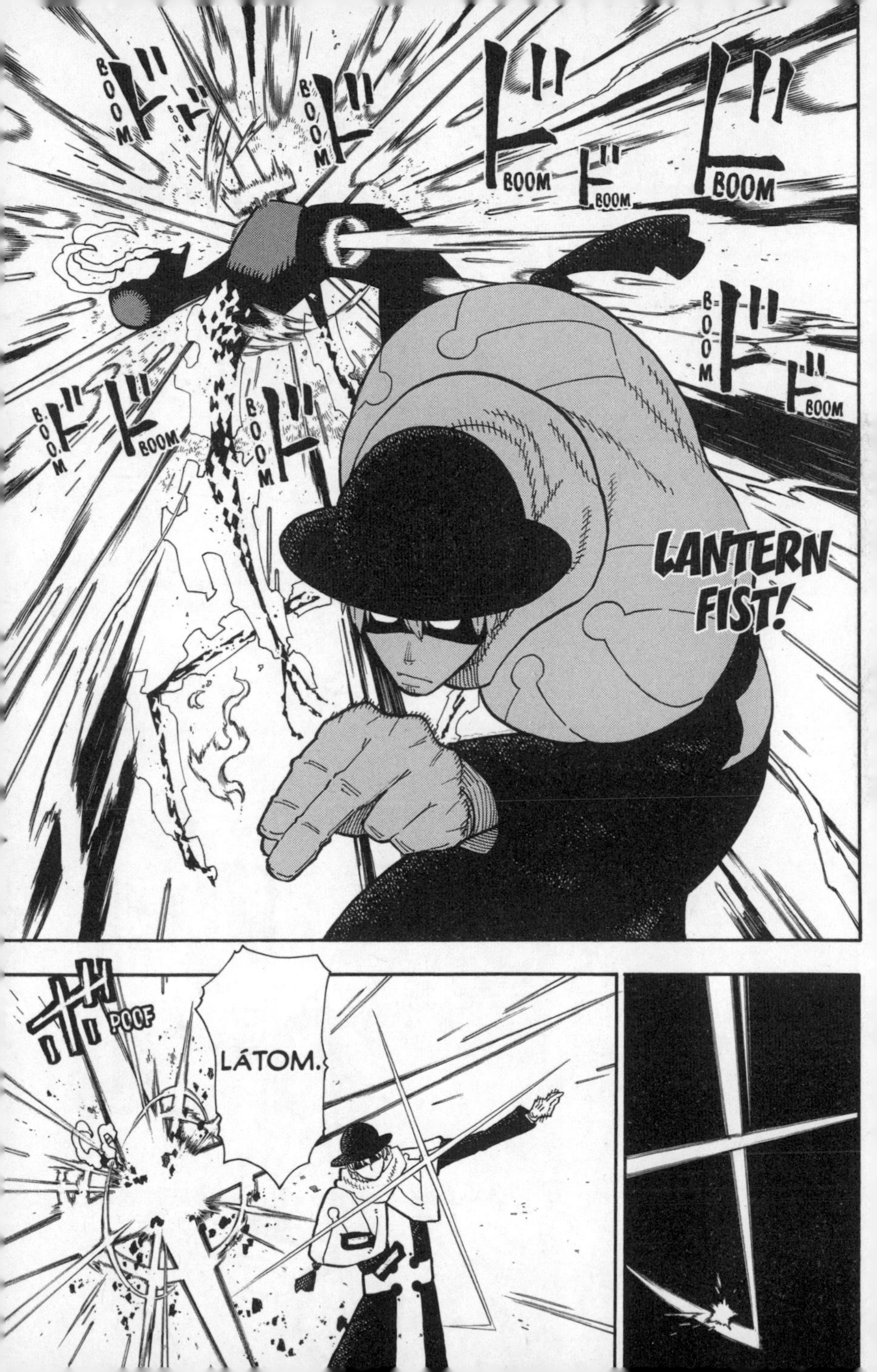
BOOM
BOOM
BOOM
BOOM
BOOM
BOOM
BOOM
BOOM
BOOM
BOOM
BOOM
BOOM
BOOM
LANTERN FIST!
LÁTOM.
POOF

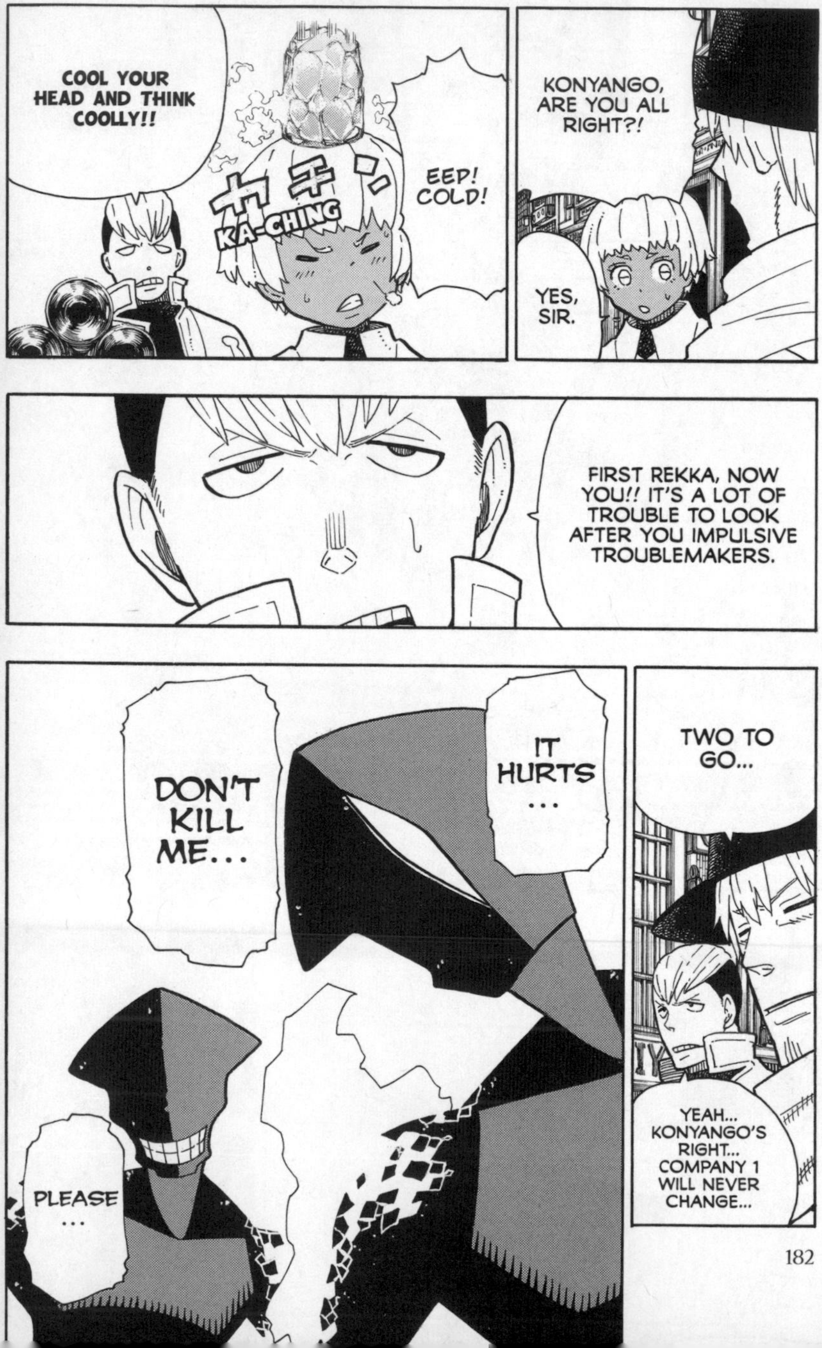
KONYANGO, ARE YOU ALL RIGHT?!
YES, SIR.
EEP! COLD!
カチ
KA-CHING
COOL YOUR HEAD AND THINK COOLLY!!
FIRST REKKA, NOW YOU!! IT'S A LOT OF TROUBLE TO LOOK AFTER YOU IMPULSIVE TROUBLEMAKERS.
TWO TO GO...
YEAH... KONYANGO'S RIGHT... COMPANY 1 WILL NEVER CHANGE...
IT HURTS ...
DON'T KILL ME...
PLEASE ...

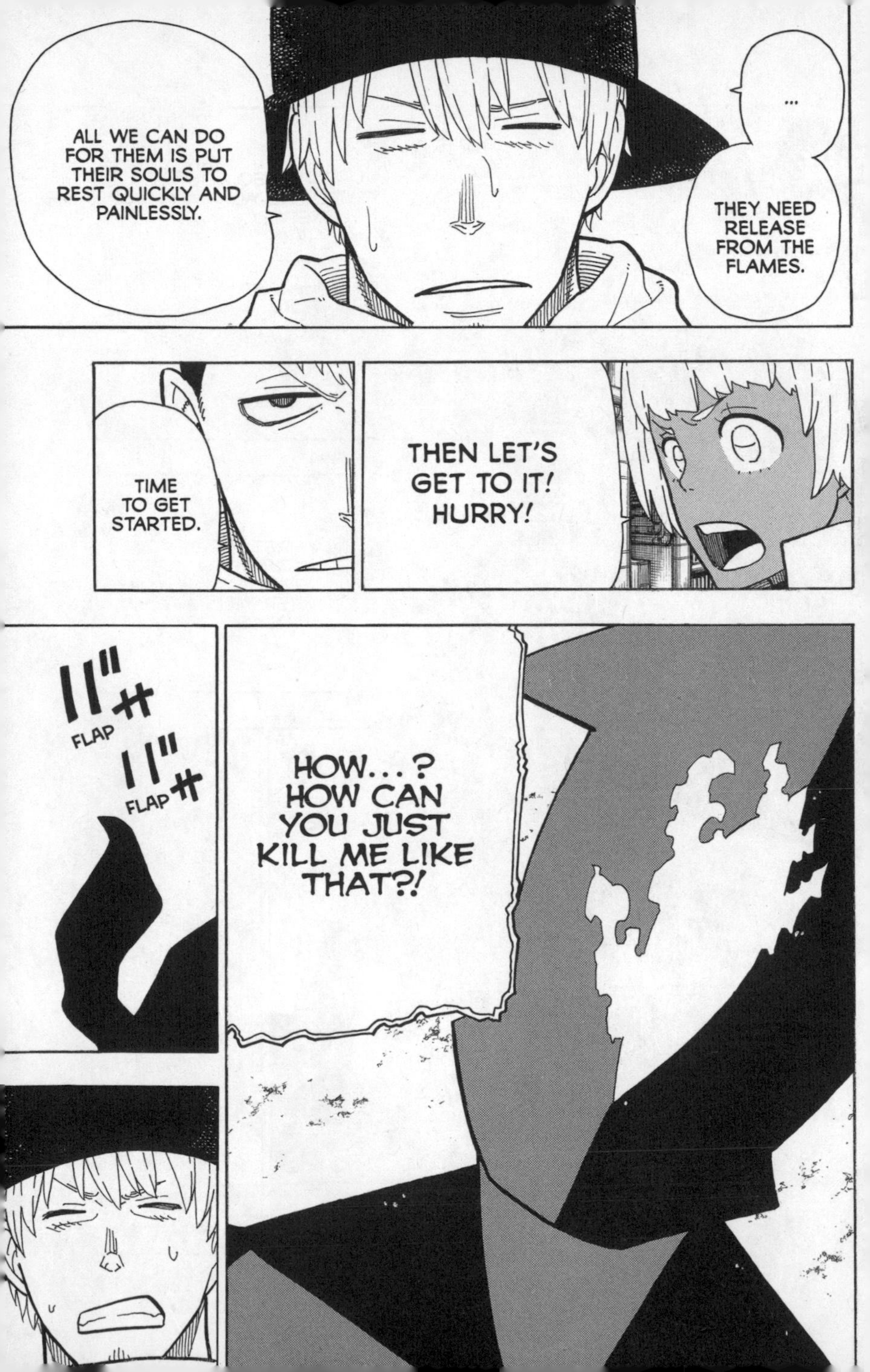
...
THEY NEED RELEASE FROM THE FLAMES.
ALL WE CAN DO FOR THEM IS PUT THEIR SOULS TO REST QUICKLY AND PAINLESSLY.
THEN LET'S GET TO IT! HURRY!
TIME TO GET STARTED.
HOW...? HOW CAN YOU JUST KILL ME LIKE THAT?!
FLAP
FLAP

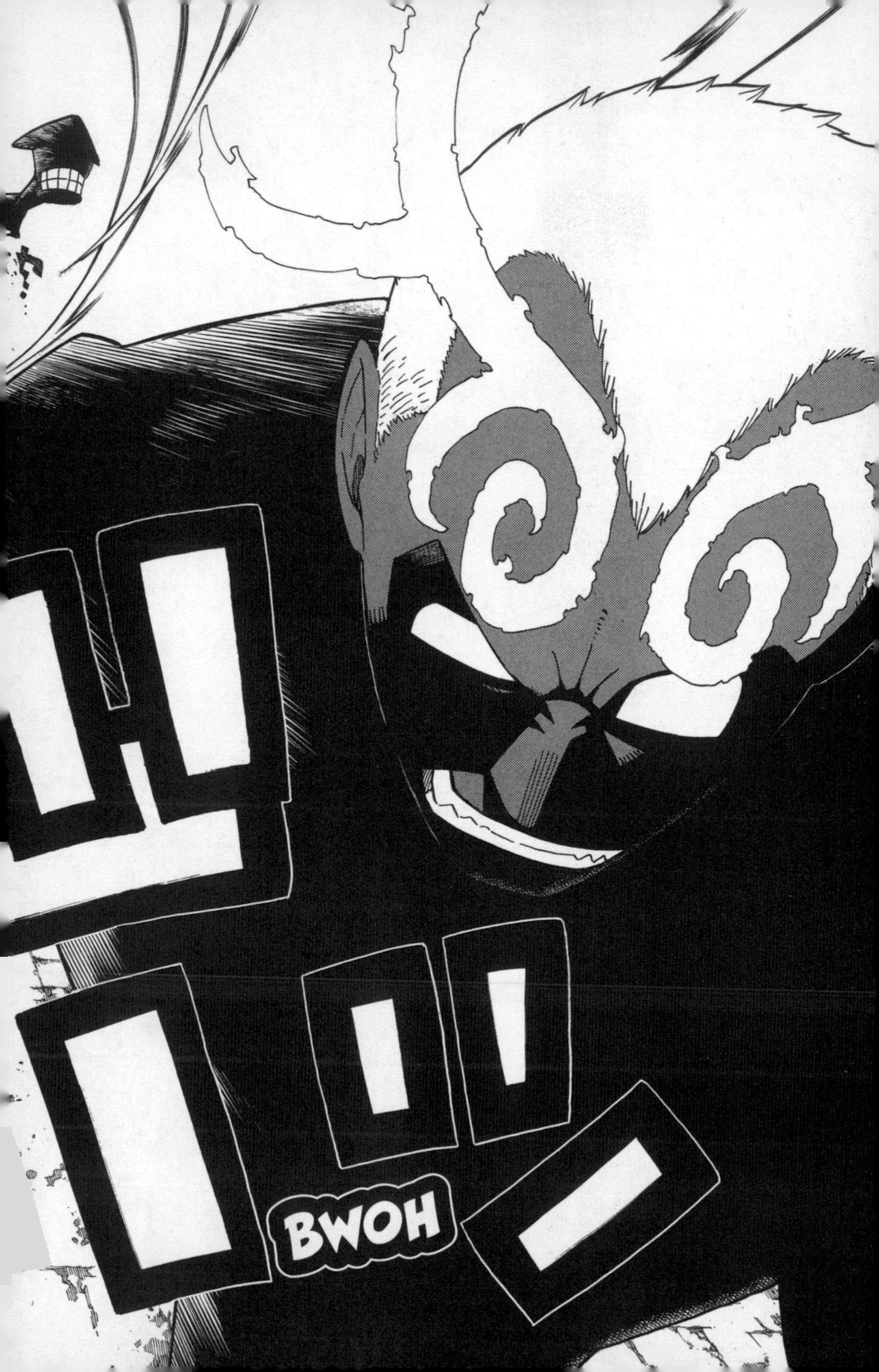
BWOH

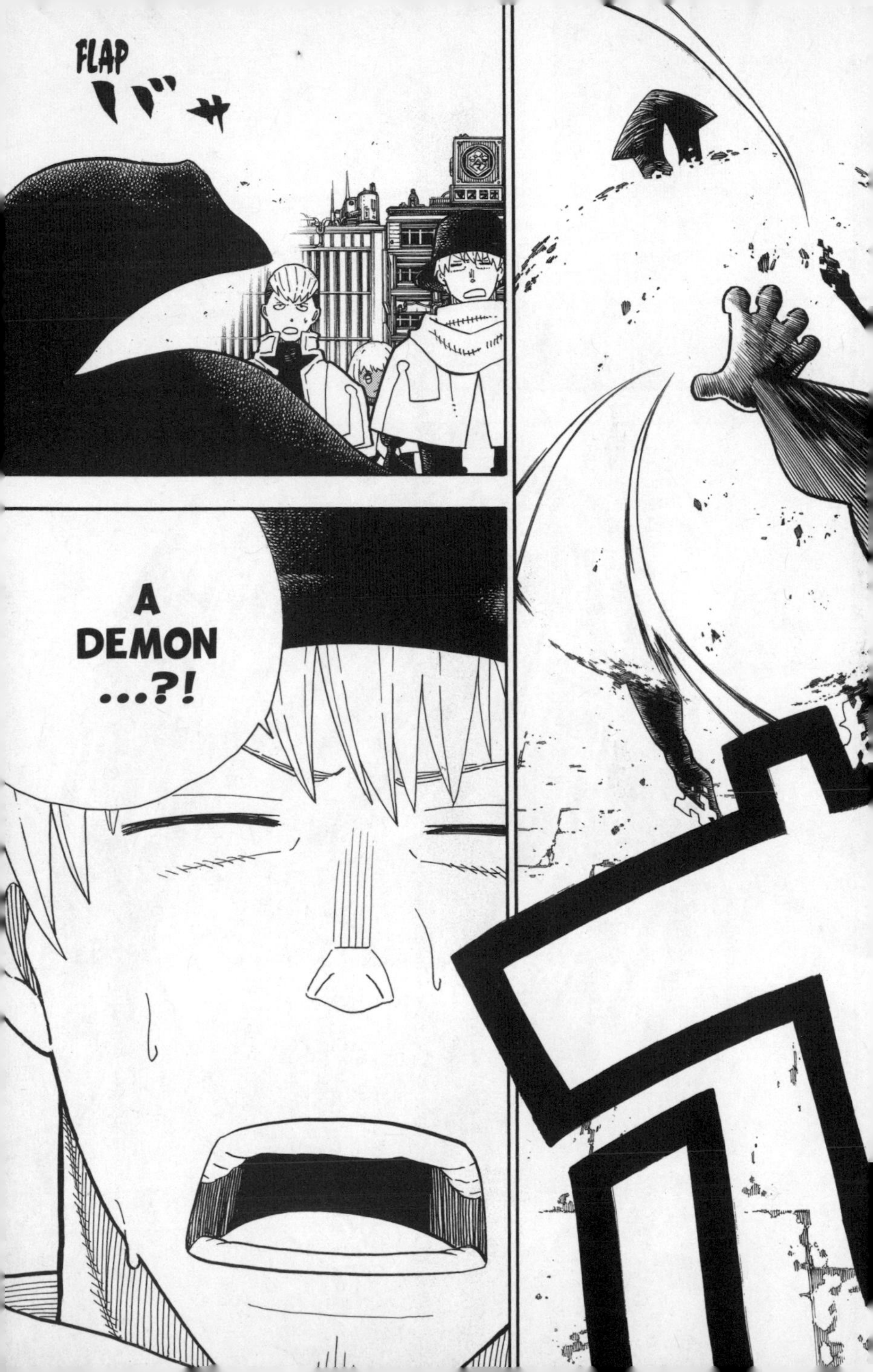
FLAP
A DEMON ...?!

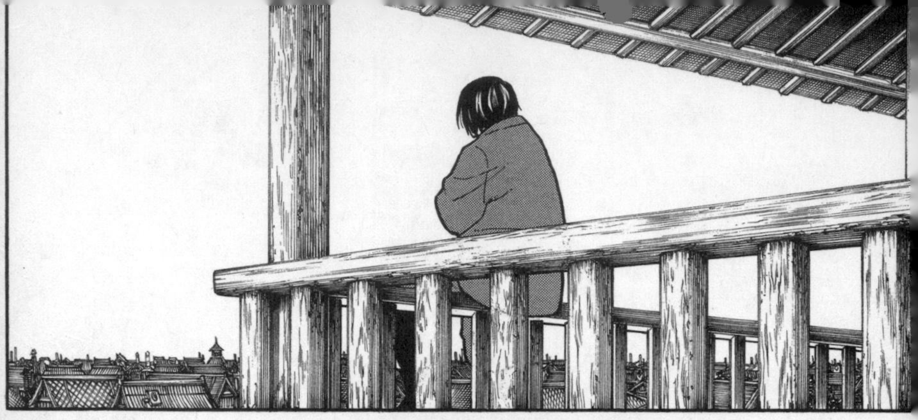
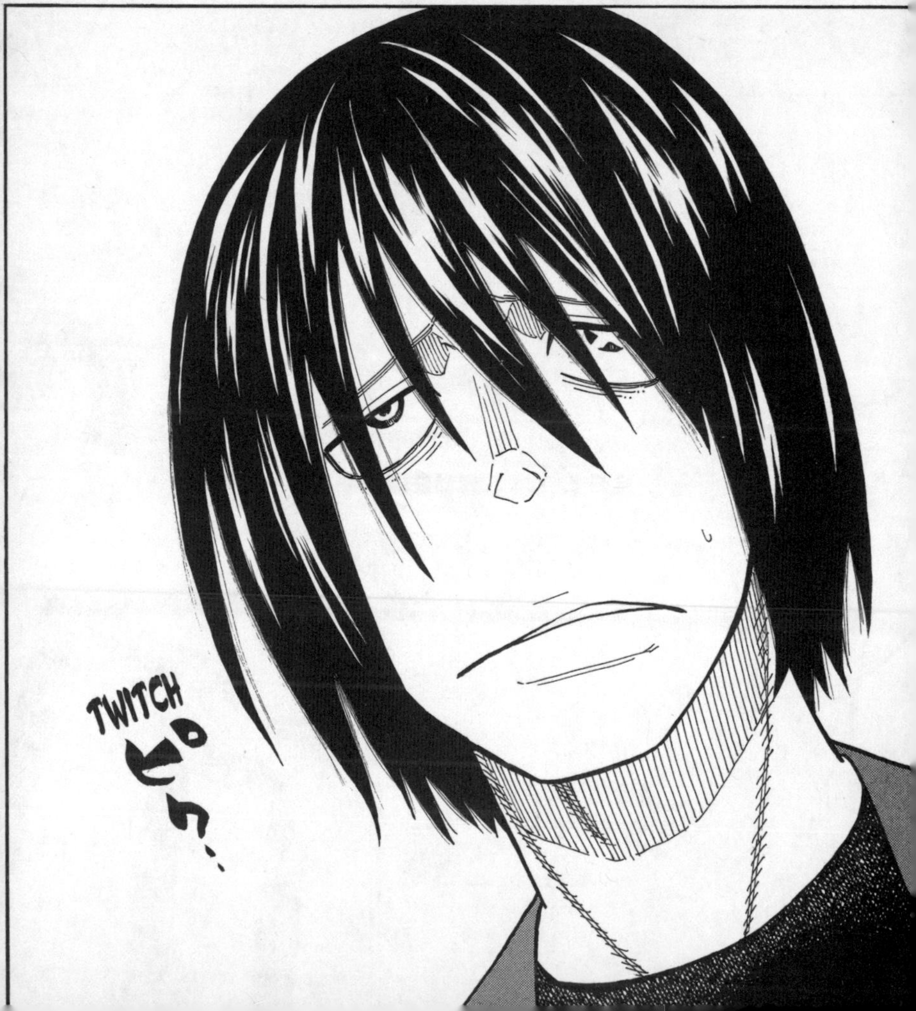
TWITCH

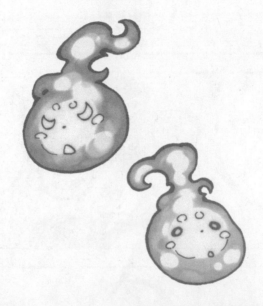

TO BE CONTINUED IN VOLUME 26!!

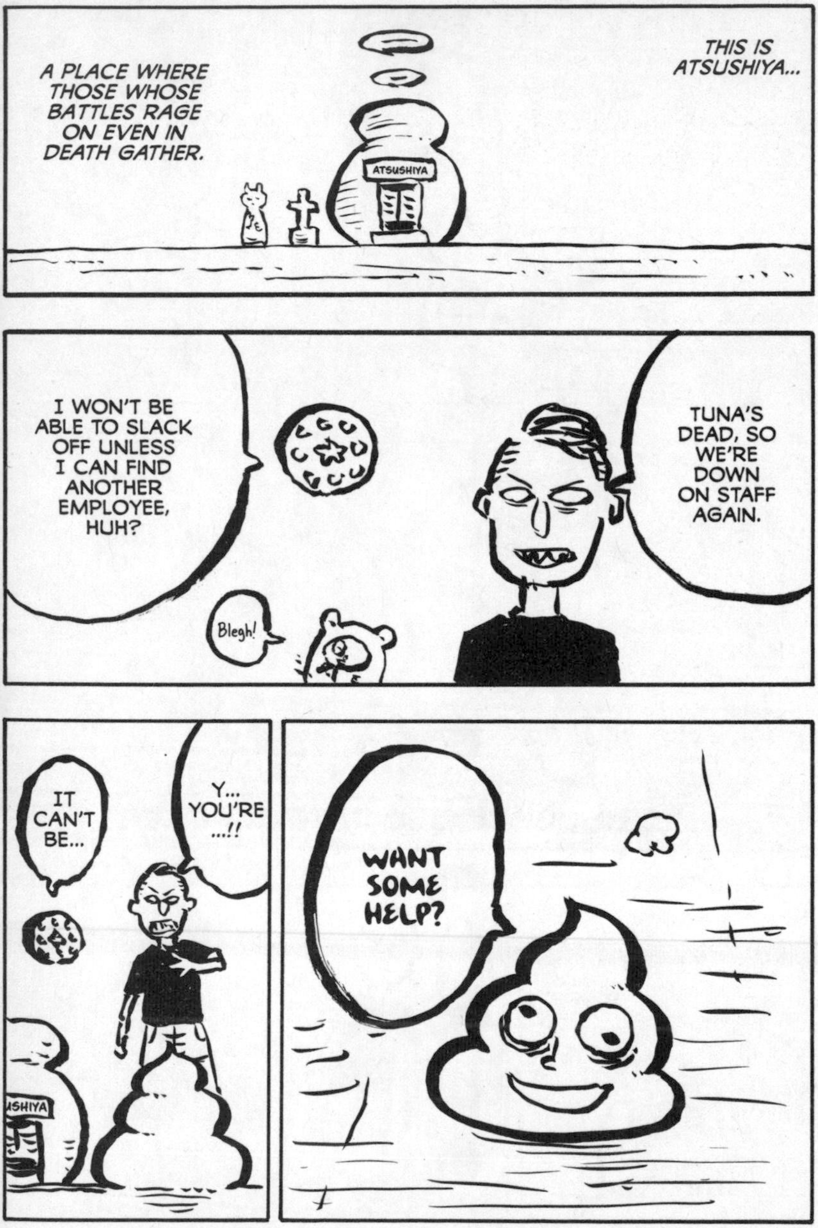
THIS IS ATSUSHIYA...
A PLACE WHERE THOSE WHOSE BATTLES RAGE ON EVEN IN DEATH GATHER.
ATSUSHIYA
TUNA'S DEAD, SO WE'RE DOWN ON STAFF AGAIN.
I WON'T BE ABLE TO SLACK OFF UNLESS I CAN FIND ANOTHER EMPLOYEE, HUH?
Blegh!
WANT SOME HELP?
Y... YOU'RE ...!!
IT CAN'T BE...
SHIYA

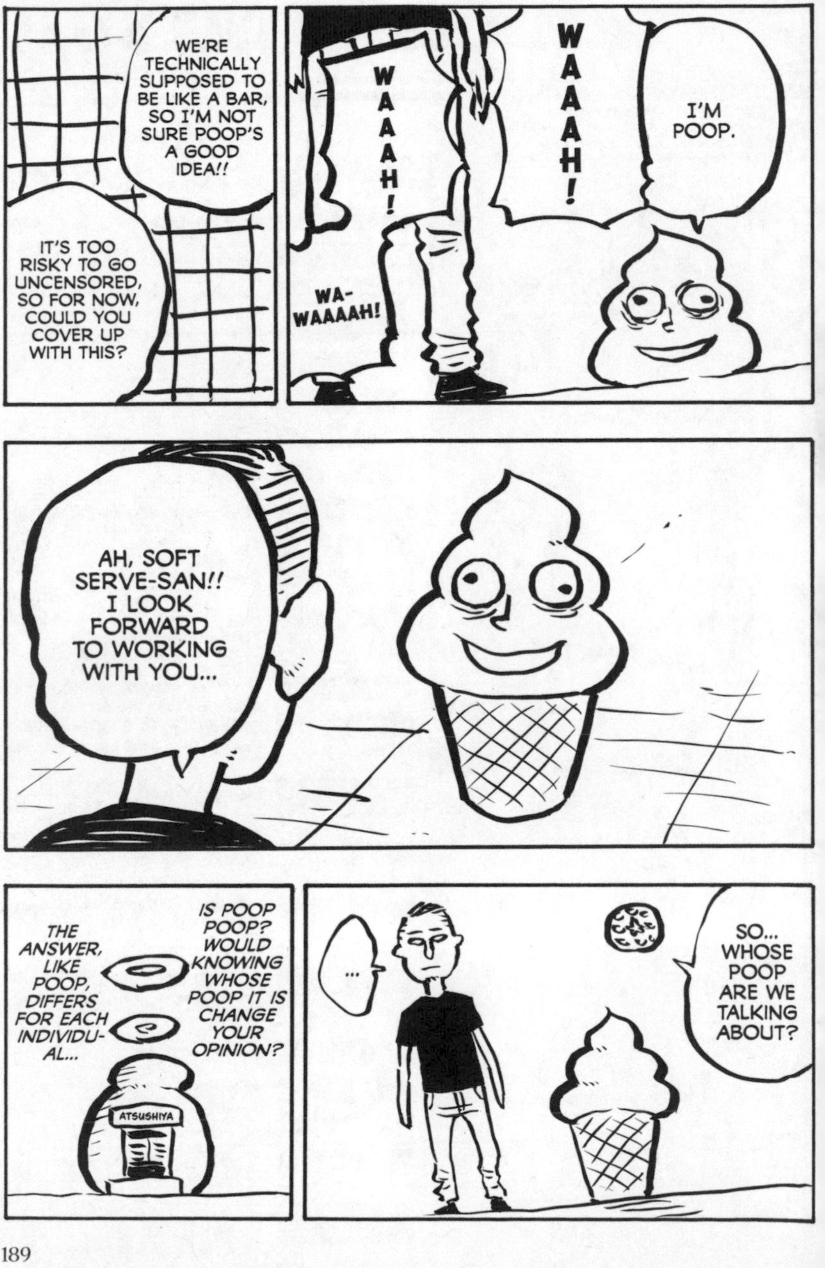
I'M POOP.
WAAAH!
WAAAH!
WA-WAAAAH!
WE'RE TECHNICALLY SUPPOSED TO BE LIKE A BAR, SO I'M NOT SURE POOP'S A GOOD IDEA!!
IT'S TOO RISKY TO GO UNCENSORED, SO FOR NOW, COULD YOU COVER UP WITH THIS?
AH, SOFT SERVE-SAN!! I LOOK FORWARD TO WORKING WITH YOU...
SO... WHOSE POOP ARE WE TALKING ABOUT?
...
IS POOP POOP? WOULD KNOWING WHOSE POOP IT IS CHANGE YOUR OPINION?
THE ANSWER, LIKE POOP, DIFFERS FOR EACH INDIVIDU-AL...
ATSUSHIYA

FIRE FORCE

TAMAKI KOTATSU

AFFILIATION: **SPECIAL FIRE FORCE COMPANY 1 (CURRENTLY IN THE CARE OF COMPANY 8)**
RANK: **SECOND CLASS FIRE SOLDIER**
ABILITY: **THIRD GENERATION PYROKINETIC**
(changes flames into cat ears, tail, and claws)

Height	156cm [5'1"] (I wish I were a little taller!)
Weight	41kg [90.41lbs.]
Age	I'm seventeen!
Birthday	February 22
Sign	Pisces
Blood Type	A
Nickname	Cat Girl, Tama-chan
Self-Proclaimed	I don't wanna be a lucky lecher lure!
Favorite Foods	Fishies ♥
Least Favorite Food	Celery, carrots, peppers…blegh
Favorite Music	Pop
Favorite Animal	Kitty ♥
Favorite Color	Hmm…I can't choose! If I had to pick, white and yellow!
Favorite Type of Guy	Someone with no secrets, someone who's not too fired up
Who She Respects	Daddy, Mommy, Captain Burns, Lieutenant Karim, Lieutenant Huo Yan
Who She Has Trouble Around	Lieutenant Rekka
Who She's Afraid of	People who suddenly change their attitude, Lieutenant Rekka
Hobbies	Napping in the park So relaxing! (@ ￣ρ￣ @)
Daily Routine	Caring for my hair and fingernails. I never miss a day!
Dream	I want a kitty cat!!
Shoe Size	23.5cm [7]
Eyesight	0.9 [20/22]
Favorite Subject	Music Any class where the girls and boys are separated
Least Favorite Subject	Co-ed P.E. Seriously, it should be illegal ♯

A Kodansha Comics Trade Paperback Original
Fire Force 25 copyright © 2020 Atsushi Ohkubo
English translation copyright © 2021 Atsushi Ohkubo

All rights reserved.

Published in the United States by Kodansha Comics, an imprint of Kodansha USA Publishing, LLC, New York.

Publication rights for this English edition arranged through Kodansha Ltd., Tokyo.

First published in Japan in 2020 by Kodansha Ltd., Tokyo.

ISBN 978-1-64651-283-6

Printed in the United States of America.

www.kodansha.us

9 8 7 6 5 4 3 2 1
Translation: Alethea Nibley & Athena Nibley
Lettering: AndWorld Design
Editing: Greg Moore
Kodansha Comics edition cover design by Phil Balsman

Publisher: Kiichiro Sugawara

Director of publishing services: Ben Applegate
Associate director, publishing operations: Stephen Pakula
Publishing services managing editors: Madison Salters, Alanna Ruse
Production managers: Emi Lotto, Angela Zurlo

Translation Notes:

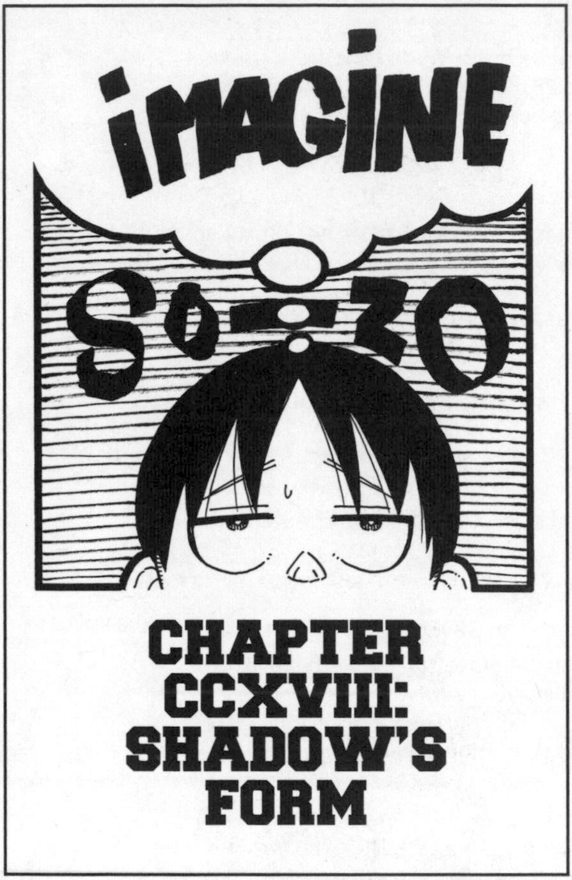
IMAGINE
SO-ZO
CHAPTER CCXVIII: SHADOW'S FORM

Shadow's Form, page 87

The title of this chapter, *Kage no Katachi,* literally translates to "the shape (or form) of a shadow," indicating that perhaps someone is going to define the shadow that has appeared in the Company's midst. The Japanese phrase is also used as part of an idiom that translates roughly to, "stays with you like a shadow," and describes something that is constantly with you.

Beloved, page 140

This saké is very similar to a real-world pre-Cataclysm saké called Saiai, meaning "beloved." The same *kanji* characters that make up its name can be pronounced Moa, which is the name of a member of the pre-Cataclysm band, BABYMETAL. Notable differences between what Benimaru drinks and the original are that, instead of the Kiso Three Rivers and Aichi brewery, the places listed are the Mizuno Three Rivers and Nakamoto Brewery. As it so happens, these place names coincide with the surnames of other members of BABYMETAL.

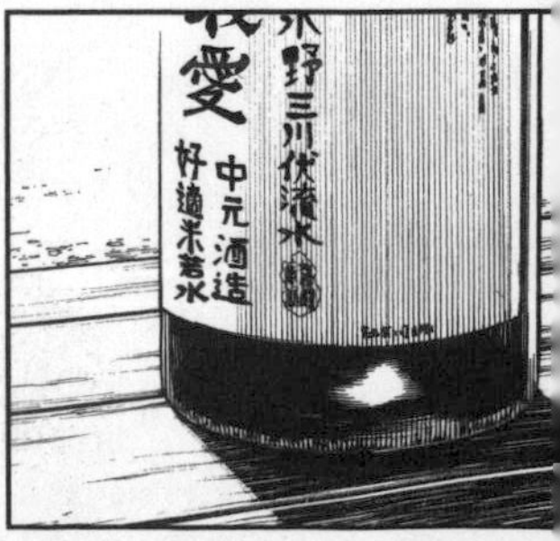
愛
中元酒造
好適米若水